THE
DISMISSAL

IN THE QUEEN'S NAME

PAUL KELLY
AND
TROY BRAMSTON

PENGUIN BOOKS

PENGUIN BOOKS

UK | USA | Canada | Ireland | Australia
India | New Zealand | South Africa | China

Penguin Books is part of the Penguin Random House group of companies
whose addresses can be found at global.penguinrandomhouse.com.

Penguin
Random House
Australia

First published by Penguin Group Pty Ltd, 2015
This edition published by Penguin Random House Australia Pty Ltd, 2016

10 9 8 7 6 5 4 3 2 1

Cover design by Adam Laszczuk © Penguin Random House Australia Pty Ltd
Text design by Samantha Jayaweera © Penguin Random House Australia Pty Ltd
Cover photographs: Gough Whitlam: Guy Wilmott/Newspix; Malcolm Fraser: News Ltd/Newspix,
John Kerr: News Ltd/Newspix
Typeset in Adobe Garamond Pro by Samantha Jayaweera, Penguin Random House Australia Pty Ltd
Colour separation by Splitting Image Colour Studio, Clayton, Victoria
Printed and bound in Australia by Griffin Press, an accredited ISO AS/NZS 14001 Environmental
Management Systems printer.

National Library of Australia
Cataloguing-in-Publication data:

Kelly, Paul, 1947– author
The dismissal : in the Queen's name / Paul Kelly and Troy Bramston
9780143574088 (paperback)

Kerr, John, Sir, 1914–1991
Whitlam, Gough, 1916–2014
Prime ministers – Australia – Biography
Australia – Politics and government – 1972–1975

Other Creators/Contributors:
Bramston, Troy, author

320.994

penguin.com.au

Contents

Preface

The dismissal of the Whitlam government on 11 November 1975 never loses its capacity to astonish from one generation to the next. It remains Australia's greatest political crisis. This book reinterprets the 1975 political and constitutional showdown in a way that makes this event even more surprising.

While the central characters – Sir John Kerr, Gough Whitlam and Malcolm Fraser – have departed the scene, the story of their confrontation continues to generate revelations.

The book offers a fresh account of these extraordinary events. It draws upon new documents – diaries, notes, minutes, memos, correspondence and oral history interviews – from archives in Australia and the United Kingdom, new interviews with nearly forty participants, in addition to published material over the past four decades. Much of this material comes from the pen of Sir John Kerr documenting his calculations, dilemmas, planning and, after the event, his agonising self-justifications.

These documents and interviews recast the story in vivid ways. They challenge our previous understanding of the crisis and the interplay among Kerr, Whitlam and Fraser. This book also offers different perspectives of the crisis: from Buckingham Palace, Government House and Australia's High Court, in addition to the Whitlam government and the Fraser-led opposition. Forty years later, it entrenches some of the prevailing orthodoxies about 1975, yet shatters many others.

Paul Kelly and Troy Bramston, 9 September 2015

Introduction

The dismissal is the most dramatic event in Australia's political history – the moment when our parliamentary institutions and constitutional system were put under their greatest strain. Gough Whitlam's political death in the afternoon of 11 November 1975, dismissed by Governor-General Sir John Kerr, was caused by a cocktail of ruthlessness, incompetence and deception. Forty years later, when the passion and tumult have died, there is a fundamental truth: this was a highly unsatisfactory solution for Australian democracy.

The dismissal was a monumental train wreck, in its prelude, its execution and its consequences. Neither inevitable nor necessary, it was inferior to other options available to resolve the four-week parliamentary deadlock. The crisis can only be understood in terms of the ambition and character of its principals: Whitlam, Kerr and Malcolm Fraser. As Kerr's predecessor, Sir Paul Hasluck, later told Buckingham Palace: 'The wisdom of a constitutional monarchy is to avoid confrontation.' Australia in 1975 failed this test.

The rage and delight about 1975, depending on your perspective, has expired. But the story has not settled. The passage of four decades has not brought reconciliation over these events. A permanent chasm still exists among the different interpretations of what happened, why it happened and who carries the blame. The dismissal sits on our historical landscape like a gigantic expended yet unexplained volcano. It is too big to forget but too lethal for a settlement.

As the Queen, in blissful ignorance, slept in her bed in Buckingham

Palace, the governor-general used the Crown's power to terminate the prime minister's commission in Canberra. Kerr acted in the Queen's name but one could not expect the Queen to have taken such action herself. This crisis was about the exercise in Australia of the royal prerogative without warning.

It was one of those rare occasions when the Crown's intervention was decisive in settling a great contest. The governor-general called his memoirs *Matters for Judgment*. This was Kerr's call; it was Kerr's test; it was Kerr's judgement. He had the power and the influence. Yet Kerr's solution – changing the government at the stroke of a pen – divided the nation, embittered the politics and compromised our institutions.

No matter how many people try to evade the issue, the final responsibility can rest only with Kerr as governor-general.

The 1975 crisis was about the political system. It was not the usual stuff of party conflict – tax, spending, jobs, war, growth or fairness. In that sense it transcended the ideological confrontations of the age. It was both less, yet more serious. The escalating tensions between institutions vested the crisis with its lethal nature.

The originating conflict was between the Senate and the House of Representatives over the blocking of supply – the funding of general government services. This triggered the next conflict – whether the governor-general was obliged to follow the advice of his prime minister. In turn, this provoked another issue – whether the governor-general was entitled to seek advice from the chief justice of the High Court. The final question became whether the governor-general in exercising the reserve powers of the Crown had an obligation to give Whitlam the choice of going to the election as prime minister.

The key to understanding the crisis lies in its dual nature: this was a struggle between men and a conflict between institutions. It is unparalleled in our history as a gladiatorial struggle between two wilful leaders. It is equally unparalleled for the pressure it applied to the principal institutions of the state – the parliament, the office of the governor-general and the High Court – and its destructive effect on the series of conventions that underwrite the consensus and stability required in a constitutional democracy.

Whitlam and Fraser were titans from an era long passed. They were authentic leaders convinced of their mission, ready to invoke political violence for their cause and prepared to push the constitutional system to breaking point in their rivalry. As governor-general it fell to Kerr – talented, ambitious and cunning – to manage the deadlock.

It is a tribute to our politics and society that Whitlam and Fraser reconciled. Few participants and observers of the crisis would have imagined such an event. With their deaths in 2014 and 2015 and Kerr's earlier death, the dismissal has consigned its last living secrets to the grave. It belongs to our history and our memories, the product of a place and time that will be contested as long as Australian democracy is alive and pulsating with its endless disputes over power and values.

At the fortieth anniversary the power questions from 1975 remain unresolved. The Senate can still block supply to force an election; a prime minister can still defy the Senate, precipitating a deadlock; and a governor-general can still sack a prime minister. In theory, it could happen again. In practice, that is extremely unlikely. The 1975 crisis was the product of three extraordinary personalities – Fraser, Whitlam and Kerr – unlikely to be replicated as individuals, let alone as a troika.

Predictions that the crisis would permanently undermine our democracy have proven unfounded. Other prophecies that none of this sequence of events can happen again are absurdly complacent.

But the 1975 crisis created a new set of 'understood' yet undefined working rules – that the Senate should not again deny supply; that the High Court should not again advise the governor-general; and that the governor-general should represent the nation by shunning any repeat of Kerr-type interventions based upon the reserve powers of the Crown. This constitutes recognition by subsequent leaders that 1975 was an exercise in brinkmanship that went too far and did endanger the institutions and the culture.

There were winners and losers in the 1975 power struggle but there were no heroes. This book exempts none of the three principals from blame. Indeed, the follies of the three dominant figures only loom as more extraordinary in the years since.

The originating blame rests with Fraser, whose decision to block supply to force a late 1975 election was an issue of choice, neither essential nor irresistible at the time. Fraser was the last embodiment of the 'born to rule' Menzian age, convinced Labor was unfit to govern and, as a consequence, self-righteous in his convulsive bid to force an election by denying through the Senate the funding for government salaries and services.

The litany of conventions Fraser demolished has no precedent in the nation's history – he relied upon a 'tainted' Senate, blocked supply, sought to sabotage a Senate election and drove Kerr to the dismissal by a masterful mixture of persuasion and threat.

This book is about the real Malcolm Fraser who once strode the political stage – strong, ruthless, manipulative and fixated on power, not the cultivated compassionate convert of his retirement phase. Those who saw him in action will never forget him. Fraser later launched many attacks on the Liberal Party by invoking moral principle – yet that same party under its many subsequent leaders never contemplated for a moment the serial smashing of conventions and moral norms that Fraser made his signature path to office.

Whitlam was the self-styled man of destiny who led his party to power from the political wilderness but whose grandiose transformations were often flawed. The excitement he engendered was matched only by the incompetence he displayed. It was Whitlam's follies that left his government in October 1975 discredited and morally bankrupt, a tempting target for Fraser's strike.

While Whitlam was justified in refusing an election and seeking to break Fraser's nerve, he had no justification whatsoever for assuming that as prime minister he had no obligation to solve the crisis by either advising an election or obtaining supply. It seems incredible but it is true – Whitlam misunderstood the battle he was fighting. Because his government was denied funding, he had only a limited time in which to prevail. And he failed, the final proof being his absurd journey to Yarralumla on 11 November to seek a half-senate election, without guarantee of supply for the election period, a request no responsible governor-general would grant.

It is past time that Whitlam's inexcusable blunders of strategy were catalogued and that is what the new documents and interviews do. His wordsmith and confidant, Graham Freudenberg, says: 'We never saw an independent role for the Governor-General in the crisis. That was our downfall.' Most of all, Whitlam misjudged Kerr as a man and governor-general. Addicted to the idea Kerr was weak, Whitlam practised public intimidation and private aloofness. He thought the crisis was about willpower, not judgement, and he was wrong. Whitlam failed to reassure and advise his governor-general, the condition for a solution short of dismissal. The upshot is that Kerr was filled with suspicion and hostility towards him.

In his dismissal of Whitlam, Kerr used a valid constitutional power following the Senate's use of a valid constitutional power to block supply. The central issue in the 1975 crisis was not the powers of the Senate or the governor-general, but the way they were exercised.

This book, however, rejects the view that Kerr was a victim of history, trapped between two fanatics on a collision course. This is the enduring falsehood of the crisis. Fraser and Whitlam would have had no option but to accommodate a persuasive governor-general who had the influence of the Crown at his disposal, had Kerr chosen to use that influence.

For the rest of his life, Kerr delighted in outwitting and outlasting Whitlam. 'I felt he at all times did not think I would have enough guts to do it,' he wrote in his journal years later. He refers to Whitlam's 'euphoric megalomania' and his delusion 'that he was unassailable' – with the satisfaction of having shattered that psychology.

Kerr, in fact, had a flawed understanding of his position. He had the powers of a king but not the permanence – a paradox that drove him over the edge. Infatuated by the idea of a monarchical solution through the reserve powers, he was simultaneously obsessed by insecurity and fear that Whitlam would sack him. This contradiction led Kerr to a catastrophic conclusion: dismissal in a constitutional ambush planned in secret in order to preserve his own position.

Kerr operated as a judge rather than a governor-general. He assumed his task, at some point, was to pass sentence. His real responsibility, however, was the exact opposite: to use his influence to procure a political solution without resort to the Queen's dismissal power. The magic of monarchy is beauty concealing lethality. The Crown's influence is maximised not by using the reserve powers but by not using them – it is a golden rule arising from political and monarchical history missed typically by clever lawyers.

Along his bumpy journey during the crisis, Kerr created havoc. He refused to trust Whitlam; he signalled his fears to Fraser; his dialogues with both leaders were inept and compromised; he sought comforting advice from friends such as Sir Anthony Mason, a High Court judge; he fixated on implicating the High Court by obtaining an opinion from its chief justice, Sir Garfield Barwick; and finally, in the cause of protecting the Queen from involvement in Australian politics, he dismissed Whitlam in an action that flouted the principles consistently displayed by that wise monarch, Elizabeth II. Kerr agreed to leave the office less than eighteen months after the dismissal, with his successors openly declaring their mission 'a healing process'.

What happened in 1975 is that the system was threatened not by masses in the street but by the nation's leaders who staged an eruptive confrontation that tested the Constitution and its institutions. It was a struggle rare for the purity of its ruthlessness.

This is the story we tell in five parts. Part one identifies the keys to the crisis based on new archival material and interviews. These themes focus on Kerr and his critical interactions with the Palace, Fraser, Whitlam and the High Court. The remaining parts sketch the prelude to the crisis, the dynamics that led to the dismissal, Kerr's fateful decision and the aftermath.

The skeletons from 1975 still hang in the cupboard. At the fortieth anniversary it is time to get them out, dust them off and bring them to life. Their story will shock, astonish and provoke. It is a perpetual reminder of the strength of Australia's democracy. But it is also a reminder that institutions cannot be abused and constitutional powers cannot be pushed to their limits. Political leaders must recognise this and governors-general must live with the obligation to rectify Sir John Kerr's legacy.

PART ONE

The Legacy Forty
Years Later

I

Kerr and The Queen: Dismay at The Palace

The Queen was keen to see the back of Sir John Kerr as governor-general and was relieved when he resigned as her representative in Australia in 1977. The Palace had worried about Kerr's behaviour, reliability, and his apparent pursuit of his self-interest, and believed the Kerrs, as a couple, were greedy.[1] The decision that Kerr would quit as governor-general became irrevocable at a meeting he had with the Queen on board the royal yacht *Britannia* at Fremantle, Western Australia, on 30 March 1977.

An insight into the attitude of Buckingham Palace towards Kerr was provided in an intimate meeting on 1 August 1977 at the Palace between the Queen's trusted private secretary, Sir Martin Charteris, and Sir Paul Hasluck, Kerr's predecessor as governor-general of Australia. Hasluck had dealt with the Palace as the Queen's representative in Australia from 1969 to 1974. He remained on good terms with Charteris and was a confidant who had access to the Palace's thinking and, by implication, the Queen. As an historian, Hasluck made a note of his August 1977 meeting with Charteris. It has been provided to the authors by his son, Nicholas.

Hasluck wrote: 'It was also apparent that at some stage some pressure had been applied from the Palace to bring about his [Kerr's] resignation. Charteris – and by implication the Queen – had a poor opinion of the Kerrs.'[2]

This appears no casual remark.

Hasluck had also met Charteris on board the royal yacht *Britannia* when it docked at Fremantle in March 1977 as part of the Queen's Jubilee tour. From both these conversations Hasluck 'gained the impression that the Palace had brought pressure to bear on Kerr to retire'. Charteris told him the Palace's judgement had been to defer Kerr's retirement until after the Queen's visit to Australia and to accommodate Kerr's wish to visit London in mid-1977 for the Jubilee celebrations. Charteris said this gave 'the right public appearance' ahead of the resignation and Hasluck had agreed.

These are remarkable admissions. The governor-general is appointed and removed by the Queen only on the advice of the prime minister. That the Palace wanted Kerr gone suggests an unusual degree of dissatisfaction. By early 1977, not only Buckingham Palace but Australia's prime minister, Malcolm Fraser, whom Kerr had installed in office, saw Kerr as a chronic liability. It had been a rapid, sad and divisive descent.

Interviewed for this book, Fraser's senior adviser and former Howard government minister David Kemp said: 'Fraser did not have regard for Kerr and welcomed his departure.'[3] Official secretary to Kerr and other governors-general, Sir David Smith said of Fraser: 'How many Governor-Generals did he have? Kerr, [Sir Zelman] Cowen and [Sir Ninian] Stephen. My impression of Fraser was that he was always ready to treat each of them with disrespect if it suited his purposes. He had no particular respect for them and he expected them to do what he wanted.'[4] Fraser's private secretary, Dale Budd, said of Fraser and Kerr: 'I think it was just a formal relationship. They never celebrated together. And Fraser tried to ease him out into the UNESCO job which I guess was a way of giving him the blue water treatment.'[5] Fraser confidant Tony Staley, who saw a lot of Kerr as governor-general, said: 'He made it plain to me that he felt un-liked by Malcolm . . . I think in a way Malcolm despised him.'[6]

The Palace's motives are likely more subtle. In recording the views of the Palace, Hasluck wrote:

> We discussed the Kerrs, both man and wife, the conclusion being that it was 'a good thing' that they were going, that up to date it was a relief to know that his resignation was being handled smoothly, and that the Palace was fervently hoping that at the time he left office or immediately thereafter he did not doing anything that was improper, either in publication or in public activities. It was apparent that at the Palace the chief fear arose from a belief that the Kerrs and, especially, Lady Kerr, were 'very greedy'.[7]

Has any recent governor-general inspired such a contemptible opinion from Buckingham Palace? The answer is no. Ironically, Kerr's justification for dismissing Whitlam without telling the Palace before-hand was to 'protect' the Queen from any involvement and safeguard the Crown. In the end the Palace was deeply equivocal about the merits of both Kerr's intervention and his justification.

At the time of his departure Kerr had a 'trust' problem with the Palace. Charteris left Hasluck in no doubt of the Queen's concerns. He said the Palace was worried about media reports 'that Kerr was going out of office with a book already written under his arm and that very high bids were being made for the right to publish it'. Hasluck wrote: 'Charteris said the Palace had been in touch with Kerr about this and had reminded him of his assurances and the position of The Queen in respect of any communications to and from the Palace.' But Charteris worried about Kerr's character: he told Hasluck that Kerr was 'greedy' and Lady Kerr was 'much more so'. Charteris said that during their earlier talks on *Britannia*, the Queen and Charteris had obtained an 'assurance' from Kerr not to publish any of the correspondence between himself and the Queen about Whitlam's dismissal. This revealed not just the sensitivity of the Palace about the correspondence but its fears of Kerr's reliability and pursuit of his self-interest.

In the end Hasluck felt he had to defend Kerr, saying he would know what was 'discreet and proper'. Charteris was not so sure. 'We shall wait and see,' he replied. But Hasluck then expressed his own insightful doubts about Kerr. 'I thought that self-justification might be his strongest temptation,' Hasluck said. He recalled that on two social occasions at Government House in Perth, 'Kerr was going from guest to guest asking in effect "Did I do the right thing?"' One can imagine what the Palace thought of this.[8]

Kerr himself insisted he had only highly cordial relations with the Palace and the Queen. And the Queen, obviously, would never contradict this. Kerr always maintained his decision to resign was 'upon my sole initiative'. In narrow terms this is correct – but Fraser and the Palace felt the argument for departure had become compelling.

In his self-justification Kerr wrote in his memoirs that resignation was an act of 'duty'. He wrote that his motive was to help 'our national politics to return to normal'. He asserted that resignation was 'contrary to all the advice I had so far received' and highlighted the views of a long-retired Sir Robert Menzies, who had urged him to stay 'for years'.

Kerr said that during the Queen's visit in March 1977, he had an audience with her at Yarralumla. He later spoke to Fraser about his position. The meeting on *Britannia* soon followed. Kerr has disclosed no details of this meeting except to say 'there was at no time any direct or indirect suggestion from the Queen' about what he should do.[9]

This is no surprise. One could not envisage that the Queen, a wise monarch, would ever reveal her hand. In a letter to Menzies, Kerr said he raised the issue of resignation with the Queen and Fraser. 'I had the distinct impression that both felt that I was adopting a very honourable role,' Kerr wrote. Of course, they would say that. Even if they wanted him gone. Kerr added that he was resigning out of 'duty' but that 'if I had been asked to stay on I should have done so'. Tellingly, he was not asked. It is a pivotal point. Kerr – blinded by pride – also relays to Menzies that Charteris had called his decision a 'noble' one.[10]

According to Kerr, it was only after the *Britannia* meeting that 'I told Mr Fraser what I wished to do and why.' Fraser agreed. He too made no effort to dissuade Kerr.

This is significant not just because it was only sixteen months since the dismissal, but because on several earlier occasions Kerr had discussed the question of resignation with Fraser who, on each occasion, had advised him to stay. These discussions, according to Kerr, occurred immediately after the dismissal during the caretaker period and again soon after the 13 December 1975 election that confirmed Fraser as prime minister.

Bill Hayden, later governor-general himself, believed that Kerr should have gone then, announcing that for 'the reputation of the office he occupied and for the comity of the Australian community he would therefore step down as Governor-General as soon as it was clear a government had been elected'.[11]

The issue of resignation had been permanently on Kerr's mind. In a thirteen-page handwritten note at the time of the Queen's visit in March 1977, he said: 'The subject of resignation and its timing has always been with me from 13th December until the present time. I have often discussed it with the Prime Minister, in correspondence with the Palace and in discussions with the Queen and Sir Martin Charteris. All advice until now has been against such a move.'[12]

Facing a sustained boycott on the vice-regal office by the Labor Party, hostile demonstrations and heavy media criticism, Kerr said he would not be driven from office. He feared an early resignation in 1975 or 1976 might seem an admission that the dismissal had been a mistake.

Kerr had been tormented during early 1976 by the resignation question and was driven to a decisive discussion with Fraser about his future. His worries were revealed in a twelve-page handwritten note dated 20 April 1976 in which he confirmed his future was 'under constant review'.[13] Kerr related a confidential discussion with Sir James Plimsoll, a friend and senior Australian diplomat, who told him that John Menadue, the secretary of the Prime Minister's Department, had expressed the view that Kerr 'might have to go before the Queen's visit because the country was polarised'. Kerr was alarmed. He confided in Plimsoll his fear – that he had 'to consider the risk of my position being weaker later in the year and a retreat being pressed upon me from various quarters for the country's sake including from government quarters'. In short, he feared losing Fraser government support.

It was just six months since the dismissal and Kerr in April 1976 brought the issue to a head with Fraser. He wanted to know where Fraser really stood. Kerr wrote that 'my purpose was to give him a real opening in frankness to say what he and his government thought'. But Kerr's note said he indicated that he 'would not want to go later from a position of possible greater weakness'.

With relief, Kerr described Fraser's reply: 'he was adamant that he and his government and the Coalition parties wanted me to stay . . . he had never heard any suggestion with the Coalition parties except that I was widely popular in the country'. The point is that in April 1976, Fraser wanted Kerr to stay since a departure at that time would have reflected on the dismissal. Kerr, reassured that he would still be in office at the time of the Queen's 1977 visit, made plans accordingly.

But by 1977, Fraser had changed his mind. Both Fraser and the Palace were involved that year in managing Kerr's departure. In Kerr's thirteen-page note written in March 1977, after meeting the Queen at Yarralumla, he is preparing the ground for resignation.[14] He writes that 'the "battle of the streets" was won in 1976 and the royal visit was an outstanding and enthusiastic success'. The day after meeting the Queen, Charteris told Kerr the issue 'was one I had to decide for myself' in the light of discussions with Fraser. But Charteris raised with Kerr the possibility of him being appointed to the World Court as his next career move. Fraser told Kerr at this time the Palace was 'very grateful' for all his efforts during the year. Kerr felt that with an election due in 1978, any resignation had to occur in 1977. He wrote: 'The reason would be that I had achieved all that could be expected or asked of me.'

Kerr had a comparatively short period as governor-general. It spanned just three and a half years, from July 1974 to December 1977, contrasting with the contemporary practice of a five-year term. That Kerr had made extensive representations to Whitlam before his appointment saying he wanted ten years in the office, double the normal period, only accentuates the extent of his change of mind after the dismissal. He had become a tainted figure.

The strain on Kerr had been immense. Fraser, finally, came to the view that he was a broken man.[15] There would be no political peace over the office of governor-general until Kerr left the stage. Fraser's support for Kerr lasted for as long as it was useful to have him in place and no longer. Yet in notes to himself, Kerr rationalised his 1977 departure decision: 'I had not retreated; the battle had been won on my front.'[16] This was self-delusion at its most conspicuous.

David Smith said he discussed the issue of resignation with Kerr. Interviewed by the authors, Smith conceded the office was 'inevitably' damaged by the dismissal because anything that 'brings the governor-general into public controversy damages the office in the minds of some people'.[17]

In a letter Kerr drafted to Fraser dated 10 June 1977, he sought to confirm before history that the resignation was his own initiative: 'I feel I should state in this personal letter to you what is clearly understood between us, namely that this development was initiated by me and not in any other ways in discussions with the Queen and yourself.'[18] Kerr said that the 'battle of the streets' during 1976 was now behind them. With the Queen's successful 1977 visit he could look forward to a new chapter in his life with 'my dearest wish' being to serve in an official capacity, 'preferably outside Australia'.

The reality, however, is that the Palace and the Queen wanted a 1977 departure. Their concerns about Kerr arose far earlier. They originate with the dismissal itself. This is revealed by a series of interviews the authors have separately conducted over the years with Sir William Heseltine, assistant private secretary to the Queen at the time of the dismissal, working closely with Charteris. An Australian who had joined the Prime Minister's Department in 1951 and later worked for Sir Robert Menzies, Heseltine had entered the Royal household in 1960 on a two-year secondment. He returned in 1965 to work in the Queen's press office, before switching to the private office in 1972, becoming assistant to Charteris, and from 1986 to 1990 he was private secretary.

Heseltine knew better than virtually anybody at the Palace how the vital relationships worked in theory and practice: between the Queen and the governor-general and between the Queen and the prime minister. He knew Kerr personally and in early 1975, during a visit to Australia, had stayed at Admiralty House, the governor-general's Sydney residence.

Asked how he felt at the time about Kerr's dismissal of Whitlam, Heseltine said: 'I didn't think it was very prudent. I thought with a little bit more subtlety he could have delayed the event for a few more days when it was my impression that the Senate would have caved in.' Heseltine said that at the Palace 'we talked about virtually nothing else for the next few days'. He was sure that Charteris had the same reservations: 'I think that we both felt exactly the same about it.'[19]

In an earlier interview, Heseltine said that if the governor-general had sought the Queen's advice – which he didn't – obviously he could not 'say categorically' what the Queen would have advised but he had a view on what she was likely to have said. 'My own feeling is that she would have advised him to play out the situation a little longer,' Heseltine said. 'I do suspect that in the course of another day or two a political solution rather than this drastic imposed solution would have been found.'[20]

In short, Heseltine says the Queen would not have done what Kerr did. The constitutional irony is Kerr sacked Whitlam in the name of the Queen, yet the Queen would not have done this herself.

This reticence reflects the culture of the Palace: supreme caution, extreme reluctance to even contemplate resorting to the reserve powers and the imperative of monarchical impartiality. Kerr's action in its surprise, shock and divisive impact contradicted this culture. This is the origin of the tension that arose between Yarralumla and the Palace. It was never resolved.

This is not to deny the Queen's appreciation that Kerr had protected her from involvement in the crisis. Kerr got this strategy correct. He decided the governor-general, not the Queen, would determine the result. The crisis would be resolved in Australia not Britain. Amid the criticisms of Kerr there is no gainsaying the importance of the political shield he gave the Queen. This was recognised and valued by the Palace. Interviewed in June 1995 Charteris told Paul Kelly: 'The Queen did appreciate Sir John's desire to ensure she was not involved. There's no doubt about that.'[21] The point, however, is that Kerr was protecting the Queen from involvement in a surprise dismissal.

After the dismissal Prince Charles and Kerr had a cordial correspondence. Charles wrote a personal letter to the governor-general expressing his appreciation and conveying his moral support. He urged Kerr 'not to lose heart' in the teeth of domestic hostility. This letter was valued by Kerr and, in particular, by Lady Kerr. It showed the Prince of Wales was sympathetic to the tribulations Kerr faced having done what he felt was his duty in the Queen's name.[22]

It was Heseltine and Charteris who broke the news of the dismissal to the Queen. When David Smith, as official secretary, rang the Palace during the afternoon of 11 November, Australian time, it was Heseltine who took the call in the middle of the night in London:

'I was asleep in my virtuous bed in an apartment in St James' Palace when the telephone rang. It was an extension from the Buckingham Palace switchboard and the operator told me that Mr David Smith was on the telephone. I said, "Hello David, what on earth are you ringing for at this time of night?" And he said, "Well, the Governor-General has dismissed the Prime Minister." The double take of all time. I can't remember what I said to him but the reaction was stunned surprise because in all the lead up to this I personally, and I don't think my colleagues, had any indication it was happening.'

'I deliberated wondering whether I should try and call the Queen and tell her the news. Well, I thought, 2.30 in the morning I wouldn't be a very popular caller and there was nothing she could do about it. I resolved the sensible thing was to get up and make sure I got to the Palace before she would be awakened listening to the news. I think I even went back to sleep again for a while digesting this news.'[23]

The decisive encounter at the Palace came in the early morning. Heseltine said: 'It would have been the eight o'clock news I knew she [the Queen] listened to. So it was probably about half past seven in the morning and I found that Martin Charteris was already there. He had no immediate explanation of why he hadn't been available at two in the morning but I knew he had been at the Lord Mayor's banquet that night. Anyway, he was seething with rage when I got there.'[24]

Charteris already knew of the dismissal – he had been told by Whitlam. The former prime minister had rung Charteris, whom he regarded as a friend, and Charteris, a civil servant with an appreciation of protocol, had addressed Whitlam as prime minister. Whitlam now referred to himself as the Member for Werriwa. 'He informed me that Sir John had terminated his commission,' Charteris said. 'That was the sole purpose of his call.' Heseltine said that 'Martin was very cross at being taken unawares.' Asked if Whitlam made any requests of the Palace, Charteris said: 'He didn't ask me to do anything.'[25]

Heseltine said of the next step: 'We got her on the telephone immediately. We then went up and saw the Queen. I can't remember whether she was in her dressing gown, I think she had got dressed already for breakfast, I think it was probably in the private dining room. We went in together because she was anxious to hear my account of my conversation with David Smith and fascinated equally by Martin's having addressed Mr Whitlam as Prime Minister. I think she was indeed surprised, as surprised as we had been. She certainly gave no indication to me that there had been any thought that something like this would happen.'[26]

Asked about the Queen's view of the dismissal, Heseltine said: 'Ha, ha, I think she is an old and wily bird about her own views. She certainly wouldn't have stated it categorically.' Heseltine said that 'to the extent that I could divine what she felt I think she felt the same' as himself and Charteris.[27] Heseltine also said: 'I'm reasonably confident myself that she thought it could have been handled better.'[28]

In previous interviews with the authors, Heseltine said of the Queen: 'She was very interested in the news but also concerned about it. But she felt, as we did, there was little she could do about it.'[29] Heseltine also said of the Queen's reaction: 'I would hesitate to say that she was shocked. It would be true to say that none of us at the time thought that this was an ideal solution to the crisis. It would be fair to say, however, that both Sir Martin Charteris and myself felt that it was a pity that this very drastic solution was applied exactly when it was and that a little bit more political leeway would have enabled a political solution to emerge in Canberra and that would have been a very much more desirable outcome.'[30]

Indeed, Charteris said in 1995 that 'there was plenty of drama in Buckingham Palace after it became known'. But in keeping with her practice, the Queen has not disclosed her actual view of the dismissal of the Whitlam government.

A few weeks after the dismissal the official secretary at Australia House, London, Tim McDonald, had a discussion with Charteris, whom he knew well. McDonald was the official channel with the Palace on a range of protocol-related issues such as the Order of Australia. In 1995 he relayed this conversation with Charteris to Paul Kelly and John Menadue in separate notes:

> 'It was a few weeks after the dismissal that I asked him for his personal view of the events. What, I asked, would have been his

advice to the Queen in a comparable situation? His reply suggested that the Palace shared the view that Kerr acted prematurely. He said that if faced with a constitutional crisis which it appeared likely to involve head of state his advice would have been that she should only intervene when a "clear sense of inevitability" had developed in the public that she must act. This had been Kerr's mistake.'[31]

McDonald said the comment from Charteris 'made such an impression on me at the time that I am confident that the recollection is accurate'. He said the import was that the head of state must only act 'independently' and 'in accordance with public opinion' not 'as the instrument of political forces'.[32]

During their 1977 Buckingham Palace discussion Charteris asked Hasluck whether, when Kerr sacked Whitlam, he acted as a politician or a judge. Charteris was inclined to the view that Kerr 'had acted judicially on the facts' but Hasluck felt Kerr's thinking had been 'more political than judicial'.

Hasluck told Charteris: 'It seemed to me that in the period leading up to [the] crisis the Governor-General had either acted politically or had been neglectful. Of course, this view arose from my view that in a constitutional monarchy the wisdom is to avoid confrontation and never let an issue come to a crisis in the political sense.' He noted that Charteris 'was in general agreement with my doctrine and we recalled the words about "counsel, advice and warning."'[33]

In response to Charteris, Hasluck expounded on the political skills a governor-general required to avoid a confrontation. He told Charteris that Kerr had not been sufficiently 'diligent and attentive to the duties of his office'. He believed the heart of the problem lay in the lack of trust and confidence between Whitlam and Kerr and, if this had existed, 'there never would have been a crisis'. Charteris endorsed Hasluck's conception of the role of governor-general.[34]

Heseltine captured what was the hardly repressed orthodoxy at the

Palace: 'I think that had there been a different Governor-General, as I say had Paul Hasluck agreed to stay on a few years, the events would not have transpired as they did . . . They [Whitlam and Hasluck] would have had a relationship which would have precluded the turn of events which took place.'[35]

It is a revealing assessment. It shows the considered view of the senior officials advising the Queen was that a prudent governor-general would have likely averted the confrontation, given priority to a settlement short of a surprise dismissal and that the solution Kerr hit upon exposed his own deficiencies – the Hasluck argument.

After the event and in private, Kerr had many doubts. His notes and diaries reveal a degree of agonising and obsession. There are long handwritten notes that become harder to decipher as they get longer and, presumably, as the night grew older.

In his thirteen-page handwritten note of 1977 he pondered 'the legitimacy of everything done by me' and confided he had long thought about 'the effect of dismissal of the Whitlam Government upon the position of the monarchy in Australia, the effect upon the governor-generalship, possible moves for a republic or an elected governor-general and the constitutional impact, generally, on the decision, both before and after it was made'. He did worry that he may have damaged the standing of the monarchy and eroded public trust in the office of governor-general.[36]

Kerr, in a 1977 letter to Menzies, wrote: 'I have several times since 1975, including immediately after November 11 and immediately after 13 December raised the question whether this nation would be helped by a resignation, not myself wishing to resign, but to give the Queen and the Prime Minister an opportunity to express an opinion.' He worried about the impact of his continued presence upon the monarchy and whether he had 'a duty, independent of party political interests to help to heal wounds'.[37]

But Kerr deluded himself about the Palace. The treasure-trove of private notes left after his death shows his conviction that the Queen and Charteris had been with him. He was proud of the letters he wrote to the Queen during the crisis, keeping her informed. 'Conversations with the Queen and with Sir Martin Charteris, as well as questions raised by me in the correspondence itself left me with the comfortable assurance that what I was writing, and the way I was going about the task, were welcomed in the Palace,' Kerr wrote.[38]

Kerr stunned the Palace when he dismissed Whitlam. The monarchy recovered from this event but its judgement of Kerr did not. The Palace engaged in a reassessment of Kerr as the Queen's representative. The consequences spoke for themselves. No prudent monarch, and Elizabeth II was nothing if not prudent, would have risked the fallout Kerr provoked by the dismissal.

In the end it is apparent that Buckingham Palace, suspicious of Kerr's character, worried about his reliability and concerned about his legacy, wanted him gone. 'Everybody was extremely relieved when he indicated that he was going to go,' Heseltine said.[39] And Kerr, by his own admission, felt his time had come. In his epic *The English Constitution*, Walter Bagehot said: 'We must not let in daylight upon magic. We must not bring the Queen into the combat of politics or she will cease to be reverenced by all combatants; she will become one combatant among many.'

The test required by monarchy is that of constitutional tranquillity and confrontation avoidance. As the Queen's representative, it is the test Kerr failed.

Kerr and Fraser:
The Tip-Off

At 9.55 a.m. on the morning of 11 November 1975, three hours before the governor-general dismissed the prime minister, the private phone rang in the Parliament House office of the leader of the opposition. It was Sir John Kerr ringing direct from Government House. This would be the most significant conversation Kerr and Malcolm Fraser had prior to the dismissal. It has been an issue of fierce controversy since it was first revealed in 1987 – but substantial new evidence puts the issue beyond any doubt.

In this call Kerr tipped off Fraser about his plan to dismiss Whitlam that afternoon. The extraordinary feature of the dismissal is not just that Whitlam did not know he was going to be dismissed – it is also that Fraser was forewarned. Kerr was not just defying the advice of his prime minister. The governor-general was in collusion with the opposition leader over his intention to commission Fraser that afternoon and gift him victory in the greatest political contest in the nation's history.

Kerr's motive was obvious. He was worried the sacking of Whitlam might be undone that afternoon. Kerr wanted a quick political execution. This meant preparing the pathway with Fraser. It was a double operation: the dismissal of Whitlam and the commissioning of Fraser. The two would occur within minutes of each other. In order to guarantee a smooth event Kerr had two imperatives: to take Whitlam by surprise and to forewarn Fraser about the terms of the caretaker commission he must accept.

Fraser was ready and prepared. The defeat of Whitlam was comprehensive – it was a joint Kerr–Fraser effort.

An earlier meeting that morning between Whitlam and Fraser had failed to break the deadlock. Kerr was proceeding with his plans. The prime minister rang the governor-general on his private line to confirm what Kerr expected – Whitlam would visit at lunchtime to advise a half-senate election. Whitlam explained he would need to brief his party room on this decision mid-morning and wanted to ensure Kerr felt no discourtesy. Kerr agreed. He had no problem with Whitlam's timetable. In truth, Kerr had no interest in Whitlam's half-senate election. He was planning a spectacular event. Whitlam was left believing that Kerr would authorise the Senate poll.

Fraser was in his office preparing for his own joint party meeting. The building was engulfed in drama. Whitlam was expected to call a half-senate election. The moment of truth was at hand – if Kerr gave Whitlam his election, Fraser's strategy was defeated. Labor MPs felt on the brink of victory in their struggle against Fraser. The press gallery, humming with excitement, assumed the momentum lay with Whitlam. Fraser knew that internal discipline was paramount: he had to keep his party room united and stifle any panic.

Kerr confirms that he rang Fraser at this point. 'He opened by saying that this [call] would have to remain confidential,' recalled Fraser.[1] As Kerr spoke, Fraser looked for a piece of paper. He picked up the one-page, three-item agenda paper for the joint party meeting scheduled at 10 a.m. Fraser turned it over and recorded the essence of their discussion. Fraser was not alone. Senate leader Reg Withers and opposition whip Vic Garland were both in the office.

Kerr, as Fraser recalled, asked his response to a series of undertakings put as questions. This is how Fraser recalled those questions: 'If Whitlam was dismissed and Fraser was made prime minister, would he agree to call a double dissolution election? Would he agree to run a caretaker administration, making no policy changes? Would he obtain supply straightaway? Would he advise a dissolution on that very day? [And] Kerr asked Fraser to guarantee that no action would be taken against the ministers of the Whitlam government over the loans affair, and that there would be no royal commission.'[2] Fraser answered 'yes' to each of these questions.

As they spoke Fraser jotted down six points summarising what Kerr told him. The authors now have in their possession a copy of both sides of this note, which is part of the Malcolm Fraser Collection at The University of Melbourne. The note is made in Fraser's handwriting. It is a shorthand version of the phone conversation. It records six clear points (although two are numbered five): 1) double dissolution bills; 2) caretaker; 3) no policy changes; 4) no royal commissions; 5) plus supply; 5) dissolution today.

Later that day, Fraser made an additional note on the sheet of paper in a different pen recording the time as 9.55 a.m., the date as 11 November 1975, and signed it. It was a memento of a pivotal phone call. He had stepped closer to the prime ministership.

Fraser said he now knew this 'was the day Kerr intended to act'. Clearly, he knew this as a fact, unlike Whitlam. Fraser, however, tries to excuse Kerr as well. He said Kerr made it clear no final decision had been taken. He says he could not be certain from this call that Kerr would dismiss Whitlam. '[I] still wasn't certain that, once faced with an ultimatum, Whitlam would not back down and choose to go to an election as prime minister,' Fraser said.[3] But this is wordplay on Fraser's part.

Fraser now knew what Kerr was planning. The conditions Kerr was imposing on Fraser's caretaker commission were vital and he wanted to ensure they would be accepted in full without problems or negotiations. Fraser understood this. Fraser also knew the chance of Whitlam backing down was remote: he had just come from a meeting with Whitlam where the prime minister's determination was undiminished. The scenario Kerr put to Fraser that morning played out in this exact manner in the afternoon. There can be no other conclusion: Fraser was tipped off in order to make the operation as smooth as possible.

This call is a matter of disagreement between Kerr and Fraser. Kerr said he called Fraser that morning but they did not discuss any undertakings as Fraser outlined. The purpose of the phone call, argued Kerr, was to confirm that the meeting with Whitlam that morning had failed to produce a circuit-breaker. 'I next spoke to Mr Fraser who confirmed that the position and the opposition policy remained the same,' Kerr wrote in his memoir *Matters for Judgment*. 'I said nothing else to him about the situation.'[4] Kerr said these questions, or undertakings, were only put to Fraser in the study at Government House before he was commissioned as caretaker prime minister.

When Paul Kelly interviewed Fraser in May 1995, he said he had absolutely 'no doubt' about the matters discussed in that morning phone call. Asked what he felt when being presented with those questions, Fraser said: 'I felt then that unless Whitlam changed and recommended something sensible, Whitlam was going to get dismissed.'

The doubts about Fraser's account of this phone call were given weight because Fraser, over many years, could not find the note he made of the conversation. Indeed, in 1995 Fraser told Kelly that he had lost the handwritten note. Eventually the note was rediscovered. Fraser told Troy Bramston he had found the note when he began sorting his papers in the 2000s and gave Bramston a copy of it in 2013.

The weight of evidence overwhelmingly supports Fraser's view against Kerr. Fraser argued that of all the discussions in his political life this is the one he would be least likely to forget. He has no ulterior motive since the revelation is a potential embarrassment for him as well. But Fraser is scathing of Kerr's version of events. 'Look, denying it was a sign of weakness,' Fraser said of Kerr. 'There are many signs of weakness in his character, and that is probably true of most of us. It was an error of judgement and it was a weakness not to explain it how I've explained it.'[5]

Fraser's explanation is that Kerr did nothing improper; he merely checked to be sure Fraser would accept the terms of the commission. But Fraser also offers another explanation for Kerr's dissembling: that Kerr was under such pressure post-dismissal 'with conspiracy theories being floated' that he preferred denial to fanning another conspiracy.

In 1997–98, Reg Withers gave an oral history interview to the National Library of Australia. Revealed here for the first time, Withers recalls he was in Fraser's office with Vic Garland when Fraser's private line rang. 'He took up his big felt pen,' ready to make his note, Withers said. 'Vic and I could read it upside down. It was the four or five points that Kerr had laid down . . . he [Fraser] agreed when Kerr said they'd be the conditions . . . Anything that Kerr and Fraser said since has been . . . none of them told the truth about that.' Withers said that 'Malcolm was so excited he didn't realise we were there' but 'he came to and took the paper aside'.[6]

Withers believes Kerr had previously rung Fraser on his private line. He recalls being in Fraser's office a number of days before the dismissal when Fraser took a call, had a short conversation and told Withers: 'You never heard that.' Withers had initially thought it might be his wife, Tamie, but Fraser had said, 'No, no, it wasn't.' Withers had no doubt he and Garland were eyewitnesses to a significant phone call.

Vic Garland is the only one of the three Liberals in Fraser's office who is still alive. Interviewed in July 2015, Garland said: 'I do have a recollection of that morning. I was standing in Fraser's office with Reg Withers. In terms of this dispute it is Fraser and Withers who are right and it is Kerr who is wrong. These were important items being discussed and this event has stuck in my mind. I recollect Malcolm making a note. But I don't think he said much at the end of the conversation. Malcolm was always reticent about these things.'

Garland pointed out that he had no disrespect for Kerr. When he was high commissioner in London the two men saw each other and would reminisce on the events. But Garland, like Fraser, said that 'it made perfect sense for Kerr to ask these questions'.[7]

In the afternoon of 11 November, Dale Budd, Fraser's principal private secretary, saw the note scrawled at 9.55 a.m. sitting on Fraser's desk. It was already signed and marked by Fraser in bold pen at the bottom right-hand corner. Budd had not been in the room during the phone call. But he describes the call as Kerr indicating to Fraser 'the provisions applying to a caretaker government, should Fraser be commissioned in that role'.[8] Budd told the authors he photocopied the note that afternoon. 'I thought it was an interesting and potentially historical document,' he said. The authors have a copy of Budd's photocopy.

During 2005 and 2006 a public dispute arose between Sir David Smith and Dale Budd about some of the events and phone calls between them on the morning of 11 November, including the 9.55 a.m. Fraser–Kerr call. The debate was conducted in the pages of the *Sydney Institute Quarterly*. As a result Budd decided to contact Fraser. He asked whether Fraser would provide him a letter to substantiate the position Budd had been taking against Smith and to verify the note. 'To my surprise instead of giving me a letter he sent a statutory declaration,' Budd said. He told Fraser he didn't want to use the statutory declaration in his dispute with Smith. He didn't want to create a bigger public event. Budd just sat on the statutory declaration.

Budd told the authors he spoke to Fraser at the time about the note and the circumstances of the Kerr call: 'Fraser told me that Kerr hadn't made up his mind. But Kerr wanted to be assured that if Fraser was sworn in as a caretaker Prime Minister that he would be agreed to the provisions. I've always regarded that as fair enough. But it was absolutely an indication of the way he was thinking. Fraser had no doubt about that.'[9]

Asked why he thought Kerr had denied the details of the call, Budd said: 'He probably felt he would have been strongly criticised for, in effect, telling Fraser what was going to happen when he hadn't warned Whitlam. I think he felt it was better to deny it.'

Fraser swore and signed the statutory declaration at Balnarring, Victoria, on 2 June 2006, affirming his version of the phone call.[10] Revealed here, we believe for the first time, Fraser declared that:

> Governor-General Sir John Kerr rang me at 9.55 am on 11 November 1975. The following is my recollection of the substance of the conversation that I had with the Governor-General and the undertakings which I gave to him.
>
> He wanted to know what actions I would take if I were Prime Minister. He emphasised that no decision had been made.
>
> I knew quite well at this point that, if Mr Whitlam were prepared to recommend a double dissolution, he would go to the election as Prime Minister.
>
> The main commitments I made were:
> · to pass supply.
> · to dissolve the Parliament.
> · a Fraser Government would act as caretaker only, making no new policies and no personnel changes in the Public Service.
> · there would be no police charges in relation to the Loans Affair.[11]
> · there would be no Royal Commission in relation to the Loans Affair.

This call made by Kerr to Fraser was first revealed by Philip Ayres in his book *Malcolm Fraser: A Biography*, published in 1987.[12] Ayres describes this as 'the most momentous call Fraser had ever taken'. Ayres notes that when Kerr wrote that he had 'said nothing else' about the situation he was referring to the opposition's policy on supply.

The Ayres account has Kerr putting the four questions that Fraser lists in his statutory declaration. 'He can't go to the end of the road with Whitlam,' Fraser told Ayres, 'and find that he's got an unacceptable situation as far as I'm concerned.' Fraser's biographer concluded that 'although he now felt sure of the outcome', Fraser 'did not yet have knowledge of it'.

There is validity in this fine distinction. But it cannot disguise the reality: Kerr had tipped off Fraser.

In the mid-1980s Fraser was interviewed by former Labor minister Clyde Cameron for the oral history program at the National Library of Australia. It has not previously been fully accessible. In that interview, Fraser spoke of the phone call with Kerr. 'He said something to the effect that I probably knew that the time was coming when he, as Governor-General, would have to make a final decision,' Fraser told Cameron. Fraser outlined the undertakings that Kerr sought if he were to appoint him caretaker prime minister. 'I thought it was entirely reasonable for the Governor-General wanting to know,' Fraser said. 'But he conducted that part of the conversation in ways that still left me not knowing, in any sense, what his own final decision would be. I think he did it in a way which was saying it would be wrong for him to make his final decision not knowing my response to these questions.'[13]

There is a recurring pattern: Fraser keeps depicting Kerr's approach as reasonable. Obviously, Fraser wants to avoid implicating himself in what many would see as a plot by Kerr to forewarn Fraser of the dismissal of Whitlam.

David Kemp, Fraser's senior adviser, was aware of the call and that Fraser took a note of it.[14] In an interview with Troy Bramston, Kemp said: 'This call was, I believe, interpreted by Fraser as a signal that Kerr was planning to act against Whitlam. The matters discussed and noted in Fraser's handwritten notes at the time, make this clear.' Kemp recalls that when news came through that Whitlam was to see Kerr that afternoon, Fraser phoned his wife, Tamie, in Melbourne.

'Whitlam is going to see the Governor General,' he said. 'You may see a prophecy fulfilled.'[15]

For nearly thirty years there has been controversy over the veracity of Fraser's account. It has been challenged by two notable supporters of Kerr: Gerard Henderson, author, commentator and executive director of the Sydney Institute, and David Smith, former official secretary to the governor-general.

When Ayres' biography was published, Henderson contacted Kerr and he agreed to an interview for *The Australian*. Kerr rejected Fraser's account. 'For one thing, I was still keeping open the possibility that Mr Whitlam would change his approach when he learned that the alternative was his dismissal,' Kerr told Henderson. 'Secondly, in all the circumstances it would have been extraordinarily unwise of me at that stage to have signalled my intentions to either political leader.' Henderson had extensive contact with Kerr at this time and reported that the former governor-general was 'full of contempt' towards Fraser for the account he had given Ayres.[16]

Henderson was given access to a twelve-page note written by Kerr about his discussions with Whitlam and Fraser on 11 November 1975. In that note, written on 16 November 1975, Kerr recalled: 'I rang Mr Fraser to find out whether it was true that they had got nowhere and whether it was the opposition intention to continue to refuse supply. His answer to both questions was "yes".' This note is now accessible in the National Archives of Australia.[17] But it does not reveal anything substantially different to what is in Kerr's memoir.

Henderson argued that Kerr's account is more believable than Fraser's. He pointed to Kerr's contemporary note. He highlighted the fact that Fraser apparently no longer had his own handwritten note. He put weight on the account given by political journalist Alan Reid, who wrote that Fraser assured him that he had no prior knowledge of Kerr's intentions.[18] Finally, Henderson argues that Kerr, an obsessively cautious man, would have taken an 'extraordinary risk' to signal his intentions to Fraser. There is, of course, another interpretation – as

Fraser has said, Kerr was actually being careful by ensuring the commissioning of Fraser would proceed smoothly.

Smith also disputes Fraser's account.[19] Smith says that when Kerr informed him about the phone call at the time, he did not mention any undertakings to Fraser. He describes Fraser's note as a 'recent invention'. Significantly, Smith was not present for the phone call. 'I was not in the study at that time,' he said.[20]

Smith cannot vouch for every call that Kerr made. Other important phone discussions have been omitted from Kerr's memoirs, for example, his early 11 November call to Sir Garfield Barwick, revealed in Barwick's files. Kerr may have a note dated 16 November but Fraser has a note dated 11 November, made at the time of the call, verified by several witnesses.

In relation to Alan Reid, the veteran journalist said Fraser made clear to him when leaving the building at lunchtime on 11 November that he had no idea what the governor-general wanted and that, subsequently, Fraser had also told him he had no knowledge of Kerr's plan. Frankly, this is hardly significant. It is nonsense to think Fraser would have told Reid while on his way to see the governor-general that he had been tipped off. It is also unremarkable that Fraser declined to reveal the content of this phone call for many years – until after he ceased being prime minister.[21]

There is no doubt that the conversation took place and no doubt that Fraser believed, as a result, that Kerr planned to sack Whitlam that afternoon. Fraser's note is authentic and constitutes powerful evidence. It has been validated by eyewitness accounts of the call and note, other sightings of the note and a statutory declaration from Fraser. In addition, since Fraser first revealed this story his account of the conversation has been remarkably consistent.

When Paul Kelly interviewed Fraser for the twentieth anniversary in May 1995 he gave an account of the discussion and the following exchange occurred:

Kelly: I would like to get this right. You've got a clear recollection in your mind?

Fraser: Yes. On this point absolute. There is no doubt . . . There were some people in my office at the time . . . They would have seen me take a few notes on a piece of paper . . .[22]

In Fraser's 2010 memoir co-authored with Margaret Simons, he provides another detailed account of the conversation with Kerr making clear that, as a result, he knew Kerr intended to act. In his interview twenty-five years ago with a doubting Gerard Henderson, Fraser was emphatic: 'But that conversation I'd be most unlikely to forget. And if it were not correct why in hell's name would I fabricate it . . .'[23]

After the phone call Fraser went into the joint party meeting. If anything was to go wrong, this was the moment. It was a strange event. They stood silent for two minutes to honour Armistice Day. Fraser and his deputy, Phil Lynch, had taken a tactical decision – they would say nothing to the party room about their earlier meeting with Whitlam and nothing about Whitlam's intention to call a half-senate election. Indeed, they wanted no discussion of the crisis. Their greatest fear would be expressions of alarm and unrest within the party room suggesting Fraser might not be able to hold his troops together.

Fraser had moved with a deliberative confidence during the morning and early afternoon of 11 November. He knew Kerr was about to act. He was alerted by a phone discussion that should not have occurred. It was an improper act by the governor-general. The terms of Fraser's commission should not have been canvassed at 9.55 that morning – only when Kerr commissioned Fraser at Government House that afternoon. Kerr's action constituted an unjustified tip-off to Malcolm Fraser.

3

Kerr and Whitlam:
The Deception

Sir John Kerr said in his memoirs that by Thursday, 6 November, with Gough Whitlam and Malcolm Fraser on a collision course, he had to take a decision. His guiding principle was to keep this decision secret from the prime minister. The reason was that Kerr feared dismissal by Whitlam if the prime minister had any inkling of his plans. Kerr was frank about concealing his plans from Whitlam – it is the first stage in a process legitimately called deception.

Kerr was explicit about his decision and his motive: 'I believed, quite starkly, that if I had said anything to Mr Whitlam about the possibility that I might take away his commission I would no longer have been there. I conceived it to be my proper behaviour in the circumstances to stay at my post and not invite dismissal . . . If Mr Whitlam or any other minister was deceived, he deceived himself.'[1]

It is true that Whitlam deceived himself but it is also true that Kerr, by what he said and failed to say, encouraged this deception. The heart of the crisis was Kerr's decision to deny Whitlam access to his judgement of the situation. He treated the prime minister as a dangerous potential adversary. In the end, he sacked Whitlam in what is correctly described as a constitutional ambush. This violated the convention and practice whereby the governor-general acts on the advice of the prime minister and engages frankly with the prime minister.

Nevertheless, Kerr justified his secrecy by saying that once Whitlam began to assert publicly that the governor-general 'had no choice but to adopt his advice', then Whitlam had 'disqualified himself' from access to Kerr's thinking. Kerr's belief that Whitlam was prepared to sack him became an abiding obsession. 'Mr Whitlam was not entitled to receive a running report on how I was wrestling with the problem he had set,' Kerr wrote with supreme arrogance.

In fact, the governor-general was damned by his closest friend during the crisis, High Court judge Sir Anthony Mason. When Mason explained his role in a 2012 statement, he said he told Kerr he should give Whitlam the chance of going to the election as prime minister, an option Kerr did not follow. Mason said he told Kerr that 'if he did not warn' Whitlam then 'he would run the risk that people would accuse him of being deceptive'.[2] It was a prophecy of startling accuracy. Whitlam hung the charge of deception around Kerr's neck.

Central to Kerr's strategy was his conditioning of Buckingham Palace. He devoted countless hours writing letters to the Palace designed to keep the Queen informed of events. These letters, despite their importance to Australian history, are still secret forty years later, in a self-serving deal negotiated between Government House and the Palace that mocks Australia's sovereignty. However, in a presumed oversight by officials at the National Archives, selected extracts from these letters were made available to the public in 2012. The extracts are sufficient to reveal that Kerr was implying to the Queen that Whitlam was beyond the limits of reason.

On 20 October 1975 Kerr wrote to the Palace: 'The Prime Minister's position has hardened and changed considerably in the last forty-eight hours. He has now decided that he will advise no election of any kind whatsoever. On Saturday he told me that he is determined to break the alleged power of the Senate to force an election, at its whim, of the House of Representatives by denying supply . . . He has, so he says, finally and irrevocably decided never to take the House of Representatives to the people because the Senate denies it power to govern by cutting off money. He will not do this now, not next May, nor ever. He has said something along these lines publicly and has been accused by Mr Anthony, the Leader of the National–Country Party, of attempting to stand over the Governor-General.'[3]

In short, Kerr was telling the Queen that Whitlam was seeking to intimidate him. There is no doubt he felt this. His conditioning of the Palace, however, was subtle. A constitutional ambush conceived in secret would be a remarkable event, but Kerr could not foreshadow any dismissal since that would implicate the Queen. He depicted Whitlam as an unreasonable man prone to intimidation, laying the basis for his justification, though the full import of his letters cannot be assessed until they are released. Under current policy that is after 8 December 2027, fifty years from Kerr's retirement as governor-general.

Not only did Kerr omit to inform Whitlam of his views but he selected his own constitutional advisers from outside the government. His principal personal adviser was his old friend Mason and his ultimate constitutional adviser became the chief justice, Sir Garfield Barwick. Kerr's separate and initial contacts with Mason and Barwick came before the blocking of supply in mid-October. Whitlam was in complete ignorance that the governor-general, supposed to take advice from the government, had initiated his own advisory arrangements within the High Court.

How did the government perceive Kerr?

The head of the Prime Minister's Department, John Menadue, wrote a document during the month between the dismissal and the subsequent election assessing the crisis, relating a number of personal discussions and reviewing what had happened. Referring to the period before supply was blocked, Menadue said: 'There was no doubt that Mr Whitlam believed that the Governor-General was sympathetic to his position and the problems with the Senate. In conversation also with me the Governor-General gave the very clear impression that he regarded the course proposed by the Opposition as being quite improper. This arose during discussions I had with him at briefing sessions in the months leading up to the crisis . . .'[4]

Menadue said that when Whitlam, in an act of folly, authorised Kerr to begin talks with Fraser: 'He [Whitlam] believed that the governor-general would encourage Mr Fraser to desist from the course he was following.' Interviewed in 1995, Menadue made clear that Kerr's tactics, up to the dismissal on 11 November, had succeeded brilliantly. 'We were still trusting,' he said. 'I certainly was . . . [Kerr] deceived the prime minister without any doubt whatsoever and insofar as it was relevant, he deceived me.'[5]

A minister who actually opposed Whitlam's 'tough-it-out' tactic of not going to an election, John Wheeldon, said: 'I was at Government House chatting to Kerr . . . He said to me, "How are *we* going?" It struck me at once – how are *we* going? When I got back to Parliament House I bumped to Jim McClelland and said to him, "Well, your friend Kerr is onside all right". . . McClelland replied, "That's good. I'm just on my way to see Gough, so I'll tell him."'[6]

McClelland, also a minister in the Whitlam government, had been Kerr's personal friend, an enthusiastic supporter of his appointment to the office, and spoke with Kerr several times during the crisis. 'I wouldn't have held it against Kerr if he had just been honest,' McClelland said later. 'If he had said to Gough, "Prime Minister, I'm in a dilemma and I might soon have no option but to dismiss you." But he didn't. Instead he planned an ambush. He did his best to deceive us and mislead us about his intentions on the reserve powers.'[7]

Interviewed for this book, Whitlam's speechwriter, Graham Freudenberg, offered his personal diagnosis of Labor's tragedy: 'We thought, for instance, that Kerr was an honourable man. We were not going to be diverted from our course by facing up to the fact that we were dealing with a lot of bastards. It all goes down to what I now admit was our culpable blindness during the crisis. It was our willingness to suspend our judgement about people.'[8]

The two Labor prime ministers most influenced by the dismissal were Whitlam and Keating, the most senior and junior ministers at the time. Keating was sworn in as a minister on the eve of the crisis. He has a memorable recollection of attending Government House with Whitlam for an Executive Council meeting on 6 November. Interviewed by the authors in 2015, Keating told the story. Whitlam and Kerr had a private discussion first and then Keating was ushered into the room:

'As the door opened there's huge guffawing going on, huge – not just chuckles but huge laughing going on. So I take my seat and I finally get let into the secret. The laughter was about their view that [Lionel] Murphy and [Garfield] Barwick deserved each other, and that Murphy was having an argument with Barwick about the uniform for a female tipstaff. At some point, maybe seven or eight or ten minutes into this yarn, the governor-general said, "Well, we should transact the business of the day." A couple of minutes after that we all get up to leave and as we are walking I'm to the right of Gough, and Gough is between me and Sir John Kerr. And Gough says to me, "Look at his leonine mane, the big silver crop of hair." What can you say? I said, "He can lend me some," making a joke, so there was much goodwill on the way to the door.

'When we get in the car Gough sits in the front. I get in the back. Gough has the habit of immediately going back and having a slight nap, so we turned the circle and were about to leave the gate. I said, "Gough, he seems all right," referring to the crisis. He turned round and said, "He's entirely proper, he'll do the right thing."'[9]

This was the day Kerr began planning to dismiss the government.

When Whitlam was dismissed five days later, Keating was enraged. 'It was a premeditated and an elaborate deception,' he said of Kerr. 'I absolutely knew [Kerr] had garrotted [Whitlam].'

'Sir John Kerr's deception was twofold,' Whitlam later said in his memoirs. 'At all stages, he failed to "counsel and warn"; he never disclosed to his constitutional advisers his concerns or the course he had in mind. It follows by necessary inference that he deliberately misled us: at the very time he had determined to dismiss us, he consciously and deliberately left us to believe that he understood and supported what we were doing. His was a double deceit – by omission and commission.'[10]

It was the fusion of two elements in Kerr that fuelled Labor's post-dismissal rage – deliberate concealment of his thinking and the pretence of friendship. The evidence is manifest on both counts. That is the reason Keating was angry.

On 30 October Whitlam and McClelland went to Government House for an Executive Council meeting and, at Kerr's instigation, they stayed for lunch afterwards. It was a jovial and friendly event with plenty of banter and flattery. McClelland said, 'I had a glass of wine with [Kerr]. Whitlam didn't.' At one point Kerr, looking at Whitlam and then nodding towards McClelland, asked, 'Well, how's he going?' Whitlam paused and replied, 'Good, bloody good, but he gets a bit histrionic at times.' They chatted about the crisis and the governor-general sought Whitlam's approval to meet Fraser again to explore a possible compromise. Whitlam and McClelland assumed that Kerr was helping, trying to do them a favour. Whitlam remembered Kerr saying Fraser 'had to have an escape' or his leadership would be threatened.[11]

This lunch had an impact on the ministers. McClelland later said: 'The only deduction which could *not* be drawn from what he said to us was that he contemplated in any way exercising the option which he ultimately exercised.' After the dismissal McClelland remembered a remark Kerr made when they left. Turning to McClelland and referring to his job as a minister, Kerr said: 'Of course all this . . . is just gloss on your career.' McClelland later called this a 'preparatory apology' for what might come.

But McClelland's anger was prompted by a phone call Kerr made one night to his Sydney home. It was another discussion about the possible compromise: 'The Governor-General spoke to me about Mr Fraser having painted himself into a corner and how we could get him off the hook, how he and I and the Labor Government could collaborate to solve the problem by finding a solution for Mr Fraser which would not involve a total loss of face . . .'[12] McClelland never forgave Kerr for his tactics.

There were several remarks Kerr made to Whitlam that encouraged the prime minister. Early in the crisis on Sunday, 19 October, Kerr complained to Whitlam in a phone discussion about newspapers, notably from News Limited, seeking to 'intimidate' him by implying he had to act. The upshot was that Whitlam incorporated into his speech for the following Tuesday a critique of the papers, thinking he was assisting Kerr. The prime minister said in parliament: 'Now we have the headlines: "Will Sir John Kerr act?" and "Fraser says Kerr must sack PM". Where will this intimidation stop?'[13]

Two days later Kerr rang Whitlam, who left a caucus meeting to take the call. The governor-general raised the publicly released opinion by opposition frontbencher Bob Ellicott QC, on whom Fraser was relying, arguing for Kerr to dismiss Whitlam because he could not obtain supply. Ellicott's opinion went to the heart of the crisis. 'This Ellicott opinion . . . it's all bullshit, isn't it?' Kerr asked. Whitlam could only be encouraged. He took great hope from this remark – yet it proved a false hope.[14]

On the morning of 11 November, Whitlam rang Kerr to make arrangements to visit Government House to advise on a half-senate election. Whitlam explained his intention: he cleared with Kerr the fact that the Labor caucus was going to be told. Did Kerr have any objections? No, Kerr said, that was fine. Whitlam assumed, falsely, that his recommendation for a half-senate election would also be fine.

Fundamental to these political and social exchanges Labor ministers describe with Kerr is the absence of any direct comment by the governor-general in which he rejects dismissal as an option. He did not rule out dismissal because dismissal was an option. Kerr did not lie to Whitlam. He did not have to lie because Whitlam never engaged him directly on the key issues. This aversion to any intimacy with Kerr was Whitlam's blunder, and turned their interaction into a flawed psychological drama. Having decided not to speak frankly with Whitlam, Kerr said that 'any guesses' the prime minister made about the governor-general's thinking were Whitlam's own responsibility. This is far too cute. Kerr was encouraging Whitlam and his ministers. He did not lie but he did mislead.

The evidence is overwhelming from minister after minister. So is the behaviour pattern – it fits with Kerr's character as a social being who liked to chatter. Labor assumed he was its friend and that assumption was correct – Kerr was its friend until he dismissed the government. If Fraser and the Senate had folded, then Whitlam and his ministers would have known Kerr only as a loyal and true friend. If Whitlam had won this battle, he would always have seen Kerr as an unwavering supporter. All the signals Kerr sent to Whitlam and his ministers were about assurance and Labor, in turn, seemed pathetically grateful.

But being governor-general in the 1975 crisis was not about friendship. It was about responsibility. This reveals the shallowness of Whitlam's thinking. As prime minister, Whitlam was officially Kerr's adviser. He should have engaged Kerr on the fundamentals of the crisis: his view of the situation, his role as governor-general and of the reserve powers. 'It could perhaps have been different if he had asked me,' Kerr said. 'Mr Whitlam's failure to ask my view of the Reserve Powers must, I have always believed, have been deliberate avoidance.'[15] This is Kerr's strong point: it is where Whitlam deceived himself as much as Kerr deceived him.

In the end, however, the issue of deception turns on Kerr's refusal to counsel or warn Whitlam before resorting to the reserve powers. When all the views are read and re-read, when all the analysis is completed, this is the sticking point. Kerr as governor-general violated the classic texts and conventions surrounding the Crown's discretion.

Walter Bagehot wrote in *The English Constitution* that the Crown has three rights – 'the right to be consulted, the right to encourage, the right to warn'. It is the enduring rule. There is simply no justification for the failure to apply this on the ultimate question of dismissal. Kerr's obligation was to tell Whitlam that, without a solution, he might need to dismiss him and obtain a prime minister who would advise an election. That would have given Whitlam the opportunity to respond to this reality. No amount of Whitlamesque lofty intimidation can exempt Kerr from this responsibility.

Bill Hayden, drawing upon his own later experience as governor-general, said, 'Kerr should have had the courage and conviction about his own role in the crisis to express himself frankly to Whitlam.'[16]

There were two governors-general under Whitlam – Hasluck and Kerr. The problem in Kerr's self-defence is that Hasluck enjoyed a frank, cooperative and honest relationship with Whitlam. Hasluck recalled they discussed policy, politics and personalities 'in a fatherly way', which Whitlam welcomed. During Hasluck's 1977 discussion with the Queen's private secretary, Sir Martin Charteris, he said he found Whitlam 'very responsive to a question or a cautionary word' – the complete opposite of Kerr's obsessive depiction.

As Hasluck said, the art of the job is to find political solutions short of confrontation. He explained the rules: 'With the Prime Minister, the Governor-General can be expected to talk with frankness and friendliness, to question, discuss, suggest and counsel.'[17] Kerr should have been straight instead of playing a double game. Because Kerr decided he could not talk frankly with Whitlam, he was locked into deceiving Whitlam, an untenable position for the Crown.

In his retirement years, Kerr's obsession was with self-justification. Nobody was spared. On 3 November 1983 he wrote to his son, Philip, from his third-floor flat in Pall Mall, London, about the publication in *Quadrant* of an article by Hasluck:

He, I believe, got on quite well with Whitlam during his day; indeed, he told me his relations with Whitlam were easier and better than his relations with Coalition Prime Ministers who were in office during his Governor-Generalship. However, the Whitlam I knew was a totally different person from the one he knew. It was impossible to talk to him about the crisis. He was determined to "smash the Senate", quite willing to "crash through or crash". There was no possibility whatsoever of getting him to listen to any views of mine on any aspect of the crisis. This he made perfectly clear. The whole business was beyond argument, beyond talk. I did what I could do; in fact, I did rather more than might have been wise, bearing in mind the risks I was running.[18]

It is a father's defence to his son. Sadly, it is misplaced. Whitlam was a difficult and overbearing man. Because the governor-general, like the Queen, has the dismissal power, he has the necessary lever to engage the prime minister. Kerr choose concealment in dealing with Whitlam and, as a consequence, became an agent of deception.

4

Barwick, Mason and the High Court

Forty years after the intervention by Chief Justice Sir Garfield Barwick in the 1975 crisis, the values and norms of the High Court have changed significantly. Barwick's more recent successors have asserted that any comparable event is inconceivable or at least most unlikely. This is because after the events of 1975, the separation of powers doctrine and the imperative for the court to be impartial have gained fresh intensity.

Barwick made little effort, then or later, to conceal his enthusiasm for a role in dispatching the Whitlam government. While the advice he provided was a legal opinion on the constitutional powers of the governor-general, Barwick believed he had an influence on Kerr's action. Barwick knew that Kerr shunned conflict and tended to 'temporise'. He believed he 'stiffened' Kerr to the task.[1] The chief justice became, in the public's mind, an authorising agent for the governor-general.

This is exactly what Kerr wanted – his resort to the chief justice invested the dismissal with constitutional weight and the perception of High Court consent, which was intended to increase his leverage over public opinion. Kerr did not need Barwick's opinion to act. Yet

Kerr, a prudent man despite this audacity, wanted to implicate the High Court in his decision – and Barwick, eyes wide open, was a willing participant in this collaboration. It is absurd to believe Barwick did not strengthen Kerr's personal resolve.

Former High Court chief justice Sir Gerard Brennan (1995–98) and current High Court chief justice Robert French, appointed in 2008, argue that the reaction against Barwick has also changed the High Court since the 1975 crisis. Brennan told the authors: 'The reaction to the events of that date demonstrates that there is now a public expectation that the Chief Justice will not participate, whether by advice or otherwise, in an exercise of a prerogative or reserve power.' This is an unqualified repudiation, if not of Barwick's action, then of the so-called Barwick 'rules'.[2]

Interviewed by the authors, French said: 'Obviously I cannot speak for future chief justices but I think that the controversy attaching to the events of 1975 would be a significant disincentive against the provision of advice quite apart from the absence of any constitutional warrant for doing so.' French starts with the Constitution: 'There is nothing in the Constitution to suggest that it is part of the function of the chief justice to provide independent advice to the governor-general in relation to the powers of the governor-general or the discharge of those powers.'[3]

While French declines to address Barwick's action directly, he repudiates any remnant of the Barwick 1975 principles that saw the chief justice advising the governor-general.

The 'new' post-Barwick rule was famously and initially put when Chief Justice Brennan delivered a eulogy in Barwick's honour on 5 August 1997. He made a pithy comment about Barwick's 1975 advice: 'It was, and remains, a controversial matter but, if only on that account, will not happen again.'[4]

Brennan's prediction is almost certainly accurate. In a 2009 speech, French quoted Brennan's remark on Barwick's intervention and said: 'I agree with that sentiment.'[5] French's position entrenches the contemporary High Court's belief that Barwick's advice reflects standards now obsolete that would no longer pass the tests of judicial impartiality and proper behaviour for a chief justice.

Asked about Barwick's involvement, former High Court chief justice Murray Gleeson (1998–2008) said: 'I think the public reaction to what Barwick did would constitute a very substantial warning . . . I was twenty years the chief justice (in NSW and in Australia) and I was never asked to advise any incumbent governor or governor-general on the exercise of any power. Now, maybe one reason I wasn't asked was because of the public reaction to what Barwick did. That is not to say I never had conversations with people about matters relevant to their office.'[6]

Gleeson said one reason he may not have been asked for advice was because no issue or crisis arose. 'But another reason, I think, would be that there would be caution about it because of the reaction to what Barwick did.'

However, Gleeson sounded a note of caution about Barwick's intervention: 'I wouldn't go so far as to say it is impossible that it would ever arise again. I am cautious about saying never.' Gleeson explains the main reason for his caution: 'If the governor-general can't go to the chief justice, to whom can the governor-general go? It can't be the case that the governor-general is legally bound to rely only on the advice of ministers.'

So the defect in the system revealed by 1975 is still unresolved. The reaction against Barwick's actions makes any future resort by a governor-general to a chief justice almost certainly untenable – yet there is no obvious alternative source of independent advice if the chief justice is ruled out.

Reflecting on the events of 1975, Gleeson highlighted the role of personalities: 'Barwick had been a prominent politician. He had political involvement and political associations. The relationship, for example, between Barwick and Menzies, would have been entirely different from any relationship I ever had with a prime minister.'[7]

This identifies the different culture that prevailed in the 1975 era. Barwick was sharp and domineering. Virtually everybody in law and politics, except Sir Robert Menzies, was treated as his junior. He was a legal technician but highly political in his views. Barwick's life had been based on giving advice to lawyers and politicians. Instructing them was his second nature and it had made him rich and famous. Kerr had known Barwick for many years and their friendship had grown over time. Many observers felt that Kerr seeking advice from the chief justice was a contentious step. For Kerr, however, given he intended to dismiss the prime minister, it was a protective move. He knew his man – as colleague, judge and former Menzies minister.

Barwick, having been approached by Kerr, said the 'safe' option would be to refuse to give advice but that would have been the action of a person of 'craven spirits'. The chief justice could not conceal his enthusiasm. Aware that his role would be contentious, Barwick was nevertheless confident that 'my office and my own reputation would more than survive any unreasonable and partisan assault'.[8] But such confidence was, at least to a degree, misplaced.

Central to the Barwick controversy is the nature of the opinion he gave – it was contentious and, in the view of many, flawed. Its content inflamed the debate about Barwick's involvement and helped to cast the chief justice as a partisan figure, an argument addressed later in this book.[9] Fundamental to the changed culture of the High Court since 1975 has been the absence of another appointment from politics like Barwick and the diminished probability of any such appointment from partisan politics in future.

The extent to which Kerr involved the High Court is unappreciated. As well as formal advice from Barwick, Kerr had a more sustained yet informal dialogue with Sir Anthony Mason, then a judge of the High Court who later became its chief justice.

While Barwick's meetings with Kerr were publicised and his advice became public, the details of the Kerr–Mason dialogue before and during the 1975 crisis on the governor-general's options have been a tightly held secret for much of the past forty years. The public reluctance to address Mason's role in Whitlam's dismissal has been extraordinary. This appears an unjustified oversight. During our interviews there was a palpable distaste on the part of other judges to address the question of Mason's involvement. This is partly because they feel unsure of the full story and Mason has not sought to enlighten the public beyond a single public statement in 2012. This reveals a reluctance on Mason's part over many years to provide the public with the full story. The lack of discussion about Mason's role is partly a function of his reputation: he is widely seen as leading one of the most innovative and progressive High Courts in our history.

In his 2012 statement, Mason confirmed he and Kerr had a number of discussions between August 1975 and Whitlam's dismissal. Mason said he was not advising Kerr but outlined a number of views he expressed at the time to the governor-general. These discussions were deliberately confidential. According to Mason, Kerr said he might have to exercise the reserve powers and dismiss Whitlam, that he was thinking of consulting the chief justice, that Whitlam had told him he was not to consult with Barwick, that he nevertheless believed Barwick would be willing to advise him and that Kerr feared Whitlam might seek to remove him from office.

One of the most important discussions between Mason and Kerr occurred on 9 November 1975 when the governor-general told Mason he had decided to dismiss Whitlam. Kerr asked Mason for his opinion on the 'draft' advice from the law officers and Mason told Kerr he did not agree with it. Mason said that Kerr asked him for a written opinion to that effect, which Mason said he could not provide without consulting Barwick. However, Mason did agree at Kerr's request to draft a letter terminating the prime minister's commission, although his version was not actually used. Mason said he disagreed with some aspects of Kerr's 'account of events'. Importantly, Mason said that he advised Kerr on more than one occasion that he 'had a duty to warn the prime minister of his intended action' so that Whitlam had the opportunity of remaining prime minister.[10]

In 1981, Kerr wrote a detailed note about his discussions with Mason during the crisis. Kerr said Mason had no difficulty discussing the governor-general's options in the crisis. Kerr said that they had a 'running' dialogue and Mason 'never felt that his position on the court rendered that course of action undesirable or impossible'. Kerr said his dialogue with Mason was 'historically important' and that there was no other person who 'could better, by conversation, help me to sort out my own thoughts on the constitutional powers of the governor-general'.[11]

Yet Mason has offered no explanation of how a confidential 'running' dialogue with Kerr, involving the reserve powers and the circumstances in which Whitlam might be dismissed, was consistent with his role as a High Court judge.

Neither Barwick as chief justice nor Whitlam as prime minister had any knowledge of this 'running' dialogue. It is reasonable to assume they would have been unimpressed, even shocked.

This raises the question: if Kerr and Mason felt there was no impropriety involved, why have those meetings and discussions been kept secret from virtually the entire public for so long? Whose interest did this serve? No convincing argument has been made that it served the public interest. There is considerable evidence that Mason's silence over this issue has been to his benefit. Mason was appointed chief justice by the Hawke cabinet and began his term in February 1987. His appointment was universally applauded. The Labor cabinet that appointed him had no knowledge of his intimate consultations with Kerr leading to Whitlam's dismissal. The pivotal question is: would Mason have become chief justice if a full disclosure had been made?

The authors put this question to former prime ministers Bob Hawke and Paul Keating. Hawke was precise and emphatic in his answer. Asked if it was appropriate for Mason to counsel Kerr extensively in 1975, he said: 'No, I don't think so. It's going beyond the line of duty.' Hawke says that his government would not have appointed

Mason chief justice in 1987 if his consultations with Kerr had been known at the time. 'In terms of his acceptability to a Labor government, it would have brought him undone,' Hawke said.[12]

Keating was treasurer at the time. His answer to this question about Mason's appointment was 'definitely not'. Pressed on how sure he could be that the cabinet would not have appointed Mason, Keating said: 'I'd be completely certain. And I'd be among those most well disposed towards him. But were the current matters known, I think it would have disqualified him. I don't think it would just simply have defeated him in a cabinet room discussion. It would have been a disqualification – this man has virtue and substance, but there are events and those events are a disqualification.'

Keating said he had 'always had a high regard' for Mason. 'He seemed to be on the right side of most of the big legal arguments from the point of view of the Labor Party,' Keating said. Explaining his view about Mason's role in the 1975 crisis, Keating said: 'If [Mason] was personally friendly with Kerr as a former barrister friend and Kerr approached him to speak about this subject, most friendships would accommodate a conversation like that. But the moment the conversation turned on the use of the reserve powers in a really serious way – for the same reason I think Barwick should have dissociated himself from it – I think Mason should have too.' For Keating, this is the point at which Mason crossed the line.[13]

The comments by Hawke and Keating settle the matter: had the Hawke cabinet known, there is no way Mason would have been appointed as chief justice.

Other interviews by Troy Bramston of senior Hawke ministers offer even more weight to this view. The communications minister at the time and later attorney-general, Michael Duffy, said: 'Because of his involvement in the dismissal, I don't think he would have been appointed by the Hawke cabinet had we all known that at the time.' Resources and energy minister Gareth Evans, a former attorney-general, also doubted whether the appointment would have been made. Evans said the government 'would have thought long and hard' about any Mason appointment as chief justice not because of his politics but 'rather the extraordinary level of indifference to constitutional convention his behaviour revealed'.

Minister for employment and industrial relations Ralph Willis was indignant. His comments reveal that within the Labor Party, emotions about Mason's failure to disclose run high. Willis said Mason 'should have come clean' at the time of the appointment. 'Mason kept quiet about his influential role in the dismissal,' Willis said. 'In so doing he deceived two Labor governments.'[14]

Bill Hayden, a former foreign minister and governor-general, did not approve of Mason's role. 'I think it was unwise in case [the dismissal] ended up before them on the court,' he said in a new interview. Hayden recalled he had a 'very high regard' for Mason but not for Barwick whom he saw as 'a bumptious little bastard'.[15]

There is a uniform theme in these responses – anger at Mason's failure to disclose his role. Senior Labor figures drew a distinction between Mason's competence as a chief justice and the fact that his behaviour in 1975 would have ruled him ineligible for appointment had a disclosure been made.

The event reveals the different norms and culture on the High Court in 1975 compared with the contemporary institution. Mason acted as Kerr's friend during the toughest decision of his career. His role has raised serious questions about judgement. Mason was more than a friend; he was also a High Court judge. On the one hand, such consultation likely represented just one part of a long tradition of private counsel between legal colleagues. On the other hand, it had the capacity to prejudice the doctrine of separation of powers, and the ethical duties requiring such a distinction to be maintained. That any High Court judge in future would replicate Mason's behaviour seems remote.

Barwick advanced a core principle to justify his involvement as chief justice. He was sure the issue was not 'justiciable': that is, the question of any dismissal could not come before the court. That meant, he said, his advice 'would in reality not be advice given in a judicial capacity'. It would rank 'no higher than personal advice' though it might carry more weight because of his office. He argued that 'if I were asked for advice on a justiciable question or matter, I would decline to give it', and, therefore, the issue was clear-cut: to give the governor-general advice on a non-justiciable question did not compromise the independence of the chief justice. 'I did not breach the strictest view of the separation of powers,' Barwick said.[16]

He also addressed the issue of precedent. Barwick said that contrary to views that his intervention was unusual or unprecedented, there was, in fact, a series of 'useful precedents' for a chief justice to offer advice to a vice-regal officer. He noted them but he did not rely upon them.

The High Court in 1975 was deeply divided over Barwick's role. It was supported by Sir Harry Gibbs, who succeeded Barwick as chief justice in 1981, and by Mason, who approved Barwick's letter and also collaborated with Kerr on the timing of his approach to Barwick. Gibbs supported the dismissal and later publicly defended Kerr and Barwick.[17] Gibbs said the governor-general 'was entitled to seek advice from Sir Garfield and Sir Garfield was entitled to give it'.[18] It is noteworthy that the two chief justices who followed Barwick have endorsed his role.

Another two judges on the Barwick court are known to have opposed his intervention: Lionel Murphy and Sir Kenneth Jacobs. The antagonism between Barwick and former Labor attorney-general Murphy ran deep. Barwick was outraged at Murphy's appointment to the court. 'He is neither competent nor suitable for the position,' Barwick told Whitlam when the prime minister rang to inform him of the appointment. Barwick said in his memoirs he was 'considerably upset'.[19] That is an understatement.

The day after the dismissal Barwick sent a memorandum to his fellow judges explaining his involvement and attaching his advice to

Kerr, which argued dismissal was consistent with his constitutional authority and duty. On 13 November, Murphy wrote back to Barwick, delivering a strong rebuke: 'The advice itself was, in my opinion, wrong and, by its disregard of options open to the Governor-General, seriously prejudicial to one side in the political controversy. I dissociate myself completely from your action in advising the Governor-General and from the advice you gave.'[20]

On 14 November, Barwick circulated two notes. In a memorandum to the other judges, he dismissed Murphy with contempt. 'I am sure no other Justice thought I was either seeking or treating myself as having received approval of any Justice for my personal actions as Chief Justice,' he said. 'I regret that my courtesy has seemed capable of misunderstanding.' In a direct response to Murphy, copied to the other justices, Barwick was more scathing. 'I note your remarks,' he said to Murphy. 'I fundamentally disagree with them, both as to any legal opinion they involve and as to any matter of the propriety of my conduct. I see no need to discuss with you either question.'[21]

In April 2015, former High Court judge Michael Kirby had a meeting in Brighton, England, with fellow former High Court judge Sir Kenneth Jacobs, who was on the bench in 1975. Kirby spoke to Jacobs on behalf of Troy Bramston for this book. Jacobs died several weeks after his meeting with Kirby, and Kirby subsequently told Bramston by email he believed it would be appropriate for their conversation to be reported in this book.

Jacobs told Kirby he was 'extremely shocked' by Whitlam's dismissal. He said, Kirby reported in a note, 'that he has rarely been so shocked by any news of a similar non-personal kind.' Jacobs said he did not know in advance of Barwick's role and learned of the dismissal during the court's lunch break on 11 November. Kirby said: 'He believed that the court should not get involved in the slightest way in such matters because they were deeply divisive and politically partisan.' When Kirby offered an excuse for Barwick's action, Jacobs said he was being 'very kind'. Kirby wrote that 'by "kind" I took him to mean "naïve"'. Jacobs said 'he felt that he would be tarnished if he had anything whatever to do with the provision of advice'. He declined to endorse either the Barwick or Murphy letters in their exchange.

Kirby said such criticism as Jacobs voiced was directed 'solely' at Barwick's actions. Jacobs was 'very fond' of Mason and 'did not criticise him'. Indeed, Jacobs had told Kirby on many occasions of his high regard for Mason's subsequent service as chief justice. Kirby reported that Jacobs spoke 'clearly and firmly', aware his answers were 'for the sake of history'. In summary, Kirby reported that Jacobs indicated 'his strong opinion that it was wrong for judges to have anything to do with the unfolding political events'.[22]

Kerr's papers seek to implicate the High Court in Whitlam's dismissal beyond Mason and Barwick. Kerr claims that another judge, and future governor-general, Sir Ninian Stephen, was aware of Barwick's advice and did not dissent.[23] Kerr said he lunched with Stephen in London on 15 May 1981. He claimed in a note that Stephen was in court on the morning of 10 November with Mason and Barwick, and told them he was pleased to have been asked for his view. Kerr noted: 'It is clear from my conversation with Stephen that he did not attempt to dissuade Barwick from giving the advice and my understanding of what he said was that he, as well as Mason, saw the draft [Barwick] prepared that morning.'

This is an extraordinary claim. Kerr's effort to implicate a third judge – as endorsing Barwick's advice at the time – contradicts an interview Stephen gave to Paul Kelly in September 1995 when he denied any prior knowledge of Barwick's advice and of the dismissal. 'The whole thing came as a complete surprise to me,' Stephen said. 'I have no recollection of being consulted. I think I am quite clear in my own mind that I knew nothing until the news broke publicly.'[24] Given this statement, contrary to Kerr's claim, the weight of evidence is that Stephen had no knowledge. Indeed, Barwick said in 1994 that he had shown Stephen a copy of his letter 'some days later', another implied contradiction of Kerr's version.[25]

The view of the remaining High Court judge from 1975, Edward McTiernan, is not known. Michael Sexton, who worked as an associate to McTiernan in 1971–72, said: 'It's more a matter of speculation, I think, but he certainly would have disapproved of any involvement by any members of the court.'[26]

Having made justiciability the 'make or break' test for his intervention, Barwick's memoirs argued that the Constitution was clear: prime ministers held office at the governor-general's pleasure. 'No court can decide that question,' Barwick said of Kerr's exercise of the dismissal. 'Whether or not an incumbent minister can secure Supply is a matter for the decision of the Governor-General' under the executive powers of the Constitution. That is, it could not be reviewed by the High Court. Kerr and Barwick were convinced on this matter.[27]

Elaborating on his theme, Barwick said: 'It would be strange if the Governor-General were unable to seek the advice of the Chief Justice on a non-justiciable question . . . If Sir John Kerr could not seek such advice, neither could a Governor-General with no legal training . . . Surely, such a Governor-General would be entitled to seek the advice of the Chief Justice on a non-justiciable question.'

Gleeson said of Barwick's view of justiciability: 'I can understand why Barwick would have been confident in his view at the time. But in the light of later legal developments I think you can't be completely categorical . . . The scope for judicial review has developed since 1975 and that is why I would not be so categorical about it.'[28]

Asked about justiciability, French said: 'It is sufficient to say, that even the most confident judgement, that a matter upon which advice is sought is not justiciable or unlikely to come before the court, may be confounded by events.' This is surely the prudent outlook for a chief justice. At a philosophical level, French said the law as experienced, rather than in theory, 'suggests the exercise of caution before taking an absolute position on anything'. And Barwick took an absolute position.

French warned that despite the confidence of lawyers, 'someone might bring a challenge to the court which might be required to determine whether the action was justiciable'. And a chief justice who had provided advice in relation to the action 'could hardly sit in judgement even on the question whether the action was justiciable'.[29] Brennan said: 'A chief justice is expected to remain uncommitted and available to preside at any judicial determination of the existence of such a power or the legitimacy of its exercise.'[30]

These views tend to undermine Barwick's certainty on the question of justiciability. The more recent chief justices are agreed that attitudes have changed over the past forty years. In interviews for this book, Barwick's recent successors agree his advice provoked an adverse reaction that reveals a dramatic change in the norms of the court since 1975.

Basic to this process is a strengthening in the separation of powers doctrine. Brennan puts this proposition forcefully: 'In recent years, the concept of the separation of powers has been popularly understood to require not only that judges should be immune from political bias and political influence in making decisions but should themselves avoid conduct that may give rise to a reasonable apprehension of political bias (or any other form of bias) that might affect judicial impartiality . . . In earlier times, popular understanding did not insist on such a rigorous standard.'[31]

This can only be interpreted as a rejection of Barwick's behaviour. This implies that Barwick's behaviour, which was contentious in 1975, would not be acceptable today. Brennan further states: 'As public confidence in judicial impartiality is essential to the rule of law, a chief justice would be unwilling today to give advice that would impair public confidence in his or her own impartiality or in the work of the courts over which he or she presides.'

Coming from a former chief justice in office twenty years after the 1975 crisis, nothing could reveal more explicitly the view that Barwick's intervention reflected behaviour no longer acceptable.

Brennan's implication is that the current judiciary thinks any such repetition would be inconceivable. In assessing the changes in public attitude, Brennan nominated a series of causes – greater political polarisation, worries about judicial impartiality, more emphasis on transparency. He said 'whatever the factors may be' the upshot is 'they have undermined public confidence in the propriety of the practice of the giving of advice by a chief justice to a governor-general or governor'.[32]

This is also the view of French. 'I offer no judgment on the events of 1975,' French said. But he offered a sustained judgement on the Barwick assumptions if applied to the present day. French said: 'It is difficult to conceive of circumstances today in which it would be necessary or appropriate for the Chief Justice to provide legal advice to the Governor General on any course of action being contemplated by the holder of that office, whether such advice was tendered with the prior consent of the Government of the day or otherwise.'[33]

French argued that there was no constitutional basis and no convention for such action by a chief justice. In this new interview and in an earlier 2009 speech, French said: 'There is nothing in the Constitution or the *Judiciary Act* (1903) or the *High Court of Australia Act* (1979) to support the proposition that it is an incident of the office of the Chief Justice that he or she can be called upon to provide independent legal advice to the Governor-General relating to the discharge by the Governor-General of his or her powers.' He said such advice, if given, would have 'no constitutional standing to distinguish it from legal advice received from a senior barrister or a constitutional law expert or a retired Chief Justice of the High Court or any other court'.

There is no doubt French makes a strong case – yet the precedents on Barwick's behalf are also powerful.

In his memoirs, Barwick cited the well-known case of the first chief justice, Sir Samuel Griffith, advising the governor-general Sir Ronald Munro Ferguson over the 1914 double dissolution. Barwick noted a number of instances of state chief justices giving advice to their governors. These included the NSW governor Sir Philip Game getting advice from the chief justice Sir Philip Street in 1932 before dismissing the premier, Jack Lang. In 1952, the governor of Victoria received advice from both the chief justice of the High Court, Sir Owen Dixon, and the chief justice of Victoria, Sir Edmund Herring, over the blocking of supply and the method of granting a dissolution of parliament. It is also known, as French has observed, that in a different situation Lord Casey as governor-general sought Barwick's advice following the drowning of Harold Holt as to who he should appoint acting prime minister.

In one of the best expositions of the role of governor-general, Sir Paul Hasluck, in a 1972 lecture addressing the options facing a governor-general on the question of an early dissolution, said it was 'open' to the governor-general to seek advice from a number of quarters including 'perhaps the Chief Justice'.[34] During the 1975 constitutional crisis, the Liberal Party sought a legal opinion from three highly regarded lawyers, Keith Aickin QC, Murray Gleeson QC and Professor Pat Lane. It said: 'The Governor-General is entitled to seek advice on his powers from sources outside the Ministry. There is, for example, precedent for the seeking of advice from the Chief Justice of Australia.' In Gleeson's 2015 interview with the authors, he repeated this view, saying there was 'a good deal of precedent' for consulting a chief justice.

The best academic authority on this issue is Professor Anne Twomey from Sydney University. Her research identified eighteen occasions before 1975 when judges advised vice-regal officers.[35] In short, the practice was not unusual. She also suggested there would be other instances of unrecorded oral advice. Twomey referenced the comment from the former official secretary to a number of governors-general, Sir Murray Tyrrell, who served in this capacity from 1947 to 1973 and had unrivalled vice-regal access, that past incumbents had requested advice from the chief justice 'many times'. Tyrrell said he had done so on behalf of the governor-general on half a dozen occasions.[36]

According to Barwick, precedent meant there was 'no impropriety' in him giving advice. It is true he had both precedent and significant learned opinion on his side. However, Kerr sought Barwick's advice in defiance of Whitlam's view.

In his interview with the authors and in a 2009 speech, French said: 'Undoubtedly there have been historical precedents. But the nature and circumstances of those precedents are not such as to provide any sound foundation for the existence of a convention' that the chief justice advises the governor-general. French says the precedents derive from colonial and state chief justices and represent a different constitutional context: the early post-federation era represented by Sir Samuel Griffith was a period when the separation of powers doctrine 'was not developed to the extent it is today'.

French, therefore, rejected both a constitutional foundation for Barwick's intervention and equally rejected any notion of a convention that justified it. He said: 'It is difficult to see any basis' that would entitle a governor-general 'to seek such advice with or without the consent of the Prime Minister'.[37]

The High Court experienced a decisive evolution in the 1980s. In 1986, the *Australia Act* was passed, terminating any prospect of Privy Council appeals, and entrenching the High Court as the nation's final court of appeal. Chief Justice Mason said the *Australia Act* 'marked the end of the legal sovereignty of the Imperial Parliament and recognised that ultimate sovereignty resided in the Australian people'.[38] This produced a High Court more aware of Australian sovereignty and more alert to its separation from the other arms of government.

As the High Court has evolved, the behaviour that Barwick felt was justified in 1975 seems unacceptable forty years later. Indeed, the split in the 1975 court over Barwick's action is testimony to an evolution that was already underway.

Gleeson, like Brennan and French, agreed the separation of powers doctrine has become stronger since 1975. 'You are right to have identified such a trend,' he told the authors. Asked if Barwick's action had compromised the High Court, Gleeson said: 'No, I don't think so.'

Developing this point, Gleeson said: 'This is purely hypothetical. But let's suppose Kerr had another friend at the Bar, someone who wasn't a judge, wasn't a chief justice, would it have been improper for Kerr to have spoken to that person? Personally, I would prefer to see the governor-general going to the chief justice and getting a written opinion that people would contemplate and be made public rather than ringing his friend at the Bar . . . what Barwick did he did openly and in writing.'

Gleeson was not as categorical as Brennan and French in rejecting a role for the chief justice in advising the governor-general. 'I would not dismiss the possibility that such circumstances could arise,' he said. It is an important warning. The unknown issue is where a governor-general goes to get independent advice. French suggested an 'agreed mechanism' be established for any such 'rare event'. He said: 'A small group of independent experts, perhaps even including one of more retired Justices of the High Court, could be established for the purpose.' Yet no such mechanism exists, nor is there much prospect that it will.

One of the lessons from 1975 is the need for such advice in any crisis. Whitlam's obsession in denying Kerr access even to the law officers (the attorney-general and solicitor-general) for nearly the entire crisis only drove the governor-general to look elsewhere. Kerr remarked of the crisis that there were 'no legal advisers' to whom he could turn 'in any institutional way'.[39]

Kerr felt that, having decided to exercise the reserve powers, he was entitled 'to take unofficial advice from anyone' whom he trusted. He said this was one of those 'rare but real' occasions when, acting against the prime minister's advice, the governor-general 'can go where he believes he will get the best help'. He went to Barwick.[40] There is one certainty: at some point another crisis, though probably different from 1975, will arise and advice will be needed.

The reality is that political and personal ties were pivotal to the advice Kerr sought and got from Barwick. Those ties are a theme of this book. It was part of Kerr's plan to involve the High Court in any dismissal and he did that to protect himself.

Barwick was willing to respond – as a highly political chief justice, keen to participate in Whitlam's demise and sure he could justify his intervention. It has fallen to his successors to try to construct new and better 'rules' to ensure the separation of powers doctrine.

PART TWO

The Prelude

Kerr's Journey: Dreaming of Menzies

John Kerr found his liberation when he deserted the Labor Party. The jurist whom Gough Whitlam appointed as governor-general in 1974 was a lifelong political obsessive. That was unsurprising given that Kerr's home, the Sydney Bar, was a cauldron of networks and political flirtations. But Kerr was different – he was a Labor man who changed sides, even to fantasise that he might replace Sir Robert Menzies.

There were two standard yet contradictory views of Kerr – that he became an orthodox establishment figure and that his heart was still with Labor. Both were wrong. As a lawyer, Kerr was a frustrated politician. As a frustrated politician, he had undergone a transition from Labor to the social and political comfort of the Liberals. As a man, Kerr was an adroit opportunist, a beneficiary of patrons and a man who liked running with the winning team.

A Labor devotee for the first forty years of his life, Kerr from the late 1950s entered a new domain that he loved: being courted by Liberal Party ministers and party chiefs. There were offers to enter both the NSW and national parliament. Kerr was flattered, recorded the approaches and indulged his fantasies.

'It was always discussed in terms of the top leadership with me,' he said in a revealing oral history interview made available to the authors in 2013. A number of prominent Liberals saw him as either a future NSW Liberal premier or a potential successor to Menzies. Kerr said that his friend Sir John Atwill, later Liberal Party federal president during the Fraser era, 'really believed that the top job was within my grasp'.[1]

The most detailed account of Kerr's life comes from this interview he recorded for the National Library of Australia during many sessions. Asked whether he was seen 'as a second Menzies', Kerr said: 'It's an immodest thing to talk about . . . but I think most of those who were seeking me out to consider joining the Liberal Party and going into politics, especially federal politics, had in mind the top leadership roles . . . I was thought to be a person who could get in there in the way that [Sir Garfield] Barwick had done . . . Everybody knew that Menzies would some day go and where was the leadership to come from? Nobody really seemed to think of [Harold] Holt as a long-term prospect.'[2]

At his peak, in the late 1950s and early 1960s, Kerr was an imposing figure. His friend Jim McClelland said Kerr 'exuded physical and intellectual vitality'. A classical face, thick maze of white hair and roving intellectual range vested Kerr with a standout physical presence that made only more improbable his incongruously high-pitched voice. Kerr was never a narrow legal technician but a man of diverse interests and social charm. Prone to pomposity too early in life, his ability carried him to the epicentre of events and this was where he thrived. Known for much of his legal career as 'Jack', he cultivated friends, spent money freely and was fascinated by politics.

He took delight in describing an approach from senior NSW Liberal and future prime minister Billy McMahon, who asked whether he would put his name forward for Senate preselection. McMahon had spoken to Menzies first to secure the great man's consent. Kerr told McMahon he didn't want the Senate. He could picture himself only in the House of Representatives. According to Kerr, McMahon confessed to him that Menzies had predicted Kerr would say no. For Kerr, this confirmed he and Menzies had a common view: that to be 'big in politics' you must have your 'eye on the House'.[3]

In these Liberal approaches to Kerr there was a consistent pattern: proposal, dalliance and rejection. Kerr wanted to leap yet realised it would be unwise. He had the brains but not the toughness for politics. It became the fantasy life he would never have. But the fantasy was elaborate.

'I think I could have made a good job of leadership in the sense of taking people along behind me,' Kerr said. Conceding he had 'been through this many times in my own mind', Kerr identified his core defect: 'not ruthless enough'. He confessed his admiration for Whitlam's strength and toughness: 'I doubt if I would have enough strength of egoism, egoism or drive, to put up with what he went through for twenty years before he got there.'[4]

McClelland said Kerr never 'concealed his interest in becoming Prime Minister' when talking to his intimates.[5] When Kerr was governor-general, Whitlam teased him, saying: 'Everybody tells me that if things had worked out right, you'd be in my job.' Kerr passed it off but Whitlam then got serious: he told Kerr he didn't have the ruthlessness for politics. It was true, yet it was a misleading truth. Whitlam never grasped that Kerr was capable of a single act of pure ruthlessness.[6]

While unsuited for politics, Kerr longed to leave his mark on Australia. His successor as chief justice of New South Wales, Sir Laurence Street, told the authors: 'He was a political figure. He knew politics. He was a vain man. I think he wanted to go down in history as a man who made a decisive action.'[7] Kerr's second wife, Anne Robson, had this core insight into him. Robson married Kerr in April 1975 but had known him since they first met at a lunch in Sydney in January 1941. Interviewed by Paul Kelly, Robson retold a conversation she had with Kerr after World War Two: 'John said very intensely, "There is something in me that has got to come out in this country." '8 Robson remembered this line nearly forty years later. But ambition and pretension would constitute a fatal chemistry in Kerr's character.

On 28 December 1974, Kerr, as governor-general, relaxed over drinks on the sandstone verandah at Kirribilli House, the prime minister's Sydney residence. With the prime minister away, Kerr had popped over from his even more magnificent Admiralty House residence to socialise with two of Whitlam's female staffers. It was after the recent death of his first wife and before his marriage to his second wife. One of the staffers later told Whitlam that Kerr recalled that 'as a penniless student he had taken his first wife on ferry trips . . . she liked the look of what was to become the official residence of our Prime Ministers. It was the house she dreamed of living in as they viewed it from the harbour. When he was appointed governor-general, Sir John said, he had apologised to his wife that the job took him to the wrong house.'9

Kerr was born in Balmain in 1914 to working-class parents: his father was a boilermaker and his mother had been a dressmaker. When young John was ten or eleven years old, his parents became campaign supporters of a young ALP barrister, Dr Herbert Vere Evatt. 'Evatt had gone to Fort Street Boys High School,' Kerr said. 'I concluded that I would have to go to Fort Street too.' The school was a pathway for working- and middle-class boys into the professions such as law. As an outstanding student, Kerr gained entry to Fort Street.

A gifted student who won the university medal, Kerr studied law part-time while working as an articled clerk but absorbed the intellectual and social currents of the 1930s. He read widely, from Bertrand Russell to Leon Trotsky. For a while, like many students in the 1930s, Kerr became 'a kind of fellow-traveller of Trotskyism' only to reject Marxism. Finally, Kerr's political philosophy was set: he called himself 'a strong anti-Stalinist social democrat'.10

When he went to the Bar, Kerr joined a team of Evatt-orientated Labor lawyers thriving off trade-union business. Family ethos, intellectual conviction and Evatt's role as patron had crystallised Kerr's political brand: 'I was a supporter of the Labor Party; I wanted to identify myself with the Labor Party and the trade unions and for a number of years I did.'[11]

From an early stage, the great tension in Kerr's life became apparent: he was a Labor man but he wanted to succeed within a conservative profession. Kerr concluded he was on the wrong track as a lawyer; his decision to commit to the Labor floor had been a mistake. 'This really said to the whole of Sydney that although I had got first-class honours and a Medal, all I really wanted was Labor work,' Kerr said. 'That was silly. I should never have done it.' He felt it took him years to escape this pro-Labor label within the profession.[12]

It was the conflict between his origins and his ambitions. So Kerr moved to another set of chambers. He was geared to the expectations of the establishment. He was still a Labor man but he wanted success and freedom.[13]

Describing himself at the outbreak of World War Two, Kerr said: 'I was a Socialist, a Social Democrat, a so-called radical with no orthodox and well-defined ideology of a revolutionary kind. I was just ready, as it were, for Labor politics if things moved me in that direction.'[14]

He married in November 1938, having met his wife at university. Alison, usually known as Peggy, had become a friend of Margaret Whitlam's at university, and this connection continued throughout their lives. Kerr had a stimulating war. He worked for the enigmatic Alf Conlon in the Directorate of Research and Civil Affairs with a range of experts in administration, geography, economics and law under the overall direction of Commander-in-Chief Sir Thomas Blamey. In effect, Kerr became Conlon's deputy and was promoted to colonel as they grappled with complex postwar problems of military government in the Pacific. It was here he got to know his second wife, Anne, an expert in French territories and language. After the war Kerr turned down the option of a diplomatic career but did not return to the Bar until 1948, when he quickly entered a new phase dictated by Cold War politics.

Calling himself 'a fairly orthodox right of centre Labor lawyer', Kerr took his only step towards a political career. With a winnable seat unavailable, friends proposed he stand for an unwinnable seat at the 1951 election to build political capital for another day. As an ALP member and rising barrister he was endorsed for Lowe, held by Billy McMahon, who had been elected in the 1949 Menzian landslide.

It was a bizarre event. Describing the situation later, he seemed embarrassed at his nomination. 'I had no urge to stand for pre-selection,' he said. 'I didn't stand against anyone.'[15] In the end he volunteered to step aside for Dr John Burton, the high-profile former head of the External Affairs Department who was short of an electorate in which to run. Kerr's only step towards a political career had come to nothing. 'I cannot say that I regretted it or regret it,' he said.[16]

Yet the convulsive event in his political life was at hand. This was the great Labor Party split of 1954–55 – it finished Kerr with the Labor Party, sowed the seeds for his separation from Evatt and left Kerr with no direction but the sunlit uplands of the Liberals.

Since being visited by right-wing trade unionist Laurie Short in December 1949, Kerr had been involved in legal efforts to overturn the ballot that gave the communists control of the Federated Ironworkers Association. The solicitor with whom Kerr mostly worked in this endeavour was McClelland. They were part of a fierce and wider struggle over communist influence in the unions, which had damaged the Chifley government before the 1949 election and would cripple the ALP for a generation. Short won and overturned communist control of the union. Kerr was drawn into contact with right-wing ALP figures and intellectuals determined to purge the unions of Stalinist-driven control.

He gradually became aware of the Catholic-inspired campaign – the Movement – against communists inside the unions and the ALP, with the Melbourne-based BA Santamaria as its disciplined and tactical genius. After his defeat at the 1954 election – a poll he had expected would make him prime minister – an enraged Evatt declared an internal political war on Santamaria's Movement. The result was a split in the Labor Party and the creation of a breakaway, the Democratic Labour Party (DLP), whose role was to keep the ALP in opposition on the assumption it was communist-influenced.

Kerr had met Santamaria a few times before the split and was introduced to him by a capable organiser of the anti-communist industrial groups, Jack Kane, later a DLP senator. A close friend of Kerr's, the iconoclastic James McAuley, whom Kerr knew both at university and in Conlon's wartime outfit, had committed to Santamaria. Later Professor of English at the University of Tasmania and a poet of renown, it was McAuley who in the 1950s persuaded Kerr to join the Australian Association of Cultural Freedom, a group of anti-communist intellectuals associated with the publication *Quadrant*.[17]

The symbolic turning point in Kerr's political life came in 1955 when he was invited to a meeting in a suburban cottage in Sydney's inner west that included Santamaria, McAuley, McClelland and Kane. The purpose was to discuss the future of the DLP. Kerr was asked to join the party and accept a leadership role as its president.[18]

Kerr later recalled: 'I said I would not do that. In fact, I would not have anything to do with it. I said that I can see from your point of view you've got to go on with this. The way you see it, it's necessary to prevent Evatt from becoming Prime Minister, it's important to prevent the Labor Party from ruling whilst it is in the hands of the left-wing where it now firmly is. I can see what you think you have to do but you will do it as a Catholic party and I will not be with you.'[19]

McClelland later said he had never heard Kerr speak 'so forthrightly'. He said Kerr's robust reply to Santamaria 'took the wind out of the Movement boys' sails'.[20]

Kerr's true character now emerged. Faced with two opposing Labor parties, he found both of them repugnant. As a non-Catholic he saw the DLP as a sectarian party with an ideological obsession. As a pragmatist he had no interest in attaching himself to a minority party and cause that would doom his future career, social standing and political options. Kerr was not a man to make such a sacrifice. He wanted to be with winners. His friends had misjudged him.

'Apparently they'd expected I might be seduced into that position,' Kerr said.[21] But McAuley would understand. More than twenty years later McAuley wrote of Kerr's stand: 'His decision was not unreasonable. Kerr had a lot to throw away: would any use he could have been really have justified the sacrifice in a perfectly honourable commonsense view?'[22] Kerr's decision was vindicated. It is inconceivable had he pledged to the DLP that he would have become either chief justice of New South Wales or governor-general.

Kerr was now finished with the Labor Party. 'I was no longer interested in being a member of the Labor Party because, as I saw it, the Labor Party was now firmly in the hands of its own left-wing,' he said. 'It wasn't viable, it wouldn't be for many years as a party capable of attaining power. Many people disagreed with me on that and thought like other splits this group splitting off from the Labor Party would wither away and die and the Labor Party – the great Labor Party – would come back as a coalition of all the forces that were anti the Liberals. My view was that it would take twenty years, that the DLP was too well organised and too strong and too likely to survive.'[23]

The nakedness of his turn against Labor was startling: 'I wasn't interested in spending years hanging on around the edge of a left-wing led party in which Communist views were strong and Communist fellow-travelling views were strong. So I said this was goodbye as far as I was concerned. It was goodbye to them . . . The Labor Party itself no longer attracted me; the DLP certainly didn't attract me . . . I was getting right out of Labor Party politics and industrial group politics altogether.'[24]

Kerr grasped that under Evatt the ALP had made a catastrophic blunder. The result was a broken ALP weak on communism. Kerr claims that he confronted Whitlam with this argument on the beach in the mid-1950s. He said he told Whitlam: 'If you really believed in the Labor Party you would give leadership to this. You would not leave it to the Catholics . . . It's a fight that you don't carry on yourself and if it's not carried on by them, it would be carried on by nobody.'[25]

His declaration after these events – 'I was free' – is revealing. The Labor chains were broken. Kerr felt liberated to be himself. He embarked, in his own words, on a life that was 'entirely different'.[26] His rejection of the ALP and the DLP was comprehensive: intellectual, self-interested and visceral. Kerr did not just leave Labor. He rejected Labor and turned in another direction.

Twenty years later, during his seven months as a lonely widower locked in the vice-regal office, Kerr spent time, professionally and socially, with Elizabeth Reid, Whitlam's adviser on women's affairs. He was at his most vulnerable and, to an extent, opened his heart. Reid later said: 'He had a very strong need to make his mark as governor-general . . . but he saw himself as quite separate from the Labor Party that appointed him. He talked to me about this a lot. Kerr wanted to rise above his roots and repudiate his origins. It wasn't just a rejection of the Labor Party; he rejected that ethos.'[27]

From 1955 onwards Kerr built a big legal practice, taking briefs from the Menzies government and the NSW ALP government. The money was good. He bought a large home at Turramurra on the upper North Shore and the family lived there for twenty years before he went to Yarralumla. They entertained regularly and Kerr presented as a man of the world. He lived a full life. His wife knew legal method alone could not sustain him. He had friends on both sides of politics but his social life drew him into contact with influential Liberals. Kerr said during the 1960s he was 'tempted to submit myself in the Liberal interest' – an unusual position for somebody once pledged to Labor for so long.

The first Liberal approach came from lawyer Jack Cassidy, who suggested Kerr nominate for Wentworth, a blue-ribbon Liberal seat in Sydney's east. It is doubtful if Kerr would have had much of a chance. He didn't take it too seriously and Leslie Bury, a future treasurer, won preselection and the seat at a 1956 by-election. The next offer, as already outlined, was the McMahon approach for a Senate seat. In the early 1960s, NSW Liberal president Jock Pagan and general secretary John Carrick lunched with Kerr and discussed a move into state politics. For Kerr, the message was 'if I went into state politics the leadership of the state Liberal Party would be within my grasp'. Yet he had no interest in state politics.[28]

Kerr said Pagan subsequently asked him to stand for a NSW House of Representatives seat, with North Sydney and a couple of other seats being mentioned. Again, Kerr baulked. 'Menzies was a lawyer,' Kerr said. 'The mixture of law and politics, that is the orthodox way to leadership in this country.' Menzies was in his mind yet beyond his reach. Kerr fancied himself within that classic operation – the transition from the Sydney Bar to the House of Representatives, the path of Sir Percy Spender, Barwick, Sir Nigel Bowen, Bob Ellicott and Tom Hughes. He could imagine himself fitting into this constellation.

According to Kerr, the closest he came to taking the plunge was in 1964, when Barwick retired to become chief justice and his seat of Parramatta was vacant. 'Had I been here I think I would have probably stood,' Kerr said.[29] The problem this time was that Kerr and his wife were deep in Afghanistan, attending an international conference. Replacing Barwick would have been a real temptation. But Kerr, if at home, would have found another excuse to absent himself from a choice that always beckoned but was never taken.

Kerr said he felt comfortable with the Liberals but could not give them his political soul. 'I would in my own heart have felt it was a kind of act of apostasy,' he said. He felt Liberal endorsement would have been 'a kind of final, definitive, irreversible abandonment' of the last vestiges of his youth. He felt trapped, a victim of the ALP split, 'emasculated' by his past. 'I always had some reason for not doing it,' he said of the Liberal career.[30] The 'eternal question' in the family discussions was 'whether I would or wouldn't go into politics'.[31] But Kerr knew professional politics was not his life.

In 1965 an event occurred that Kerr called 'the great tragedy of my life'. His wife suffered a subarachnoid haemorrhage and was paralysed down her left side. It took her two years of treatment to return to a 'reasonable' condition and complete mobility was never restored. Kerr now decided for financial reasons to accept the next offer to the Bench.[32]

In 1966, he was appointed by Liberal attorney-general Billy Snedden to the Commonwealth Industrial Court. For the next eight years he lived the life of a judge. In 1972 came the decisive event: the Askin Liberal government made Kerr the chief justice of New South Wales. It was the Liberals who gave his career an elevated prestige. This position put Kerr on a logical shortlist as contender for governor-general. As chief justice he would serve as lieutenant-governor during the governor's absence. But the experienced NSW governor, Sir Roden Cutler, was unimpressed, saying, 'to be frank, I thought his understanding of politics was weak . . . I often found that his judgement was wrong'.[33]

Kerr succeeded on the Bench yet he felt a sense of loss. 'I didn't want to go onto the Bench,' he said. 'I didn't intend to go onto the Bench. I liked my freedom too much. I liked controversy. I liked stating my own position.'[34]

Kerr was Whitlam's third choice as governor-general. His first preference was for Sir Paul Hasluck to extend his term but, for personal reasons, mainly Hasluck's wife's health, this was not possible. Had Hasluck remained in office, there would have been no dismissal.

Whitlam sought Hasluck's advice about his successor. In June 1973, Hasluck presented Whitlam with a list of eight names he had handwritten on Government House letterhead. The outgoing governor-general described them as 'classes to be considered'. They were: Frank Crean or Kim Beazley (ministerial); David Derham or Kenneth Wheare (academic); John Kerr (judiciary); Vincent Fairfax or Ken Myer (business); and Harold Souter (unions).[35]

Whitlam offered the post to the youngest man on the list who was also his personal choice, Myer. When Myer declined, Whitlam went to another name on the list, Kerr.

Whitlam and Kerr had been acquaintances. Their paths had rarely crossed. They knew of each other but they did not know each other. Kerr said Whitlam had never been involved 'in any of my own life activities in any way'. They did not visit one another; they had no social life together. McClelland said Whitlam 'only knew Kerr casually'.[36]

Yet they shared a mutual regard. Kerr said of Whitlam: 'I think we've always rather admired one another and, at the same time, stayed away from one another.'[37] Whitlam knew the contours of Kerr's life. He had admired some of Kerr's industrial rulings from the Bench. In May 1973, Whitlam was guest of honour at a NSW Bench and Bar dinner with Kerr attending as lieutenant-governor. Whitlam began his speech with a joke: with Kerr sitting to Whitlam's right, the prime minister said he had observed the chief justice moving further to his right for the last twenty years. Everybody laughed, including Kerr.[38] But Whitlam would later make too many jokes at Kerr's expense.

In September 1973, Whitlam offered Kerr the post of governor-general. Kerr had not sought it. He took a long time to decide and extracted a series of concessions from Whitlam. The negotiation was protracted because of Kerr's concerns about salary, pension and tenure. Kerr, fifty-eight, said he was entitled to remain until age seventy as chief justice. While there was no fixed term as governor-general, the convention was five years, and Kerr asked Whitlam for a double term. Whitlam agreed and Bill Snedden, as opposition leader, also agreed. Whitlam further agreed to increase the salary and provide a retirement pension. Kerr was sworn in on 11 July 1974 at a time of rising turbulence in national politics. Labor Party opinion was also broadly supportive.

Kerr said it was his record in the years from 1954 to 1974, not his earlier Labor history, that constituted the reason for his appointment. This is correct. Whitlam did not appoint Kerr on the basis of past

Labor ties. It would be ignorant of human nature, however, to think his long Labor links were irrelevant. They were seen as integral to Kerr's character.

Whitlam wanted a candidate who guaranteed bipartisan support and Kerr met that test. There was no suggestion of 'jobs for the boys'. Kerr's wife, Peggy, had reservations, yet Kerr wanted the job. This was confirmed by his close friend Sir Anthony Mason. At Kerr's initiative, they discussed the offer and Mason doubted that Kerr would find the office a sufficient challenge. But Kerr told Mason 'he thought there would be opportunities to contribute to policy issues' – a strange remark since the governor-general has no policy role.[39]

In his memoirs, Kerr said while he knew the office did not involve the exercise of power, he was attracted by the return to work 'at the national level and to interest myself in national problems'. He envisaged the 'occasional opportunity to offer comment or advice'.[40] His friend and lifelong supporter Ken Gee, an activist and then a judge, said: 'John wanted to be at the centre of power. He knew the governor-general did more than open bazaars. He wanted influence and a new challenge.'[41]

Whitlam never asked Kerr his view of the office. But Whitlam did talk up the significance of the office of governor-general. Kerr was attracted by Whitlam's proposal that the governor-general, from time to time, should represent Australia overseas. Australia's head of state cannot do this, because whenever the Queen travels abroad she is treated as Queen of Britain, not Queen of Australia. Whitlam wanted to enhance the office of governor-general as opposed to the Queen of Australia. It was an integral step in making Australia a more independent nation. Kerr understood. He saw the point: the office of governor-general was a developing institution, an Australian institution and held by a prominent Australian.[42]

For Kerr, there were convenience and ceremonial factors. Whitlam said Kerr put to him the advantages of having a domestic staff, given his wife's poor health. Gee said that Kerr 'had a belief in ceremony, ritual and order' and that he 'relished ceremonial functions'.[43] Kerr disputed the view of legal colleagues that the office was essentially a rubber stamp that would not satisfy him. There was a Whitlam–Kerr unity ticket for an enhanced office of governor-general.

There were two common, yet false, assumptions made about Kerr during the 1975 crisis. The first was that Whitlam and Kerr had a strong personal relationship based upon a long association. The second was that Kerr in any showdown would be swayed by his long ties to the Labor Party. Neither assumption had any validity. Indeed, what was far more important was Kerr's opportunism, his ambition to make his mark and being on the winning side, a consistent theme in his career.

Whitlam's critics said later he should have recognised the risks in Kerr's outlook. But this was never going to happen given Whitlam's patronising view of Kerr. In his oral history, Kerr said of Whitlam: 'To me he represents something that perhaps I might have been, had I stayed in the party as he did at the time of the Split . . . he's symbolic, as it were, of that other way of life that I rejected.'[44]

This is precisely how Whitlam saw Kerr: as a man who wanted a political life but lacked the courage, strength and temperament for it. He would never take Kerr seriously as a power player. It was a fatal mistake.

When Bill Hayden and Hasluck left politics to become governor-general, neither would have looked upon the job as a chance to exert influence. But from the time Kerr took office, this was his preoccupation. The secretary of the Prime Minister's Department, John Menadue, saw Kerr regularly for discussions and said: 'He was an able, articulate man, still quite young. And he did not see himself as a person retiring to Yarralumla. He was seeking to make and find a role for himself. He asked on many occasions what his role should be in speaking engagements and the extent to which he should discuss public issues in a way which, whilst not causing embarrassment to the Government, demonstrated that the Governor-General had a view of his own. He asked my advice on whether he should hold press conferences and how he should respond to press queries.'[45]

Kerr never became prime minister, but he now lived next door to the prime minister in Sydney. Fundamental to his life story, his pride and his conception of the new office was the belief that the role had substance. Nothing was more certain to antagonise Kerr than public declarations by the prime minister that he was nothing but a rubber stamp – Whitlam's position in the crisis.

Unbeknown to Whitlam, Kerr was searching for a legacy. Given a chance, he would leave his mark. That is what his second wife, Anne, felt. And McAuley, writing after the dismissal, felt Kerr 'would enjoy the opportunity for a grand dramatic moment'.

The Guiding Stars: Evatt and Barwick

In John Kerr's real life as a lawyer and fantasy life as a politician, there were two towering role models who shaped his aspirations – HV 'Doc' Evatt and Sir Garfield Barwick. Evatt's influence came in the first part of Kerr's life, while in the second part he aspired to walk in Barwick's footsteps.

Evatt and Barwick were ideological opposites and political rivals. Yet they had a fundamental agreement on the central issue of the 1975 crisis: they believed in the existence of the dismissal power that Kerr exercised. Both men influenced Kerr's decision – Evatt from the grave and Barwick from the High Court.

They were Kerr's companions in Whitlam's sacking. Evatt, Barwick and Kerr testified to the power of the law in Australian politics. The nation's longest-serving prime minister, Sir Robert Menzies, was a lawyer. Nearly two generations later another lawyer, John Howard, became the second-longest-serving prime minister. The leader who had returned Labor to office after twenty-three years in the wilderness was Gough Whitlam, another lawyer. In the only time he was able to appoint a governor-general, Whitlam selected

Kerr after his illustrious legal and judicial career.

In retrospect, Whitlam's effort in 1975 to persuade Kerr that the reserve powers of the Crown were obsolete was a doomed project. How could Whitlam compete against the combined forces of Evatt and Barwick, who had dominated Kerr's life? Kerr's entire legal life had told him the opposite. He knew the reserve powers existed and he was as certain about this as anything in his legal life. He had the intellectual edifices of Evatt and Barwick behind him.

Kerr was at home in the 1975 crisis. It became a lawyer's picnic with opinions dashed off morning, noon and night. This was a crisis where lawyers thrived – Whitlam, Kerr, Barwick and Bob Ellicott were lawyers with a fixed view. Only Fraser, a farmer, was the odd man out. Evatt and Kerr had both served as chief justice of New South Wales. As a young man, Kerr took Evatt as his patron and guiding star. As his life approached full circle at the Bar and Bench, Barwick became the role model. Former chief justice Murray Gleeson likened the Barwick–Kerr relationship to that 'of senior and junior counsel'.[1]

The patronage of Evatt had been critical in Kerr's early life. When he had faced financial difficulties in doing law at university, Kerr approached Evatt, at the time a High Court judge. He found Evatt's Mosman address in the phone book, arrived, rang the doorbell, met Evatt's wife, Mary Alice, and was told to ring that night after the judge returned home. They subsequently met, talked and Evatt volunteered to fund a scholarship for the young Kerr of fifty pounds a year, an arrangement Kerr needed only for the first year of university, at the end of which he won a paying scholarship.[2]

When Kerr went to the Bar in the late 1930s, Evatt virtually delivered him his chambers, since a group of Labor lawyers close to Evatt had been getting established and Kerr joined them as a junior. The group included Clive Evatt, Doc's brother, and Richard Kirby, later president of the Conciliation and Arbitration Commission. 'Clive

Evatt was in charge of an enormous practice and was making a fortune,' Kerr said. They mobilised the unions and secured 'an enormous amount of business' in workers compensation.[3]

Calling himself an 'acolyte' of Evatt, the young Kerr was influenced by his career path. They would lunch regularly at Rainaud's, a restaurant at the top of Sydney's King Street. Yet Kerr was soon looking to bigger opportunities. He was attracted to the 'big end of town', a phrase Jim McClelland frequently used and attributed to Kerr.

Evatt, as Labor leader during the 1950s, had been vanquished by Menzies while Barwick, after a short political career under Menzies, was appointed by him as chief justice of the High Court. The scale of the legal conflict between Evatt and Barwick was unprecedented. They fought each other in courtroom battles in Australia and Britain over bank nationalisation, the banning of the Communist Party and the Petrov defection. They were combatants in the great ideological struggles of the 1950s.

By contrast, the reserve powers seemed an abstract, even arcane, issue. They transcended contemporary debates and were irrelevant to the raging ideological conflicts of the age.

The reserve powers derive from the medieval Crown and are deemed to be those discretions that still reside with the Crown after the transfer of its powers to the parliament, executive and judiciary within a system of democratic constitutional monarchy. In 1936, Evatt published his classic book *The King and His Dominion Governors*, which he was partly motivated to write after the spectacular May 1932 dismissal by the NSW governor Sir Philip Game of the firebrand Labor premier Jack Lang. Evatt wrote as a constitutional scholar and a social democrat worried about the implications for reforming Labor governments.

For Kerr, the book was 'of great autobiographical significance'. Kerr had discussed these issues in detail with Evatt at the time he was writing the book. Evatt wanted Kerr to collaborate with him in preparing the book for publication. But Kerr, while flattered, was too busy.

However, he said the question of the reserve powers 'became a reality for me from my early student days'. Kerr said of Evatt: 'I could not have had a better or more realistic introduction to the subject of the Reserve Powers than I received from him.' For Kerr, the personal ties with Evatt made the entire debate 'far more vivid to me'.[4] Indeed, Kerr fancied himself as an expert on the reserve powers from this time on.

After reviewing their application in Commonwealth nations, Evatt concluded that the powers, including the dismissal power, did exist. This position was contrary to that adopted by Whitlam and attorney-general Kep Enderby during the crisis. Their view reflected that of British Prime Minister Herbert Asquith during the 1909–11 constitutional crisis, when Asquith, in Evatt's words, subscribed to the 'Whig view of the Constitution'. Asked by Paul Kelly in 1995, twenty years after the dismissal, whether he believed in the reserve powers, an unforgiving Whitlam gave an emphatic answer: 'No.'[5] In his memoir of the crisis, Whitlam elaborated: 'It is absurd to suggest that the Governor-General is exercising in the Queen's name powers which she does not possess and would not presume to invoke.'[6] This was an intellectual and power contest that Whitlam lost.

In his book, Evatt said: 'What may fairly be called the extreme Whig view of the Monarchy, whatever validity it is thought to have in point of theory, is not true in point of fact.' Evatt attacked the theory, saying it sought 'to reduce the power of the Monarch to a nullity in those very times of great crisis when his intervention alone might save the country from disaster'. Evatt said the historical experience revealed 'an immense amount of sheer uncertainty and confusion' surrounding the powers and, as a consequence, he proposed their codification in the form of rules of law.[7]

As a Sydney-raised lawyer fascinated by politics and knowing Evatt, Kerr was profoundly influenced by the Game–Lang crisis. He saw the practical use of the dismissal power, recognised it could protect the institutions and realised its application would always be contentious.

In summary, Kerr had forty years of knowledge of the reserve powers when he became governor-general. He knew that despite Evatt's arguments, no codification of the reserve powers had occurred in Australia. For Kerr, this did not relieve the governor-general of potential responsibility for using the powers but meant any application was sure to be divisive because the 'uncertainty' to which Evatt referred still existed. Kerr had re-read the literature supporting the notion of the reserve powers before arriving at Yarralumla. In particular, he was familiar with the successive introductions to Evatt's book by Sir Kenneth Bailey, who had been solicitor-general, and Professor Zelman Cowen, who would follow Kerr as governor-general. Indeed, Kerr said that in deciding to accept the office of governor-general he 'took what Sir Zelman had written into account'.[8]

In an extraordinary revelation, Kerr's friend Sir Anthony Mason said that during their discussions about the offer of appointment, Kerr 'thought there would be opportunities to contribute to policy issues and he referred to the Reserve Powers and the possibility that an occasion could arise for their exercise'. Mason said he didn't interpret Kerr's remark as a 'prediction' but more of 'an argument that I was underestimating the importance of the office of Governor-General'.[9]

It was a remarkable situation. Not only was Kerr convinced the reserve powers were real, but he was updating himself on their application before taking office and telling his intimate Mason the possibility of their use could not be ruled out. Whitlam would have been astonished had he known. In truth, given Kerr's history, he was about the last person in Australia likely to be persuaded by a headstrong prime minister that the reserve powers no longer existed.

Whitlam had never foreseen the problem. Why would he? For Whitlam, if the thought had ever crossed his mind, the notion that he should assess the new governor-general's attitude towards the reserve powers would have been fantastic nonsense. Whitlam did not think about the reserve powers because he assumed, like many Labor lawyers, politicians and journalists, that they were anachronisms, not just outdated but probably extinguished in the same way that property franchise or denial of female suffrage had been extinguished.

While a man of his times, Kerr would not succumb to such fashion. He saw it as intellectual softness or ignorance. The reserve powers had been part of his life in theory and in practice, given he had lived through Game's dismissal of Lang in 1932.

From the time of Kerr's appointment, there was a disguised yet gigantic crack in the foundations of the Whitlam–Kerr relationship. In any crisis their opposing views about the reserve powers would become an unbridgeable gulf – and this is exactly what happened. Kerr, in fact, was an unfortunate option for Whitlam in Yarralumla. A military man, with a sense of hierarchy, uninterested in second-guessing government legal advice, would have been ideal.

Kerr said his ties with Evatt were 'never close again after my early days at the bar'. He distrusted Evatt's increasingly erratic behaviour, calling him 'in many respects a psychopathic person' who was 'very suspicious and trusted nobody'. This political alienation and their personal alienation went in tandem. 'There was a drifting apart,' Kerr said. 'I didn't have anything to do with him, as far as I can remember, after I left the Labor Party in 1954–55.'[10]

Kerr left Evatt but he kept an Evatt legacy, the reserve powers doctrine, with its repudiation of the Whitlam–Whig position.

As Kerr climbed the ladder of legal success, the spectre of Barwick was ever-present. Biographer David Marr captures the aura of Barwick in the early 1950s: 'He commanded the sort of practice the Bar only dreamed of: a choice of the finest work, a stupendous income, the leaders of the community queuing for and deferring to his advice. In a way never equalled, Barwick was the leader of the Australian Bar.'

He was an aristocratic larrikin with a killer instinct. Marr said Barwick 'strode down Phillip Street to court still cocky and abrasive, proud of a certain roughness at the edges'.[11] He held sway from the Privy Council in London to the High Court in Sydney. Whenever his government faced a decisive event in the courts, Menzies engaged

Barwick as his advocate. The man radiated self-importance with a tart, domineering manner, buttressed by a ferocious work ethic. Nearly everybody was a junior to Barwick and nearly everybody courted his approval. Kerr was far from immune.

Barwick was sharp, forensic and radiated animal spirits. He loved a contest and expected to win. When justifying his intervention in the 1975 crisis and advice to the governor-general, Barwick said only a 'timid or too self-protective' man would have declined. Barwick was not such a man.[12]

'Barwick, I think, played a role in my life, indirectly, similar to the role played by Evatt in earlier years,' Kerr said in an oral history interview for the National Library.[13] It is a revealing comment but an exaggeration. Kerr sought Barwick's approval but he never achieved with Barwick the intimacy he had enjoyed with Evatt. Jim McClelland said: 'Kerr, throughout his career, always sought Barwick's esteem and approval.'[14]

'I had always known Barwick,' Kerr said. 'We were not friends in any detailed way. But we went to the same school . . . We would yarn and have contacts with one another. My really detailed connections with Barwick began in connection with the leadership of the profession.' They were involved together in the Bar Council. It was a contact that Kerr valued. He sought Barwick's approval and liked to think Barwick held him in high regard: 'I think Barwick had a kind of, not admiration, but I think he had a kind of mixed feeling of liking and appreciation of my general style,' Kerr said.[15]

Barwick affirmed much of their contact was over the affairs of the NSW Bar Association and the Law Council of Australia. Barwick said Kerr 'was never in any sense a protégé of mine'. He encouraged Kerr but never promoted him for any office. Barwick said they were 'friends' and believed they 'entertained a mutual regard', thereby confirming Kerr's assessment.[16]

In 1958, Barwick made the move into federal parliament at a by-election for the seat of Parramatta, standing as a Liberal Party candidate. Mason joined Barwick on the campaign trail, spruiking his candidature. Menzies attended the opening of his campaign and a young John Howard, also in attendance, felt the great man radiated 'an air of self-satisfaction' at having snared such a star candidate. Howard said many NSW Liberals saw Barwick as a rival to Harold Holt when Menzies retired.[17] He served as both attorney-general and minister for external affairs in a short career of achievement.

When Sir Owen Dixon retired as chief justice, Barwick told Menzies he knew of nobody at the Bar suited for the office and that a promotion from within the Bench was inappropriate. What else would Barwick say? He told the prime minister that what was needed was an administrator for the court and 'only the two of us, Menzies and myself' might meet the requirement. Barwick said Menzies was 'indispensable' to the government 'and I was not' – hence he became chief justice.[18]

In the end Kerr was explicit: Barwick was the man he wanted to follow. Kerr had worked with Barwick as attorney-general and had been briefed by him. After Barwick went to the High Court, Kerr said, 'I continued my association with him.' These were different men with contrasting personalities. 'His style had, from the beginning, not been mine,' Kerr said. But over time he viewed Barwick 'more sympathetically' and 'occasionally' they would visit one another. 'I enjoyed his company anyhow,' Kerr said. 'I always held him in high esteem.'[19] Kerr said that 'in a very real sense when I lost Evatt as a person in whose path to follow . . . in many ways I adopted Barwick as a kind of pattern. Everything that he did I, in due course, did.'[20] Barwick was the model.

As governor-general, Kerr enjoyed a bonus: Barwick as chief justice. In any crisis his instinct was to mobilise Barwick on his behalf. Kerr knew it would be a mistake to leave Barwick alone. He was too dangerous to be ignored. Kerr instinctively grasped he needed Barwick with him. And if he had Barwick in any crisis, he had the prestige of the High Court.

Kerr had not the slightest doubt about Barwick's view of the reserve powers. 'The power to withdraw the [prime minister's] commission is always available as a last resort,' Barwick said. 'Its existence is, in my view, beyond question.'[21]

Once in office, Kerr's fascination with the reserve powers was further revealed when he took the initiative for the Australian National University to conduct a seminar on the subject. In March 1975, long before there was a crisis, Kerr approached the acting vice chancellor, Noel Dunbar, with an unusual request. He wanted 'a group organised within the university' to meet with him to 'discuss the constitutional position and powers of the Governor-General.'[22]

Mason, pro-chancellor of the ANU, played a key role in organising this group. He identified participants to Kerr after consulting with professors Geoffrey Sawer and Leslie Zines. Mason told Kerr that as discussions could involve 'important questions which may sooner or later come before the High Court for decision' he would limit his attendance to just the initial meeting. But Mason wasn't going to miss out. 'On the other hand, as Pro-Chancellor, I am anxious to ensure that the university makes a comprehensive contribution to the discussions which you have initiated,' he wrote Kerr.

After some delay, the first lunchtime meeting took place on 2 September 1975, with a second meeting on 10 September. Supply would be blocked just a month later and the government dismissed two months later. In addition to Sawer and Zines, the other attendees at meetings were: Jack Richardson, Francis West, Colin Hughes, Finlay Crisp and Dennis Pearce.[23]

Geoffrey Lindell, then a senior lecturer, was aware of the meetings. He recalled: 'I was mildly surprised that so early in his term Sir John sought guidance on the powers of the Governor General given that the office was largely ceremonial subject to the existence of the reserve powers which could and should only be used in exceptional circumstances.'[24]

Pearce, who recalls attending at least one meeting, describes

what took place. 'We chatted informally about John Kerr's powers as Governor-General. He was very interested to know what we
all thought. He gave no indication what he was thinking. He mainly
listened.'[25] Pearce says it is likely the issue of dismissal was discussed.
'He wanted to canvass the extent and scope of the reserve powers. I am
sure Jack Lang's dismissal would have come up, as it inevitably did in
discussions about the reserve powers. I don't think any of us were even
considering the possibility of dismissal of Whitlam at that time.'[26]

Sawer said Crisp 'strongly urged the case for denying any such
powers' while others thought 'there must be some "reserve" power,
though we differed a good deal about the definition of its extent'. The
university became uneasy about the talks. 'It soon became evident
that the course of politics was moving in the direction of crisis,' Sawer
wrote in a note. 'Sir John gracefully agreed to ceasing our tutorials.'[27]

At around the same time, however, Kerr had made a decisive
approach to Barwick. It is illustrative of their pattern of social contact
that his first conversation with Barwick about the 1975 crisis was at the
annual dinner of the NSW and ACT group of members of the Order
of St Michael and St George, held on the evening of 20 September at
the Union Club, Bent Street, Sydney. It was three weeks before the
Senate acted to delay supply. Barwick presided as chairman at the high
table. On his right was the governor-general and on his left was the
governor of New South Wales, Sir Roden Cutler.

Kerr confided he was 'very worried' that Whitlam and Fraser were
on a collision course and that 'serious difficulties were likely to arise'.
He asked Barwick if he foresaw any way in which the High Court
could be called upon to resolve any deadlock. Barwick was reluctant to
be drawn. 'But I said that the matter appeared to be for the Parliament
itself and not for the Court to resolve,' he said. Barwick said that
'in the long run' the matter might land on the Governor-General's
desk – a reference in Barwick's mind to the double-dissolution provisions to resolve a deadlock between the houses.

Barwick said: 'The Governor-General then asked me if I would

be prepared to advise him as to his own position if the need arose . . .
I was content to temporise. I said that would depend upon what I was
asked and the circumstances in which I was asked. There the matter
rested and nothing more was said that evening. I am bound on reflection to say that I had left the door open for the Governor-General to
approach me.'[28]

This reveals Kerr as a prudent, cunning and independent
governor-general. He had not yet asked Whitlam where, as governor-
general, he might seek advice. He had not sought Whitlam's approval
to speak to Barwick. But he had enlisted the chief justice as a potential
adviser even before the crisis was triggered. Solicitor-General Maurice
Byers said: 'Kerr must have known what sort of advice Barwick would
give.'[29] The dismissal was not an issue at this point. But nobody would
doubt, given Barwick's career and allegiances, his willingness to support an intervention by the governor-general at some stage.

Kerr, in effect, was lining up Barwick for one of several roles – as
an informal adviser or even a constitutional guarantor in a crisis of
unpredictable dimensions. It was a good night's work. A cautious
Barwick had left his door open. Kerr understood.

He had drawn the High Court into his net. It was Kerr who took
the initiative, not Barwick. It was Kerr who expressed concern about
the situation, not Barwick. It was Kerr who said he wanted to get
Barwick's advice rather than Barwick volunteering his own advice.
After the dismissal, Whitlam was obsessed with the idea that Barwick
had put the steel into Kerr. But this view doesn't fit the evidence.

The reality is that Kerr, given not just his belief but his obsession with the reserve powers – and that was a rare obsession in those
days – was virtually the most unsuitable person in Australia to appoint
as governor-general given Whitlam's viewpoint. It is tempting to see
the dismissal as Kerr engaging in an act of intellectual homage to those
patrons he honoured: Evatt and Barwick.

The exchange with Barwick shows Kerr preparing for a possible crisis. His preparation was superior to that of Whitlam. If his

intervention was required, Kerr wanted Barwick with him. This was the action not of a weak man but of a calculating man.

If Whitlam had known about this exchange, he would have been incensed. He would later instruct Kerr not to consult the chief justice. But Kerr was lining up Barwick for advice – not Whitlam, not the attorney-general, not the solicitor-general. After the dismissal the Labor minister Joe Riordan, who knew Kerr well from their industrial relations days, said: 'I heard Kerr speak of him when they were both barristers. Kerr was in awe of Barwick.'[30]

Kerr now saw Barwick as a potential ally to be used. Kerr would exploit Barwick in the showdown. He would convert his relations with Barwick into an instrument of insurance for himself in the crisis.

Fraser Strikes,
Whitlam Resists

While John Kerr was the linchpin of the 1975 crisis, Malcolm Fraser was its engineer. It was Fraser who initiated the crisis by trying to force a late 1975 general election. In an act of self-righteousness and self-interest, Fraser convinced himself that the Whitlam government had forfeited its right to govern and had to be terminated. This decision belongs to another political age: it was the final deluded gasp of the 'born to rule' ethos of the Menzian era and the Liberal and Country parties of that time who believed only they could properly govern Australia.

The paradox of Fraser was his simultaneous dedication to high principle and predilection for political violence. Fraser, like Whitlam, believed in the 'great man theory of history' where strong leaders could make or break their nations. He decided his mission was to save the nation and that it must be saved at once. Only a ruthless leader of high-minded principle could justify the inflamed public mood, social divisions and throttling of the governing institutions that Fraser triggered. The legacy became a permanent shadow on his prime ministership. He would defend his actions until his death in March 2015.

Fraser's mechanism was to use the Senate's power to block bills appropriating funds for the ordinary services of government, thereby blackmailing Whitlam into an election. Such a method had not been implemented since federation. Fraser used a constitutionally valid Senate power over money bills to smash an established convention, assert the Senate's right to declare 'no confidence' in a government, terminate the House of Representatives term and force an election at a time of his choosing.

By this action Fraser triggered the greatest deadlock between the House of Representatives and the Senate. He triggered a fierce clash between competing views of the Australian Constitution. It was a grab for power, pure and simple. But Fraser invoked high principle and justified his action by the damage wrought by the Whitlam government.

Fraser's decision to block supply was neither inevitable nor essential. By late 1975, there was near universal agreement that Whitlam would be defeated at the next election whenever it was held. Announcing his decision, Fraser made the absurd claim, 'the Opposition now has no choice'. As a leader of immense authority, Fraser had every choice. He could allow the normal parliamentary term to continue, or he could deploy the Senate to destroy the Whitlam government, which he denounced as the 'most incompetent and disastrous' since federation.[1]

In assessing Fraser over this decision and the bitter month-long struggle that followed, his main adviser, David Kemp, captured the intense admiration for Fraser's leadership in many conservative circles and in much of the nation: 'Fraser's leadership was daring and heroic. It was the kind of leadership Rudyard Kipling described in "If" – he kept his head when all around him were losing theirs and blaming it on him. He was desperately concerned at the damage Whitlam was doing to the country by his misgovernment and even fearful at what Whitlam might do to the Constitution and the federation by his attack on the powers of the Senate.'[2]

Elected to parliament in 1955, Fraser was a wealthy farmer and cultural product of the age of Sir Robert Menzies. He was fashioned by an era of sustained Liberal success, chronic Labor failure and entrenched distrust of Labor as an economic manager or national-security guardian. As a senior Coalition minister before the 1972 election, Fraser was a vigorous right-winger who never concealed his belief that Labor would not be able to govern the country with success for any length of time.

His personal philosophy, developed in the postwar period, enshrined the ideas of sacrifice and fortitude. In his famous 1971 Deakin Lecture, Fraser warned of the stoic nature of the national challenge and said: 'There is within me some part of the metaphysic and thus I would add that life is not meant to be easy . . . we need a rugged society but our new generations have seen only affluence.' He feared that 'people or leaders can be trapped to take the easy path' when this was 'the high road to national disaster'. Fraser pledged to 'overcome' – here was a politician who would ask the nation to confront the tough options it needed.[3]

As he rose, Fraser developed a deep self-assurance. In the late 1960s and first half of the 1970s, he triggered the most violent party and political upheavals since Billy Hughes. Fraser was the instrumental figure in the downfall of John Gorton as prime minister in 1971, in the overthrow of Billy Snedden as Liberal leader in 1975 and, finally, in the destruction of Gough Whitlam.

The method of Whitlam's defeat brought Fraser's ruthlessness to a new intensity: after blocking supply in the Senate, he pressured and persuaded Kerr to dismiss Whitlam and, finally, he connived in the act. In a 2013 interview nearly four decades after the event, Fraser said: 'It would have been very wrong to leave that government in power one day or one week longer if I could prevent it.'[4]

The combination of Fraser's personal aloofness and proclivity as a manipulator in such contests made him a polarising figure. Yet his strength of purpose, policy grasp, political aggression and dedication meant nobody else in the relatively weak Liberal Party of the 1970s could match his leadership ability. While Fraser led the assault on

Whitlam, he was never alone. On the contrary, this campaign became a fierce and spontaneous movement, one of the most remarkable events in the history of Australian conservatism.

It was provoked, in large part, by Whitlam. He lacked cunning and any sense of calculated self-protection. As a passionate reformer, Whitlam seemed uninterested in the hostility his proposals generated among his opponents. As a rhetorician he inspired fear in Coalition ranks, but as a strategist he became their gift. While a measured reformer in most respects, Whitlam, a born actor, was addicted to alarming his conservative enemies.

The Whitlam government had become discredited on multiple and lethal fronts. Its convoluted economic policies against a backdrop of global stagflation saw both unemployment and inflation surge to unacceptable highs. As a centralist Whitlam spread fear on the non-Labor side that he wanted a fundamental change to the federal system, thereby alienating the Coalition parties at state level, in particular, in New South Wales and also Queensland where Nationals premier Joh Bjelke-Petersen became a virulent enemy. Finally, Whitlam created the impression he was unfit to govern because of a series of improprieties, the nadir being the Tirath Khemlani loans affair, which was financially unjustifiable, legally dubious and politically irresponsible, at which point much of the governing elite decided that extreme measures to remove Labor were legitimate.[5]

Labor had been put on notice by the 1974 double dissolution, a warning it failed to heed. Indeed, the tactic of mobilising Senate powers long pre-dated Fraser's March 1975 elevation to the Liberal leadership. The story is astonishing.

The Senate did not face the people at the 1972 'It's Time' poll that had brought Labor to office. There was no euphoria in the red chamber. With the government in a minority, the Senate majority (the Coalition, DLP and independents) had a distaste for the speed, style and content of the Whitlam government. The newly elected Liberal Senate leader, Reg Withers, was a virtual unknown, a Jackie Gleason lookalike with a self-deprecating smile who said: 'I'm just a boy from Bunbury. I'm not a clever man.' But Withers, a politician with cunning in his blood, had mastery of one subject: Senate powers and procedures.[6]

From the start, Withers saw the Senate as the key to Whitlam's destruction. For the Coalition, the Senate would be recruited to fulfil two functions: to defeat Whitlam's contentious bills and then to force an election to terminate his government.

During 1973, a conservative revolution in political and parliamentary thinking took place with Withers at its epicentre. Its essence was the full exploitation of the Senate's constitutional powers to ruin the Whitlam government. No rule or convention, no matter how valid, long or sacred, was to block this objective. At the time of Labor's first budget in 1973, Withers said he looked 'at the possibility of using a future financial bill to force an election'. He concluded it was a mistake to reject a budget. The right technique, Withers decided, was rather to defer budget or appropriation bills in the Senate until Whitlam agreed to an election. 'This became the foundation of what we did in both 1974 and 1975,' he said.[7]

In March 1973, ALP Senate leader and attorney-general Lionel Murphy visited ASIO headquarters in Melbourne, the so-called ASIO 'raid', thereby convincing the Coalition that Labor was untrustworthy on security grounds. In October 1973, the Country Party room decided unanimously that the opposition should block supply and force an election. Country Party leader Doug Anthony said the electorate felt Whitlam 'had been given long enough'. He had been prime minister less than a year.

By April 1974, the legislative deadlock between the two houses was the greatest since federation. The Senate had twice rejected ten bills and another nine bills had also been rejected. Six of the rejected bills constituted grounds for a double dissolution – they included bills to introduce Medibank and reform the electoral system on the principle of 'one vote, one value'.

On the morning of 2 April 1974, when journalist Laurie Oakes broke the news that Whitlam was planning to appoint DLP senator Vince Gair as ambassador to Ireland, Snedden snapped: 'I'll take the bastard to the country.' The 1974 double dissolution was a political chemistry of anger, opportunity and blunder.

Thinking he was engaged in a masterstroke with Gair's appointment, Whitlam's aim was to secure a Senate vacancy in Queensland. Using this, he planned to turn the coming Senate election in that state into a contest for six seats, not the normal five seats, thereby achieving a likely three-all result instead of three–two against the ALP. The extra seat would give Labor a chance of winning control of the Senate at the election. This was his justification for giving a diplomatic bauble to Gair, a hated Labor defector and 'rat'.

The Coalition leaders, Snedden and Anthony, were enraged and decided to block supply. Snedden called Gair's appointment 'the most shameful act ever perpetrated' by a government. Rivers of political poison were unleashed. Snedden and Anthony felt they would win an election, but they miscalculated. Whitlam, furious and supremely confident, embraced the election Snedden was forcing and moved first. He went to Yarralumla to advise the governor-general, Sir Paul Hasluck, on a double dissolution. Seizing the chance for a May election, Whitlam foresaw a victory that would see the eventual passage of his cherished double-dissolution bills. It was a classic in Whitlam's 'crash through or crash' technique. He prevailed on each count.

This meant, unlike in the events of 1975, that the opposition never actually blocked supply. Whitlam's joining of this contest was a sublime and stark contrast to his refusal to accept the forced election of 1975. The ironies abounded. The DLP senators who backed the 1974 election saw their party eliminated from the parliament. Subsequent events revealed that Snedden's premature strike came just three months before growing economic tribulations would have guaranteed Whitlam's defeat at the polls. Snedden's election loss put him on a trajectory of decline that saw Fraser depose him in early 1975.

But Whitlam had only just won. His majority was reduced from nine to five seats. Labor was left in a situation of knife-edge vulnerability. The opposition was disappointed but unrepentant.

Amid the turmoil there was one constant: the Coalition parties stood by the validity of their tactic to halt supply and force an election. This tactic, far from being repudiated, became entrenched. In his speech to the Senate, Withers said: 'We have wanted for a long time to go to the polls . . . We are not doing anything unusual. Let me put it this way: we are not doing anything that is unconstitutional.'[8] Using the word 'unusual' was misleading, since denying supply to force an election was unprecedented. The only mistake the Coalition conceded was that of poor timing. The dominant sentiment was that the move on supply had been successful because it had weakened Whitlam overall.

Labor had just failed to secure the Senate it needed. The new Senate was twenty-nine Labor, twenty-nine Coalition, one Liberal Movement (Steele Hall) and an independent who joined the Liberals post-election, taking their numbers to thirty. After the election, Snedden insisted that 'we were not defeated'. He denied Whitlam had any mandate and refused to concede Whitlam's right to a three-year parliamentary term. This was important: it was a denial of the legitimacy of Labor's election victory.

When Fraser became Liberal leader, the question of blocking supply was front and centre. He adopted a formula to turn the political heat back on Labor. Fraser said he wanted election talk 'out of the air' and announced that governments were entitled to their three-year term unless 'quite extraordinary events intervene'. Fraser was stronger and more resourceful than Snedden. Whitlam faced a far more formidable opponent.

The Coalition states now became vital players as the anti-Labor movement spread across the nation. With Lionel Murphy's appointment to the High Court, the NSW parliament, under section fifteen of the Constitution, had the task of filling this casual Senate vacancy.

The convention was for a replacement from the same party to maintain the status quo. But the NSW Liberal premier, Tom Lewis, broke with convention and appointed an independent, Cleaver Bunton, the mayor of Albury. While this reduced Labor's numbers to twenty-eight, it would not matter on the supply issue because Bunton voted with Labor. But the Senate casual-vacancy convention had been breached.

Interviewed in March 2011, former premier Lewis was unrepentant: 'I appointed whoever I thought was correct,' he told Troy Bramston. 'I was appalled by what was happening in Canberra. The fact that they didn't belong to the same party didn't have much to do with it.'[9]

This breach of convention became pivotal when a Queensland ALP senator, Bert Milliner, died in June 1975. The power to determine the successor lay with Bjelke-Petersen via his control of the Queensland parliament. This would become decisive in the subsequent crisis. Bjelke-Petersen now had his fun. He tortured and tormented the Labor Party. He rejected Labor's candidate, Mal Colston, and asked Labor to submit a panel of names from which he might pick a new senator. The Queensland ALP, irrational with rage and standing upon its pride, refused. It was a serious blunder. They should have given Bjelke-Petersen the names and even tried to find some ALP candidates he might like. Only one thing mattered: sheer, raw, Senate numbers.

In the end Bjelke-Petersen repudiated Labor, smashed the convention and appointed a French polisher by trade, Albert (Pat) Field, who had rung his office to offer his services. Having been given his background, Bjelke-Petersen said 'he sounds a true-blue Labor man'. En route to Canberra, Field said in interviews he would never vote for Whitlam, attacked him for calling the premier a 'bible-bashing bastard' and backed an early election. He was sworn in amid a walkout of Labor senators. Labor challenged Field's eligibility to sit, and he was given a month's leave. He never voted on supply but his appointment changed the numbers.

On the supply issue, the vote was now thirty to twenty-nine the Coalition's way, with Steele Hall voting with Labor. If Bjelke-Petersen had followed convention and appointed an ALP senator, the vote would have been thirty-all. Bjelke-Petersen had delivered a majority Senate vote to Fraser and Withers. It was this majority that enabled them to defer supply. A split vote can block a bill or resolution, but a majority vote is needed to carry a bill or resolution and Fraser needed that majority for his deferral motion.

This was the origin of Steele Hall's emotive yet understandable claim that Fraser denied the budget 'over a dead man's corpse'. The Liberals professed to be dismayed at the smashing of the Senate casual-vacancy convention. Yet their hypocrisy was undisguised. They were so dismayed they relied upon the majority gifted in a moral and political atrocity by the Queensland parliament. As Whitlam often said, the Senate that denied the 1975 budget was 'corrupted' and 'tainted'. It was not the Senate as elected by the people. The vote that forced the crisis was secured by a negation of democracy.

Fraser could have instructed a Coalition senator to abstain. But morality was not allowed to interfere with self-interest. The 1975 crisis was driven by Fraser's strength, Withers' tactics and Bjelke-Petersen's corruption of the Senate's numbers. It is true that Fraser, as prime minister, later sponsored a 1977 referendum to write the convention into the Constitution, thereby preserving it forever. It was a worthy reform that ensured the Senate abuse of power that Fraser deployed to take office could not be repeated.

By October 1975, the momentum to deny supply was mounting. Two events this month tipped a calculating Fraser over the edge. They were the High Court's 10 October ruling that validated the creation of two Senate places each from the Australian Capital Territory and Northern Territory, and the resurgence of the Khemlani loans affair, which saw the resignation of minerals and energy minister RFX (Rex) Connor, nicknamed 'the Strangler'.

The High Court decision on territorial senators revealed the obsession within the Coalition over future Senate numbers. It meant that at the next election, four new senators would be elected. While the new Senate as a whole would not be constituted until 1 July 1976, the territorial senators would take their places immediately. So would two new senators replacing the casual vacancies filled from New South Wales and Queensland. If Whitlam called a Senate election early and constituted the interim Senate before mid-1976, there was a fear he might have a remote chance of having the Senate numbers for a short period.

For the Coalition parties, this remote possibility assumed the status of an unacceptable nightmare. By this stage, the deadlock between the House of Representatives and the Senate in the current parliament had far exceeded the deadlock over the six double-dissolution bills in the previous parliament. There were now twenty-one bills on the double-dissolution list. The Liberal and National parties had used the Senate, time and again, to deny Labor's bills. They would not tolerate any chance of Labor winning Senate control and passing its detested legislation.

On 13 October, the Liberal Party Federal Council approved a motion to deny Whitlam the option as prime minister of calling a half-senate election. Since writs for Senate elections are issued by state governors on advice from state governments, the plan was to have the four non-Labor premiers use their constitutional powers to sabotage an election by advising their governors not to issue election writs. It was an extraordinary motion that testified to the atmospherics of fear and hostility generated by the Whitlam government. It was a call for the breaking of another convention that governed the process for Senate elections.

The crunch event, however, was Connor's 14 October resignation. At this point, the loans affair claimed its most famous victim: the architect of the deluded search for overseas funds via Khemlani, a shadowy Pakistani middle man. Whitlam forced Connor's resignation on the grounds that he had misled the parliament in denying his ongoing contact with Khemlani.

The affair revealed the Whitlam government stayed true to its character: proving its impropriety at a moment of maximum danger. In political terms, this closed the debate about whether or nor Fraser would deny the budget. Fraser was handed an embarrassment of political weapons. It became easy for him to justify blocking the budget and hard to reject this option. Connor's enforced resignation satisfied the test Fraser had required: that he would need 'extraordinary' or 'reprehensible' events to force an election through the Senate. Those events were now a stage-and-screen spectacular. It was as though the Greek gods had conspired to doom Whitlam in a performance of tragedy, farce and incompetence.

But the founder of the Liberal Party, Sir Robert Menzies, had serious reservations. He expressed them to Doug Anthony, leader of the National–Country party, when Anthony visited him in Melbourne before the decision to block supply. 'Pleased to see you Douglas,' Menzies said. Anthony recalled: 'He started to lecture me and said that we shouldn't be acting the way we were. It wasn't the job of the Senate to dismiss the government Menzies said.' But Anthony held firm, saying the opposition should not 'let Australia disintegrate with the wild policies of [the] Whitlam government.' As Anthony was leaving, Menzies said: 'Douglas, you've made my day!'[10]

The Whitlam government had offended the public's sense of morality. For Fraser, the unprecedented step of blocking a budget now assumed an air of legitimacy. The few doubters within Liberal ranks were left without an argument. The immortal ineptitude of the Whitlam government was its worst enemy.

The next day, 15 October, the Coalition leadership group met and decided to block the budget. This was endorsed by the shadow ministry. There were no dissenters. The minutes of the shadow ministry meeting say: 'Mr Fraser went around the table and all [shadow] ministers indicated their support for the move. Mr Fraser said he shared Mr [Jim] Killen's reluctance about taking this course of action but, following the sacking of Connor, the Opposition would have little respect if it did not try to get rid of the government.'[11] John Howard recalled: 'I thought it was justified in the circumstances. I was very conscious it was a big thing and, like a lot of the members, I was nervous about what the impact would be on the body politic and the fabric of the system. I was not gung-ho.'[12]

The recommendation then went to the joint party room where there were only two dissenters, Senator Don Jessop, who indicated he would not create trouble, and Senator Alan Missen, a cogent and courageous Victorian Liberal who argued at length this would leave 'great scars' on the nation and was betraying the supremacy of the House of Representatives. But Missen told Fraser privately he would not launch any unilateral revolt. He would respect the collective decision.

Fraser, as near as possible, had achieved unanimity across the Coalition. He had worked diligently for this purpose and it became fundamental to his success. The conservatives had become constitutional radicals. Their justification was the need to satisfy and safeguard the country by terminating the Whitlam era. At 4.35 p.m., Withers rose in the Senate to fulfil the mission on which he had embarked long before. His amendment deferring the appropriation bills pending an election was carried by one vote.

Withers said Whitlam 'is not a President, he is not a dictator and he is not a king' – he was a prime minister with a duty to go to the people. The budget had been deferred, not rejected. This was a considered tactic – the bills remained alive, ready to be passed contingent upon an election.

Fraser had evaluated the consequences of his momentous step. He was better prepared than Whitlam, far less emotional and a clearer thinker. Fraser felt that, provided the opposition kept its nerve and kept deferring the budget, ultimately, it would get the election it wanted. Fraser judged there was no alternative. But he knew Whitlam was planning a political onslaught that meant an epic encounter.

A month earlier, on 12 September, Whitlam had delivered a speech in Goulburn that foreshadowed his tactics. They were the reverse of autumn 1974, the reason being that Whitlam, like Fraser, knew Labor would now lose any election. His plan, therefore, was to resist the election. He wanted to buy time till the government, with Bill Hayden as treasurer and Jim McClelland as labour minister, recovered in the polls. But Whitlam was also planning his greatest audacity.

This arose from the deepest instincts of his political and parliamentary life. The central organising principle of Whitlam's career was to modernise Labor and its policies to secure a House of Representatives majority. His field of vision was executive government and the House of Representatives, where he became the supreme parliamentarian of his time. As prime minister he now found his life's work threatened by a Senate, elected on a state-based, undemocratic franchise, purporting to turn its constitutional powers into a weapon to terminate the term of the House of Representatives that he controlled. It was a negation of everything he had striven to achieve, of everything he believed.

Whitlam's career revealed a penchant for brinkmanship under pressure. His description of his method as 'crash through or crash' was not hyperbole. A wilful personality with a sense of destiny and a leader alert to constitutional powers, Whitlam embarked upon the grandest application of 'crash through or crash' in his career.

He said: 'There are no laws applying to a situation where supply is refused by an Upper House, no laws at all. There is no precedent in the Federal Parliament . . . and there is, in fact, no convention because people never used to think it could happen, so it's never been discussed. And accordingly one can only say that there is no obligation by law, by rule, by precedent or by convention for a Prime Minister in those circumstances which are threatened, to dissolve the House of Representatives and have an election for it.'[13]

This was a declaration that he would not be intimidated. The Senate might pass its motions but Whitlam would ignore them. He asserted his right as prime minister to defy them. Whitlam had two motives. The first was to persuade Fraser against blocking supply, a ploy that failed. The second was to equip his campaign to break

Fraser and his senators with a constitutional legitimacy and popular appeal. Whitlam was going to 'tough it out'. He judged that if such brinkmanship forced Fraser's retreat, then his leadership would never recover and Labor would enjoy a transformation of its fortunes.

Whitlam intended to teach Fraser that using the Senate to break convention was not cost-free. His plan was to transform the issue from Labor's unpopularity to the integrity of Australia's democracy.

He took his stand on the principle of responsible government implicit in the Constitution: a prime minister was commissioned because he commanded a majority in the House of Representatives. The government was made and unmade by its confidence in the lower house, the 'People's House'. Whitlam said while he had the confidence of the House, he was entitled to govern.

However, this view was qualified by the federalism principle. The founding fathers created the Senate as a states house with virtually equal powers with the House of Representatives. This was a political bargain that made possible the creation of the nation. The Senate was given such powers to protect the states and preserve the federal nature of the Constitution. In practice, however, the Senate operated as a chamber governed by party and party interests.

The architects of the Constitution knew that they had implanted a contradiction at its heart. The conflict between responsible government and the Senate's powers in the name of federalism was a political time bomb. In an immortal passage, those great scholars of the constitution John Quick and Robert Garran wrote: 'In the end it is predicted that either Responsible Government will kill the Federation and change it into a unified State or the Federation will kill Responsible Government and substitute a new form of Executive more compatible with the Federal theory.'[14]

Whitlam now became a killing agent in the cause of responsible government. He was asking the people to resolve the contradiction by repudiating Fraser's use of the Senate to force the House to submit. This was the epic nature of the 1975 crisis. Whitlam's aim was to break

Fraser, break the Senate's position and, beyond that, resolve the constitutional contradiction in favour of the House of Representatives.

As their titanic battle was joined, Fraser and Whitlam had a shared view – Sir John Kerr would be pivotal in deciding the outcome.

8

Kerr Turns
Against Whitlam

Even before supply was blocked Gough Whitlam had lost the trust of John Kerr, who had become wary and resentful of the prime minister. Kerr had reached a fatal conclusion: there was no point in him speaking honestly to Whitlam. He decided not to try. The trust between the Queen's representative and her chief adviser was broken. Incredibly, Whitlam knew nothing of this, nor that the problems originated in Kerr's early days in office.

Kerr stayed friendly and jovial with Whitlam but kept secret his heart and calculations. The authority for this is Kerr himself: he said by 14 October, on the eve of the Senate's action, he felt Whitlam was beyond reason. 'From that time forward my opinion was that he was beyond the reach of any argument of mine or even discussion,' Kerr said. 'Everything he said publicly, or privately to me, thereafter strengthened me in that view.'[1]

Whitlam had lost Kerr. He had not necessarily lost the coming struggle. But his assumption that 'Kerr would do the right thing' was false. The story of how Kerr's early worries grew into distrust is riddled with vanity, complacency and deception.

Within weeks of coming to office Kerr was worried to find that, on a vital action he was required to perform, he felt he was given unsatisfactory advice by the attorney-general and solicitor-general.

After the 1974 double-dissolution on six bills, Whitlam proceeded to a joint sitting of both houses to pass the bills, and Kerr was advised to issue a proclamation for the sitting. But he claimed to be 'extremely doubtful' whether one of the bills, the *Petroleum and Minerals Authority (PMA) Act*, was a valid double-dissolution bill. Kerr felt it did not satisfy the double-dissolution provisions because three months had not elapsed between the two relevant failures of the Senate to pass the bill. The opposition was making this argument at the time and Kerr felt its pressure.

The sensitivity arose because Kerr's predecessor, Sir Paul Hasluck, had approved the double dissolution on the six bills, acting on the government's advice. Kerr, however, believed the advice had been invalid. He sought fresh legal advice on whether the PMA bill 'could properly be dealt with at a Joint Sitting' and he was left unimpressed with the advice he got.

In a note on this issue left in his personal papers, Kerr said the law officers advised that 'I was bound' by Hasluck's decision and 'could not act inconsistently with the way in which he had acted'. Given an election had been held on this basis, the advice seems sensible. Kerr accepted the advice but said 'my own view' was that the *PMA Act* 'would be declared to be invalid by the High Court' if challenged. The *PMA Act* was challenged a year later and was found to be invalid as Kerr had predicted.

Kerr said with disdain this was his first exposure to the way Attorney-General Lionel Murphy gave advice and that he was 'surprised' that Maurice Byers, as solicitor-general, failed to express a view on the issue of substance of the PMA. Kerr wrote a pompous letter to Hasluck about these events. He said: 'I may say, as between the two of us, that even had the law permitted it and even if I had the independent power and duty to apply my mind to the matter, I should have found it as a matter of discretion almost inconceivable that one Governor-General – and a new one at that – should review so recent a decision of a previous Governor-General on a high act of State involving the dissolution of parliament.'[2]

The point is that both Hasluck and Kerr did the right thing. They acted on advice and left the High Court to pass judgement on the act's validity. That was the court's job, not the governor-general's job.

But a doubt had crossed Kerr's mind about the law officers. Its magnitude was apparent when Kerr, in a speech on 25 August 1975, after the High Court's decision, said that 'advice given to my predecessor, Sir Paul Hasluck . . . was held to be legally wrong'. For Kerr, there were two lessons: be wary of the law officers and ensure that any major decision taken by the governor-general was not undone by the High Court. These lessons would be fundamental in the great crisis.

Far more significant, however, were the events of 'Black Friday', the night of 13 December 1974 at the Lodge, when one of the most infamous events in Australian political history occurred. Senior ministers gathered in secret to authorise the raising of a US$4 billion loan for natural-resource projects through a highly dubious middle man, Tirath Khemlani, bypassing the Treasury's orthodox financial channels. Veteran correspondent Alan Reid called this event the 'death warrant' of the Whitlam government. Authorisation took the form of an Executive Council minute that required the governor-general's signature. The Whitlam–Kerr relationship never recovered from this night.

Each man made grievous mistakes in dealing with the other: Whitlam treated Kerr with a complacency that assumed he was a cipher and Kerr failed to raise the necessary questions with Whitlam that would be expected from a competent governor-general.[3]

The executive power of the Commonwealth is vested in the Queen and exercisable by the governor-general as her representative. The Constitution created a Federal Executive Council as the instrument through which the governor-general is advised of executive decisions and gives his assent. Ministers are sworn in as executive councillors before they are sworn as ministers. In practice, the Executive Council (ExCo) meets about once a week, normally the governor-general presiding with two ministers. It is served by a secretariat located in the Prime Minister's Department.

During the afternoon and evening of 14 December, the four most senior ministers were at the Lodge: Whitlam, Murphy, Treasurer Dr Jim Cairns, and the architect of the scheme, Minerals and Energy Minister Rex Connor. In frantic events over the previous days, the Attorney-General's Department had expressed grave misgivings about the legal basis of the plan. The Treasury, led by Sir Frederick Wheeler and John Stone, was alarmed and tried to scuttle the project. On the night, Wheeler advised Cairns not to sign the minute, advice he ignored.

The loans affair, as it became known, destroyed the careers of Connor and Cairns, provoked a campaign to remove Murphy from the High Court, fatally damaged Whitlam, gave Fraser his single-most powerful reason to block the budget and drove a wedge between the governor-general and the prime minister. There has been nothing like it before or since. If Whitlam had appointed Bill Hayden as treasurer in late 1974, not Cairns, then history may have been different as Hayden would have fought this travesty.

One of the most contentious aspects of a proposal riddled with contention was the legal advice from Murphy to the effect that the loan was for 'temporary purposes'. The real purposes of the loan, mainly resources projects, were not temporary. The significance of such advice was that Loan Council approval, involving the states and the premiers, was not required under the financial agreement if the purpose was 'temporary'. Loan Council approval would have taken time and generated political problems. And the government was in a rush. It is significant that Murphy's advice was not written. It was oral and was later mocked as a 'curb-side' opinion.

The head of the Attorney-General's Department, Sir Clarence

Harders, said later that Murphy put his view 'with his customary vigour'. Murphy said that what counted in legal terms was the purpose not the duration of the loan, and the broad purpose was described as meeting immediate economic problems. Harders said Whitlam 'expressed doubts' about Murphy's opinion but finally accepted it. He said both Whitlam and the solicitor-general, Maurice Byers, questioned Murphy closely. The attorney-general conceded there was a risk of legal challenge by the states but asked: 'How could the hostile states possibly prove it wasn't for temporary purposes?' Byers said the government was 'drawing a long bow' but the opinion was 'arguable'. Harders said later the department 'did not support [Murphy's] argument regarding temporary purposes'.[4]

The Lodge meeting was held under extreme conditions. Whitlam was due to leave on an overseas trip the next day. Connor believed the funds were now available through Khemlani and haste was essential, though this information was later proved to be false. Early that afternoon Kerr and his secretary, David Smith, had left for engagements in Sydney. At about 7 p.m. Whitlam sought an ExCo meeting; it had to be held that night at the Lodge. But Kerr's approval for a meeting had not been obtained before he left for the Opera House. Efforts by Whitlam and officials to reach Kerr or his secretary had not been successful. The ExCo meeting proceeded with the four ministers signing the document only after midnight.

When an official finally reached David Smith at 2 a.m., he was incredulous, saying: 'There couldn't be an ExCo meeting unless the Governor-General was informed.' Standard procedure for ExCo meetings is that while the governor-general is not required to attend every meeting, his approval is obtained before a meeting occurs and he signs the relevant documents after any meeting.

In the morning Smith briefed a disturbed Kerr at about 8 a.m. A short time later, Whitlam rang Kerr at Admiralty House in Sydney. Whitlam said that because of exceptional circumstances it had been necessary to hold an urgent ExCo meeting. Kerr said Whitlam told him because of the hour it was decided not to wake the governor-general but seek his approval after the event. Whitlam said the four ministers agreed on the decision and its urgency. They had all signed the ExCo minute. Whitlam, according to Kerr, said that 'if I would have been prepared to give approval in advance I could do so afterwards though it certainly was unusual to ask for it'. He explained the purposes and reasons for the loan. According to Kerr, Whitlam said the attorney-general's advice was that the loan could be regarded as for temporary purposes. He said a special messenger was en route to Sydney with the documents and would arrive soon. Whitlam advised Kerr to approve the meeting and sign the minute.

In a lengthy nine-page note written in July 1975 about these events, Kerr said that after the minute arrived, he examined it 'and came to the conclusion that the Attorney's legal advice was by no means certainly correct and was probably wrong'. Kerr spoke several times that morning to the secretary of the ExCo. He established that various Crown law officers had been at the Lodge meetings. He tried to speak to Harders but he was unavailable. Kerr reached Byers to clarify what had happened, and Byers told him that Murphy's advice was 'arguable'.

Kerr concluded the legality had been 'clearly canvassed at the officials level and the Attorney-General's opinion had prevailed'. He said: 'The point here was that the act proposed was not plainly illegal and the point of law was not plainly unarguable on the facts as known to me.' His view was that future legality could be tested in the courts. It was not his job 'to usurp the role of the High Court in constitutional matters'. He concluded that if the loan was raised the 'legal error' would be addressed in the courts.

In deciding what to do, Kerr asked himself two questions: if awakened in the night would he have authorised the meeting, and if he had attended the meeting would he have accepted the advice of ministers and signed the minute? He decided the answer to both question was yes. Kerr said he was 'confronted by a solid political and formal decision made unanimously'. He decided it would be 'absurd' to insist upon another ExCo meeting. Kerr said his signature did not constitute 'personal approval' but reflected the convention of acting on ministerial advice. He decided, therefore, 'to excuse the lapse' of not being informed of the ExCo meeting beforehand.[5]

The governor-general took two decisions: he authorised the loan raising and he raised none of his doubts with Whitlam.

In his July 1975 record, Kerr said he felt the loan 'could run into political and legal trouble' but that Whitlam's position was firm. Kerr wrote that he contemplated whether to resort to the Crown's 'advise and warn' doctrine but rejected this option as 'useless' and impractical since it meant intruding into the policy and politics of the issue.[6]

In his memoirs Kerr went a step further: 'The purported meeting of 13 December 1974 was in my view invalid.' He decided this because his prior consent as governor-general had not been obtained. In effect, he was accusing Whitlam of misleading him and of giving him invalid advice. Yet Kerr conveyed no such concerns to Whitlam on the day. His rationale was that the issue of whether or not the meeting was valid was one 'to be left to the courts'.[7]

The loan authorisation testified to Connor's ability to hijack the government, the extraordinary naivety of the senior ministers, the catastrophic misjudgement of Whitlam and the irrational hostility towards the Treasury that fought, correctly and courageously, against the proposal. When the loan authorisation became public, Whitlam's defence was that the money had never been procured. In no way did this constitute an excuse.

When news of the loan was leaked during 1975, with reports of Treasury opposition, Kerr came under collateral attack: he was criticised in public and private for signing the minute and not questioning the government about the policy and process. This had a profound impact on Kerr – he looked complicit in one of the greatest follies in the nation's political history.

In his memoirs, Kerr took his concerns to a new intensity – saying the circumstances of the ExCo meeting were a 'great shock' to him. He felt the government failed to respect him or his office. 'My deepest concern,' he said, was not the legal issue, but whether the 'proper attitude' was taken towards his office. The more he had learned about the loan, the more he feared Whitlam's attitude was that the governor-general could be 'increasingly ignored'. Kerr says he now worried the office might be 'diminished' during his tenure.[8]

Harders affirmed later that Kerr's 'deepest concern' was whether Whitlam had a 'rubber stamp' approach to his office. He said Kerr worried whether the governor-general could on occasions be 'forgotten rather than being kept fully informed'.[9] John Menadue, the head of the Prime Minister's Department, reveals Kerr's changed behaviour after the ExCo meeting: 'Almost from that meeting on, the Governor-General was very particular about Executive Council meetings and was more careful and probing.'[10]

In an effort to save his government, Whitlam convened on 9 July 1975 a special sitting day devoted exclusively to putting on the table all details of the loans affair. It was at this time that Kerr wrote his nine-page document, a methodical and self-justifying missive, explaining everything that he had done.

During the special sitting day, future Liberal attorney-general Bob Ellicott delivered his withering condemnation of the Whitlam government:

'I cannot believe that any honest man could advise the Governor-General to approve of that minute if he knew that the borrowings were for 20 years and were to meet the long-term energy purposes of the Government. I do not believe an honest man could do it. I believe it was an illegal and unconstitutional act . . . I cannot imagine that His Excellency, a lawyer of great eminence, would have approved this minute unless he had received assurances and advice that satisfied him that this was indeed a borrowing for temporary purposes. To satisfy him that it was, was to deceive him . . . That is the charge. The action was unlawful, unconstitutional and based on deception.'[11]

Given Kerr's long association with Ellicott, a former solicitor-general, this speech would have had a profound impact on him. While it was an attack on Whitlam, the governor-general hardly appeared in a flattering light.

After the dismissal, however, Whitlam laid a lethal accusation against Kerr: that the protests in his book about the loan were retrospective. Whitlam said of Kerr: 'He became concerned about his complicity in the events of 13–14 December 1974 only when they became a matter of political controversy and when the people with whom he wished to ingratiate himself starting ribbing him about it. Legality and propriety had nothing to do with it.'[12]

The loan authorisation was revoked on 7 January 1975 at an ExCo meeting attended by Kerr, at which he said nothing about the process. On 28 January, Kerr presided at another ExCo meeting attended by Connor and Murphy, which reinstated the authority for half the amount. At this meeting, in response to Kerr's question, Murphy gave the same opinion – it could be regarded as being for temporary purposes. In his private notes, Kerr later wrote he concluded 'it would be useless for me to try to discuss policy and of no relevance what my own legal opinion might be'.[13] He did not even ask Murphy to put his opinion in writing. When the meeting broke, Kerr's social discussion with the ministers confirmed their determination on the loan. Kerr decided 'there was nothing I could do about it'.[14] Again, he had not raised any doubts with them.

Whitlam later mocked Kerr's hypocrisy. How, he asked, could the matter that caused Kerr 'great shock' on 14 December apparently deserve his 'approval and acquiescence' on 28 January? Whitlam was enraged by Kerr's claim that the original meeting was invalid and by his justification for not raising this at the time: that it was a matter for the courts. He branded this a 'monstrous' argument. Whitlam is surely correct: the idea that a governor-general would decide an ExCo meeting was invalid but not raise this with the prime minister is untenable behaviour. At face value, it is an abdication of constitutional responsibility. This is either a post-event fabrication by Kerr or confirmation that Kerr was weak and frightened of Whitlam.

In assessing Kerr's attitude at the time Whitlam said the governor-general in discussions with ministers in December had been enthusiastically canvassing the loan's potential. Whitlam said that 'at no stage' did Kerr raise with him 'the slightest doubts about any aspect of the matter' though he had 'plenty of opportunities' to do so. Whitlam documented his frequent meetings with Kerr over January and early February and said there was no sign of any tensions. In his book about the crisis, Whitlam said 'it surprises me to discover nearly four years later that Sir John Kerr was a deeply troubled man at that time'.[15]

Fraser, following Ellicott's line, said the original ExCo minute raised the possibility of 'a deliberate conspiracy to deceive and defraud'. The public servants involved were later called to the bar of the Senate and quizzed. Whitlam laid his own charge against Kerr: if the governor-general had such doubts then, as a man of honour, it was his duty to raise them.[16]

It is obvious that Kerr's doubts intensified over time as he discovered more about the bitter internal row over the loan. For example, on 14 February 1975 the Reserve Bank governor, Sir John Phillips, during a courtesy call, told Kerr 'that the Bank and Treasury were very worried about the transaction and that it was doing us no good in Europe and in the classical money markets'.

Kerr was correct to accept Whitlam's advice, sign the minute and authorise the loan-raising. He is correct in saying the substantive legal issue was for the High Court. But the contradiction in Kerr's account is unsustainable: he claims to be shocked, offended and worried the office is being diminished yet he says nothing to Whitlam. The contradiction is untenable. The more Kerr escalated his concerns over time, the more he condemned himself.

Given the gravity of his concerns, what should Kerr have done? He should have told Whitlam the depth of his concern about the

ExCo meeting. He should have asked on the Saturday morning for the attorney-general's advice to be put in writing. He should not have signed the minute until the written advice was provided. He could have spoken to Connor to get a fuller explanation of the purposes of the loan and spoken to Cairns to get an explanation for the unusual channels being used to raise the funds. He spoke to Byers but missed the main game: the Treasury and the treasurer.

Hasluck said the governor-general should function as a 'watch-dog over the Constitution and laws for the nation' not by rejecting advice outright but by ensuring advice is 'well-founded'. Despite his hand-wringing, Kerr did next to nothing.

His personal records, correspondence, journal and memoirs are tedious in the gravity of his concerns yet near empty in tangible actions. These concerns should have been put to Whitlam on the Saturday, both orally and in writing. Harders nailed the issue: 'I think a Governor-General who had the concerns about the ExCo minute and its legality along the lines expressed by Kerr in his book should have raised these concerns at the time with the Prime Minister.'[17] Indeed, if the concerns were genuine at the time, Kerr was irresponsible not to do so.

During Hasluck's August 1977 meeting with Sir Martin Charteris, he argued that the Whitlam–Kerr difficulties went back to the loans affair, and that, at the time, Kerr should have been more 'diligent and attentive to the duties of his office'.[18]

This penetrates to the supreme lesson from the loan crisis – Kerr felt he could never influence Whitlam. His writing is thick with self-justification for inaction. In the end, Kerr never tried to influence Whitlam. Kerr keeps saying that raising issues would be 'useless' and 'pointless' and that because Whitlam and his senior ministers had made up their minds 'there was nothing I could do about it'.[19]

A king without influence erodes respect for the Crown. The same applies to a governor-general. Hasluck queried and counselled as governor-general. On a number of occasions he declined to sign ExCo minutes until more information was provided or procedures were changed. Hasluck had influence and a governor-general without influence is useless. Yet facing Whitlam, with his intimidating manner, Kerr seemed paralysed. The office of governor-general as the Queen's representative is designed to carry influence and, if a governor-general presses a point, the government has no option but to respond. In the end, Kerr had no stomach to raise the concerns he felt, and he calculated, no doubt, that damaging his relations with Whitlam would be unwise.

In his portentous style, Kerr said in his memoirs he 'had learned some lessons from the loans affair'. He felt the need to be more vigilant. He feared being taken for granted. He was less trustful of Whitlam and suspicious of his advice as prime minister. Aware of a likely supply crisis, Kerr 'stiffened' himself for further troubles. Above all, he decided he would not tolerate becoming 'a rubber stamp for whatever the Prime Minister might advise'.[20]

Kerr was turning against Whitlam.

His doubts were accentuated on the eve of the supply crisis. In his memoirs, Kerr says that shortly before the 14 October resignation of Connor, he had a conversation with Whitlam in which the prime minister said he would defy the Senate if supply was blocked and 'destroy forever' the Senate's power. Kerr claimed he asked Whitlam whether 'that is the wisest course'. Kerr said he suggested it might be better to go to an election. He argued that Whitlam was still young, and even if Whitlam lost an election, he would have a good chance of returning, as did Harold Wilson in Britain in 1974. He says Whitlam rejected this approach 'out of hand'.[21]

The governor-general believed this was an important exchange. He said it was one of the first conversations when an 'implacable element' began to appear in Whitlam. 'He made it clear that my suggestion was not discussable and never would be,' Kerr says. He gave no date or location for this exchange.

Kerr claimed that this view was confirmed when Whitlam came

to Government House on 14 October for the swearing-in of Senator Ken Wriedt as Connor's successor. He wrote that Wriedt said he was against the 'toughing it out' policy and preferred going to an election if supply was blocked. Kerr gave no details of this further discussion with Whitlam. But his conclusion is breathtaking: he decided Whitlam was beyond reach of any argument 'or even discussion'.[22]

Kerr said in his memoirs that these exchanges saw him 'going as far' as he 'could prudently go in the exercise of my right to "advise and warn"'. This is a ludicrous statement. In no way does it constitute a serious example of the Crown's 'advise and warn' doctrine.

This purported exchange is Kerr merely engaging in political speculation. His version is reminiscent of a journalist chatting with Whitlam over a drink. If Kerr had been serious, he would have warned Whitlam that, in any supply crisis, it was the prime minister's ultimate responsibility to resolve the deadlock before funds expired. This would be the natural expectation of any monarch or governor-general. It would be consistent with Bagehot's classic refrain that provided a king exercised 'the right to warn' then 'he could not help moving his ministers'.[23]

Accepting Kerr's version at face value, it reveals a governor-general alarmed about the position of the prime minister but deciding he had no ability to discuss the issue. It was a certain recipe for trouble and misunderstanding.

A contemporary twelve-page handwritten note in Kerr's papers, dated 16 November 1975, reinforces his core claim. Kerr said that from 'the beginning of my relevant talks' with the prime minister before the blocking of supply, 'Mr Whitlam told me he would never agree to an election for the House or a double dissolution election whilst supply was being denied as a means of getting supply'. The note continued: '[Whitlam] told me he intended to "tough it out" and if necessary to govern without supply . . .'[24]

Whitlam, however, disputed the facts in Kerr's memoirs. He said no such discussions took place. He said he would have remembered any reference to Wilson and it was not made. He said that on the occasion of Wriedt's swearing-in, the supply issue was not canvassed.[25]

Accepting Kerr's version, it does not constitute a serious example of the 'advise and warn' doctrine. Indeed, it reveals the farcical nature of the situation and Kerr's behaviour. These exchanges, if they occurred, were before supply was even blocked. Kerr's admission that he never subsequently counselled Whitlam in a frank manner reveals the extent of the governor-general's deception of the prime minister. His justification was Whitlam's intransigence. But that was no justification whatsoever. Having an intransigent prime minister is hardly unique and did not absolve Kerr of his responsibility. Everybody had to deal with Whitlam's overbearing personality: his staff, ministers, party officials, public servants and journalists.

Indeed, governors-general are selected supposedly because of their experience, maturity and wisdom. The office possesses the ultimate constitutional powers as well as an influential seat from which to engage, counsel and warn. Kerr's failure on the latter drove him to the former.

The position Kerr now took followed his outlook from the loans affair. He internalised his concerns, built up his private resentment towards Whitlam and, after a disputed but forlorn effort to raise his doubts, kept quiet, using the impossibility of influencing Whitlam as his justification. According to Kerr's own account, he had lost confidence in Whitlam before the budget was blocked.

But there was a deeper and more explosive factor at work: it was the dynamic behind the dismissal.

PART THREE

The Crisis

9

Kerr's Fear
of Recall

On New Year's Eve, 31 December 1975, just two weeks after his rejection by the public at the general election, Gough Whitlam wrote to British Labour prime minister Harold Wilson, exposing his still raw feelings about the dismissal. He said this would not have happened in Britain because 'the Queen would never have done it – a feeling I know you will share'. But Whitlam made a revelation to his counterpart.

He said: 'I made a fundamental mistake in recommending to the Queen that she appoint a judge as her viceroy. In Australia judges suffer the corruption of knowing that on the High Court they can with impunity make propositions and dispositions of a political nature. The Governor-General was persuaded that he could do the same. He deceived me – realising, I'm sure, that I would have been in touch with the Queen if my suspicions had been aroused.'[1]

Whitlam, in effect, was telling Wilson he would have moved against Kerr if he had had any notion of the governor-general's intentions. The letter was discovered by the authors in the National Archives in the UK. It is significant because it was written close to the events, Wilson was a reliable confidant, and the tone shows Whitlam was exposing his heart. It penetrates to the psychological paradox of the dismissal.

Kerr believed he was under threat from Whitlam. He was convinced that Whitlam, if he had any inkling of Kerr's plan to use the reserve powers, would contact the Palace to have Kerr recalled. It is the reason Kerr deceived Whitlam. The governor-general's protection of the Queen from any involvement is the justification Kerr openly offered for his dismissal by deception. He wanted to surprise Whitlam and he did surprise Whitlam.

In his letter to Wilson, Whitlam was contained yet poured out his emotions. He said Kerr's action meant no reforming government in Australia was safe in future and that republicanism had got 'a very significant boost'. There is no reason to think Whitlam's comment about contacting the Palace did not reflect his views in late 1975, a few weeks after the crisis.

In his memoir of the crisis, published in 1979, Whitlam denied outright any interest in removing Kerr: 'At no time during the crisis had the possibility of replacing Sir John Kerr been a significant element in my thinking. I never bothered even to inquire into the legal or practical procedures for so drastic and unprecedented an action. I have not to this day.'[2]

Comments from John Menadue in a document he wrote in late 1975 throw light on this contradiction. Menadue said the possibility that the governor-general might seek to dismiss Whitlam was considered early in the crisis but 'as time passed, however, [Whitlam] became less concerned with the question'.

Menadue wrote: 'On a couple of occasions I asked him if he had considered the mechanics of contacting Government House if he had to move quickly. He merely said he would have to ring Martin Charteris but believed that this was a hypothetical and theoretical possibility which he did not consider likely. I suggested early after the Opposition had moved to refuse supply that perhaps Sir John Bunting [High Commissioner in London] should be briefed on the subject and, if necessary, I could go to London for this purpose. He thought that this would be quite unnecessary.'[3]

In short, Whitlam had no contingency plans for Kerr's recall. The reason is that he was sure he had Kerr's measure. Seeing Kerr as a weak man, Whitlam never took seriously the idea of dismissal by the governor-general. And, as Menadue indicated, the prime minister also made no plans for a situation in which Kerr moved against him.

It was correct, therefore, for Whitlam to say that at no time was replacing Kerr a 'significant element' in his thinking. In interviews conducted by the authors at the time and since, there has been no credible suggestion of such plans in Whitlam's office or department. The modus operandi was that Kerr was 'onside'. This point was affirmed by speechwriter Graham Freudenberg: 'To the last hour Whitlam had complete confidence in Sir John Kerr.' Michael Sexton, adviser to Kep Enderby at the time and later NSW solicitor-general, said as far as he knew, there was never any consideration given to Kerr's recall. 'Most ministers and staff assumed, wrongly as it turned out, that the Prime Minister and the Governor-General were co-operating at this time,' Sexton said.[4]

During the crisis, however, Whitlam would periodically joke about having to sack Kerr. 'Yes, he would joke about it,' his principal private secretary, John Mant, said. Mant recalled this took the form of Whitlam saying, "Oh well, I might have to ring the Queen. I might have to ring Westminster about this." Nobody ever took it seriously and I certainly didn't think he ever would.'[5] Mant's comment, however, highlights one of the paradoxes of the crisis – Whitlam knew that Kerr had a technical power to move against him but he never treated this as a serious option that required any contingency planning.

What Whitlam might have done had he discovered Kerr's dismissal plan is another matter. His anger and sense of betrayal would have matched the fires of hell.

There is, however, no gainsaying Kerr's conviction on this question. In his twelve-page handwritten note dated 16 November 1975,

Kerr said: 'On several occasions, sometimes jocularly sometimes less so, but on all occasions with underlying seriousness, [Whitlam] said that the crisis could end in a race to the Palace to see who could get there first.'[6]

Throughout the crisis Whitlam sought to reinforce his confidence in Kerr with a counterproductive tactic of intimidation, in private and public. This was notable in his public declarations that the governor-general had no option but to act on the advice of the prime minister. The most famous such example was the Government House dinner for Malaysian prime minister Tun Abdul Razak on the night of 16 October, the day the Senate deferred the budget bills. Kerr recollected that Whitlam, referring to the supply crisis, 'said to me with a brilliant smile, "It could be a question of whether I get to the Queen first for your recall or you get in first with my dismissal." We all laughed.'[7]

Kerr said later he saw this supposed joke as 'a very real threat'. He said he felt 'shattered' and that it was another piece of Whitlam's 'psychological warfare'. Anne Kerr, who was there, has confirmed its impact and this interpretation. Kerr's official secretary, David Smith, said 'it was a brand of intimidation'.[8] Whitlam later dismissed his remark as flippant, but it would be a mistake to accept that at face value. Anybody familiar with Whitlam knew he used wit, sarcasm and jokes as a weapon.

Yet there is another unknown feature of this dinner. In Kerr's files is a seven-page typed note about this dinner titled 'Notes on Conversation with Mr Malcolm Fraser on Occasion of Dinner to Prime Minister of Malaysia – Thursday, 16 October 1975 and Related Matters'. Kerr reviewed the notes with a pen and made some hand-written changes.

In the note, Kerr said that before the dinner Fraser told him: (a) he was 'very worried' and 'would welcome any advice I could give him'; (b) that he was relying 'heavily' on the advice of Bob Ellicott; (c) that he had not decided to block supply until the Khemlani loans affair scandal recurred and 'after that he really had no choice'; and (d) that he thought he could 'possibly have destroyed himself' but 'he had to do it'.

This reveals Fraser at an early stage deferring to Kerr and seeking his guidance. After dinner, Fraser raised with Kerr the Ellicott opinion, released in the form of a press statement, making clear he wanted Kerr to see it. He told Kerr the Ellicott opinion was 'without any disrespect' to him.

Kerr's note said that he had not yet begun 'any process of mediation' between the leaders 'although this has been canvassed during the weekend in the press'. His note said: 'There was one element in my pre-dinner and post-dinner short conversations with Mr Fraser which for completeness I should record.' In a remarkable account, Kerr said:

> Before dinner [Fraser] was undoubtedly wishing me to know that he had confidence in me and that my presence was important and he hoped to have the benefit of my advice. Some intuition led me to make a cryptic remark about things not necessarily remaining the same. He did not understand this – I was referring to the remote possibility that I might not be there, to possible but unlikely dismissal. He did not pick this up and I could not at that time stay and elaborate . . .
>
> Having thought about it over dinner, I concluded that I should be rather more specific because I felt he was entitled to take into account a bare possibility which he had not seemed to contemplate. I therefore said to him that one conceivable but remote aspect was that as the crisis developed the Prime Minister had the option of considering the degree of his confidence in me. He said that it was inconceivable.
> I replied it was a matter nevertheless to be at least thought about.
>
> His reaction was to say the Queen would never permit it. I told him that that question was one I preferred not to discuss. It was all most unlikely but he would have to make up his own mind about it. I did this out of fairness because he could be badly caught by

ending up with a Governor-General who would not even consider ever using the reserve power however bad the situation and I had a feeling that the point would in any event break into the press as it immediately did. He should be thinking about it.

There is of course nothing he could do if things moved, as I do not believe they will, in this direction except make a fuss. There would be a very great fuss indeed. I judge that the only circumstances in which my dismissal would be recommended would be if the crisis became really drastic and the Prime Minister feared that I was about to dismiss him. He would under those circumstances undoubtedly try to get in first.[9]

The document is undated but was obviously written very soon after the dinner. It is astonishing in many respects. First, it reveals Kerr's conviction that Whitlam would 'undoubtedly' try to sack him if alerted to any planned use of the reserve powers against him. Second, despite Kerr's claims this was a 'remote' possibility, it was preying on his mind from the start of the crisis. Third, although he had decided he could not talk frankly to Whitlam, Kerr choose to speak frankly to an unsuspecting Fraser and alert Fraser to his fear of dismissal by Whitlam. Fourth, Kerr did this in a calculating manner, having thought about it during the meal. Fifth, this was invaluable intelligence for Fraser since he now knew that Kerr distrusted Whitlam on the issue of his survival as governor-general. Sixth, by depicting himself as a governor-general who believed in the reserve powers, Kerr gave Fraser more encouragement. Seventh, Kerr's justification for telling Fraser of his fears is pure sophistry, namely, that Fraser in taking future decisions had a right to know he might face another governor-general. Finally, the event reveals Kerr's style – while purporting to be highly proper, he was disposed to chat about the crisis and his situation.

Kerr often drew upon notes he wrote at the time for his subsequently published memoirs. But his book makes no reference to this discussion with Fraser. When Fraser was asked about this exchange with Kerr, he denied it. Interviewed by Troy Bramston in 2013, Fraser said: 'That conversation, in my view, did not take place. If I had that conversation with him I don't believe I would have forgotten it.' But Fraser said he knew that Kerr 'was frightened of being dismissed'.[10]

With Kerr and Fraser both dead, a degree of uncertainty surrounds this conversation. Yet the explicit and detailed nature of Kerr's note must lend credence to the view that it happened.

In his note, Kerr wrote:

> At no stage in the short discussion with Mr Fraser did I discuss any options open to me, attempt to persuade him that he should take any particular course nor did he attempt to persuade me to take any particular course. For the sake of completeness I should say that although I know Mr Fraser he is not a friend but we have had important official relations before.

Towards the end of his note Kerr referred to his 'continued firm intention to stay above the battle'.

In his 1980 handwritten journal, Kerr ruminated at length on the prospect that Whitlam would recall him. He wrote that in September 1975, when in Papua New Guinea for the independence celebrations, he told Charles, the Prince of Wales, the reserve powers might 'need to be exercised', which could heighten 'the risk of recall'. According to Kerr, the Prince said: 'But surely, Sir John, the Queen would not have to accept advice that you should be recalled at the very time should this happen when you were considering having to dismiss the government.'

Kerr's journal says that after returning to London, Prince Charles spoke to the Queen's private secretary, Sir Martin Charteris, who then wrote to Kerr on 7 October. Kerr says Charteris advised 'that if the kind of contingency in mind were to develop, although the Queen would try to delay things, in the end she would have to take the Prime

Minister's advice.' Kerr makes the point he already knew this.[11]

The suggestion that Kerr told Charles, a month before supply was blocked, that he might have to dismiss Whitlam is astonishing. Its credibility is in question. The full account is not mentioned in Kerr's memoirs or in any of Kerr's contemporary notes written during the crisis sighted by the authors. It also contradicts Kerr's golden rule in the crisis – that he did not signal his hand to the Palace. The letters between Kerr and the Palace have not been released.

Whitlam's biographer, Jenny Hocking, used this journal entry to argue that before supply was blocked 'the Governor-General had already conferred with the Palace on the possibility of the future dismissal of the prime minister, securing in advance the response of the Palace to it'. Hocking built this into a theory about 'several critical conversations and understandings reached' between the Palace and Kerr over Whitlam's dismissal. She asserted the Palace was 'forewarned about the possibility of dismissal by Kerr'. The evidence does not support this. It was denied by Kerr, by the Palace officials, and by every principal involved in the crisis. There has never been any hard documentary evidence to sustain this claim in the past forty years. What Kerr's journal reveals, above all, is his obsession about dismissal by Whitlam.[12]

During the crisis, the media made scant reference to the 1932 Game–Lang crisis in New South Wales that saw the governor sack the premier. Yet both Kerr and Whitlam were deeply aware of this precedent and had lived through these events. On 15 October, Whitlam referred to the Game–Lang event, saying he had been conducting research 'into the general question of dismissal of governments'. But Kerr had studied this crisis more deeply than Whitlam. In his memoirs, Kerr wrote that 'it is something of a mystery why Lang did not try to get rid of Game before he was himself dismissed'. Kerr was preoccupied with the idea of a premier or prime minister striking first.[13]

Around the onset of the crisis, the Kerrs dined at Admiralty House with the NSW governor, Sir Roden Cutler, and his wife. This arose because Kerr had planned an overseas trip – subsequently cancelled – and Cutler, as the senior governor, would have served in his place during the crisis. Cutler recalled: 'At one stage I said to Kerr that there was, of course, the possibility that the Prime Minister might move to dismiss him. He became very activated at this point, saying, "Yes, I know, I know." It was obvious that he had given some thought to this possibility.'[14]

The governor-general is appointed by the Queen on advice from the prime minister and can be removed by such advice. There is no security of tenure. Kerr and his official secretary, David Smith, had discussed the possibility of Kerr's removal from office. As a result, Smith contacted Charteris to inquire about the process. The advice from Charteris was that a phone call would not suffice. The Palace would require a letter. Charteris later told Paul Kelly: 'You couldn't just pick up the telephone and fix it up that way.'[15] Smith told the authors: 'The message from Sir Martin was that the Queen would have to accept any advice from the Prime Minister but in the process there could be to-ing and fro-ing.'[16]

Kerr said he had a long discussion with Whitlam on 18 October in which the prime minister talked of finding a method to enable the banks to fund government salaries and services, thereby outmanoeuvring Fraser. Kerr claimed Whitlam said, as a result, there would be 'no excuse for removing him and sending for someone willing to advise an election'. Such a remark by Whitlam would have been extraordinarily inept. He denied this conversation took place. The point, however, is Kerr's self-declared state of mind. He asserted that from this point, early in the crisis: 'I never again felt I could talk to the Prime Minister about his policy on Supply.' Kerr said Whitlam told him: 'I can and will break Fraser, if my party stands behind me and it will.'[17]

A fateful Whitlam–Kerr discussion occurred on 21 October after an ExCo meeting. At this point, Kerr was feeling pressure from an intense media campaign for him to become more active. He was worried he may have appeared 'indifferent' to the deadlock. He had been assessing from the start what role he might play. He now asked Whitlam for approval to meet with Fraser to evaluate the situation. Kerr said he merely wished to assess Fraser's intentions. He told Whitlam he believed the crisis was still 'political' and had not crossed the threshold to become a 'constitutional' crisis.

Whitlam agreed. He believed Kerr might be able to help.

It was, however, an epic blunder. At this point Whitlam surrendered one of his major advantages. The Crown acts on the advice of ministers. The Crown exists not as a constitutional umpire but as a constitutional guardian. It is the prime minister, not the opposition leader, who advises the Crown and the governor-general. The opposition leader has no direct relations with the governor-general. On those rare occasions of crisis when the Crown does mediate with both sides, the solemn responsibility on the Crown is to promote a solution yet keep the Crown impartial.

Whitlam's decision changed the atmospherics of the crisis. It brought Kerr to centre stage. It enshrined Kerr in a new role: conducting a dialogue in search of a solution. Menadue said Whitlam felt there were 'no risks' in letting Kerr see Fraser. There was almost no limit to Whitlam's naivety. Only a prime minister with total trust in the governor-general could authorise such a dialogue. Yet this trust was misplaced. Whitlam was oblivious to Kerr's suspicions about him. Now he was allowing Kerr and Fraser to consult without having any access to their discussions. Whitlam was deluding himself: the idea that Kerr would procure Fraser's retreat was wild fantasy.

Not only did Whitlam misjudge Kerr. He also grievously misjudged Fraser. Kerr and Fraser were not friends but Fraser told people during the crisis that 'I actually know Kerr better than Whitlam does'.[18] In his notes, Kerr referred to Fraser's decision as defence minister years earlier, when he appointed Kerr to chair an inquiry on defence force pay and conditions. Fraser's private secretary, Dale Budd, told the authors in 2015: 'Kerr would come into the office periodically and report to Fraser on the progress of the inquiry. He would sit down and chat with me before seeing Fraser. Fraser obviously got on well with him. He felt he knew Kerr.'[19]

The opposition spent more time and effort evaluating Kerr than did Whitlam. David Kemp, Fraser's senior adviser and speechwriter, recalled discussions about tactics: 'Following Fraser's discussion with the Federal Executive of the Liberal Party at the Federal Council in early October, I expressed my concern to Jim Carlton that there needed to be a proper analysis of the implications of a decision to refuse supply. A group was brought together comprising Ellicott, [John] Carrick, [Timothy] Pascoe, Carlton and John Atwill to assess Kerr's likely responses. Carrick and Atwill had clear views about Kerr, both believing that Kerr's character made it possible that an exercise of the Reserve Powers would be attractive to him if it were clear that he could "save" the Constitution.'[20]

Sir Laurence Street, who succeeded Kerr as chief justice of New South Wales, was approached by Atwill for an assessment of Kerr. Street and Kerr had remained on friendly terms. Street recalled the conversation in 2015. 'I told him that Kerr would not hesitate to exercise his power if he was convinced there was a stalemate, or before, but certainly if it came to a stalemate. In a personal sense, he had no inhibitions about doing what he thought was the right thing . . . Kerr knew politics. I think he was looking forward to having a hand in what was a really big issue.'[21]

The Ellicott opinion had identified the governor-general as the central figure in the crisis. This was Fraser's view. He saw communications with Kerr as pivotal. On the night of the Tun Razak dinner, Fraser had given David Smith an alarming view of Whitlam, intending it to be passed to Kerr. Kerr's notes record this view – Fraser had 'extreme fears about the Prime Minister's stability'.[22]

At the shadow cabinet meetings of both 19 October and 21 October, two of the options on the table involved Fraser, publicly or privately, seeking a meeting with Kerr. The records of the 21 October meeting show shadow cabinet canvassing 'a direct approach to the

Governor-General' but deciding against it at that stage.[23] Dialogue with Kerr was identified as an objective. Now Whitlam had solved this problem for Fraser. The idea that Whitlam should let Fraser anywhere near Kerr was pure folly.

Whitlam never grasped he was giving Fraser the chance to succeed where he had failed – to persuade the governor-general. He misread the potential Kerr–Fraser dynamic.

It is easy to see the logic Whitlam used. The Ellicott opinion argued that Kerr should dismiss Whitlam. So Whitlam cast himself as the governor-general's defender in the teeth of this opposition campaign to get Kerr to sack the government. Whitlam publicly accused the opposition of trying to 'bring reprehensive pressure to bear' on Kerr. He felt he was Kerr's champion; he hoped Kerr would be his champion in talks with Fraser.

That evening, 21 October, Fraser saw Kerr at Yarralumla. He was given a drink and they settled down. The conversation lasted more than an hour. It is unlikely that Whitlam had spent an hour discussing the crisis with Kerr. In his memoirs Kerr gave a long and revealing account of his meeting with the opposition leader:

> Mr Fraser said that a firm decision had been made to deny Supply, that this would be persisted in to the end, that whatever the press said or predicted the Bills would be deferred as often as they were presented and the Prime Minister would have to face the country . . .
>
> I asked him why deferral had been chosen. He said that Supply had been deferred so that, should it come to a dissolution, he would be able to guarantee Supply by passing the Appropriation Bills immediately.
>
> I told him not to assume I accepted the Ellicott thesis but he responded to this by saying that, if the Prime Minister tried to govern without supply – and he certainly would be forced into that position – [Mr Fraser] would need to be in the position

of being able to guarantee Supply although the Prime Minister could not . . . Mr Fraser's attitude in this first talk with me and until the end was that deferral was not a sign of weakness due to internal problems with some Senators but a deliberate and unanimous tactic . . . Mr Fraser did not at any time attempt to give me any advice . . . Mr Fraser believed at that time that there already was a serious constitutional crisis.[24]

That night the parliamentary lobbies were filled with false reports that Kerr had censured Fraser at the meeting. Hurried denials were provided by Smith and Fraser's office. Budd said: 'I think Fraser came back from the first meeting fairly relieved. He said, "Kerr just listened to a statement of my position." '[25]

Over the next two days the opposition publicly altered its message. When pressed by the media, Fraser made clear he would defer to Kerr's judgement. 'If [Kerr] gives a decision we would respect and accept it absolutely,' Fraser said. This was because 'of the respect we have for the office and the man'. The media went into overdrive. Fraser's remarks were seen as the first stage in his inevitable retreat: laying the ground for the best possible exit with Kerr as cover.

In reality, Fraser had played an astute hand. He had told Kerr there would be no retreat until Whitlam called an election. He stood by the Ellicott thesis that the governor-general had to resolve the deadlock. He made clear the deferral tactic was to enable the governor-general to commission Fraser as prime minister, confident that Fraser, unlike Whitlam, could obtain supply and end the crisis. By saying he believed there was already a constitutional crisis, he was, in effect, implying the governor-general needed to act. In short, Fraser was inviting Kerr to dismiss Whitlam without saying so. Then he went public genuflecting before Kerr's wisdom. It must have been a sobering encounter for the governor-general.

In his 16 November note, Kerr left no doubt about the significance of this meeting. He said: 'Mr Fraser referred to the Ellicott document and said that they were acting on the basis of its correctness, with all that implied for me as to what my duty was.' There is no doubt: from their first meeting, Fraser was pushing for a dismissal. And from the time he left this meeting to 11 November, Fraser remained confident that Kerr, eventually, would act.

What else was said that evening at Yarralumla? John Menadue later provided an account of this first Kerr–Fraser meeting based upon a confidential exchange with Fraser. Menadue, a Whitlam loyalist, was retained for some time by Fraser in his capacity as head of the Prime Minister's Department after the change of government. This meant he had regular contact with Fraser. Menadue claimed that at this meeting Kerr 'had indicated to Mr Fraser that he had the threat of dismissal hanging over him and that if he showed his hand to Mr Whitlam that he would be dismissed'.[26]

Menadue said this account came from an exchange he had with Fraser on 28 January 1976, two months after the dismissal, on the street outside West Block, Canberra. Menadue made a note of this discussion in June 1976. The authors have a copy of it. It reads: 'On 28 January this year Mr Fraser said that, on his first meeting with the Governor-General during the Supply crisis . . . the Governor-General had said that he could not give Mr Whitlam an inkling of what he had in mind or Mr Whitlam would be immediately on the telephone to London seeking the Governor-General's dismissal. There is a note on file to this effect in the Department of Prime Minister and Cabinet.'[27]

This exchange is credible. This is not just because Menadue felt it was significant and made a record of it, but because it duplicates Kerr's version of what he told Fraser at the Tun Razak dinner just five evenings earlier. Given that Kerr says he told Fraser on 16 October, it is hardly a surprise that he might have told Fraser again in more relaxing circumstances on 21 October about his fear of recall. In a subsequent 1995 note, Menadue calls this 'a critical clue' and says 'it was the critical meeting'.[28]

Asked why Fraser told him this, Menadue said: 'I think to justify the action he had taken.'[29] In short, if Whitlam was ready to threaten Kerr then the Kerr–Fraser outcome was justified to protect the office of governor-general and the Queen.

By telling Fraser he felt threatened, Kerr was changing the atmospherics. After all, this threat existed only in the context of Kerr using the reserve powers. This intelligence could only have encouraged Fraser. It would have reinforced his belief that, if he held firm, he would prevail. It also encouraged Fraser's public remarks supportive of Kerr: knowing Kerr felt threatened by Whitlam drove an astute Fraser to offer him public support.

In 1995, when Paul Kelly asked Fraser about Menadue's account, he insisted that Menadue had it wrong.[30] Fraser said Kerr never gave him 'explicit signals' at any of their meetings about what he planned to do. But the Fraser memoirs, significantly, provide a broad confirmation of this account. They say: 'Fraser also came away from the meetings with the strong impression that Kerr believed his own position to be at risk. We now know that Kerr believed if Whitlam suspected he was to be sacked, he would try to get Kerr sacked first. Fraser divined this at the time and realised that it would mean Kerr would not give Whitlam any warning.'[31]

On reflection, Fraser later said of the prospect of Kerr's action: 'I was convinced that he should and I believed he would. I also believed that he would do it at the last possible moment.'[32] Fraser's senior adviser, Kemp, affirmed Kerr's caution yet ultimate willingness to move: 'I had a sense early on that Kerr had flagged that the situation would need to be unconstitutional before he could act.'[33] Ellicott, who knew Kerr better than any other Coalition figure, was sure that provided the opposition held firm, Kerr would intervene. John Howard reported that his close friend Carrick, a senior Coalition figure who also knew Kerr, felt Labor 'had misread Kerr's character' and was confident that Kerr would do 'the right thing by history'.[34] Budd said: 'I would say that Fraser was reasonably confident of Kerr.'[35]

The Fraser memoirs say: 'Fraser himself was so confident that Kerr would act that he had no fallback, no Plan B. He says today that while he was sure of Kerr, he was not certain that Whitlam would be dismissed. He thought it equally likely that Kerr would give Whitlam an ultimatum and that Whitlam would then agree to call an election.'[36] Frankly, this reeks of post-event rationalisation. Towards the end of the crisis, Fraser and Ellicott were predicting a dismissal, pure and simple.

Would Whitlam have sacked Kerr?

There is unlikely to be a definitive answer to this question. Opinion is divided. Fraser, not surprisingly, said: 'I'm certain. Whitlam's whole demeanour indicated that Kerr had to do what he wanted.' Menadue said: 'Yes, I have no doubt whatsoever . . . Mr Whitlam would have taken his head off quickly if he could.' Ellicott said: 'I always thought that his bark was worse than his bite. You see, when Kerr gave him the letter there was a strange reaction. It wasn't this "smash the Senate" man at all. He walked away . . . I believe, perhaps contrary to what Kerr believed, that Whitlam would have acted more responsibly than Kerr feared.' Prominent Labor minister John Wheeldon said: 'I would have resigned from the cabinet if Whitlam had moved against Kerr.' Indeed, he predicted an internal revolt. Jim McClelland said Whitlam sacking Kerr was not 'in his nature' as a 'great constitutionalist'. Whitlam's private secretary Mant said, 'I don't really believe he would have done this.' His speechwriter Freudenberg said, in this situation, 'Whitlam would have asked for more time. I don't think his response would have been related to Kerr.'[37] In a separate interview, Freudenberg said: 'We never canvassed recall because we never calculated that Kerr would act deceitfully.'[38]

Drawing upon his experience as politician and governor-general, Bill Hayden had no doubt of the consequences had Whitlam been so rash: 'If Whitlam had sought to dismiss Kerr I am certain the Palace would have taken a deliberately careful and long look at the proposal by which time the crisis would have been well and truly sorted out within Australia.' Hayden branded any such notion as 'political lunacy' that would have created a 'whirlwind of resentment in the electorate'.[39]

As the years advanced, Whitlam accorded more weight to the arguments against sacking Kerr. At the twentieth anniversary he said: 'I don't think it would have suited me to look as if I was sacking the Governor-General.'[40] Yet the letter to Wilson, closer to the heat of the crisis, sits on the table: its implication is that he would have moved against Kerr. Whitlam's rage, if he had discovered Kerr's plans, would have been immense. Perhaps his passion would have driven him to sack Kerr but his head would have dictated a wiser course.

What would the Palace have done?

Sir William Heseltine said: 'None of us felt the Queen would have been bound to act on a telephone call without substantial support in terms of a signed written submission from the Prime Minister.'[41] Charteris said: 'I am sure that written notification would have been required.'[42] The issue was much debated at the Palace after the dismissal. Heseltine said: 'After the event, we had quite a lot of discussion about this issue and various possible scenarios were canvassed. This included recall, but we concluded that some sort of written document would be needed.'[43]

Charteris raised the issue with Hasluck during their discussion at the Palace in August 1977. He asked Hasluck directly: if you were in my position and Whitlam had rung you wanting Kerr dismissed, what would you have done? Hasluck's answer was predictable: he would have said, in 'fairness to the Queen' and to Whitlam, a submission in writing would be needed. But Hasluck told Charteris he believed Whitlam would have 'enough intelligence' to persist only 'if there were good and defensible reasons for it'. He remarked on the bizarre nature of Australia's system – a governor-general could sack a prime minister without further consideration but a prime minister had no power to sack a governor-general without resort to the Queen.[44]

In short, the reserve powers of the Crown left the prime minister exposed.

Nobody disputes that the Queen had to act on Whitlam's advice. The Palace could have demanded proper process but the Queen would have removed the governor-general. This raises another question. Who would Whitlam have appointed to replace Kerr?

In the end, these questions are hypothetical.

What matters is Kerr's conviction that he was under threat. The governor-general believed the threat was real, that it was ever present and that Whitlam would not hesitate to remove him. And Kerr signalled this to Fraser. From an early stage of the crisis, Fraser knew that Kerr's trust in Whitlam was shot. Fraser's job was to push Kerr into acting on this logic.

Whitlam's Blunders

Gough Whitlam had two fixations during the 1975 crisis – that management of John Kerr was his exclusive domain and that the governor-general had no option but to act on the prime minister's advice. They saw him overrule advisers, shut his mind to alternative options, lose his judgement and engage in a brand of kamikaze politics that virtually invited dismissal.

In a twenty-eight-page memorandum dated 11 December 1975, written soon after the dismissal, the secretary of the Prime Minister's Department, John Menadue, assessed what had gone wrong. He wrote: 'Mr Whitlam was insistent on all occasions that he was the adviser to the Governor-General on important constitutional and, indeed, other matters.' Yet Whitlam had an exceptionally narrow view of how Kerr should be advised. 'The advice given by Mr Whitlam in all instances was oral and in the expectation that the Opposition would give way,' Menadue said.[1]

In the end the Whitlam government failed to provide direct, formal written advice to the governor-general on how he should act. This omission seems incredible. It was recommended on a number of occasions by the Prime Minister's Department and the Attorney-General's Department. Giving formal advice to the governor-general during the most serious parliamentary and constitutional crisis since federation would seem the supreme act of prime ministerial logic and prudence. Yet it never happened.

The reason is that Whitlam's irrational approach towards Kerr resulted in a failure of process and policy from the prime minister. His attitude towards Kerr was patronising, contemptuous and guaranteed to provoke hostility. Whitlam's defective grasp of human nature lay at the heart of the dismissal.

His principal private secretary at the time, John Mant, depicts a bold government but plagued by dysfunction run by a prime minister crippled by personality defects and unable to organise any proper crisis management. 'He was a loner,' Mant said of Whitlam. 'He didn't get on well with people. I mean he seldom engaged. He would give you a speech but he didn't engage.' Asked by Troy Bramston how much Whitlam consulted with ministers and advisers during the crisis, Mant said: 'Not much. But it was symptomatic of the whole problem . . . there was no sense of team because Gough's view was that everyone was largely useless and they were pissants – and he was right.'[2]

Asked how Whitlam saw his relationship with Kerr, Mant said: 'As master and servant. Whitlam was Kerr's intellectual superior. He was somewhat contemptuous of Kerr because of his drinking and his pretensions but didn't see him as a class traitor.' Mant said that whatever regard Whitlam might have had for Kerr was 'disappearing' by the time of the crisis. 'I think that Kerr joined the pissant group – which was a large group – and the assumption was that he would do what Gough told him,' Mant said.

While declining to provide Kerr with considered advice, Whitlam insisted in public that the governor-general had no independent discretion and must follow what the prime minister wanted. This insulted Kerr's pride and intellect. It became, in effect, an exercise in public humiliation. It would have been offensive to most governors-general.

It was Whitlam's job to persuade Kerr to his position but he substituted intimidation for persuasion.

The solicitor-general, Maurice Byers, said: '[Whitlam] failed sufficiently, I think, to realise that, strictly speaking, there was only one important person and that was Kerr. Therefore, Kerr should have been cherished and he wasn't.'[3] At the outset of the crisis on 17 October, interviewed by Richard Carleton on *This Day Tonight*, Whitlam said the governor-general must 'unquestionably' take advice from his prime minister. Asked if there was any tolerance here, he replied: 'None whatever.' He repeatedly affirmed this position. Menadue said of Whitlam's dealings with Kerr: 'I think his attitude was there was nothing to discuss.'[4] He saw the governor-general as a rubber stamp.

It was a hopeless conception that proved fatal.

Whitlam's effort to exercise a supreme control over the situation concealed serious cracks in his government's approach. The performance of his attorney-general, Kep Enderby, was incompetent. The Prime Minister's Department under Menadue and the Attorney-General's Department under the veteran Clarrie Harders were busy producing briefs, tactics and ideas, yet they went nowhere. Harders lamented the 'lack of communications' between Enderby and Byers. He said, however, the deeper communications defect was between Whitlam and Kerr.[5] He branded this a 'real shemozzle'.[6] Mant said: 'I think it was consistent with Gough's character for him not to have had a proper discussion with the governor-general during the crisis.'[7] Mant recalled that, unlike the Liberals, who tried to understand Kerr, Whitlam's lack of any such effort was 'typical' of his approach to people.

The senior advisers were periodically worried but impotent before Whitlam's dogmatism. They sensed Whitlam's treatment of Kerr ran a risk but never grasped the full danger. Harders said: 'I kept saying the Prime Minister should not just tell the Governor-General that he must act in accordance with instructions from the Prime Minister but that the government should, to use my language, look after the

Governor-General.' Nobody performed that role, not Whitlam, not Enderby. Harders believed Lionel Murphy's earlier departure as attorney-general for the High Court had been a great loss. Murphy was a charmer and 'a talker'. Harders said Murphy's personality meant he 'would have kept talking to Kerr' and ensured the governor-general 'would not have been left in isolation'.[8]

'Certainly Whitlam was running the strategy,' Mant said. 'I don't think the private office played any great role in determining how we responded to the crisis.' During the crisis Whitlam operated as the real attorney-general. But there was a dual problem: Whitlam's judgement was flawed and Enderby was an incompetent. The softly spoken but deeply thinking Byers concluded that 'it was catastrophic to have Enderby in the job'.[9] Mant said Enderby was 'totally overwhelmed by it all'. In an unforgiving assessment of his minister, Harders said: 'I believe that the Prime Minister had been badly served by his then Attorney-General.'[10]

Anne Kerr affirmed the ineptitude in Whitlam's management of Kerr. She said: 'Gough Whitlam almost never came out to Yarralumla just to have lunch with John or to have a chat . . . Whitlam completely misjudged John. He wanted to work with people, not against them. Whitlam misinterpreted this as acquiescence.'[11]

Referring to Whitlam's view of himself as the only adviser, Menadue said: 'He kept emphasising that to Messrs Byers and Harders and myself. Mr Harders was so sensitive on the question that even when he went to see the governor-general socially he was most anxious for me to inform Mr Whitlam that he should not believe that this was in any way to give an opinion.' During the crisis Menadue avoided contact with the governor-general 'to avoid misunderstanding between the department and Mr Whitlam'.[12]

The entire government accepted that Whitlam was managing the governor-general. Michael Sexton, Enderby's adviser, explained the resulting trap: it was assumed 'that the prime minister was aware of what the governor-general was thinking and that he wasn't alarmed and, therefore, I don't think anybody else was alarmed'.[13] This was a dysfunctional government facing a constitutional crisis with Whitlam assuming exclusive dealings with the governor-general and contemptuous of virtually anybody but Jim McClelland offering him any advice on how to proceed.

Under Menadue and Harders, the departments, from the outset, were focused on two techniques: formal letters from Whitlam to Kerr and an innovation in the appropriation bills that would have kept them in control of the House of Representatives, a decisive event.

The departments were prophetic in raising the idea, as Menadue said, of inserting 'clauses in the Appropriation Bills, insisting the Bills be returned from the Senate to the House before they were presented to the Governor-General for Assent'.[14] It would have been unusual but legal. Menadue raised this option in a two-page note to Whitlam dated 2 October. By requiring the bills to be endorsed another time by the House after Senate passage, the effect, as Harders said, 'is that Mr Fraser would not have been able to guarantee to the Governor-General that he could provide Supply'.[15] This is the pivotal point.

It would have made impossible the commissioning of Fraser under the conditions required by Kerr. Labor would have retained control of the appropriation bills. The idea, debated before the crisis, was never adopted. Menadue said later: 'As it turned out, this was the greatest mistake the government made.'[16]

It would have been a contentious step. Opinion within the government was divided. At this point, Labor's hope was still that the opposition would not block supply. One concern was that insertion of such a clause would have been highly provocative. Menadue said: 'The view was expressed by some members of the government and particularly the senators [Jim McClelland and John Wheeldon] that this might only provoke the Opposition into refusing Supply.' Harders suggested the same: the fear was that by inserting the provision, some of the wavering Coalition senators who had doubts about blocking supply 'would have stiffened in their resolve'. He said, however, he 'never did ascertain' why this idea recommended by the two departments was not taken up.[17] 'We were so naive,' Menadue said.[18]

In the end, Kerr's dismissal of Whitlam depended upon control of the supply bills.

The bizarre feature, however, is the lack of any evidence that Whitlam was interested. Whitlam's focus was the authority of the House of Representatives, not the governor-general or the Senate.

In his reappraisal of the crisis, Menadue offers another perspective: if it was apparent that a dismissed Labor government could deny supply to Fraser because of its ongoing House of Representatives majority then 'it is most unlikely, in my opinion, that the Governor-General and Mr Fraser would have contemplated the action that was finally taken'.[19] This seems to be an arguable proposition.

The departments were alert to the expectation that the prime minister would provide formal written advice to the governor-general on the crisis.

For example, Menadue had proposed that Whitlam write formally to the governor-general even before supply was blocked. Menadue and Harders had their departments work on a letter for Kerr and a numbers of drafts were done. It was not formal advice. The aim was to shape the atmospherics. Menadue called it 'tactical'. He said the purpose was 'emphasising the Prime Minister's role as the principal advisor to the Governor-General'.

The files bulge with draft letters. One of the main drafts was sent to Whitlam on 7 October. Written in strong terms, the letter for Kerr warned that it would be 'unprecedented' for the Senate to reject the budget. While such a power existed it 'has never been exercised'. The draft said: 'I do not exaggerate when I say that what is at stake is the future, not only of stable government, but of democratic government, in Australia.' Another draft warned the opposition's threatened action 'could result in an unprecedented constitutional crisis'. This draft warned that if the Senate breached the convention and refused supply it 'would set a precedent for continued disruption in the future and which in its immediate effects would cause administrative chaos'. Most drafts finished by saying that Whitlam wanted Kerr's agreement to say he had raised this serious issue with the governor-general.[20]

No such letter was sent. In the period before supply was blocked this may have been wise. The critical insight, however, is that Whitlam didn't want to write to Kerr at any time, before or during the crisis. He felt it was unnecessary. He said repeatedly in private that 'Kerr would do the right thing'.[21] The prime minister was loath to take any action that conceded it was necessary for him to persuade Kerr. In its essence, this was irrational.

Because constitutional practice was for the governor-general to act on the advice of the prime minister, Whitlam had an obvious advantage over Fraser, who was opposition leader, an office with no claim on the governor-general's actions. Yet Whitlam failed to capitalise on this advantage. What should he have done?

Whitlam should have visited Kerr after the Senate's initial vote to force an election. That would have been on 16 or 17 October. He should have given Kerr formal written advice at the outset explaining his government's support for the doctrine of responsible government as embodied in the Constitution and explaining that he had no obligation, legal or financial, to buckle before Fraser at that point and recommend an election. He should have offered to make the solicitor-general available to Kerr for direct consultations. This was necessary given Whitlam's belief that Kerr must not consult the chief justice. Far better that he talk to Byers than Barwick.

Beyond this, Whitlam should have engaged Kerr as a personality. He should have spent time with Kerr, being encouraging and supportive, without jokes, put-downs or patronising asides. Kerr was a social being, he loved conversation, and Whitlam, since his survival was the issue, should have been prepared to make concessions on this front.

Yet Whitlam did none of this. He honoured neither the governor-general nor his own self-interest. Byers said: 'I think it was unwise not to give John Kerr the chance to talk to people such as myself if he had wanted. Gough was definitely opposed to that.'[22]

The singular irony is that the opposition, in the form of Bob Ellicott QC, a prominent figure from the Sydney Bar, did provide Kerr with written and public advice. The Ellicott opinion, as it became known, was a decisive yet misinterpreted event in the crisis. Coming early in the showdown on 16 October, it argued that Kerr should dismiss Whitlam.

Ellicott was the most sophisticated lawyer on the Coalition side and a former solicitor-general. He was a friend of Kerr's, a relative of Barwick's, with a bland face disguising a cool yet ruthless mind. His opinion was similar to that provided by Barwick twenty-four days later. The Labor Party and most media saw the Ellicott opinion as virtually irrelevant. They could not have been more wrong.

At the Tun Razak dinner on 16 October, Fraser told Kerr he wanted the governor-general to read the opinion released that day. Kerr asked his secretary, David Smith, to talk to Fraser about getting a copy. The upshot is that Ellicott left a copy for Smith at the Commonwealth Club.[23] Ellicott had wanted to speak directly to Kerr but the governor-general thought this would be unwise.

'I decided not to do this and told Mr Smith to say that I had read the document but that, in the circumstances, thought I should not talk to him about it,' Kerr wrote in a 21 October note. In a later note, Kerr surmised that Ellicott only wanted 'to indicate that the statement was not meant to put pressure on me'.[24]

But in a conversation with Troy Bramston in 2014, Ellicott said his memo had one purpose: to persuade Kerr to dismiss Whitlam. Ellicott, like Kerr, regarded himself as an expert on the reserve powers. Ellicott recalled: 'Fraser said to me that Kerr would like to see the legal opinion. And I said: "Yes." I couldn't see why the Governor-General couldn't have it. Everybody else had it. Let's be frank. When I put it out, I put it out there for the Governor-General to read. We wanted it to influence his thinking. We were politicians. The person who's going to make a decision was the Governor-General.'[25]

Ellicott's opinion put dismissal of Whitlam at the heart of the crisis. This was its significance, yet Whitlam and Labor never grasped the point. Ellicott argued that Whitlam's treatment of the governor-general as a 'mere automaton with no public will of his own' was wrong. He said Kerr had the power to dismiss his ministers and appoint new ministers. He argued Kerr needed to know 'immediately' from Whitlam how the prime minister would solve the deadlock and, if Whitlam refused to call a general election, then he should dismiss Whitlam and commission a new government. For Ellicott, it was time to exercise the reserve powers.

Kerr disagreed with Ellicott's view on immediate action. He did not agree that he should ask Whitlam for advice on a solution. Nor did he agree with the view that if the advice was not adequate, he should dismiss Whitlam. Kerr wrote: 'If Ellicott were hoping that his document would influence me to act immediately or very soon after supply was blocked, it in fact had the opposite effect. I strongly felt that time should be allowed to pass and action, if needed at all, should await the last possible moment. Ellicott took the opposite view.'[26]

But on the core point, the dismissal power, Kerr agreed with Ellicott: that he had the power and obligation to dismiss Whitlam if the crisis was not resolved.

The Ellicott opinion revealed Fraser's real strategy. Because Whitlam was defying the Senate, Fraser's strategy depended ultimately on Kerr being prepared to dismiss the prime minister. Ellicott had written Fraser's script. Ellicott, unlike Whitlam, did not see Kerr as a weak man. Early in the crisis, Ellicott and McClelland had an exchange at breakfast. 'You won't get away with this, Bob,' McClelland said. His recollection is that Ellicott shot back: 'Oh, yes we will. In the end this will all depend on Old Silver and he'll do the right thing.'[27]

At that time, neither the government nor most of the media grasped that the issue was dismissal. Byers said: 'The advice I gave from the start was that the Senate was refusing to exercise its law-making powers with the intention of procuring a dismissal . . .

It seemed to me to be obvious.' Asked how Whitlam and his office saw the issue, Byers said: 'I don't think this point was as clear in Whitlam's mind as it was in my mind . . . What I told them was that the actor could be and only could be the governor-general.' The material Byers sent to Whitlam's office rebutted Ellicott's opinion about dismissal. He argued the Crown should not interfere in a contest between the houses of parliament because it 'would be brought down to the same level as a contestant'.[28]

The prime minister's office discounted this, seeing it as mere intellectual rivalry between Byers and Ellicott. Whitlam, his office and the public service missed the central question of the 1975 crisis. This contest, in intellectual terms, was akin to two football teams playing on different fields. Whitlam believed the issue was the right of a prime minister to govern with the confidence of the House of Representatives, but Fraser believed it was about the right of a governor-general to dismiss a prime minister who could not obtain supply.

After the event the man who wrote Whitlam's speeches, Graham Freudenberg, saw the magnitude of the blunder with piercing clarity. He lamented the 'invincible blindness' that caused them to discard the Byers drafts that rebutted the Fraser/Ellicott view of the governor-general's powers and obligations.[29]

Interviewed by Troy Bramston, Freudenberg said: 'In retrospect, my great regret is that we focused on the principle of the House of Representatives having confidence in the government. We never saw an independent role for the governor-general in the crisis. That was our downfall.'[30]

Because they never saw it, they never argued against it. The idea seemed too fantastic. But Kerr's mind rarely left the dismissal option. Sexton said: 'I don't think that anyone on the government's side really had dismissal in their mind.' Asked about the Ellicott opinion, Sexton said: 'I think people thought that it was fanciful.'[31]

On 21 October, during a phone discussion, Kerr requested from Whitlam an opinion on the Ellicott thesis from the law officers, the attorney-general and solicitor-general. To this point Whitlam had given no advice to Kerr – now the governor-general was asking for advice. After the phone call, Whitlam asked Enderby to prepare an opinion.

Kerr said Whitlam's position during the crisis was that 'I had no right . . . to ask the law officers direct for their advice . . . he claimed it was a matter for his discretion.'[32]

In a note written on 21 October, Kerr said: '[Whitlam] said again that he was not anxious to do anything which conceded that I was entitled to have outside advice and, for example, to go to the Chief Justice. He also said that his view was that I could not ask directly for the Solicitor-General's advice. I could get that advice only through him.' Yet Kerr's scepticism of Whitlam is palpable in this written record. He said: 'The possibilities are: 1. I shall get what I asked for; 2. I shall get nothing from the Law Officers; 3. I shall get an opinion saying: Ellicott is wrong and I have no Reserve Powers at all – no discretion. In truth I do not really mind which of these three possible results flow. I have asked for the help of the Law Officers and that in itself is enough for the moment.'[33]

It is a revealing document. Kerr had no expectations about what would happen. Yet this was the governor-general seeking advice on the critical issue of the crisis. Kerr's scepticism of the law officers was apparent. He wanted to know if they would say 'there was nothing left of any substance of the reserve powers of the Crown'.[34] Such a view would have been contrary to Kerr's thinking. On the other hand, if the law officers found in favour of the reserve powers, that would strengthen Kerr's hand. He was testing them.

Whitlam and Enderby failed to grasp the importance of Kerr's request: he wanted advice on the dismissal power. A competent government would have delivered such advice promptly, clearly, persuasively. How could such a request be mismanaged? How could its significance be missed? How could the governor-general be treated with disdain?

Yet it was allowed to drift. Harders said: 'The Government was not sufficiently alert to the risk it was running through not watching very carefully the submission of the law officers' opinion.'[35]

According to Harders, Byers promptly sent his opinion to Enderby's office where it 'lay for some days'. The attorney-general and his advisers had wanted 'to see it strengthened'. There is no evidence Whitlam saw it as a priority. Sexton said Enderby felt the opinion 'conceded too much'. Menadue said Kerr's request for advice was 'badly handled' and there was too much delay from the attorney-general and solicitor-general.[36] The ineptitude is hard to grasp.

On 28 October, Kerr saw Harders at a reception for a public-service board course and asked when the advice would be ready. By 3 November, Harders had become agitated. The deadlock had lasted nearly three weeks. The government had provided no advice to Kerr despite his request thirteen days earlier.

Harders now prepared a five-page note marked 'secret'. It was infused with urgency. Devoid of usual bureaucratic language, the first sentence said: 'The Prime Minister should tender advice formally to the Governor-General now.' Harders said in this situation 'it could fairly be anticipated that the Governor-General would accept the advice and act on it'.[37] This was a remarkable assessment given coming events. On display was the optimism of the conventional wisdom with which senior public servants saw the crisis – they could not imagine the governor-general not acting on advice from the prime minister.

Even more revealing was Harders' statement: 'Whatever the position may be regarding the existence of reserve powers in the Governor-General, the stage has not been reached when any such powers could properly be invoked by the Governor-General.' This was correct at the time but only for a short time. The dismissal was just eight days away. Harders was a worried man but the public service was clueless about Kerr's thinking and outlook.

Harders, however, did appreciate the value of giving Kerr formal advice. He wrote that one of the elements of that advice should be 'that there should be no dissolution of the House of Representatives'. Harders also recommended that the law officers' opinion on the Ellicott thesis should accompany Whitlam's formal advice. Despite Harders' alarm, there was no immediate action.

Three days later, on 6 November, Enderby saw Kerr at Government House. The final stage in the 'advice' fiasco was at hand. By this stage the governor-general had almost reached his dismissal decision.

In an extraordinary performance, Enderby handed Kerr two documents. The first was an unsigned legal opinion from the law officers on the alternative financial arrangements devised by the government. According to Kerr, as Enderby handed over the document he wrote 'draft' at the top with his own pen. The second document was a twenty-eight-page opinion dealing with the reserve powers in reply to Ellicott. It had Byers' signature but not Enderby's as attorney-general.[38]

Enderby told Kerr he was providing the document as 'background'. It was not the final document. He said it contained Byers' views but would be subject to final discussions between Byers and him. 'It shows the line of advice which the Prime Minister will be giving you,' he told Kerr. Enderby then struck out Byers' signature on the document and added the word 'draft' to the heading. He told Kerr there were sections of the documents with which he disagreed. 'I treated the document as an indication of the probable views of Mr Byers,' Kerr said in his memoirs.[39]

Enderby said: 'Kerr asked me whether I had an opinion on the matter and I said to him, "I am a Whig. I believe in the Whig view of history on these matters" which obviously meant I didn't believe in the reserve powers. Kerr said nothing.'[40] That is hardly a surprise. His feelings must have ranged from distaste to contempt.

It was now sixteen days since Kerr had asked Whitlam for an opinion from the law officers on the dismissal powers. The situation on 6 November had changed significantly from the situation on 21 October. Kerr was now given a document written for both law officers to sign. But Enderby had not signed it, had deleted Byers' signature,

called it a draft, made clear he disagreed with sections and foreshadowed formal advice later. That advice had not been delivered five days
later when the dismissal occurred. There was no basis for the governor-
general to treat this as a final opinion from the law officers and he did
not make this assumption. Sexton said that when Enderby returned
from Government House 'he didn't seem concerned'.[41]

Harders later admitted the process had taken 'too long' and the
way the document was given to Kerr was 'seriously open to criticism'.[42] He was too generous. Byers was angry with Enderby for
crossing out his signature. He later called the attorney-general a 'silly
fellow'. Byers subsequently told Kerr the document did represent his
views. Enderby said: 'I left [Government House] never thinking for
one moment that he might sack us.'[43] The question left hanging is
why Enderby didn't finalise the advice and provide it promptly to Kerr
in the next day or two.

The attorney-general never understood the nature of the crisis. He
deferred to Whitlam and accepted Whitlam's judgement.

The Byers opinion addressed the dismissal issue. He said the
Senate power over supply had never before been exercised, a fact suggesting the convention claimed by Whitlam against its use did exist.
Byers said, given Whitlam's refusal to bend, the issue was a forced dissolution by the governor-general. Yet the rarity of forced dissolutions
'cast the gravest doubt upon the present existence of that prerogative'.
Byers said it was incorrect to resort to the dismissal power when supply was blocked. This was a conflict between the two houses, and the
Constitution in section fifty-seven provided a specific resolution for
such a deadlock. Attacking Ellicott's opinion, Byers said it was untenable to believe that, in this situation, there should be resort instead
'to a reserve power of uncertain existence and unknowable constituents' and, to the extent Ellicott believed this, he is 'clearly wrong'.
Finally, Byers said Ellicott's view that the Senate could defer supply
and force the governor-general's hand implied a process that 'may be
indefinitely repeated and may involve deleterious consequences'. The

legal powers had to be seen in the light of 'constitutional practice' and it was wrong to disregard such established practice that had governed the use of the powers.

There is no evidence the Byers opinion, delivered when it was and the way it was, had any impact on Kerr. Indeed, it represented a view Kerr had rejected in coming to his decision for dismissal.

The conclusion is inescapable. Whitlam abandoned his chief advantage in the crisis as prime minister able to advise the governor-general. It was a dual failing, personal and constitutional. He never treated Kerr as a colleague who would appreciate a prime minister in whom he could trust and confide. Whitlam saw any effort at persuasion of Kerr as a sign of weakness because he would never consider that Kerr had any discretion. It was a catch-22 that destroyed his government.

The refusal to provide formal, written advice – which would have necessitated a response from Kerr and hence a dialogue – was a function of Whitlam's blind dogmatism and belief that because Kerr was weak intimidation would suffice. It is false to assume such advice would have saved Whitlam, but it would have changed the atmospherics, perhaps significantly. The flawed 'advice' saga testifies to Whitlam's irrational approach to Kerr. By shunning engagement and persuasion, Whitlam failed to respect Kerr as a man and treated him with contempt as a governor-general.

Anthony Mason
and the Arch of Opinion

In his memoirs, Sir John Kerr made an intriguing and puzzling state-ment that there was another person apart from Sir Garfield Barwick who helped fortify his decision to dismiss the Whitlam government on Remembrance Day 1975:

> My solitude was tempered by conversation with one person only
> other than the Chief Justice. The conversation did not include
> advice as to what I should do but sustained me in my own
> thinking as to the imperatives within which I had to act, and in
> my conclusions, already reached, as to what I could and should
> do. The person with whom I spoke was not and has never been
> mentioned in any of the speculations about persons I might have
> consulted. The substance of our conversation is recorded and will
> some day, when for history's sake the archives are opened,
> be revealed.[1]

This person was Sir Anthony Mason. He had been appointed a justice of the High Court in August 1972. He was made chief justice in February 1987 and served until April 1995 when he retired. Mason spent twenty-three years on the court and is one of Australia's most eminent jurists. His period as chief justice is recognised as one of the most progressive and innovative in the court's history.[2] Kerr had known Mason as a 'close personal friend' over many years.

In the Kerr papers there is a pivotal document, including earlier drafts, titled 'Conversation with Sir Anthony Mason during October–November 1975' and, unless otherwise identified, Kerr's quotes in this chapter come from that document. It was written in 1981, although it includes another note written on 21 October 1975, during the crisis. In one version, Kerr has a revealing descriptor denoting the importance of this document for future historians: 'If this document is found among my archives, it will mean that my final decision is that truth must prevail, and, as he played a most significant part in my thinking at that critical time, and as he will be in the shades of history when this is read, his role should be known.'[3]

Yet a shadow fell across Kerr–Mason relations. It troubled Kerr for many years after the dismissal. He wrote of Mason: 'I feel that although he and I do not differ at all about the facts of what happened between us and are still very good friends, he would be happier for the sake of the Court if history never came to know of his role.' Kerr's implication is that Mason preferred to keep their dialogue unknown to the public and to judicial colleagues. Mason disputes this statement: he said he told Kerr his condition for the release of their discussions and Kerr did not reply.[4]

Having served in the Royal Australian Air Force during World War Two and earned first-class honours in law and arts at the University of Sydney, Mason joined the Sydney Bar in 1951. During this period he often served as junior counsel to Barwick and occasionally to Kerr. 'We frequently visited one another, with our wives, and, of course, knew one another very well professionally,' Kerr said. The bond between Kerr and Mason extended to mutual career support.

When Kerr was offered the post of governor-general, Mason

was one of the key figures whom he consulted on whether or not to accept. Years earlier, Kerr was proud to think he had delivered Mason the office of solicitor-general. That offer, from the attorney-general Billy Snedden, was first made to Kerr, who declined, because his wife was unwilling to move to Canberra. Kerr said: 'The Attorney-General told me he was considering Mason and Ninian Stephen for the job and asked me for my opinion. Both were men of ability. I knew them both but I knew Mason much better than Stephen and told Snedden this, adding that he could not go wrong with Mason. After the offer was made to Mason, he and I had some talks. Mason had really made up his mind to take the position and, as he had no domestic problems on the score of living in Canberra, I supported the tendency of his thinking.'

Mason was appointed solicitor-general in 1964, went to the NSW Court of Appeal in 1969 and was elevated to the High Court three years later, aged forty-seven. When Mason was solicitor-general, Kerr was appointed a federal court judge, sometimes visiting Canberra, 'where my friendship with Mason continued and grew and I frequently visited his home'. At Mason's initiative, Kerr was appointed, along with Mason, to a committee to review Commonwealth administrative law, whose completed work provided the foundation for administrative decision-making. They were joined by Mason's successor as solicitor-general, Bob Ellicott QC, later attorney-general under Fraser. While Mason was a NSW judge, Kerr was appointed NSW chief justice, and Kerr said that 'we were colleagues on that court working closely with one another as judges for a short time'.

In the end, Mason exceeded Kerr as a jurist. The solicitor-general at the time of the 1975 crisis, Sir Maurice Byers, described the Mason court as one of 'the most gifted and courageous' in history. Its judgements included the 'free speech' cases (1992), which found an implied freedom of political communication in the Constitution, and Mabo (1992), which overturned the notion of terra nullius.

Describing their relations in the years preceding the 1975 crisis,

Kerr said: 'Our friendship continued to grow. When he became a member of the High Court and later I became Governor-General, the intimacy of our friendship was maintained and we and our families . . . enjoyed private social life together. I think I can fairly say that we struck sparks off one another in conversation and enjoyed enormously our many talks. Our conversation ranged over the issues of the day in law and in political and constitutional affairs. I came to value his opinions and to appreciate the breadth of his experiences and the maturity of his judgement.'

It was Sir Garfield Barwick who first revealed Mason had a role in the dismissal in an interview with Bruce Donald on the ABC in January 1994.[5] Political commentator Gerard Henderson soon after disclosed that Kerr had told him some years earlier that he had sought Mason's advice prior to the dismissal, and that they had engaged directly.[6]

But neither of these disclosures revealed the extent of Mason's discussions with Kerr during the crisis. The magnitude of Mason's role was revealed in Kerr's papers, deposited in the National Library of Australia, and reported by Jenny Hocking in the second of her two-volume biography of Gough Whitlam in 2012.[7]

In explaining the purpose of his document outlining Mason's role, Kerr wrote: 'In, say, fifty years' time the personalities concerned will have largely disappeared into history and the nature of the friendship between Mason and myself and of his part in my thinking in October–November 1975 will not, without this note, be known to history.'

This is a man determined to have Mason's role made public. It is impossible to miss an element of resentment towards Mason at what Kerr felt was his reluctance to have his role revealed. Kerr wrote of Mason:

> I start by saying simply that I regarded him (I still do) as a liberal-minded and progressive man and lawyer, of judgement and wisdom, as well as of learning and all-round intellectual quality

and believed that no one could better, by conversation, help me
to sort out my own thoughts on the constitutional powers of
the Governor-General in the constitutional crisis of 1975 . . . His
opinions and his role in his talks with me at that time would
certainly be regarded as significant by many who have engaged
in controversy about the events of that time and from my point
of view it is unfortunate that they are unknown . . . It is only
the magnitude of the 1975 crisis itself which makes historically
important what happened between Mason and myself. But it is
truly relevant because my conversation with Mason helped me
to fortify myself for the action I was to take.

These comments reveal so much. Kerr needed help in the crisis. He
felt lonely and confided in his memoir about the burden of 'intense
mental solitude'. He needed a trusted figure as sounding board and
adviser. Kerr could see the controversy to come; it required resilience
and strength and he sought counsel from a trusted friend to help him
translate his words to deeds. From Whitlam, he got nothing but denial
of access to any legal adviser within the government. Mason was Kerr's
key confidant, not Barwick. He was not talking to Barwick. Barwick's
role was to offer formal advice at the end when Kerr had made up his
mind. But the person whose advice he valued most during the crisis was Mason. With Mason, Kerr found a meeting of minds sealed
by friendship and trust. Kerr believed it was important for Mason's
role to become public and for people to know that a prestigious figure
such as Mason had fortified him in the dismissal decision.

Kerr said that at the outset of the supply crisis, he decided to
talk with Mason. He said they 'had a running conversation' from 12
October to 10 November. A vital theme of their talks was the reserve
powers. 'As to the Reserve Powers, as I have said elsewhere, I believed
that the Governor-General could properly seek help where he wished,'
Kerr said. Yet Kerr insisted of these talks: 'I always said first what
I thought.'

Their talk on Sunday, 12 October was described by Kerr as 'long, private and personal'. It preceded the blocking of supply by a few days. Kerr said: 'It had nothing to do with legal problems but only with the possible or probable future course of events and discretionary alternatives open to me. It was a helpful conversation the main purpose of which was to enable me to talk aloud to a friend.' That it involved the 'discretionary' options for Kerr – even before the blocking of supply – reveals Kerr's assumption that he may have become the decisive actor and he may have had to use the reserve powers. That he told Mason 'I had decided to do nothing yet' suggests a governor-general who felt that, at some point, he may have to do something.

Mason, however, offers a different version. He says their first conversation about the potential crisis was much earlier, in August at Yarralumla.

This comes from Mason's account – a nine-page statement with numbered paragraphs written by Mason, dated 23 August 2012 and deposited in the National Library of Australia. It is Mason's written response to Kerr. An almost identical version of Mason's statement was published on 27 August 2012 in the *Sydney Morning Herald* and *The Age*. Unless otherwise identified, Mason's quotes in this chapter come from this document. Mason did not provide his own account until after Kerr's death, and then only when Kerr's documents concerning Mason were revealed.

In response to an interview request for this book, Mason said: 'In declining previous requests for an interview in relation to my participation in the events leading to the dismissal of Mr EG Whitlam by Sir John Kerr, I have taken the view that it was preferable that I should make my own comprehensive statement of my discussions with Sir John Kerr.' Mason added: 'It may be that I shall add to the existing statement. If so, it will not add anything to my conversations with Sir John Kerr, rather it will mention matters not discussed with him and respond to other matters.'[8]

'I was, as Sir John says, a close friend, as was my wife,' Mason writes in his 2012 statement. He explains his dialogue with Kerr in terms of friendship and intellectual partnership. Having noted that he spoke with Kerr about taking the office of governor-general, Mason says, 'and I was willing to talk to him about the issues that were to confront him in October–November 1975 and to give him my views on the exercise of the Governor-General's Reserve Powers to dismiss a Prime Minister'.

This statement from Mason puts the subject of their talks beyond doubt: as a High Court judge, Mason was holding discussions secret from the Australian public with the governor-general about the possible exercise of the reserve powers against the prime minister.

While Mason and Kerr agreed on the essentials of their discussions, there are discrepancies on several points, some minor but others fundamental. It would be a mistake, however, to interpret Mason's statement as downplaying his role. Taking Mason's reply to the authors at face value, he evidently has no intention of explaining himself further to the Australian public. So far, Mason has not been prepared, in the cause of history, to expand upon his role.

Referring to their August meeting, Mason says: '[Kerr] mentioned that an occasion might arise for him to exercise the Reserve Powers, dismiss Mr Whitlam and commission Malcolm Fraser to form a caretaker government for the purpose of securing supply and holding an election.' This is an extraordinary statement from a then serving judicial officer about events of which the public (and Whitlam himself) was otherwise unaware.

The political mood in August was not focused on dismissal. Indeed, Whitlam had not yet made his declaration that he would defy the Senate if supply was blocked. There was virtually no public debate at this time about a possible dismissal. It was not on the radar. Yet this statement suggests Kerr's mind had focused on a dismissal option many weeks before the crisis. That is what makes this statement from Mason so extraordinary.

Mason, moreover, claimed that in this discussion he told Kerr 'that in my view the incumbent prime minister should, as a matter of fairness, first be offered the option of holding a general election to resolve any dispute over supply between the two houses and be informed that if he did not agree to do so his commission would be withdrawn'. Mason said that he pointed out to Kerr the 'advantage' of the incumbent prime minister going to the election rather than facing the poll as a dismissed prime minister. 'Sir John did not question my view then, or at any time in his discussions with me,' Mason wrote.

This statement is damaging to Kerr because it suggests he got sound advice and did not heed it. Mason claimed that from the start he told Kerr that Whitlam must be given the chance of going to the election as prime minister – and that Kerr never challenged this proposition in their talks despite not doing it on 11 November 1975. With Kerr dead, this point cannot be tested. The authors cannot find anywhere in Kerr's papers any reference to Mason taking this position during their talks. This is not to say he did not. That Mason claimed to be arguing this to Kerr in August when there was virtually no discussion anywhere of a dismissal is extraordinary. If this was Mason's consistent proposition – as he claimed – then Kerr would have had a motive not to mention it in his documents.

Mason also provides more details than Kerr of their 12 October discussion. Yet Mason's account of this discussion is inaccurate, because he referred to events that had not yet happened. Mason said that on or before their 12 October discussion, Kerr told him he 'had it in mind' to consult Barwick 'in the event that it became necessary to resolve a crisis over supply'. He intended to do this despite 'concern over possible perceptions' arising from Barwick's past links with the Liberal Party. Mason also referred to the Ellicott opinion, yet this opinion was made public only on 16 October four days later. Mason's timing is confused.

Kerr, in fact, revealed he had further discussions with Mason on both 20 and 21 October, a week into the crisis, and he did so in a long document dated 21 October, which, because of its contemporaneous nature, has credence as an account of events. It is likely that some of their discussions that Mason locates on 12 October actually occurred at these later October talks. Much of their 20–21 October talks focused on the Ellicott opinion. In this note, Kerr branded the opinion as a 'constitutional absurdity' in as much as Ellicott suggested immediate action by Kerr – dismissal. Such speed went against Kerr's nature. Yet while Kerr broke with Ellicott on timing, he asserted in this note his belief in the reserve powers and the possibility of their use.

On 20 October, Kerr said he told Mason he was still following the 'same line' as before and Mason agreed. They discussed the Ellicott opinion and 'Ellicott's motivations in producing it and his relations with Mr Fraser'. Kerr said that overnight – without prior consultation with Mason – he decided to ask Whitlam for an opinion by the law officers on the Ellicott opinion. He told Mason of his decision by phone the next day, 21 October. Mason agreed with this move. Kerr said he told Mason he would organise to have a copy of the Ellicott opinion delivered to his home. Kerr said he asked Mason whether he would be prepared to give a personal opinion on both the Ellicott document and the law officers' opinion when finalised. 'I did this because of his undoubted integrity, ability and impartiality,' Kerr wrote. He said Mason was 'prepared to allow publication if it were ever needed to enable me to defend my own integrity if it came under serious attack'. Again, these are extraordinary claims by Kerr.

It has produced another sharp difference of view. In Mason's account he said he did not receive the Ellicott opinion from Kerr. He also said that 'I did not agree' to provide any such opinion on either the Ellicott document or the law officers' opinion. Mason recalled Kerr telling him about Whitlam's comment at the dinner for the Malaysian prime minister and said that Kerr was 'very much aware' of the possibility that Whitlam might seek to remove him. Mason confirmed there was discussion of Barwick.

It is Kerr's account, however, of their discussion about Barwick on these two days that is riveting. According to Kerr, he and Mason spoke about 'the desirability or otherwise of seeking Barwick's formal advice'. It is obvious that any resort to Barwick was in the context of the reserve powers. Kerr wrote: '[Mason's] assessment was that I should only do so, if I felt otherwise at liberty to take this step, if I had assessed (a) what advice I really needed and (b) what [Barwick] would be likely to advise. Today he said he believed it to be possible that Barwick believed and would advise immediate radical action – dismissal etc. He agreed with me that to get such advice would be disastrous at this stage.' While confirming Kerr's account, Mason claimed he did not use the words 'radical' or 'disastrous'.

This is evidence that Mason was advising Kerr on how to deal with Barwick on the issue of a Whitlam dismissal. And the crisis was not yet a week old. Kerr wrote of his talks with Mason: 'The existence of the Reserve Powers was taken for granted – both of us knew of the relevant constitutional principles.' In his note Kerr highlighted Mason's attitude: 'He saw no difficulty in my consulting Sir Garfield Barwick except considerations of time and tactics.' Mason did not contradict this.

While speaking with Kerr as a trusted friend, his position as a High Court judge could not be ignored. Mason spoke to Kerr on a regular basis, and he was discussing when Kerr should approach Barwick. On tactics, Kerr knew he must not risk going to Barwick too early and being told by the chief justice to act immediately. Kerr said Mason's agreement with him on this tactical point was 'comforting'.

The sequence of events is important. On Sunday, 19 October, Kerr had asked Whitlam if he could consult with Barwick. Whitlam had refused. But Kerr didn't mind. He had, in many ways, a better alternative: he spoke with Mason. And what was their discussion? According to Kerr, it was about how to consult with Barwick.

He understood the prime minister had told him in the firmest terms not to consult Barwick, and Kerr had no time for this instruction. He wrote that Whitlam 'had made it clear to me on several occasions' he was not to consult Barwick. Indeed, when Kerr described the situation two days later, he wrote that Whitlam took a view that 'contrary to [Paul] Hasluck's opinion and despite what Sir Samuel Griffith did early in the century, I was not entitled ever to ask for the advice of the Chief Justice'. It was obvious Kerr would ignore Whitlam's instruction and consult with Barwick whenever he wanted.

The Kerr–Mason dialogue would culminate on 9 November, the day Kerr decided to engage Barwick to give the dismissal legal sanction and began preparing the documents for the dismissal.

An assumption in Kerr's dialogue with Mason was his alienation from the law officers, Kep Enderby and Maurice Byers. He had no personal bond with them. The people to whom Kerr turned in the crisis were his old friends and colleagues from the Sydney Bar, some long gone, others now located in powerful places. This was where he drew, in different measure, emotional, personal and intellectual support. In one of the several drafts he wrote of the 1981 document is a typed passage, later crossed out by pen:

'There is one final point I should like to make. Mason is the keystone in the arch of opinion which was at the time important to me on the Reserve Powers of the Crown. That arch consisted of Evatt, Bailey [a distinguished solicitor-general], Sir Garfield Barwick, Bailey's successor Mason, Mason's successor as Solicitor-General, Ellicott (on all points except timing) and Forsey the great Canadian authority.' Sir Kenneth Bailey was solicitor-general for many years and also head of the Attorney-General's Department. Both Bailey and Evatt were dead by 1975. The inclusion of Senator Eugene Forsey, a scholar of the reserve powers, is because of his intellectual influence on Kerr, not any personal ties before the dismissal. Forsey wrote the epilogue to Kerr's memoirs, *Matters for Judgment*.

Kerr's 'arch of opinion' is an artificial concept and probably had a dual purpose. It refers to individuals and scholars who helped to shape his attitude towards the crisis and, in retrospect, it is a list of the luminaries Kerr invoked to sustain his role before history. The 'arch' is a reminder that Kerr's emotional and intellectual ties lay far beyond the narrow circle of Whitlam and his advisers.

Mason was at its apex and unrivalled. Between 1974 and 1977, according to the vice-regal notices, Mason was often a guest of Kerr's for lunch or dinner at Government House or Admiralty House. He seems to have been with Kerr at critical moments. When Kerr spoke with Mason about accepting the office of governor-general, he confided about the possibility of using the reserve powers, an astonishing thing to say. On 12 November 1975, the day after Kerr terminated the Whitlam government, there was only one visitor to Government House: Anthony Mason. The vice-regal notice, published on 13 November, stated: 'The Governor-General, Sir John Kerr, and Lady Kerr entertained Sir Anthony Mason at dinner at Government House, Canberra last night.'[9] It would have been a fascinating discussion. As far as the authors know, neither Mason, nor Kerr, has referred publicly to this dinner.

In his oral history, Kerr recalled with affection his days at the Sydney Bar: 'We built a common room and a dining room and a big section of the Bar had lunches together every day. It's a very in-bred profession, the Bar, you've got three and a half to four hundred people living and working within a square half mile . . . we live, work, fight, eat, drink together.'[10] This was where he remained anchored.

Kerr's instincts told him, correctly, that the law officers would be sceptical about the reserve powers while his 'arch of opinion' gang would be certain about them. Nothing better illustrates this sentiment than the 21 October note: 'I have no escape from the duty to assert that the Reserve Powers of dismissal and dissolution still exist and can in extreme circumstances be exercised and a joint opinion of the Law Officers to the contrary would certainly not deter me if the moment arrives for action.'

In this sense Mason's role, for Kerr, was to function as an alternative intellectual source to what he suspected was the attitude of the official advisers.

Kerr was deliberative in the two documents he prepared on

Mason's role – in 1975 and in 1981. Yet not everything went to plan. For instance, in 1981 he wrote: 'The present note will go into my archives but will not be opened until after the deaths of Barwick, Mason, Ellicott and myself.' Yet Mason and Ellicott were alive when the material became available from the National Archives.

Kerr wrote this fuller document, he said, in England after a holiday in Australia from November 1980 to March 1981 'during which I saw Mason several times'. He said: 'In the light of the enormous and vicious criticism of myself, I should have dearly liked to have had the public evidence during my lifetime of what Mason had said and done during October–November 1975.'

There is evidence Mason was concerned about what Kerr would publish in his memoirs. On 25 October 1978, Mason, in a handwritten letter to Kerr, says the chief justice had told him the memoirs would be 'a good book'. Mason said: 'I should like to read it before it is published in Australia. Could you send me a copy of it?' It is not known whether Kerr did this. But the explicit nature of the request suggests Mason had his reasons.[11]

At the launch of Whitlam's account of the dismissal, *The Truth of the Matter*, in Sydney in 1979, the dismissed prime minister was still smouldering with contempt for Kerr's secret co-conspirator, a person whose role was alluded to by Kerr in his memoirs but whose identity was then unknown. Whitlam said: 'Who for instance, is "the third man" – Sir John Kerr's other secret adviser? It is just not good enough that his name, his position and the nature of his advice should be preserved in some sort of time capsule, to be opened only when all of us are dead. By all the constitutional rules, I was certainly entitled to know then, as prime minister, who was advising Sir John Kerr, but all of us are surely entitled to know now.'[12]

And now we do.

Yet Whitlam had trouble coming to grips with Mason's role. He remained unblemished in Whitlam's eyes.[13] 'I have had some interest in constitutional and administrative matters for sixty years,' Whitlam said in July 1993. 'For the first time in my lifetime the High Court has in Sir Anthony Mason a Chief Justice who is adequate in both national and international terms.'[14]

Graham Freudenberg, Whitlam's speechwriter and confidant, said in an interview for this book: 'I don't think Gough did change his view of Mason. I don't think he really took onboard the full extent and significance of Mason's involvement. I think he was always in denial about that. He was content to downplay Mason's involvement. He preferred to stick to his high opinion of Mason. And in that sense, it was the last of the many denials we had. It was this denial of reality that dogged us throughout the whole crisis.'[15] Current NSW solicitor-general Michael Sexton, an adviser to Enderby in the 1975 crisis, said of Mason: 'Although a judge of the High Court, he advised Kerr constantly in the weeks prior to 11 November and even drafted a letter on 9 November, which Kerr ultimately did not use, terminating Whitlam's commission . . . This was a clear abuse of Mason's position on the High Court and constituted a complete confusion about judicial functions and responsibility.'[16] Sexton commented further in an interview for this book on Mason's discussions with Kerr: 'I think it is one of the most surprising exercises in modern Australian history, really. But it's interesting that it's been completely ignored in the legal profession.'[17]

On 24 March 1991, Kerr died at age seventy-six. His memorial service was held on 6 April at St James Anglican Church in Sydney. The principal eulogist was Mason.[18] More than eight hundred mourners filled the pews for the high Church of England service in Sydney's legal precinct, including Malcolm Fraser, Doug Anthony, Bill Hayden and Bob Hawke. Whitlam did not attend. But he obtained a copy of the order of service. On a single page torn from a lined notepad and attached to the service booklet, Whitlam wrote: 'Note page 8 re Sir Anthony Mason address.'[19]

After the singing of a Welsh hymn, Mason addressed the congregation. He called Kerr a man of 'exceptional talents' but did concede a flaw – at times he 'seemed pre-occupied with the need for self-justification'. Mason has avoided such a flaw. There was no mention of Mason's own role in the events of 1975. 'A history of his Governor-Generalship must necessarily focus upon his decision in November 1975 to dismiss the Prime Minister and the events which led to the making of that decision,' Mason said. 'John Kerr profoundly and sincerely believed that the action he took was in conformity with his constitutional duty. He believed also that the correctness of his action would be vindicated by the judgement of history.'[20]

There are many unanswered questions for Mason. How accurate is his account? Did he keep notes of these conversations, at the time and later, as did Kerr? Why did he conduct this dialogue? Why did he refrain from telling the Australian public for so long and not share his own account earlier? Did he keep a copy of his draft letter of dismissal he says he provided to Kerr?

There are precedents for judges advising vice-regal figures. But, as far as the authors can establish, there is no precedent for a High Court judge, who was not chief justice, extensively advising a governor-general without the knowledge of the chief justice, on the possible use of the reserve powers to dismiss the prime minister. Despite referring to the dismissal in subsequent decades in his writings and speeches, Mason never disclosed his own role until his 2012 statement.

There is no question Mason has sought to keep his role a secret from public view. He could have disclosed it, certainly after his retirement from the High Court. It was only the availability of Kerr's documents from the National Archives that prompted Mason's August 2012 statement, the only detailed statement he has made. It came long after Kerr's death, thereby denying Kerr, his friend, the chance to answer the contradictions that Mason identified.

If it was not for Kerr's documentary time bomb Mason's role might never have been fully revealed. Kerr was not to be denied: he unmasked the full extent of the Kerr–Mason dialogue from the grave.

PART FOUR

The Resolution

Kerr's Decision

Sir John Kerr's decision to dismiss the Whitlam government was the consequence of two events – Fraser's month-long command of his own forces in blocking the budget and his superior reading of the governor-general's mind and character. Fraser's tactical management of Kerr was perfect, a blend of public persuasion and private threat. In retrospect, Whitlam seems clueless. He shunned any compromise, failed to devise an effective strategy and was blind to his alienation of Kerr.

A savvy prime minister with a modicum of human understanding would have heard the alarm bells long before lunchtime on 11 November. But Whitlam heard and saw nothing, earning a zero for emotional and political intelligence. He was victim of his own propaganda. By insisting that Kerr had no discretion, Whitlam was unable to think rationally about what a governor-general willing to exercise his discretion might actually do.

The key to the 11 November climax is that both Fraser and Whitlam were convinced they would prevail. The longer the crisis extended, the greater the stakes for both men – the more they had to lose but the more they had to gain. The usual story in a great political contest is that one leader gains the ascendancy and this reality imposes itself as events are played out. But the 1975 crisis negated such orthodoxies. 'The two leaders were stubborn and proud men,' Kerr wrote five days after the dismissal. He believed they were 'on a collision course which, if maintained, could cause enormous chaos and even political disorder'. He lamented that 'when one is dealing with intransigent men it is almost impossible to get alternatives considered'.[1]

Fraser won because his grasp of the power realities in the 1975 crisis was superior to that of Whitlam. In the end, Kerr acted upon Fraser's view of those realities and repudiated Whitlam's view of them. The pivotal point was obvious: Fraser said that if Whitlam could not obtain supply he must advise an election or resign, while Whitlam said he could remain in office while he had the confidence of the House of Representatives even if supply had run out. As a constitutional and political fact, Fraser's view was correct and Whitlam's view was wrong. And Kerr acted on this basis.

On 20 October, Kerr wrote to the Palace: 'I said to the Prime Minister today – "You say you intend to break the power of the Senate to force the Lower House to the people. Ultimately you can do that only by getting a constitutional amendment or by breaking Mr Fraser." He said, "I cannot get a constitutional amendment but I can and will break Mr Fraser, if my party stands behind me and it will." I replied "What about his?" He said, "It will break."'[2]

This is as good a summary of the elemental nature of the crisis as we are likely to get. As Paul Keating told the authors: 'This gets back to a classic judgement about power: who has it, who uses it and how it is used.'[3]

Whitlam misread Kerr. But his greater blunder was to misread the basic power equation. Whitlam failed to realise he had only a finite time to break Fraser before supply was exhausted. Once this time had expired then Whitlam, his strategy having failed, would need another strategy. Labor was optimistic for most of the crisis period from 16

October to lunchtime on 11 November. This is because the polls were running Labor's way and it assumed, sooner or later, that Fraser would crack. Fraser's political achievement was immense: as leader, he held his side together for nearly a month.

The extent of Fraser's problem was best illustrated by *The Age–Herald* poll, published on 30 October, showing that 70 per cent of people in capital cities wanted the budget passed and only 25 per cent said it should be blocked. More people blamed the opposition for the crisis than the government. While 44 per cent said Labor should call a general election, 55 per cent said it should be allowed to govern. Such polls created a false sense of confidence, sometimes euphoria, in Labor ranks. They fed Whitlam's conviction that the opposition would collapse. Because the blocking of the budget was deeply unpopular, Fraser faced a difficult management challenge to calm his own troops.

Tony Eggleton, who was the Liberal Party federal director and served as secretary to the shadow cabinet during the crisis, said of internal sentiment: 'The concern and worries about [blocking supply] were still very, very raw, right up until 11 November.'[4]

There was concern in the Liberal Party organisation in a number of states. Eggleton said the branches were more worried than the parliamentary party and shadow cabinet members were 'really quite concerned about the feedback they were getting from their electorates'. In fact, there were two concerns – that blocking supply was unpopular and that it was morally wrong. From the first weekend after the decision, Liberals returning to their electorates were worried by party and public opposition.

Given this problem, Fraser consulted widely and frequently with the shadow cabinet to keep the parliamentary party united. This is exemplified by Eggleton's briefing notes spelling out options for the shadow cabinet meetings of 19 and 21 October. The meeting of Sunday, 19 October in Melbourne widely canvassed the situation and Fraser began with a list of options:

One: we can sit tight. Two: we actually reject bills in the Senate, thus fulfilling Whitlam's condition for an election of some kind. Three: we withdraw as gracefully as possible. Four: we give him supply until February – invite the government to accumulate as many bills as it likes for a double dissolution on the basis that there will be a double dissolution in February. We could say we'd guarantee that if we failed to get a majority in the Reps, we would pass all the double dissolution bills even if we had a Senate majority. Five: agree to a full half-Senate, if that is what Whitlam asks for. Six: I publicly seek an audience with the Governor-General – to explain our actions and seek advice. Seven: I see the Governor-General privately.[5]

Eggleton's record says the shadow cabinet was 'united and determined' to stay on course. But there was 'some disquiet at the doubts and uncertainties' at the grassroots of the parties. Tactics were agreed in relation to media and the party base. But Eggleton's record of the 21 October shadow cabinet meeting shows a more aggressive outlook with 'complete solidarity' backed by the view that 'far from weakening in their resolve, they were twice as firm as they were when they made their original decision last week'.[6]

Eggleton said of Fraser: 'Once he had made up his mind about something he was hard to move.'[7] Fraser's judgement was that bad polls over supply were unavoidable, but once the crisis was resolved and an election called, the opposition's polling dominance would return. This is exactly what happened. Labor's pollster, Rod Cameron from ANOP, told Labor's national secretary David Combe that the government must not confuse public support on the supply issue with its standing in an election. They were separate: Labor would still lose an election.[8]

Labor's tactic was to highlight the public grief that would arise from the Senate's action. From the start Treasurer Bill Hayden hammered home the consequences: 'The economy of this country, if the present course of action which the Opposition has set in train is pursued, will get out of hand, there will be a major economic collapse, a substantial number of enterprises in the corporate sector will fail, there will be an upsurge in unemployment and generally there will be the worst deepening of the recession that we have seen at any time since the great Depression of the 1930s . . . Aged persons hostels, aged and disabled persons homes, organisations for assistance to the handicapped . . . will not obtain the money necessary to pay the people who provide the services . . . Hospital services will grind down . . . Education in the states will be short of some $360 million at least . . . People throughout the country will find that they will not be able to obtain their Medibank medical benefits.'[9]

The question of 'who's to blame' was pivotal. Convinced he was prevailing, Whitlam's mood became more dogmatic. On 21 October, during the second great parliamentary debate over supply, Whitlam said Fraser's action, if successful, would divide the nation 'and leave a legacy of bitterness unequalled since 1916', a reference to the conscription plebiscite. Hardening his position, Whitlam ruled out not just any House of Representatives election as sought by Fraser but any half-senate election 'until this constitutional issue is settled'. Whitlam felt he was turning the screws on Fraser, denying Fraser anything but ignominious retreat.

Standing to his full height on the floor of parliament, with the pent-up passion of the Labor benches behind him, Whitlam, in words drafted by Graham Freudenberg, now elevated the historical dimensions of the contest: 'The message from the Senate constitutes an act of constitutional aggression . . . Not for the first time is government of the people for the people by the people – and in our case, by the people's house – at stake. In the words of Lincoln when he was trying to avert the greatest constitutional convulsion in the history of democracy, let me say to the Leader of the Opposition and his followers: In your hands and not mine rests this momentous issue. You can have no conflict without yourself being the aggressor. You have registered no oath to destroy the Constitution, while I have the most solemn one to preserve and defend it.'[10]

Writing to the Palace on 20 October, Kerr said: '[Whitlam] has come to the conclusion that this is a great moment of history like the position in the United Kingdom in 1909–1910.' In the same letter he said Whitlam had said to him, 'You are in the position of George V,' to which Kerr replied, 'But you are not in the position of Asquith. You cannot pack the Senate' – a reference to Prime Minister Asquith's appointing new peers to the House of Lords in order to get the numbers during its conflict with the House of Commons.[11] It is a conversation that Whitlam denies.

Whitlam's office chief, John Mant, said Whitlam saw the crisis as being about the power of the House of Representatives. 'Right through to the moment of dismissal that was the governing thrust of what drove Whitlam,' he said.[12] It was Whitlam's vision as a parliamentarian. Yet this vision obscured the real power dynamic: it was the governor-general's discretion.

On 30 October, Kerr had lunch with Whitlam and McClelland at Yarralumla after an ExCo meeting. While the governor-general did not see himself as a mediator in the crisis, he felt the need to test the leaders on a compromise. It involved Fraser making the major concessions. The idea was that Fraser might grant supply if Whitlam agreed not to hold any half-senate election until close to mid-1976, which meant Labor would forgo any option of constituting the so-called interim Senate before 1 July and thereby gaining temporary control of the Senate. Fear of this possibility had been a factor in Fraser's decision to block supply. Because some senators would take their seats immediately – rather than after 1 July – there had been a slight risk Whitlam might enjoy a brief period of Senate control.

At lunch, Whitlam authorised Kerr to speak to Fraser on this subject. He made an appointment to see Fraser as soon as lunch broke. It was their second official meeting during the crisis. On 2 November, three days later, Kerr made a five-page handwritten note of his talks on this issue. He floated the idea but Fraser seemed unimpressed. Kerr's notes, however, have Fraser saying that if he 'had a watertight guarantee that the Senate would not meet, even for a day, till after July 1, once the election was held, he would be prepared to consult his colleagues about granting supply on these terms'.

Kerr said he would discuss this position with Whitlam if Fraser had no objections. Fraser agreed. The governor-general's notes say he put this position to Whitlam that evening. Kerr wrote: 'but [Whitlam] said he could give no undertaking that carried the implication that he got supply by making promises. Nothing but absolute surrender by the Senate was a possibility from his point of view.'

The final sentence of Kerr's handwritten note reads: 'I shall be seeing Mr Fraser tomorrow and shall tell him the Prime Minister's attitude. It will doubtless be no surprise to him.'[13]

There are several conclusions from this event. Kerr said in his memoirs he was offering Fraser 'an opportunity for retreat'. This is also the impression Whitlam and McClelland got from the lunch. Indeed, McClelland got excited and told Paul Kelly at the time that 'this is the Governor-General's solution'. In fact, Kerr probably thought it had little chance. Fraser was careful. The proposal, in effect, meant a defeat for him. He got virtually nothing in return, since any chance of Labor temporary control of the Senate was remote. Yet, managing Kerr cautiously, Fraser kept the proposal alive. The only interpretation from Kerr's note is that Whitlam killed it. Kerr was unsurprised by this – he understood Whitlam believed the Senate would crack, and he would settle for nothing but total victory. By demanding 'all or nothing', Whitlam's risk was that he would finish with nothing.

Whitlam's fatal misreading of the power dimension of the crisis was apparent in two areas – the half-senate election tactic and the alternative financial arrangements. These are two of the most extraordinary aspects of the story highlighting the monumental ineptitude of the government.

A half-senate election was due before July 1976. One of Whitlam's options – about which he changed his mind – was whether to call this election in order to put Fraser under more pressure. For most of the crisis Whitlam's position was 'no election' for either the House or Senate. His priority was the 'tough-it-out' strategy to force Fraser to retreat.

During Fraser's first meeting with Kerr to discuss the crisis, the opposition leader spent some time explaining his hostility towards a half-senate election as a proposed solution. Fraser was worried that instead of calling a House of Representatives election, Whitlam might seek a half-senate election before Christmas as an alternative. This issue, in fact, would become critical.

The point Whitlam did not grasp was that any half-senate election, in order to be a viable proposition, had to be called at the start of the crisis in mid-October. This timetable would allow the Senate election to be called and held before supply expired. However, a Senate election called on 11 November – the option that Whitlam finally embraced and the reason he went to Government House at lunchtime that fateful day – was not a tenable proposition because supply would expire during the campaign.

In Kerr's twelve-page handwritten note of 16 November (which includes revisions made on 13 September 1976), he explains his thinking about the half-senate election, revealing the extent of Whitlam's folly. Kerr said: 'At a fairly early stage it would have been possible for Mr Whitlam to decide on a half Senate election and so to advise whilst the crisis was still a political one and not a constitutional one . . . My own view was that Mr Whitlam made a tactical mistake in not having an early Senate election when there was money and I was under no deep need to make a final decision about supply . . . Had he come to me in the second half of October and asked for a half Senate election in November I should probably have been bound to take his advice because the Senate election would have been over before a real supply crisis arose.'[14]

In short, Kerr would have granted Whitlam a half-senate election in the early stage of the crisis but not on 11 November, because that would see the exhaustion of supply before the vote. Any Senate election called in mid-October would have been dominated by the Senate's blocking of supply. It would have put Fraser under intense pressure and may have broken him. It would have been an audacious tactic by Whitlam. But he declined to do this.

He waited for nearly a month while striving to crack the Senate. It was only when that tactic had failed to deliver that Whitlam decided to call a half-senate election, the purpose being to pressure the Senate via an election campaign to pass the budget. No responsible governor-general, Kerr or anybody else, would have accepted this advice on 11 November, because supply could not be guaranteed for the campaign.

Kerr wrote in his 16 November note:

> The other fundamental mistake made by Mr Whitlam was to believe, as he apparently did, that whatever happened I would do exactly what he advised and let him govern without supply and without going to the people. I should like to make it clear that at all times during the crisis Mr Whitlam stated in the clearest terms that he intended to govern without supply and that he would never recommend a dissolution of the House or a double dissolution because supply had been denied.

This statement by Kerr is credible precisely because by seeking a half-senate election to be called on 11 November, Whitlam was assuming he could govern, at least for a time, after supply was exhausted.

This reveals Whitlam's deeper tactical blunder. He failed to discriminate between Fraser and Kerr. Whitlam's task was to crack Fraser, to convince Fraser that the government would never retreat, to persuade Fraser that he was dealing with an unreasonable man and, as a consequence, that retreat was Fraser's wisest course. What Whitlam did, however, was frighten Kerr. He persuaded Kerr that he was an unreasonable prime minister, and he cracked Kerr's nerve when he should have been calm, friendly and reassuring in dealing with the governor-general.

In summary, Whitlam and his advisers (to the extent he listened to any advisers) failed to grasp their real options in the crisis. Those options from mid-October were: (1) to 'tough it out' or (2) to 'tough it out' with a half-senate election. But if these options failed there was only one fallback – to admit defeat and call a general election as Fraser demanded.

Yet the prime minister was a study in confusion. On 15 October, he said a half-senate election was a possibility. On 17 October, he said he would call a half-senate election only if the Senate rejected, not just deferred, the budget. On 21 October, he said he would offer no advice for any election until the crisis was over and supply was passed. And on 11 November, he went to Yarralumla to advise a half-senate election. It was a strategic farce. Whitlam made it up as he went along. The contrast with Fraser's consultative and measured decision-making was conspicuous.

Whitlam's related blunder was to think he could devise an alternative funding arrangement once funds from parliamentary authorisation had expired. The purpose of the so-called alternative financial arrangements was to enable the government to meet some of its obligations without parliamentary appropriation. Soon after the budget was blocked, a cabinet committee was devised to formulate a scheme. The concept was to replace government spending by bank credit.

It worked as follows: a certificate of indebtedness would be presented to a bank by public servants and suppliers, thereby obtaining a loan with the government prepared to pay interest to the bank at the end of the crisis. The law officers gave an opinion saying it was legal. The political purpose was to 'buy time' for the government in its struggle with the Senate. On 31 October, Whitlam said: 'If it comes to the crunch, it is probable that the government can govern without the budget . . . it's inconvenient to a lot of people, but nevertheless the Australian Government's obligations will be met.'[15] This was not a sustainable solution to the crisis.

Fraser was enraged by this plan: 'This scheme tells us more about the Whitlam Government than anything else in this whole issue. It was a giant step towards a dictatorship. It was one of the most serious actions by a government since Federation.'[16] Kerr believed it would result in illegalities. Treasurer Bill Hayden said: 'I had large doubts, although I could bear with the proposal as a political bluff, a legitimate political tactic. I am afraid I would have retreated from any effort to have it go much beyond that. In my view, this system could only function briefly and not happily and would have broken down early in the New Year.'[17]

Interviewed in 1995, Hayden said: 'I made it clear I'd go along with [the measures] for a period which I believed was justified. After that I wouldn't.'[18] In Hayden's view the scheme was 'doomed before it started'. Labor's Senate leader, Ken Wriedt, had similar concerns. 'It seemed to me that we were being manipulated in the cause of survival,' Wriedt said. 'I felt the politics worked best for us without the scheme.'[19] Senior minister Joe Riordan said: 'Nobody could imagine any of the banks lending money for such a purpose.'[20] A number of staffers had reservations about the arrangements, Michael Sexton calling them 'a tactical mistake'.[21]

State governments were ready to challenge the scheme's legality. The banks were extremely unlikely to cooperate. They were obtaining their own legal advice, some highly sceptical of the arrangement. Law professor Geoffrey Sawer said: 'The banks were being asked to accept a business risk.'[22] That the Whitlam government believed the banks – institutions antagonistic to Labor – would engage in an administratively complex, legally dubious scheme to circumvent Fraser's blocking of supply revealed the delusion that pervaded this desperate government.

It is difficult to see how the scheme would have become operational. Forty years later, Labor prefers to forget about this aspect of

the deadlock. Yet it was pursued with vigour at the time. It is critical, however, in grasping the tactical and strategic folly of Whitlam's
approach to the crisis.

First, the plan was unlikely to be realised. Second, it would have
unsettled virtually everyone associated with its attempted implemen-
tation. Third, it reinforced all the doubts about Labor – at the time
Whitlam was attacking Fraser for damaging the Constitution, Fraser
could argue that Whitlam was guilty of the greater abuse, planning
to govern without parliamentary appropriation of funds. Fourth, it
alarmed a cautious lawyer such as Kerr, haunted by the loans affair,
and reinforced every suspicion he harboured about Whitlam. During
their lunch on 30 October, Kerr told Whitlam he wanted a briefing
from Hayden on the measures. In Kerr's words he had been given 'no
information whatsoever' about the scheme to that stage.[23] Fifth, it was
yet another example of Whitlam's mismanagement of Kerr, with the
governor-general having to seek information from the government.

Wriedt's assessment was correct. The scheme undermined rather
than strengthened Labor's position. The conclusion Kerr drew was the
opposite of what Whitlam wanted: the governor-general felt the talks
with the banks were a clear sign that Whitlam's efforts to obtain supply by cracking the Senate had been unsuccessful. In short, it was an
admission of Labor's failure and resort to unworkable measures. At no
point did the governor-general regard the measures as an alternative to
supply. And nowhere in this disastrous saga did the government evaluate the impact which the scheme might have on Kerr's thinking.

In his letter to the Palace of 20 October, Kerr included a long section on the alternative arrangements and quoted from the *Audit Act*.
He wrote, in conclusion, that Whitlam's purpose was to circumvent
the denial of supply so 'there will be no excuse for me to demand evidence from him that he can get supply and no excuse for removing
him and sending for someone willing to recommend an election'.[24]

In short, Kerr had a conspiratorial view of the scheme. This letter
shows, again, that Kerr saw Whitlam's dismissal as an option from the

start. It reveals his chronic distrust of the prime minister and offers the view that the scheme, in fact, was designed to prevent him from doing his job. It is hard to imagine a more damning initiative during the crisis than Labor's alternative financial arrangements.

As the crisis intensified, however, adverse polls put more pressure on Fraser to retreat. The upshot was typical of Fraser's approach during this period – mobilising a united front across the entire conservative side of politics. Fraser grasped that unity was critical to his success. And unity was the key to persuading Kerr.

On Sunday, 2 November, Fraser chaired a summit of Coalition leaders in Melbourne. This became an important event given that Fraser faced a critical public, a frightened party room, an ebullient Whitlam on the rampage and a governor-general discussing compromises.

During the three-hour meeting, the Queensland premier, Joh Bjelke-Petersen, and the NSW premier, Tom Lewis, were strong supporters of Fraser's position. But Victoria's Dick Hamer was keen to defuse the confrontation. The final communiqué offered unanimous support for Fraser's stand to obtain an election and condemned Whitlam's plan to govern 'without a budget'. But the meeting, worried that the opposition looked too dogmatic, embraced a compromise offer.

Fraser now put a velvet glove over his iron fist. It was a significant concession. The opposition said it would pass supply if Whitlam agreed to a House of Representatives election at the same time as the Senate poll that was due before mid-1976. The idea originated with Hamer, who said: 'I wanted to avoid a head-on collision.'

This offer is one of the most overlooked yet most decisive events in the crisis.

Fraser was retreating to the extent that he would now accept a general election anytime before mid-1976. It was designed to cast Fraser as Mr Reasonable, always a hard call. The problem, as Fraser knew, was that this concession would make him look weak. Fraser suspected that

Whitlam would interpret the offer as proof that he was crumbling, a correct conclusion. He suspected, therefore, that Whitlam would reject the offer, another correct conclusion. Having rejected Kerr's compromise, Whitlam would now reject Fraser's compromise.

But Whitlam had drawn the wrong conclusion: this offer did not presage an opposition collapse. The Senate opposition leader Reg Withers said: 'Fraser was being tactical. He certainly wasn't looking for a way out and he wasn't about to back down.'[25]

Fraser briefed the governor-general on his offer on Monday, 3 November, having secured shadow cabinet approval. Fraser was unambiguous with Kerr. 'Mr Fraser said that this was as far as the Opposition parties were prepared to go and that if it were rejected they would unfailingly stand firm on the refusal to pass supply,' Kerr said. There is no suggestion Kerr saw Fraser's offer as weakness. Indeed, Kerr saw the significance of the summit meeting, describing it as designed 'to settle, in a way binding on all concerned, a final coalition policy for the crisis'.[26]

In short, Whitlam could accept Fraser's compromise or face ongoing deferral of supply.

During his talks with the governor-general, Fraser moved the subject to Whitlam's alternative arrangements via the banks, arguing this was in breach of the Constitution. According to Fraser's biographer, Kerr told Fraser he believed 'the government might have real legal difficulties with that' – another small yet encouraging signal to the opposition leader. As far as is known, Kerr had not raised such legal concerns with the government but was now mentioning them to Fraser. His biographer said that for Fraser it was a 'token of sympathy'.[27]

Kerr saw Whitlam thirty minutes after Fraser left Government House, Melbourne, just before a Melbourne Cup reception. Whitlam rejected the compromise proposal out of hand. Kerr wrote that Whitlam said 'he would never advise an election for the House of Representatives until he himself was ready to do so and certainly not at the behest of Mr Fraser or the Senate'. This is consistent with Whitlam's account.

For Whitlam, only total victory would suffice. This event confirms Whitlam's real objectives during the crisis went far beyond avoiding an immediate election. Those objectives were, first, to break the Senate's power over supply for all time and ensure no opposition would repeat the tactic – in effect, to alter the power balance between the houses and impose a constitutional change on the system of government. Second, he sought to damage Fraser permanently and, by achieving a complete victory, ensure the opposition was discredited in a way that would alter the atmosphere of politics in Labor's favour. Given these objectives, it made sense for Whitlam to reject the compromise but with a critical proviso: he had to be sure Kerr would comply. And Whitlam assumed this.

The stupidity of the exercise, in retrospect, is almost beyond belief. If ever Whitlam should have engaged Kerr, this was the time. Fraser had offered a major concession. If Whitlam was rejecting it, he needed to be certain of Kerr's thinking. He needed to test Kerr's willingness to support him. He could have used the Fraser offer to open up a discussion with Kerr on how the governor-general saw the crisis and the options. But Whitlam declined to use his position as prime minister for genuine dialogue with Kerr.

Whitlam had got into his head that he was going to resolve forever the contradiction embedded in the Constitution between federalism (represented by the Senate's powers) and responsible government (that assumed the primacy of the House of Representatives). It was a lofty way of saying he was going to smash Fraser and the Senate.

Kerr claimed that during this discussion Whitlam said the only way an election would be obtained was if Kerr 'were willing "to do a Philip Game"'.[28] If true, this remark would be reckless, almost taunting the governor-general, the implication being 'you wouldn't be bold enough to sack me'. This was a phrase Whitlam sometimes used; he had used it in private discussions at the time with a number of people.

If Whitlam said this to Kerr, it could only be interpreted as foolhardy intimidation. Interviewed in 1995, Whitlam said: 'I never spoke about Game to him.' It was a denial but not a comprehensive denial of the assertion.[29]

The Kerr files show the governor-general mentioned this exchange in a letter to the Palace. On 6 November, according to Kerr's files (which include only an extract from the letter), Kerr wrote: '[Whitlam] later said that the only way in which an election for the House could occur would be if I dismissed him.'[30] In his 16 November handwritten note, Kerr said: 'Mr Whitlam towards the end whilst implacably maintaining his policy said that there would be only one way in which an election could be obtained and that was by his dismissal – if I were willing to be a Sir Philip Game.' There is only one conclusion: this meeting with Kerr was exceptionally counterproductive from Whitlam's perspective.

Yet if Kerr's version is true, then Kerr is also to blame. No responsible governor-general should have let Whitlam's remark pass without responding. Kerr could see the dismissal option getting closer for him. Indeed, the dismissal came eight days later. If Whitlam had raised the question, even in such a provocative manner, then Kerr should have engaged the issue. That was his job as the Queen's representative.

Kerr fixated on the idea that Whitlam was unreachable. His 16 November note says: 'Mr Whitlam was engaged in a crusade based upon a single minded determination to destroy the power of the Senate on money bills. No one talking to him privately at that time would come to any other conclusion. The matter was not discussable.'

By staying silent and refusing to discuss the central issue of the crisis, Kerr only encouraged the confrontation. In describing the Philip Game reference, Kerr said: 'I made no comment.' He seemed proud of his silence. But that silence meant he allowed Whitlam to reject Fraser's compromise on the false assumption that Kerr acquiesced in Whitlam's approach.

Indeed, it is tempting to think that Kerr understood what he was doing. Kerr was happy to let Whitlam destroy himself. Kerr, as the key player, had the best vision. He knew what was unfolding. Kerr was close to forming the view that Fraser would hold firm. Within a few days, he set about the task of dismissal. He wasn't going to talk honestly to Whitlam. He would let Whitlam carry the full consequences of his misjudgement. This was the real meaning of Kerr's conviction that Whitlam had 'no claim' to know his thinking and that Kerr had no obligation 'to advise and warn him'.[31] Whitlam did deceive himself, as Kerr said later. But Kerr also sought to fool Whitlam. His silence at this point was an elaborate deception of Whitlam and sinister in its implications.

Withers said of the Fraser compromise: 'Of course, Whitlam should have taken the deal.' Bob Ellicott said: 'In retrospect, it was a very reasonable proposal.' If Whitlam had agreed then the budget would have passed, he could have declared victory, the country would have broken for summer, and in 1976 the 'new look' government with Hayden as treasurer and McClelland as labour minister could have advanced its agenda and prepared for a general election before mid-year. What would Whitlam have done if there had been no crisis? Given that a half-senate election was required before mid-1976, it is likely, therefore, that Whitlam would have called a double dissolution before mid-1976 anyway, if given a completely free hand.[32]

In summary, the Fraser compromise offered Whitlam an opportunity that he refused to seize – to either engage Kerr or snatch a partial victory short of his ultimate objective of smashing the Senate.

As Melbourne Cup Day dawned, Fraser and Whitlam set upon their collision course with renewed intensity. Compromise was finished and confrontation was enshrined. The stakes had escalated.

It was a time for the torching of even more conventions. At their 2 November summit, the Coalition leaders had urged the non-Labor premiers to advise their governors not to issue the writs for any half-senate election sought by Whitlam. The Senate still had the constitutional structure of a states house. The states issued the writs for a

Senate election and the Fraser-led conservatives decided to sabotage any such election. This caused merry hell.

Whitlam branded this tactic an 'outrage'. Victorian premier Hamer now drew the line. He would give no such advice to his governor: if Whitlam called a Senate election then Victoria would conduct a Senate election. NSW governor Sir Roden Cutler was not going to be pushed around by advice from Premier Lewis not to issue the writs in New South Wales. In 1995 Cutler revealed that he would have discussed the issue with Lewis; he would have informed Lewis of his position; and if Lewis persisted then Cutler would have advised the Queen of the reasons for his position and resigned as governor.[33]

During the Cup festivities, Kerr stayed at Government House in Melbourne where he discussed the situation with Cutler and Victorian governor Sir Henry Winneke. It was not a meeting of minds. Cutler said that he and Winneke believed Kerr should 'call Whitlam in and explain the situation' then 'ask Whitlam to consider his position and tender advice'. That meant warning Whitlam and giving him the chance to go to an election as prime minister. It was anathema to Kerr. He told Cutler that Winneke didn't understand the situation. Hamer said later that Winneke told him Kerr's dismissal of Whitlam was 'wrong' and that Whitlam should have been warned.[34]

In parliament on 4 November, Whitlam was almost triumphant. Indeed, he seemed consumed by false euphoria. Having rejected Fraser's compromise, he taunted the opposition and now opened up, as a trump card, the option of calling a half-senate election. He said he would never surrender to the Senate's blackmail. But Fraser hit back: 'The one threat to democracy is when one gets a Prime Minister of this kind who is terrified to face the electors of Australia, terrified to face his masters, because he knows that he would be banished.'

The decisive day was Thursday 6 November. Sensing a collision, Kerr had a final meeting with Fraser to ask, again, whether he would accept the compromise that Kerr had floated on 30 October. The governor-general was not hopeful and he was right. Kerr said: 'Mr

Fraser was not interested at all. He said the terms he had already announced were final.'[35]

Now Fraser made his big play. He felt Kerr was sympathetic. He knew Kerr was worried about job security. He knew Kerr believed in the dismissal power. Fraser felt he had convinced Kerr the opposition would not crack. It was time to push Kerr over the edge. His fear was Kerr's weakness. David Kemp said: 'Fraser told me on November 1 that Kerr was being very weak: he will not act until there is chaos all round.'[36]

The two men were alone. The crunch was coming. Fraser said: 'I now told the Governor-General that if Australia did not get an election the Opposition would have no choice but to be highly critical of him. We would have to say that he had failed his duty as Governor-General to the nation. I made it clear that the Opposition would have to defend itself and its actions to the people . . . if there wasn't an election the Opposition would need to explain itself . . . I told him we'd be saying he had failed in his office because he had not given the people an election.'[37]

Fraser also told Kerr the Coalition would win any election. He said once the crisis was over, public opinion would swing strongly against Whitlam. It was vital reassurance. Fraser was telling Kerr the public would vindicate his actions at a subsequent election.

Kerr's own account of the meeting reveals Fraser's skill: '[Fraser] realised that he could not advise me but felt he should say that if I failed to act in the situation which existed I would be imperilling the Reserve Powers of the Crown forever.'[38] In his 16 November note, Kerr said Fraser told him the 'last moment' was arriving when the reserve powers could be exercised. If Kerr did not act, Fraser told him he would be saying publicly this was 'a grave blow to the powers of the Crown' which everyone of substance admitted did exist but which Kerr's failure to exercise had 'destroyed forever'.

Fraser, in truth, was advising Kerr and he was threatening Kerr. Fraser was telling Kerr he must accept his responsibility as governor-general. The political message was obvious: if Fraser failed, he would blame Kerr. Kerr would be depicted as a weak governor-general who succumbed to Whitlam's intimidation and refused to do his duty. Kerr understood.

'I repeated the only thing the Opposition was asking for was an election,' Fraser said. 'I told him frankly that this was a wretched government, that Australians want to vote . . .' It was the fourth official Fraser–Kerr meeting during the crisis. This was the most important.

Fraser's career hung in the balance. His Liberal colleague and confidant Tony Staley said he and Fraser discussed a plan for failure. Staley explained what Fraser would do and say: 'Basically Malcolm resigns [the leadership] and then stands. "I take responsibility. If you want to get rid of me, this is your chance." Who else? . . . Anyone could stand against him. He wouldn't have lost the leadership.'[39]

What did Fraser feel when he left the meeting? 'I left Kerr confident,' Fraser said. 'I was confident because of my judgement about John Kerr's character.'[40] Fraser and Kerr both said the governor-general gave Fraser no indication of his intentions.

That evening Paul Kelly had a ten-minute off-the-record discussion with Fraser in his office at about 7 p.m. It had a lasting impact. Sitting across the desk from Fraser, Kelly was told that the governor-general would 'do the right thing'. Fraser said the issue would be resolved by Christmas and that Kerr would intervene to deliver a general election. When pressed further, Fraser said he believed 'the Governor-General . . . will sack the Prime Minister'. He spoke with authority, as a professional political leader in a 'make or break' crisis. His confidence was striking.

Fraser felt he understood Kerr's psychology. He had been supportive and encouraging, and now he was being assertive. Staley said that when senior Liberals had canvassed the tactics for handling Kerr there had been a critical issue: 'It was fundamental, absolutely fundamental, that [Fraser] had to settle in Kerr's mind . . . that once Whitlam had to go, was sacked, that it would reverse our decline and we would go on and win. There was no question that we would win.' That is, if Kerr delivered the election, he was running with the winning side. 'Kerr liked winners,' Staley said. 'Things about his life suggested he would go with the establishment or conservative side, as long as they were going to win.'[41]

In the end, Fraser was appealing to Kerr to do what he knew was right. None of this means there was any warmth or affinity in the Fraser–Kerr relationship. The men had little in common. Staley said that years later in their talks, Fraser 'said to me he thought Kerr was "weak and lonely, always seeking reassurance". He made it pretty clear to me that he had exploited that in his character.'[42]

But Fraser had a far superior grasp of the power reality. Despite all the options, tactics and speculation, the crisis boiled down to a simple proposition: provided the Senate held firm, there had to be an election. If Whitlam denied that, then Kerr must procure it.

Kerr told Whitlam the same day that Fraser was not compromising. The prime minister said he would probably advise a half-senate election to be held on 13 December. Kerr, unlike most of the Labor Party, realised this was a sign of serious weakness. Assessing the situation he now faced, Kerr said that 'if I acquiesced' then 'the election would be held after the money had run out'.[43] Obviously, Kerr would not agree to Whitlam's half-senate election proposal. But he avoided saying this to Whitlam. He let a deluded Whitlam think he would have his way.

Whitlam had got advice from the chief electoral officer, Frank Ley, about timetables. The last practical election date before Christmas was 13 December, and a poll on that day had to be called by 11 November. It was D-day. Kerr was aware of this timetable.

The governor-general had a meeting with Hayden that afternoon to be briefed on the alternative financial arrangements. Attorney-General Enderby spoke to Hayden before he went: 'Don't worry,' he told Hayden. '[Kerr's] one of us. You can trust him. He's on side.'[44]

Hayden described his meeting with Kerr: 'He was relaxed, quite genial, he asked me if I wanted a drink . . . I was taken by surprise to find Sir John apparently little, if at all, interested in what I had to say . . . He unexpectedly embarked on a discursive commentary about how highly he regarded Gough Whitlam's magnificent fighting ability, especially with his back against the wall. He said that Gough Whitlam fought like a lion, but even if he were defeated next time he would certainly fight his way back the time after that . . . Sir John dismissed, graciously, but quickly, discussion about different Senators retreating from the brink as too uncertain.'[45]

Hayden had no history with Kerr. He wasn't an old mate. He wasn't steeped in the romance or sophistry of the good old days. He looked Kerr in the face and he knew. This man wasn't 'on side'.

In a story the stuff of legend, Hayden said: 'I left [Government House] with a sense of agitation. I went straight to Whitlam's office instead of going out to catch a plane to return home. Whitlam was in a meeting so he came out of his office . . . He was a wearing a blue and white striped shirt. He was standing against the wall, even more larger than life. I said to Gough, "My copper instincts tell me that Kerr is thinking of sacking us and calling an election" – or words to that effect. Gough looked at me. He was fiddling his spectacles around in his hand. He said to me, "No, comrade. He wouldn't have the guts for that."'[46]

Whitlam was beyond logic. In order to convince Kerr, he had convinced himself. If Hayden drew this conclusion from one chat with Kerr, then what had gone wrong with Whitlam's instincts? And if Hayden had drawn this conclusion, what conclusion might Fraser have drawn the same day? In fact, Fraser and Hayden felt sure Kerr would move against the government.

From 6 November onwards, in moving towards his decision, Kerr made a number of assumptions. On timing, he decided the issue must be resolved by a pre-Christmas general election and that meant a decision by 11 November. The government still had supply for another fortnight beyond that. Moving before supply was exhausted was a significant

disadvantage to Whitlam. Kerr believed he had discretion on the timing question and said he had waited till 'the national purse was almost
empty, which was as long as, for the safety of the country, I could'.[47] His
justification, explained in the official dismissal documents, was that he
was 'satisfied' Whitlam could not obtain supply, that is, that the opposition would not crack.[48] In truth, Kerr did not know and he could not
know this, because neither Fraser nor Withers nor anybody else in the
opposition knew. It was a day-by-day, hour-by-hour operation.

Yet Whitlam, by deciding on a half-senate election, was also forcing
the issue. The reality was that Kerr could not wait beyond 11 November,
because Whitlam was seeking a half-senate election on that date. Kerr
had to either grant the election or impose another solution that day.
Whitlam and Kerr both made 11 November the decision day.

The reality was the Senate had held long enough. That is all that
mattered. It had held long enough to drive Whitlam into seeking a
half-senate poll and forcing Kerr's hand.

For Kerr, there was a personal element at work – witness Kerr's
statement that he would not stand idle and allow Whitlam to engage
in 'the effective smashing of the power of the Senate on supply and of
the Reserve Powers of the Crown'.[49] Kerr felt Whitlam was threatening the Constitution. He felt Whitlam was reckless in his campaign,
in effect, against the Senate and the reserve powers. He saw himself as
their guardian against a dangerous prime minister.

The pivotal assumption on which Kerr relied was that a government denied supply had to either advise a general election or resign.
This was constitutional and parliamentary orthodoxy. Kerr was correct in deciding the alternative financial arrangements were not a
satisfactory option. Because Whitlam had refused to advise a general
election or resign, Kerr's decision to force the issue was justified.

The fatal defect was how Kerr forced the issue. He decided on a
dismissal without warning. Few constitutional authorities would
agree with the view that if supply is blocked and a prime minister does
not resign or advise a general election, he must be dismissed without

prior discussion. The first stage of Kerr's intervention had to be to counsel Whitlam about the situation and for the governor-general to explain the options.

The reserve powers must be the final resort. They cannot be used before every other option is exhausted. Yet because Kerr decided not to warn or confide in Whitlam and give him the chance of going to an election as prime minister, he settled upon an even more extreme position – dismissal by ambush. It was spectacular in its unorthodoxy. Even worse, it was the action of a coward. Because Kerr feared his own dismissal, he would not warn or counsel Whitlam. The belief, indeed the obsession, that governed Kerr's approach from start to finish, was that Whitlam, if given any inkling, would advise the Queen to remove him. 'I had not the slightest doubt that if he felt the need the Prime Minister would seek to have me recalled before I could dismiss him,' Kerr said.[50]

Kerr's logic made dismissal by 'stealth', as he described in his journal, inevitable. That would inflame emotions and have political consequences. The truth is, despite his claims, Kerr didn't *know* what Whitlam would do. His justification for keeping the dismissal a secret was to protect the Queen from involvement. That meant protecting the monarchy in the Australian constitutional system. 'In this way I could hope to protect the Crown in Australia from any serious risk of being weakened by events,' Kerr said. The irony is that in order to save the Queen's impartiality, Kerr, as the Queen's representative, acted in a partisan manner. This point seemed to escape him. Nowhere did Kerr address this problem.

Kerr was correct to ensure the governor-general, not the Queen, took the dismissal decision. The powers of the Crown in this country are exercised by the governor-general. The Queen has no involvement in the daily business of government. The governor-general's decision not to inform the Palace in advance of the dismissal was correct – any advance notice would have endangered the Crown in Australia.

Kerr's critical mistake was to believe a dismissal by ambush was legitimate in order to protect the Queen from the possibility that Whitlam would approach the Palace to remove him. Kerr reduced the issue to an elemental power contest: he decided to dismiss Whitlam before Whitlam had a chance to dismiss him. This was exactly how he reasoned. It was the essence of his position. In the process, he debased the office and the obligations of the governor-general to be an impartial and unifying figure.

Manipulating a
Willing Chief Justice

The governor-general now sought the authority of Sir Garfield Barwick, the chief justice of the High Court, for his dismissal of the prime minister. Sir John Kerr followed up on the understanding he had reached with Barwick at the 20 September dinner of the Order of St Michael and St George. He would formally seek advice from Barwick on the governor-general's dismissal power. But Kerr went beyond seeking formal advice – he also sought tactical advice from Barwick about the handling of Whitlam's dismissal.

In this chapter, the authors draw upon the memoirs and more recently released archival notes of Barwick and Kerr, in addition to Sir Anthony Mason's 2012 statement. Unless otherwise identified, Mason's account comes from this document.

Kerr was astute in his management of Barwick. He wanted assurance and insurance, and he got them both. As Kerr wrote in his 1981 note, he and Mason had canvassed the resort to Barwick and its timing.[1] They knew when the time came that Barwick would affirm the dismissal power. Kerr had long admired Barwick. He now sought a de facto alliance with him. Kerr knew the combination of the governor-general and chief justice, united on the dismissal issue, would constitute an almost certain guarantee of a successful operation.

The crisis had a fascinating legacy: it drew the two men closer. Long after Barwick had left the bench, he continued to advocate for Kerr. They wrote to each other. They found solace in each other from their thunderous critics. And they praised each other's fortitude.

Barwick would have been waiting for Kerr's call. He had considered his position since their 20 September talk and had become 'convinced' it was his duty to offer advice if asked. Barwick's compulsion to be at the epicentre of great events was engaged.[2]

Kerr made his fateful call to Barwick late on Sunday, 9 November. But Kerr's account said there was another person with him when he rang Barwick – it was Sir Anthony Mason.[3] This is an extraordinary situation if true. The Kerr–Mason dialogue reached its zenith on this day.

'I rang Barwick in Mason's presence,' Kerr said in his seventeen-page memorandum written in London in the first half of 1981. However in Mason's statement of August 2012 he disputed this point. Mason said he was not with Kerr when the Governor-General had rung Barwick. The purpose of his note, as Kerr said, was to explain before history 'what happened between Mason and myself'. It is apparent from Barwick's memoirs he knew nothing of the intense Kerr–Mason dialogue, much of which dealt with him.

Kerr and Mason have both provided accounts of their 9 November conversations. They concur on the main narrative, but there are some gaps and inconsistencies, hardly surprising given the passage of the years. In his only detailed statement of his role in the crisis, made in 2012, Mason said that after he arrived at Kirribilli House Kerr told him that he had rung Barwick. Mason also said he had two conversations with Kerr that day.[4]

He said the first was at Lady Kerr's house in North Sydney where Kerr had asked to meet him. Mason said: 'On my arrival, Sir John said that we were meeting at the house because the Prime Minister was at

Kirribilli House [next to Admiralty House] and he (Sir John) did not want the Prime Minister to know of our meeting.'

Mason said the discussion began with Kerr saying 'he had decided that he had no alternative but to dismiss Mr Whitlam and to commission Mr Fraser to form a caretaker government'. Kerr explained the timing to Mason – he had information from the electoral commission that the last feasible pre-Christmas election date was 13 December and that meant a decision within the next few days.[5] Kerr's version is similar: it has him telling Mason he planned to commission Fraser as prime minister and have the parliament dissolved on 11 November if there was no earlier resolution to the crisis.

Kerr recalled that Mason spoke 'quite spontaneously and with genuine relief'. According to Kerr, Mason told him: 'I am glad of that. I thought that I might this afternoon have to urge that course upon you.' These words would have been of great reassurance to Kerr.

Mason agreed in principle with Kerr's account, if not in the detail. His version is that 'I expressed my relief that Sir John had made a final decision to resolve the crisis by dismissing the Prime Minister because I thought that this crisis should be resolved by a general election held before the summer vacation and any further delay could lead to instability.' Mason recalled his expression of 'relief' came at the end of their conversation. But he was not sure he actually told Kerr why he felt such 'relief'.

However, Mason said in his 2012 statement that his comment 'was not and should not have been understood as an encouragement to dismiss the Prime Minister'. This is too precious. If a friend confides in you about the most important decision in their career and you express 'relief' in that decision, common sense tells you that is a sign of support.

Mason knew from the start of their talks that dismissal was an option for Kerr. He was involved in the tactics of when and how to engage Barwick. For Kerr, Mason was not an impartial observer but a supporting participant.

Their discussion involved two legal opinions. They were the 'draft' opinion on the reserve powers by the law officers given to Kerr three days earlier and the additional opinion by the solicitor-general on the alternative financial arrangements. Mason corrected Kerr's account that these opinions had been provided to him earlier. He said he only sighted them on the day.

'I don't agree with it,' Mason recalled telling Kerr about the much delayed and much agonised over law officers' 'draft' opinion. Once again, Kerr would have taken heart from such reassurance. The views of the law officers were being promptly dispatched by this future chief justice and iconic figure from the Sydney legal establishment. There was no doubt where Kerr's personal and intellectual loyalties lay.

According to Kerr, he discussed with Mason the law officers' opinion and the Ellicott opinion. Kerr told Mason that he had disagreed with Ellicott only on 'timing' and the timing issue was 'now academic'. Kerr said Byers had accepted the existence of the reserve powers but offered the 'non-legal opinion that they might have fallen into desuetude'. Kerr said: 'I thought this was quite wrong. They still existed and could be used.' He said Mason 'expressed agreement with this approach and said I had the undoubted power to act as I had it in mind to do'.

According to Mason's statement, Kerr asked him for a written opinion rebutting the law officers' 'draft'. Mason told Kerr: 'I could not do that without consulting Barwick.' Mason said he added that 'it would not be appropriate for me, rather than the Chief Justice, to give such a written opinion'. At this point, Mason recalled Kerr saying: 'Well, I will ask Barwick.'

Kerr, in his note, also said they discussed an approach to Barwick. He said neither had any doubt 'that Barwick would be of the same view as we held'. According to Kerr, they had canvassed the approach to Barwick in their previous discussions on 20 and 21 October. Kerr was always inclined to approach Barwick over any use of the reserve powers. He wanted any dismissal to be watertight. The issue was the timing. If Kerr had approached Barwick too early, then Barwick's advice might contradict his own plans. Kerr said he and Mason had previously agreed the governor-general should approach Barwick only when Kerr was ready to intervene. That time had now come.

'I did not want anything more than constitutional advice,' Kerr says he told Mason. 'I did not want Barwick's views on what I should do but only on what I could do.' It is a valid yet also an imprecise distinction. It is the difference between law and politics. According to Kerr, Mason said he 'would have to make that clear' to Barwick. They both knew Barwick's highly political history and driving personality. Kerr said of Barwick: 'If he were willing to confirm the existence of my powers this would be a great help generally in enabling people to understand the unusual powers involved and rarely used.'

In short, Barwick's legal authorisation, in addition to helping Kerr, would assist public acceptance of the dismissal.

According to Kerr, Mason 'did not seek to dissuade me from talking to Barwick, indeed, he encouraged me to do this'. Kerr also noted Mason did not advance any argument that this 'would damage the court'. Mason's account is conspicuous for saying little about Barwick. Since Barwick was the chief justice, this may be understandable.

Mason, however, explained something that Kerr did not mention – that they had two meetings that day. He said that at the end of the first meeting, he volunteered to Kerr that it was 'unfolding like a Greek tragedy'. At this point Kerr called out to Lady Kerr, who was upstairs. She walked downstairs and, Mason said, Kerr explained to her what he had decided to do. Mason said the decision 'was bound to be controversial and attract strong criticism'. He recalled Kerr saying: 'Tony, you don't know these people. I do. It will be much worse than you think.' At this point, Mason said, Kerr invited the Masons to dinner that night at Admiralty House.

It was a time to be with intimate and trusting friends. Kerr must have been a troubled man that evening. He had made up his mind, aware the dismissal would provoke an outcry against him. The arrangement to see Barwick had been made.

Kerr said he rang Barwick 'towards the evening'. Barwick was at home at Careel Bay, Avalon. The conversation was brief. Kerr asked Barwick if he would see him at Admiralty House the following morning. Barwick agreed. He must have assumed the purpose.

At the end of their dinner, Mason said he and Kerr resumed their discussion of the dismissal. Kerr told him his plan was to see Whitlam and simply hand him a letter of dismissal. According to Mason's account: 'I then said that before doing so he should say that he had no alternative but to dismiss the Prime Minister unless he was willing to hold a general election.' It is the pivotal point; Mason was saying Whitlam had to be warned. Mason said Kerr replied: 'I know that.'

Mason said: 'I told him that, if he did not warn the Prime Minister, he would run the risk that people would accuse him of being deceptive. I also said he would need to consider the possibility that the Prime Minister might ask for time to consider his position and, if so, what response should be made.' He said that Kerr made no comment on this.[6]

Mason's advice was prudent. But Kerr made no reference to these statements. It is a critical omission. He depicted Mason as a vital confidant and said their discussions 'sustained me in my own thinking'.[7] Yet Mason's account had him, in effect, giving Kerr decisive advice that was not followed. As Mason said, allowing Whitlam the option of going to the election as prime minister was the key issue. But the governor-general denied Whitlam this option. The question, therefore, is whether the Kerr–Mason dialogue is different on the fundamental point from Kerr's depiction. Given Mason insisted this was his advice to Kerr the question becomes: why did the governor-general refuse to act on such advice?

'He and I do not differ at all about the facts of what happened between us,' Kerr wrote in his notes of his discussions with Mason. Yet based on Mason's account, this claim cannot be sustained. Mason's account is damning of Kerr because he quotes Kerr saying 'I know that' about giving Whitlam an option and then declining to do so.

Mason said after this exchange Kerr asked him to draft a letter terminating Whitlam's commission. Incredibly, Mason said he agreed to do so. According to Mason, his draft was 'short, consisting of about three sentences, identifying the failure to obtain supply as the critical event'. He later noted the actual dismissal letter was 'in very different terms'. According to Mason, his draft letter was delivered the next morning to Admiralty House.

This draft was a mistake by Mason. A High Court judge has no role drafting a dismissal letter for the governor-general to give to the prime minister. It was unnecessary. Kerr's staff could have drafted the letter. It was not a complex exercise. The incident, however, revealed Kerr's obsession with involving the High Court and his colleagues on the bench in his dismissal project. He wanted protection at every step. It transcended mere insurance and became a psychological need. He seemed to need others to give him the strength to implement his decision.

Kerr had a different account. He said the document he discussed with Mason was the statement of reasons for the dismissal, as distinct from the letter to Whitlam. Kerr said Mason agreed to put down on paper some suggested paragraphs for Kerr's statement and that he received them the next day in Mason's handwriting. Mason, however, said this was wrong: he was not asked to contribute to the statement and provided no material in relation to it.

Barwick had had plenty of time to reflect upon the politics and legal aspects of the crisis. In October 1975, Barwick had visited Menzies in Melbourne and found him to be unwell, irritable and confined to a wheelchair. On a second visit, this time to Menzies' office in Collins House, his secretary passed the former prime minister a message from Fraser that read: 'we are acting'. Menzies, according to Barwick, was disturbed, even angered by the news. 'The young fools are too impatient,' he said. 'If they give this fellow [Whitlam] enough rope, he will hang himself.' Menzies asked Barwick what he would do. Barwick replied: 'I would not be troubled by a refusal of supply by the Senate. After all, it is the parliament's traditional and ultimate means of control of the executive.' Significantly, Barwick remarked that he believed Fraser did not realise 'how bad things are with the country'. Barwick was deeply alarmed by the Whitlam government.[8]

There was no contact between Kerr and Barwick between 20 September and 9 November. In this period, however, Barwick considered the role of the governor-general in the crisis and the possible constitutional remedies available to break the deadlock. 'I considered the constitutional possibilities which might arise from a failure to obtain supply,' Barwick recalled in his memoirs. 'These included the obligation of the ministry and the duty of the governor-general . . . I also thought about the propriety of a Chief Justice giving advice to the Governor-General.'[9] Barwick was preparing for Kerr's approach.

By 9 November, however, Barwick felt that Kerr should have already acted. He believed Kerr was being too generous to Whitlam, that he was too soft. Barwick inclined to the view that the governor-general should have acted by 25 October – when the crisis was only ten days old.[10] He was a chief justice with strong opinions and a closed mind on the issue.

Evidence of Barwick's preparation can be found in his extensive file on the dismissal titled 'Dismissal of Labour [sic] Government, 1975–1979', which is part of his papers held by the National Archives of Australia. When the authors obtained the first access to this file in 2013, dozens of pages were withheld. On appeal, five pages have been released. They deal with a joint opinion on the reserve powers commissioned by the Liberal Party in October 1975 through the law firm Freehill, Hollingdale and Page and written by Keith Aickin, Murray Gleeson and Pat Lane. The opinion confirmed the existence of the reserve powers but placed caveats on when and how they should be exercised. It also argued there is a 'precedent for the seeking of advice from the Chief Justice of Australia'. Barwick analysed the opinion in detail and unpacked the sources it relied upon to form its judgements.[11]

On his way to Darlinghurst for a Sydney sitting of the High Court on the morning of Monday, 10 November, Barwick met with Kerr at Admiralty House just after 9 a.m. Kerr told Barwick of his intention to dismiss Whitlam and commission Fraser to advise a double-dissolution election. He asked the chief justice for an opinion on his constitutional power to take this action. Barwick understood that 'it was a legal question – not a political question'.[12]

Barwick told Kerr he was able to advise him. He specified two conditions: that his call at Admiralty House that morning should be published in the vice-regal engagements and that his advice would be exclusively in writing. Both were prudent. Kerr accepted them. There would be no secrecy about their meetings.[13]

Kerr suggested they lunch that day so he could get Barwick's advice. Barwick began writing his advice while presiding over a sitting of the court. But it was not completed to his satisfaction by lunch-time. Barwick arrived for lunch at about 1 p.m. with his draft. He told Kerr his advice would be that the governor-general had the required powers. He said he would complete his letter by the end of the day. It was delivered by car to Admiralty House around 4 p.m. by Barwick's driver Bert Reid.

However, Kerr had rung Barwick earlier, at 2.25 p.m., and had spoken to an associate of the chief justice. This phone call was unknown until the discovery of these notes by the authors in Barwick's file.[14] It revealed Kerr's nervousness and his extreme sensitivity about what Barwick might write.

Barwick's associate wrote in a note to the chief justice that:

> the Governor-General just phoned and asked that the following message be sent in to you: 'I don't want to prevent by anything I do the possibility of compromise so therefore if [Barwick] would feel at liberty to use the phrase that he was contemplating using in a slightly different form, I would have some flexibility and therefore if he used the phrase "the course of action which you

have decided to take unless an immediate compromise is reached"
or something like that. But whatever you say is OK by me.'

Kerr was offering drafting instructions to Barwick for his formal
advice to the governor-general. The text reveals how awkward Kerr
felt doing this. Not surprisingly, Barwick was hardly responsive. He
made no mention of any possible 'compromise' that would avert
intervention. In 2013, Troy Bramston asked Malcolm Fraser for his
reaction to the news that Kerr was suggesting how Barwick draft his
letter. Fraser said: 'For the governor-general to suggest to the chief justice what should be in the letter, if he was going to write a letter, was
totally inappropriate.'[15]

The vital part of the Barwick's advice read:

> the Senate has constitutional power to refuse to pass a money
> bill; it has the power to refuse supply to the government of the
> day. Secondly, a Prime Minister who cannot ensure supply to
> the Crown, including funds for carrying on the ordinary services
> of government, must either advise a general election (of a kind
> which the constitutional situation may then allow) or resign. If,
> being unable to secure supply, he refuses to take either course,
> Your Excellency has constitutional authority to withdraw his
> Commission as Prime Minister.

But Barwick went further. He argued that while the British
prime minister needed the confidence of the House of Commons, an
Australian prime minister needed the confidence of both the House of
Representatives and Senate. This was a technical, legal interpretation.
The issue of 'confidence' in Australia is defined by command of majority support on the floor of the House of Representatives. The Senate has
no role or function when, after a general election, the leader with this
majority becomes prime minister. Barwick's was a flawed statement that
elevated the Senate to a role in the political system it did not possess.

Barwick finished by exceeding his brief: namely, advising whether Kerr had the constitutional power. He said that if the government failed to obtain supply then the course upon which Kerr had determined was consistent with 'your constitutional authority and duty'. Barwick could not help himself. The notion of 'duty' went far beyond the issue of constitutional powers.

It invites an irresistible conclusion: that Barwick, fearing Kerr might retreat, wanted to stiffen him. If the dismissal became his 'duty' then retreat was unacceptable. Barwick told Paul Kelly he felt Kerr desired 'that the cup would pass from him'. Barwick's view was 'not that [Kerr] was weak but that he was tempted to temporise'.[16] Barwick, by contrast, saw himself as a strong man willing to act.

After Kerr received and read the letter, he rang Barwick, late on Monday afternoon. By this time the court had risen and Barwick was back in his chambers. This call reveals Kerr as a manipulator, almost playing with Barwick. The chief justice told the story:

> I received a telephone call from Sir John Kerr. He acknowledged receipt of my letter and then said that he was curious to know what the former Solicitors-General would have thought of the matter . . . he knew what one of them, Robert Ellicott, thought because he had publicly stated his views. But he would like to know what the other retired Solicitor-General, Sir Anthony Mason, thought. He asked me would I mind asking him. I said I did not mind doing that . . . I went downstairs to Sir Anthony's chambers. Sir Anthony had been sitting with me during the afternoon though he was then unaware of what had passed between Sir John and myself earlier that day. I told him what had occurred and I told him the substance of my letter. I told him that Sir John had asked me to ask him his view and I was now doing so. He said he quite agreed with the view I had expressed and I may say he did so without any reluctance.[17]

Barwick then rang Kerr to convey Mason's view. In 1994, during an ABC interview, Barwick said he saw this as 'a great sign of weakness' in Kerr because he needed further reassurance from Mason, a man 'who was friendly with him'.[18]

In truth, Kerr was manipulating Barwick. The chief justice did not know that Kerr had been secretly consulting with Mason on the approach to Barwick. The chief justice did not know that Kerr and Mason had discussed what advice Barwick would likely offer. Obviously, Kerr knew what Mason thought. He didn't need Barwick to tell him. He decided, however, to stage this event. Why? Probably to ensure Barwick knew Mason's views, to ensure Barwick would never suspect the Kerr–Mason dialogue and would always believe that Kerr had only discovered Mason's view via Barwick himself and not by any direct Kerr–Mason contact. In his note, Kerr said that he and Mason kept their dialogue from Barwick 'because he might be offended that I had not approached him earlier and before talking to Mason'.

According to Mason's statement, the governor-general then called him. Mason told Kerr that when he read the letter his reply to Barwick had been: 'It's OK.' Mason said: 'Sir John said he had asked the Chief Justice to speak to me because [Sir John] felt embarrassed that he had first discussed the question with me and he wanted the Chief Justice to know what my view was.'

Kerr was aware that in consulting Barwick he was defying the instruction of his prime minister. On Sunday, 19 October, during a phone conversation, Kerr had asked Whitlam whether he could consult with the chief justice on the crisis. Whitlam was firm – Kerr was not to consult Barwick. There were four reasons for this stand:

1. The last Chief Justice whose advice was sought on an election was the founding Chief Justice in 1914; the Governor-General had sought his advice with the consent of the prime minister;
2. In 1921, the High Court decided that it could not give advisory opinions; if the court cannot, then no single justice, not even

the chief justice can do so;

3.   The matters upon which the Chief Justice would be asked for his opinion could well come before another justice or the full court for argument and decision;

4.   While the High Court had never invalidated any of my government's legislation, Barwick had frequently been in the minority who would have invalidated it.[19]

Since Kerr was about to dismiss Whitlam, he felt under no obligation to honour this advice. Kerr said that on a matter of such importance he felt the governor-general was entitled to 'go where he believes he will get the best help'.[20] One of Barwick's successors as chief justice, Murray Gleeson, said Kerr would have seen the approach to Barwick as 'a prudential move on his part'.[21] In 2013 Malcolm Fraser, interviewed by Troy Bramston, said: 'I think the governor-general is entitled to ask for advice. Whether it is appropriate for the chief justice to give advice might be regarded as another thing, but that is for the chief justice.'[22]

The situation with Mason was different – this was informal advice from a friend of immense legal standing. Both Kerr and Mason, presumably, felt no impropriety was involved. It is apparent Mason was more than a confidant; as their accounts make clear, he did offer Kerr informal advice.

But Mason acted without the knowledge of either the chief justice or the prime minister. For many years Kerr and Mason refrained from exposing their dialogue to the public. Why? Did they feel the revelation would damage Mason? Did they feel it would damage the High Court? If so, what does this imply about the propriety of their dialogue?

It is surely the case that Whitlam, as the dismissed prime minister, Barwick as the chief justice, the other High Court judges, the political class and the public had a right to know about this dialogue that was, in Kerr's words, both 'significant' and 'historically important' because there was nobody else better able to 'help me sort out my own thoughts'.[23]

Mason may have been misled by his close friendship with Kerr, but the nature of his participation in this dialogue over the crisis and Whitlam's dismissal must be deemed to be a mistake. It was unknown to the public at the time and remained unknown until 2012. It originated in Mason's extreme reluctance over the past forty years to reveal or explain his own role – until the recent release of Kerr's papers in the National Archives – only reinforces doubts about his behaviour. He refused to be interviewed for this book, just as he refused to be interviewed in 1995 for Paul Kelly's book on the twentieth anniversary of the dismissal. It is extremely unlikely that a High Court judge today would engage in such behaviour.

Kerr wrote in his notes that Mason 'would be happier for the sake of the Court if history never came to know of his role'. This statement does not reflect well on Mason. The implication, however, from what Kerr and Mason have said is that they disagreed over the terms on which the details of their discussions could have been released earlier. Kerr said in his notes that he felt 'the truth' of their dialogue 'should ultimately be available to history'. Yet that 'truth' is disputed.

Kerr said that Mason agreed the governor-general had a 'constitutional duty to act' in the way outlined by Barwick in his formal advice. That is, Kerr recruited Mason as a supporter of the dismissal. Yet Mason, by contrast, insisted he told Kerr on several occasions that Whitlam should be given the option of going to the election as prime minister and this revelation had to be included in any publication of their dialogue. Mason's implication is obvious: that Kerr was reluctant to publish their dialogue on this basis because he would be embarrassed.

Late on Monday afternoon, 10 November, Kerr returned to Canberra. Government House distributed the vice-regal notice for publication in papers the next morning. It read: 'His Excellency the Governor-General received the Rt Hon Sir Garfield Barwick, Chief

Justice of Australia, at Admiralty House, Sydney, yesterday. Later, the Governor-General entertained the Chief Justice at luncheon at Admiralty House.'

Lunch between Kerr and Barwick? Not just one meeting, but two meetings? Two meetings after Whitlam had told the governor-general not to seek advice from the chief justice. What was happening? The media contacted Whitlam's office. But the prime minister, while a little puzzled, was unmoved. In retrospect, it is extraordinary that on reading this vice-regal notice in the papers on the morning of 11 November, the Whitlam government did not feel the tremors. It was beyond any warning. It was deaf to any alarm. Whitlam felt no premonition that something might have gone terribly wrong.

Kerr, by contrast, like a general on the eve of battle, was cautious, calculating and obsessed. He contemplated the coming moment of dismissal: the moment when he would destroy Whitlam's hopes and expectations. It is clear from Kerr's writings that he wondered whether his plan was watertight. He reflected on the vice-regal notice. What conclusion would Whitlam draw about him seeing Barwick? Might Whitlam sense his own vulnerability? Might Whitlam outsmart him at the final moment? How would Whitlam respond to dismissal?

On the morning of 11 November, Kerr rang Barwick. He needed to talk things through. Indeed, he needed Barwick's counsel on the tactics. Barwick dictated a note at 9.45 a.m. about this remarkable discussion.[24] Its immediacy vests this document with high credibility. In their talk, Kerr seemed more than a touch paranoid.

In their memoirs, neither Kerr nor Barwick mentioned this phone call, their last conversation before the dismissal. The governor-general told Barwick that Whitlam and Fraser were now in a meeting. It was likely he would see Whitlam about 1 p.m. Barwick's note reads:

> [Kerr] said he had to consider the possibility that the Prime
> Minister might have cabled the Queen informing her that he, the
> Prime Minister, had lost confidence in the Governor-General and

perhaps seeking the withdrawal of his commission. He said that whilst that was an eventuality which might seem far-fetched it had to be recognised as a possibility. He said that nonetheless he proposed to follow the course which he had outlined to me upon which I had given him advice.

Dismissal of Kerr was the last thing on Whitlam's mind that morning. That Kerr could not purge from his head the notion of Whitlam approaching the Queen, even at this late stage, testifies to the depth of his preoccupation about his own dismissal.

Kerr told Barwick, given the vice-regal notice, that he expected Whitlam to ask whether he had consulted Barwick. If asked, Kerr said he 'would inform the prime minister that [Barwick] had been consulted and that I had given him advice'. In the event that Whitlam reminded Kerr he had been instructed not to consult Barwick, Kerr's intention was to reply that this had become an issue for the governor-general to decide.

Kerr then asked Barwick about his letter of advice. If Whitlam requested to see the letter, should he show it to him? Barwick responded: 'I said that I thought the advice was given to him and that it ought not to be publicised until he, the Governor-General, had acted in the manner which he had outlined to me; that is to say, it should be confidential to the Governor-General until the action had been taken. Thereafter it should, of course, be publicised.'[25]

This is the course Kerr took. And Barwick's advice was subsequently released by Government House on 18 November.

It is unsurprising that Kerr contacted Barwick on the morning of 11 November to brief him on events and seek his tactical guidance on the release of the advice. That was being prudent. It reinforces the fact that Barwick's role spilled over into the management of Whitlam. It is also unsurprising that neither mentions the call in their memoirs. They were finalising the rituals for Whitlam's political execution.

Gleeson posed the question during our interview: 'What would have happened if Barwick had said: "Do it, but make sure that before you do it, you give the Prime Minister a final opportunity to back down?"[26] Barwick never said this. Obviously, Kerr felt sure Barwick would not recommend that Whitlam have a chance to stay as prime minister. But if Barwick had advised Kerr to warn Whitlam, then the governor-general would have been embarrassed. It would have been difficult for Kerr to seek Barwick's advice and then flout such a recommendation. If Barwick had felt this, he would surely have had no inhibition in saying so.

In the end, Kerr won the ultimate seal of approval – authorisation of the chief justice. He proceeded to the dismissal fortified by Barwick's advice, his strength and his office. Above all, Kerr wanted the best guarantee that the High Court would not interfere if Whitlam tried to contest the dismissal. While Barwick had written in his private capacity, his authority as chief justice was stamped on Kerr's action. Indeed, it was written on 'High Court of Australia' letterhead from the 'Chambers of the Chief Justice'. It was of immense assurance to Kerr who said that on the Monday night 'the loneliness of the decision . . . was one of the most burdensome experiences I have known'.[27]

That Barwick entered the dismissal project with enthusiasm is beyond question. Barwick wrote in his memoirs: 'To the extent that [Kerr] respected and accepted my opinion, it can be said that I had some influence in his pursuit of the course on which he had decided.'[28] In truth, Barwick lusted after such a role. Ellicott got it right: 'Barwick gave Kerr comfort. It wasn't the thing that triggered the dismissal.'[29] What Barwick didn't realise was that Kerr had manipulated the chief justice, reading Barwick even better than Barwick had read himself.

On 12 November 1975, Barwick wrote to his fellow judges setting out his role and the advice he gave Kerr. He also attached a copy of his advice. His account was brief and kept to the salient points. He made no mention of the fact that he had consulted Mason who agreed with his advice. Nor did he mention the 11 November morning phone call with Kerr.

Swearing-in of the first full Whitlam ministry by Governor-General Sir Paul Hasluck (fourth from left, front row) at Government House, Yarralumla, 19 December 1972.

Source: News Corp Australia.

Meeting of the Labor Party caucus in December 1972: (from left) Deputy Prime Minister Lance Barnard, Prime Minister Gough Whitlam, Senate Leader Lionel Murphy, Deputy Senate Leader Don Willesee. Source: Australian Labor Party.

John Menadue, the head of the Department of Prime Minister and Cabinet, and Gough Whitlam enjoying a drink at a farewell party for legendary public servant HC 'Nugget' Coombs in 1974.

Source: National Archives of Australia.

Sir John Kerr after being sworn in as Australia's eighteenth governor-general on 11 July 1974. He held the post until 8 December 1977, edged out by Buckingham Palace and Malcolm Fraser.

Source: National Archives of Australia.

Sir Paul Hasluck served as Australia's seventeenth governor-general from 30 April 1969 to 11 July 1974. In June 1973, he provided Gough Whitlam with a handwritten list of possible successors, which included Sir John Kerr. Source: News Corp Australia.

Gough Whitlam and Malcolm Fraser were political titans from an era long passed.
Both were prepared to push the political system to breaking point in pursuit of their goals.
Source: News Corp Australia.

Gough Whitlam, Queen Elizabeth II, Prince Philip and Margaret Whitlam at the Lodge
in Canberra in 1973. Sir John Kerr acted in the Queen's name, but it can be safely assumed
that the Queen would not have taken such action herself. Source: National Archives of Australia.

Margaret Whitlam, Malaysian prime minister Tun Abdul Razak, Lady Anne Kerr, Sir John Kerr, Rahah Noah and Gough Whitlam at Government House, Yarralumla on 16 October 1975. Whitlam told Kerr: 'It could be a question of whether I get to the Queen first for your recall or you get in first with my dismissal.' At the dinner, Kerr confided in Malcolm Fraser his deepest fear: his own sacking. Source: National Archives of Australia.

Sir Garfield Barwick, chief justice of the High Court from 27 April 1964 to 11 February 1981, provided formal written advice to Sir John Kerr about his constitutional powers in the crisis. Source: News Corp Australia.

Sir Anthony Mason, a justice of the High Court since 7 August 1972, had 'a running conversation' with Sir John Kerr about the reserve powers during the crisis. He was chief justice from 6 February 1987 to 20 April 1995. Source: News Corp Australia.

Sir Clarence (Clarrie) Harders served as secretary of the Attorney-General's Department from 29 June 1970 to 5 July 1979. He was worried about the Whitlam government's strategy during the crisis and was later critical of Sir John Kerr's exercise of the reserve powers. Source: News Corp Australia.

Sir Maurice Byers was Commonwealth solicitor-general from 1973 to 1983. In a (draft) legal opinion presented to Sir John Kerr, he said it was untenable to believe there should be a resort 'to a reserve power of uncertain existence and unknowable constituents'. Source: News Corp Australia.

Bill Hayden, appointed treasurer on 6 June 1975, saw Sir John Kerr on 6 November 1975. He told Gough Whitlam: 'Kerr is thinking of sacking us and calling an election.' Whitlam responded: 'No, comrade. He wouldn't have the guts for that.' Source: Australian Labor Party.

RFX (Rex) Connor, nicknamed 'the Strangler', was sacked as minister for minerals and energy over the 'loans affair' on 14 October 1975. This encouraged the opposition to block supply. Source: News Corp Australia.

James (Jim) McClelland, appointed minister for labour and immigration on 6 June 1975, was a personal friend of Sir John Kerr and felt betrayed by the dismissal. He never forgave Kerr for his deception. Source: News Corp Australia.

Graham Freudenberg, Gough Whitlam's speechwriter and confidant, later conceded Labor's 'culpable blindness during the crisis'. Angry about the dismissal, Freudenberg said: 'We never calculated that Kerr would act deceitfully.' Source: News Corp Australia.

Reg Withers, leader of the opposition
in the Senate since 20 December 1972,
was a politician with cunning in his blood
who had a mastery of the Senate's powers.
Source: News Corp Australia.

Robert (Bob) Ellicott, a former solicitor-
general who in 1975 was an opposition
frontbencher, wrote an opinion casting
Sir John Kerr as the central figure in the
crisis and argued he should dismiss the
government. Source: News Corp Australia.

John Howard, an opposition
frontbencher in 1975, thought blocking
supply was 'justified' but was not
'gung-ho' about it. He was 'flabbergasted'
when Sir John Kerr dismissed Gough
Whitlam. Source: News Corp Australia.

Andrew Peacock, a shadow minister
in 1975, 'strongly' supported blocking
supply but recalled the ruthless strategy
'had a particular impact on Malcolm
Fraser'. Source: News Corp Australia.

Bob Hawke, ACTU president, and Gough Whitlam at a Labor Party federal executive meeting in late 1973. Hawke thought Sir John Kerr could not be trusted. 'What are you doing appointing that bastard?' Hawke told Whitlam. Source: News Corp Australia.

Paul Keating, appointed minister for northern Australia on 21 October 1975, and Gough Whitlam in late 1974. Keating was enraged by the dismissal. 'It was a premeditated and an elaborate deception,' he said. Keating told colleagues Kerr should be 'arrested' and 'locked up'. Source: News Corp Australia.

Gough Whitlam and United States president Richard Nixon meeting at the White House in July 1973. While the 1975 political crisis coincided with a crisis in the Australia–United States intelligence relationship, there is no evidence to suggest the Central Intelligence Agency was in any way involved. Source: News Corp Australia.

British prime minister Harold Wilson and Gough Whitlam at Number 10 Downing Street in December 1974. There was 'shock' inside the British government at the news of the dismissal. Whitlam told Wilson he 'would have been in touch with the Queen' if he knew of Sir John Kerr's plans.

Source: News Corp Australia.

Queen Elizabeth II and her private secretary in 1975, Sir Martin Charteris. 'There was plenty of drama in Buckingham Palace after [the dismissal] became known,' Charteris said. He believed Kerr 'acted prematurely'. Source: News Corp Australia.

Sir William Heseltine and Queen Elizabeth II. Heseltine, her assistant private secretary in 1975, said: 'She was indeed surprised . . . I'm reasonably confident, myself, that she thought it could have been handled better.' Source: Sir William Heseltine, National Library of Australia.

Gough Whitlam standing behind Sir David Smith, the governor-general's official secretary, outside Parliament House on 11 November 1975. After Smith read out the proclamation dissolving parliament, Whitlam said: 'Well may we say "God save the Queen", because nothing will save the governor-general.' Source: National Archives of Australia.

Malcolm Fraser, deputy Liberal leader Phillip Lynch, Sir John Kerr and National–Country Party leader Doug Anthony after the caretaker government had been sworn in at Government House, Yarralumla, on 11 November 1975. Source: National Archives of Australia.

Gough Whitlam at Labor's campaign launch for the December election in Melbourne on 24 November 1975. Source: News Corp Australia.

Malcolm Fraser at the Liberal Party's campaign launch for the December election in Melbourne on 27 November 1975. Source: News Corp Australia.

Swearing-in of the second Fraser ministry at Government House, Yarralumla, on 22 December 1975 after the landslide election victory. Source: News Corp Australia.

Tony Abbott in his final year at St Ignatius' College, Riverview, in 1975. He saw the dismissal as a 'watershed' event for the 1970s political generation and 'got swept up in the whole thing'. Abbott finds no fault with the actions of Sir John Kerr, Malcolm Fraser or Sir Garfield Barwick. Source: News Corp Australia.

Malcolm Turnbull at the *Sunday Times* in London in the 1970s. He is the Liberal leader most critical about the events of 1975 and offers a strong critique of Sir John Kerr and Sir Garfield Barwick. Turnbull 'probably' disagrees with the blocking of supply and says Malcolm Fraser paid a price for pushing the political system to the brink. Source: News Corp Australia.

Sir Robert Menzies visited at his home in Melbourne by Sir John Kerr in 1977.
Menzies, the principal founder of the Liberal Party and the longest serving prime minister,
was one of many who provided reassurance and support to Kerr in his retirement years.

Source: National Archives of Australia.

Gough Whitlam and Malcolm Fraser meeting in Sydney in 2010. They forged a remarkable
rapprochement later in life. This triumph of human reconciliation over political hostility
came, however, without either offering significant concessions about their actions in 1975.

Source: News Corp Australia.

Kerr wrote in his memoirs: 'My only discussion with Sir Garfield Barwick, on the subject of the exercise of the reserve powers, is fully related here.'[30] This statement is misleading, given the other contact and discussion between Kerr and Barwick.

After the dismissal, Barwick lavished Kerr with the respect he craved from such an eminent legal and political figure. Barwick's file on the dismissal includes several letters between Barwick and Kerr written after the 1975 crisis. 'I do not need to say again how much I appreciate what you did in my own time of crisis and how much I regret that, for this reason, you have been pursued,' Kerr wrote to Barwick from England in June 1980.[31] 'You would not have had to suffer the harassment that has fallen upon you had you not been courageous enough to enter into constitutional discussion and to give your advice as you did five years ago. I hope you do not regret it despite everything that has happened.'

Barwick had no regrets. He was proud of his role. He was a willing chief justice. And he was brilliantly recruited by Kerr.

14

The Dismissal

When dawn broke over Canberra on the morning of Tuesday, 11 November 1975 to herald a warm spring day, John Kerr was ready to strike. He had resolved to terminate the Whitlam government if the impasse was not broken. Everything had been meticulously planned. His letter of dismissal was ready. His statement explaining his actions had been finalised. Some typing was to be undertaken that morning. He had the formal advice of Sir Garfield Barwick. He weighed several scenarios that could occur with his official secretary, David Smith. And he had spoken previously to Sir Anthony Mason about how to exercise the reserve powers on this day.

Kerr's plan went beyond mere dismissal. He had to commission Fraser, ensure supply was secured and dissolve the parliament for an election. 'The time had come when I had to act and act decisively,' Kerr recalled. He was ready to face Whitlam. 'The stage was now set for our vital conversation.'[1]

Malcolm Fraser's brinkmanship had reached the decisive moment. The feeling among senior Liberals was if 11 November passed without an election, then Fraser's plan may unravel and the Liberals might need to surrender. Tony Eggleton, the party's federal director and secretary to the shadow cabinet, reveals he arranged a secret meeting of the party leadership early that morning, at around 7 a.m.

Eggleton told the authors: 'If the result had not occurred that day – that was the last chance we needed to set an election date in that same year – if Malcolm hadn't achieved an outcome that day, there were lots of people who would probably not have continued to support him with his strategy.'[2] Dale Budd, Fraser's principal private secretary, recalls they felt that 'crunch time was coming'. Asked if 11 November was the date when an outcome would be achieved, Budd says: 'We thought either that day or the next. We knew time was running out.'[3]

Tony Staley, who had engineered Fraser's rise to the Liberal leadership, made it clear to the authors that by 11 November there was only victory or defeat. Fraser had staked everything. Interviewed by Troy Bramston, Staley iterated that if Fraser was defeated he would put his leadership on the line. He said: 'The plan was if we didn't get what we were after, then Malcolm would immediately stand down and offer himself for re-election.'[4]

Eggleton said when shadow ministers met early on 11 November there was a lot of anxiety. 'I could feel the tension,' Eggleton said. 'Malcolm saying, "Well, I can't give you any assurance as to what the outcome is going to be today but you know I am hopeful but I can't be sure." And I remember the feeling around the room was well, you know, if this is not resolved in the way that you have been hoping to have it resolved, then it is all over.' He said: 'There had been quite a few people who were hanging in there who wouldn't continue to support him.'

It was extraordinary that so few people attached significance to the vice-regal notice published in the newspapers that morning, revealing two meetings the previous day between Kerr and Barwick. But Clarrie Harders, secretary of the Attorney-General's Department, was 'surprised'. Harders recalled: 'I noticed, as others also noticed, that Sir Garfield had called on the Governor-General.'[5] Harders was not aware any such meeting had been planned. John Menadue, the secretary of the Prime Minister's Department, also saw it. But no action was taken; no alarm was sounded. The Whitlam government was sunk in naivety.

Gough Whitlam, deputy prime minister Frank Crean and leader of the House Fred Daly met Malcolm Fraser, Doug Anthony and Phillip Lynch in the prime minister's office at about 9 a.m. to test whether any last-minute resolution was possible.

Whitlam proposed that if the budget were passed, he would recommend a half-senate election be held close to the expiry of the fixed term on 30 June so that an interim Senate, including territory senators, could not be constituted which might give Labor a Senate majority. If this was not agreed, Whitlam would recommend to Kerr that a normal half-senate election be held on 13 December. Fraser rejected this as he had done before. He put forward his compromise: an election for both houses of parliament by mid-1976. 'I said that we would let supply through as long as he would have a double dissolution election when the Senate had to go out next May or June,' Fraser said.[6] But Whitlam refused Fraser's offer yet again.

The opposition leaders asked Whitlam if he would be seeking supply from them to cover the half-senate election period. Whitlam said he would not be doing so. It was a decisive answer. Fraser felt sure that Whitlam had misjudged. 'You know, Prime Minister, the Governor-General can make up his own mind what to do,' Fraser said to Whitlam. 'You can't necessarily assume he will do just as you advise.'[7] Recalling Whitlam's reply, Fraser said: 'He just wasn't disposed to listen.'[8]

Interviewed in 1995, Anthony said: 'I didn't know where we were going . . . Whitlam seemed fanatical at this meeting. He was absolutely adamant that he would not bow to the Senate.'[9] Now the last living participant from the meeting, Anthony recalled the scene in a 2015 interview with Troy Bramston: 'Frank Crean was pretty silent but he looked concerned. Fred Daly was being insulting as usual, belligerent is how I'd describe him. And Gough was pretty straightforward but he wasn't going to compromise. And there was Malcolm Fraser – he wasn't going to back down either. The conversation was pretty much between Malcolm and Gough. It lasted for about three-quarters of an hour. We departed without anything positive happening. I didn't know what was going to happen. I certainly didn't think there was going to be a dismissal. But I was fully behind Malcolm. We had to get rid of Whitlam.'[10]

Daly and Crean, however, felt something was brewing. 'I was very puzzled by the attitude of Fraser, Anthony and Lynch,' Daly recalled in his memoirs. 'They gave me the impression of trying to find out what we knew whilst at the same time knowing all the answers.'[11] As the meeting broke, Crean said to Whitlam: 'They seem very confident. They seem very cocky.'[12]

A number of people felt a sense of anticipation. The night before, 10 November, the lord mayor's banquet had been held in Melbourne. Whitlam attended, addressed the dinner and offered several opposition MPs a lift back to Canberra on the VIP flight. Andrew Peacock suspected something was afoot. 'On the plane on the way back Malcolm and Phil had their heads together all the way,' he recalled. 'A couple of us sensed something was happening.'[13] John Mant, Whitlam's office chief, was also on the plane. He said there was a heightened sense of things moving to a climax. 'You could feel it,' Mant said. Referring to Fraser and Lynch, Mant recalled: 'I said to Gough, "What are those two up to?" To my mind they knew.'[14] Lynch's press secretary, Brian Buckley, said there was 'a change of mood' at this time towards a more 'optimistic' outlook. Lynch told his staff on the morning of 11 November that 'we should get a result today'.[15]

That morning there had been another warning sign that had been ignored. At 9 a.m., Menadue received a phone call from the chief electoral officer, Frank Ley. He reported he had received a phone call from Fraser, inquiring about the timetable for holding an election. 'A decision on the half Senate election,' Ley told Fraser, 'would have to be taken either today or tomorrow at the latest for an election on 13 December.' Menadue, who recorded his conversation with Ley in a file note the next day, said Fraser also inquired about a House of Representatives election – something not being contemplated by Whitlam. 'Mr Fraser asked Mr Ley whether that same timetable would be appropriate for a House of Representatives election,' Menadue wrote. Ley told Fraser that the same timetable applied. In other words, a House and Senate election could be called that day or the following day to be held on 13 December. Ley asked Menadue to convey the details of Fraser's request directly to Whitlam, which he did.[16] Whitlam said that Ley phoned him directly to inform him of the discussion with Fraser.[17]

Eggleton was waiting for Fraser when he returned to his office after the meeting. At 9.45 a.m., Fraser dictated an account of the meeting with Whitlam. Eggleton has provided this previously undisclosed document to the authors:

> The prime minister said that if the appropriation bills were not passed today, he would go to Government House to recommend a half-Senate election. If he did not get a majority in that half-Senate election, he would still refuse to recommend a House of Representatives election.
> He said if the budget bills were passed he would not have a half-Senate election until later [next year]. But [he] tried to attach a change in the voting system to that, which he did not press . . .
> He made it plain he would not accept temporary supply for the period of a half Senate election. He made it plain he would not accept supply until the end of February, on the assumption that if the budget bills or what remained of them were again deferred or rejected, that there would be a House of Representatives election. He refused to provide any technical advice or legal advice in relation to his operation with the banks, and again rejected the proposals we had put.

From the time of this meeting, Fraser knew Whitlam was in a weak position. He knew Kerr well enough to realise he was extremely unlikely to grant Whitlam's request for a half-senate election. By deciding he didn't want temporary supply to cover the election period, Whitlam believed he was intensifying the pressure on Fraser. In fact, he was convincing Kerr there was no option but vice-regal intervention. A political veteran, Daly asked Whitlam how he knew Kerr would grant the Senate election. He was told it was normal procedure. Whitlam's answer was nonsense. Fraser phoned Whitlam just after 10 a.m. to tell him there was no deal. The stalemate remained.[18]

Whitlam now asked Menadue to phone Government House to make an appointment for him to see Kerr. Menadue spoke directly to Kerr – which Menadue recalled was about 10 a.m. – and told him that Whitlam was 'anxious to see him as soon as possible', indeed 'immediately'.[19] Kerr stalled. 'The Governor-General said it would be "inconvenient" for Mr Whitlam to come at that time,' Menadue recorded in a note. Kerr repeatedly said it was 'impossible' to see Whitlam straight away. He suggested after the Remembrance Day ceremony. Menadue said the next available time would be during the House of Representatives adjournment. So Whitlam phoned Government House.

He was told that Kerr could not take his call. He was speaking to his daughter Gabrielle about his nine-year-old grandson who had been taken to hospital seriously ill.[20] Whitlam phoned Kerr on his direct line and he answered. Whitlam told Kerr the meeting with Fraser, Lynch and Anthony had failed to reach any compromise. He said he wanted an early meeting with Kerr to formally recommend a half-senate election for 13 December. Kerr apologised for not being able to take Whitlam's first call and explained his grandchild's illness. He said he had to prepare for the Remembrance Day ceremony at the War Memorial so a meeting before parliament resumed was not possible. They agreed to meet during the luncheon adjournment, at around 1 p.m. (Kerr said it was 12.45 p.m.) to enable Whitlam to give his advice.

It is significant that Kerr asked Whitlam whether supply would be available for the campaign, and Whitlam confirmed that it would not be available. Kerr now understood there was no escape from a decision: 'I had either to let him have that [Senate] election without supply, with consequent financial chaos, or to act, so as to ensure full elections for both Houses with full supply . . . Mr Whitlam had left his half-Senate election too late.'[21]

Kerr was careful not to signal to Whitlam that he would not approve the Senate election request. According to Kerr's mindset, deception at this point was essential.

It is misleading, however, to conclude that the dismissal only occurred at this time because Whitlam was coming to Yarralumla seeking a Senate election. David Smith, for example, argues 'it was Whitlam, and no-one else, who chose the fatal day'. He writes: 'Had Whitlam not decided to go to Government House on that day to ask the Governor-General for a half-Senate election, the events of 11 November simply would not have occurred. If Whitlam needed more time, he could have had it. Instead, he chose to present the wrong advice at the wrong time.'[22] The evidence, however, does not support this argument.

Kerr had his own timetable separate from Whitlam's plans. Anne Kerr wrote in her memoirs that Kerr chose the day at least forty-eight hours prior. 'On Sunday 9 November 1975, John told me of the action he had decided to take on the following Tuesday if there were no change in the position of the two leaders,' she wrote.[23] Kerr himself had circled 11 November as the day he would act. 'I thought it likely that Mr Whitlam would come to see me on Tuesday to report the result of the morning's meeting and to advise a half-Senate election,' he wrote in *Matters for Judgment*. 'If he were not to come on his own accord I should, on the worst view of it, have to send for him.' For Kerr, 11 November was the day the crisis was to be resolved.[24]

It had been a busy morning for the Kerrs. After rising early that morning to finalise the documents, Kerr later walked into the

bedroom where his wife was drinking tea and showed her the document setting out the reasons for dismissal. 'I want you to read this,' he
said. 'From today, if I have to use it, I am going to be execrated by one
half of Australia.'[25] Anne Kerr found the document to be extremely
formal and legal. She felt Kerr needed a simple sentence to explain
what he was doing. Her suggestion became part of the statement:
'It is for the people now to decide the issue which the two leaders have
failed to settle.'[26]

Kerr believed his action would be 'bitterly resented and profoundly misunderstood in some quarters'. He was anxious, as far as
possible, to protect his wife in this situation. He said that Anne Kerr
had no material influence on the dismissal and that the later claim she
exerted 'some behind-the-scenes influence is an invention'.[27]

At 9.45 a.m., Kerr phoned Barwick to clarify some tactical issues.
He revealed to the chief justice his fear that Whitlam might have contacted the Palace and put in train moves to remove him.[28]

At 9.55 a.m., Kerr rang Fraser on his direct line. This call became a
matter of high dispute between them. Fraser told Kerr there had been
no resolution at his meeting with Whitlam that morning and there
would be no temporary supply for the Senate election. Fraser says
that Kerr then asked him a series of questions – relating to the terms
and conditions he wanted Fraser to accept if commissioned as prime
minister. It was tantamount to a tip-off of what Kerr was planning.
Kerr, on the other hand, claimed he only raised these conditions at
lunchtime when he was commissioning Fraser. An arrangement was
made for Fraser to meet with Kerr also during the luncheon adjournment. Kerr says it was scheduled for fifteen minutes after his arranged
meeting with Whitlam.

Whitlam walked around to the Labor caucus meeting, which
commenced at 10.10 a.m. He advised his party-room colleagues that
he would ask the governor-general to agree to a half-senate election. There was spontaneous applause at Whitlam's announcement.
The Labor caucus unanimously endorsed this proposal and saw it

as a circuit-breaker. The mood of the party room was buoyant, even euphoric. The caucus saw this as a winning strategy.

The Coalition parties met at 10.30 a.m. Fraser opened the meeting by saying he wanted no discussion about the decision taken a month earlier to block supply. Fraser's message, feeling the pressure of the crisis, was to hold firm. He said the crisis would soon resolve itself. A brief for Fraser prepared by Eggleton advised him to say: 'this is a crucial week', 'believe we are close to a "crunch" point', 'it cannot be long before the Governor-General will feel compelled to intervene' and 'we must remain resolute and united'.[29] The official minutes record Fraser saying: 'Government may bring on censure motion today but be ready for questions – asked parties not to press him further on current events.' Anthony said 'things are building to a crisis in the next 24 hours and to stay firm and resolute.'[30]

If there had been a breakout or even minor eruption that day in the party room, the press would have known immediately and Kerr's operating assumption – that the Coalition would hold firm on blocking supply – would have been called into question. Given that Fraser knew Kerr had plans to dismiss Whitlam in a few hours, preventing any party room debate was essential. It was a critical piece of intelligence that advantaged Fraser.

That morning Lynch called his press aide, Brian Buckey, into his office. He said: 'I think something might happen today to break the deadlock. Can't tell you the details. Don't know them all myself. But we should get a result today.' After the party room broke Lynch held a briefing for the media. It was cramped and crowded. Lynch was smiling as he began. He said it would be an anticlimax: there had been no discussion of the crisis. The journalists were agog. 'We believe events will work themselves out,' a smug Lynch told journalists. 'We believe that the present course is sound for reasons which will become apparent to you later.'

Sir John and Lady Kerr arrived at the War Memorial for the Remembrance Day commemoration in a ceremonial Rolls-Royce.

Sir John wore a tall black top hat, morning dress of grey pants and black jacket with tails. It was adorned with decorative medals. Kep Enderby, the attorney-general, was with the Kerrs at the ceremony that culminated at the eleventh hour on the eleventh day of the eleventh month. Enderby recalled the scene in an interview with Troy Bramston: 'I knew John Kerr well. But at the end of the ceremony, he just walked away. He didn't shake hands. He just left. But Lady Kerr turned towards me – and I will never forget this – with a grave look on her face. She said, "Goodbye, Mr Attorney." I will never forget that. I guess she knew what was to come.'[31]

When the House resumed at 11.45 a.m., Fraser moved a censure motion against the government for planning to remain in office despite not having secured supply. '[The prime minister] has not said that he would accept the Governor-General's decision taken in accordance with his constitutional prerogative,' Fraser told the House. 'There are circumstances, as I have said repeatedly, where a Governor-General may have to act as the ultimate protector of the Constitution. [The prime minister] ignores that.' Fraser had the perfect script; he was expecting Kerr's intervention.

At 12.34 p.m. in the House, Whitlam moved an amendment to the censure motion so it censured Fraser instead. 'The Leader of the Opposition asserts that my government is threatening the Constitution through an attempt to reduce the powers of the Senate,' Whitlam responded. 'Of course the exact reverse is true. The Leader of the Opposition is seeking to reduce the powers of the House of Representatives in a way never attempted in Australia. I am not trying to reduce any legitimate legislative power of the Senate. I am determined to protect the House and to prevent usurpation by the Senate.'

Whitlam was still defending the House of Representatives, completely unaware that the entire issue was now about the governor-general's powers. The House sitting was suspended for lunch at 12.55 p.m. The Senate broke for lunch at 1 p.m.

At about 12.45 p.m., Fraser had exited the chamber, went by his office and was then driven to Government House to meet with Kerr. The plan was for Kerr to see Whitlam first and Fraser about fifteen minutes after. Government House had communicated this to Fraser's principal private secretary, Dale Budd. Fraser's staff were advised to look out for Whitlam's car departing from Parliament House, and then follow in due course. But the timing went awry, with Fraser arriving before Whitlam. The prime minister did not depart Parliament House until about 12.50 p.m. David Smith, the governor-general's official secretary, met Fraser at the state entrance and ushered him inside to a waiting room.

Contrary to Whitlam's later claim, Fraser's driver Harry Rundle was not asked to park his car 'out of sight' in case Whitlam spotted it and smelled a rat. 'I wasn't sent out the back,' Rundle recalled in 2005. 'I was sent to the side, right by the office, which meant I had a good view of what was going on.'[32] Whitlam was driven to Government House by Robert Millar. He later said if he had seen Fraser's car, which was deliberately told to park 'out of sight', then he would have instructed his driver to turn around and head back to Parliament House. 'Had I known Mr Fraser was already there, I would not have set foot in Yarralumla,' Whitlam argued.[33] But Rundle said even if Whitlam had spotted the car, he would not have realised anything out of the ordinary as it was a standard vehicle out of the car pool. 'He would not have realised,' Rundle said. 'There were always Commonwealth cars out there going to [Government House] office for various reasons.'

Whitlam arrived at Government House at about 1 p.m. The scene was set. Whitlam went straight into Kerr's study, escorted by Chris Stephens, Kerr's aide de camp.[34] Kerr knew his objective: he would not let Whitlam escape from Yarralumla without an election. What was Whitlam's mood as he walked into Kerr's study? He was supremely confident, yet he would have known this was a critical moment.

The accounts of Kerr and Whitlam about this meeting differ. Whitlam was asked to take a seat in front of the desk. Kerr's letter of dismissal was lying face down on his desk. 'I have a letter with the advice which I gave you on the telephone this morning,' Whitlam said.

According to Whitlam, Kerr then said: 'Before we go any further, I have to tell you that I have decided to terminate your commission. I have a letter for you giving my reasons.' Whitlam's response, having briefly scanned the letter, was: 'Have you discussed this with the Palace?' Kerr said, 'I don't have to and it's too late for you. I have terminated your commission.'

Kerr's version is as follows: 'Before you say anything, Prime Minister, I want to say something to you. You have told me this morning on the phone that your talks with the leaders on the other side have failed to produce any change and that things therefore remain the same. You intend to govern without parliamentary supply. He said "yes". I replied that in my view he had to have parliamentary supply to govern and as he had failed to obtain it and was not prepared to go to the people, I had decided to withdraw his commission.'

In Kerr's account he claimed that on hearing the news of his dismissal, Whitlam 'jumped up, looked urgently around the room, looked at the telephones and said sharply, "I must get in touch with the Palace at once."' David Smith spoke to Kerr immediately after Whitlam left. Smith told the authors in an interview: 'The governor-general told me that as they shook hands at the door, when Whitlam left the study, he said: "I must get in touch with the Palace."'[35]

According to Whitlam, he rose from his chair and Kerr did the same. 'The Chief Justice agrees with this course of action,' Kerr said. Whitlam responded: 'So that is why you had him to lunch yesterday. I advised you that you should not consult him on this matter.' It was done. Both men agreed on the final exchange. 'We shall all have to live with this,' Kerr said. Whitlam replied: 'You certainly will.' Kerr extended his hand to Whitlam and wished him luck. The deposed prime minister shook hands with the governor-general and then walked to the door of the office.

Smith also recalled Kerr telling him that as Whitlam left, they had a brief exchange about the coming election. 'Whitlam said: "You know, I can win this election." And Kerr said: "You probably will."'[36] Whitlam was escorted to his waiting car. It took less than ten minutes to terminate the government.

'Dear Mr Whitlam,' Kerr's letter began. 'In accordance with section 64 of the Constitution I hereby determine your appointment as my chief adviser and head of the government . . . You have previously told me that you would never resign or advise an election of the House of Representatives or a double dissolution and that the only way in which such an election could be obtained would be by my dismissal of you and your ministerial colleagues. As it appeared likely that you would today persist in this attitude I decided that, if you did, I would determine your commission and state my reasons for doing so. You have persisted in your attitude and I have accordingly acted as indicated . . . It is with a great deal of regret that I have taken this step both in respect of yourself and your colleagues. I propose to send for the Leader of the Opposition and to commission him to form a new caretaker government until an election can be held.' It was signed 'John R Kerr'.

Kerr said that Whitlam's reference to the Palace was 'as I had foreseen'.[37] He argued Whitlam's instinct was to think of dismissing him. This is designed to validate the assumption on which Kerr had operated throughout the crisis and to justify his deception. It is a highly self-serving view.

Whitlam rejected Kerr's argument: 'To imagine that I could have procured the dismissal of the Governor-General by a telephone call to Buckingham Palace in the middle of the night – it was 2.00 am in London – is preposterous; to imagine that I would have tried to do so is ludicrous.'[38]

The most contentious claim made by Kerr about this brief conversation is that he gave Whitlam the opportunity to save himself. Kerr said Whitlam was dismissed only when he was given the dismissal letter. He suggested that Whitlam could have negotiated then and there to save his prime ministership despite being told his commission had been terminated: 'He could still say, "Let us talk about this. If you are determined to have an election, I would rather go to the people myself as Prime Minister." Had he done so I would have agreed, provided he committed himself by action there and then.'[39]

Kerr constructed this argument as a face-saving device. He pretended that at the precise moment of his planned political execution Whitlam could have remained prime minister. This claim was designed to rebut criticism that Kerr had betrayed the conventions of the Crown by conducting a dismissal by ambush and without prior discussion of the situation with Whitlam. It is not believable.

If Kerr had wanted to give Whitlam such an opportunity, he had days and weeks beforehand to raise it. The entire point of Kerr's strategy – as the governor-general kept arguing – was to deny Whitlam that opportunity. Kerr could not have it both ways. He deliberately hid his intentions from Whitlam over the previous month; he encouraged Whitlam to believe his proposed half-senate election would be approved that morning; he flagged to Fraser what his intentions were at 9.55 a.m.; and he had Fraser waiting in another room to be commissioned as prime minister within minutes.[40]

Nothing was to be left to chance. The dismissal of Whitlam was devised in secrecy, in collusion with others, implemented by surprise and planned so that no recourse would undo it. Kerr's claim that he was giving a shocked Whitlam an opportunity to save himself – in the few seconds between being told he was dismissed and accepting the letter – is untenable.

In this context, Kerr's dismissal letter is misleading. In the letter, his obvious implication was that Whitlam had 'persisted' at their meeting in his attitude that he would not resign or advise an election and that the only way an election could be obtained was by his dismissal. According to Kerr's own version of their meeting, he did not put this question to Whitlam in these terms. He did not test its validity. He did not know whether Whitlam 'persisted' in this attitude. If Kerr was serious about giving Whitlam an opportunity, his obligation before telling the prime minister he was dismissed was to ask him the question and give him the chance to reassess his position on the brink of dismissal. Kerr did not do this.

Fraser had waited in another room at Government House while Whitlam was being dismissed. After Whitlam had left, at around 1.10 p.m., Fraser was escorted into the study to see Kerr by Stephens. He was informed Whitlam had been dismissed. His face showed no change in expression. 'In accordance with constitutional principle you will, if you accept the commission, have also to accept the political responsibility for my decision to dismiss and later to dissolve,' Kerr told Fraser.[41] Kerr's desire for Fraser to take 'political responsibility' for his actions was included in his draft statement of reasons for dismissal, found among his papers, but was left out of the final statement.[42] This is intriguing because Kerr writes in his memoir that Fraser gave him this verbal undertaking. Yet, as Kerr acknowledged, Fraser never made any public statement accepting any political responsibility for the dismissal.[43]

Fraser was asked the same questions Kerr had, according to Fraser, flagged earlier in the 9.55 a.m. phone call. These were the conditions of his commission as caretaker prime minister. He agreed. Smith was summoned to the study. A letter had already been prepared for Fraser giving these undertakings to Kerr in writing. It was signed without delay.

'Your Excellency,' Fraser's prepared letter to Kerr began. 'You have intimated to me that it is Your Excellency's pleasure that I should act as your Chief Adviser and Head of the Government. In accepting your commission I confirm that I have given you an assurance that I shall immediately seek to secure the passage of the Appropriation Bills which are at present before the Senate, thus ensuring supply for the carrying on of the Public Service in all its branches. I further confirm that, upon the granting of supply, I shall immediately recommend to Your Excellency the dissolution of both Houses of the Parliament.

My government will act as a caretaker government and will make no appointments or dismissals or initiate new policies before a general election is held.' It was signed 'JM Fraser'.

Kerr then moved to swear in Fraser as prime minister. They shook hands. Fraser offered a slight smile. No photographs were taken. They dispensed with the customary glass of celebratory champagne. Fraser indicated that, assuming supply was secured, he would return later that afternoon to formally recommend a double-dissolution election. Fraser took the bible on which he was sworn in as prime minister with him. 'On this Bible, I administered the oath of office to John Malcolm Fraser,' Kerr wrote on the inside cover above his signature.[44] Fraser returned to his car and Rundle drove him back to Parliament House. Not one word was spoken in the car.[45]

Before Fraser returned, Smith made a phone call to Budd. Budd said: 'I'd had a call from [Smith] before Fraser had come back, saying: "You're now working for the prime minister. He's on his way back. He wants to see [Reg] Withers and [John] Menadue and [Geoff] Yeend as soon as possible."'[46] This call became a matter of dispute between Budd and Smith, the latter denying he ever made such a call. Budd, however, made a contemporary note and gave a copy of it to the authors.

When Whitlam left Yarralumla, he went to the Lodge for lunch. The first call he made was to Margaret Whitlam, who was hosting a luncheon at Kirribilli House. 'How ridiculous,' she said when told of the dismissal. 'You should have just torn it up. There were only two of you there. Or you should have slapped his face and told him to pull himself together.'[47]

Whitlam did not contest the legality of the dismissal, even though he thought it was unjustified. The truth is he was unprepared. He had given no prior consideration to managing a dismissal in Kerr's study and, now he had been dismissed, he had no contingency plan. He did not think quickly enough. Whitlam did not return to Parliament House to confer immediately with his staff, cabinet and Senate leadership.

He phoned the head of the Prime Minister's Department, John Menadue, and his office chief, John Mant, and asked them to come to the Lodge. 'I then ate my lunch,' Whitlam recalled. 'The condemned man ate a hearty meal, although on this occasion, the normal order was reversed; I had my steak after the execution.'[48]

Whitlam sat in a glassed sunroom annex. Those also summoned were ministers Crean, Daly, Enderby, Speaker Gordon Scholes, speechwriter Graham Freudenberg and party secretary David Combe. 'I've been sacked,' he told them as each arrived. 'Kerr's done a Game on me.' Daly said they were like 'stunned mullets'. He recalled: 'Whitlam said, "I'll sack Kerr" . . . But it was too late for that even if it were possible.'[49]

The deposed prime minister drafted by hand a resolution that would form the basis of a censure motion against Fraser. It would declare confidence in the Whitlam government and inform the Queen the House had 'no confidence' in Fraser or any government he led. It was modified slightly and moved by Whitlam that afternoon.

Whitlam's strategy was to carry a 'no confidence' motion in Fraser and seek to be reinstated as prime minister. His hope was to overturn the dismissal within hours. Mant said: 'So we sat around and the focus of conversation was all about getting supply passed and moving a vote of "no confidence". Then Kerr will have to dismiss Fraser.'[50] Mant said they expected that Whitlam could be reinstated later in the day. 'There was still at that point the view that Kerr would behave properly,' he said. Mant called it a 'hammer blow' when this hope proved futile. The reality, however, was that most Labor figures knew it was over. Once removed from office by Kerr, they sensed there was no prospect of any reversal of their fortunes that day.

The motion Whitlam drafted revealed his initial thinking: he was looking to the House of Representatives and the Palace. Nothing better illustrated his lack of contingency planning – the key was the Senate. Whitlam said the House was 'the only place that had any meaningful role'.[51]

Labor's Senate leader, Ken Wriedt, was not invited to the Lodge nor was he informed about the dismissal. Indeed, no senators were informed by Whitlam or his staff before the Senate resumed sitting at 2 p.m. It was a grave miscalculation. 'Gough never thought about the Senate or Wriedt,' Mant recalled. He said Whitlam had seen Wriedt as a 'backslider' during the crisis who wanted to compromise 'so that's why he wasn't there'. The deeper reason is that Whitlam was blind to the Senate's pivotal role: it was the Senate not the House that remained the key.

Fraser knew he had to act quickly to fulfil the terms of his commission. On returning to Parliament House, he informed his staff, spoke to his parliamentary colleagues and ensured steps were in place to pass the budget. Unlike Whitlam, Fraser knew the critical issue was securing supply through the Senate. If he did not secure supply, Kerr's dismissal strategy would have been threatened. At 2.05 p.m., a press release was issued by Government House. It announced that the governor-general had terminated the prime minister's commission. The statement was delivered to the press gallery boxes about the same time, producing confusion, shock and uproar.

At his press conference that afternoon, Whitlam said: 'I am certain the Crown did not have the right to do what the Governor-General did on this occasion . . . the Queen would never have done it.'

During their subsequent late-night conversations, Kerr told Smith he had no regrets. 'They left me with no alternative,' he said, blaming Whitlam.[52] Kerr, in fact, had destroyed the sense of unity and impartiality essential for an incumbent in the office of governor-general.

Death in the Afternoon:
The Second Crisis

The great myth of the dismissal story is that it was done and dusted at lunchtime on 11 November. The reality, however, is that Sir John Kerr had a worrying afternoon. His game plan prevailed due to crafty planning and good luck. But it was not guaranteed and events could have turned ugly and unpredictable. The drama was conducted in public in the parliament and in private at Yarralumla.

The public drama was the confused, highly charged and emotional parliamentary contest. Having been outmanoeuvred in losing his commission, Whitlam was outmanoeuvred again in his effort to regain his commission. It was a bad day that exposed his limits as a parliamentarian. Whitlam never grasped the essence of his dilemma – once sacked, his only salvation was to deny Fraser supply, one of the conditions of his caretaker commission. Yet Labor voted for the supply bills in the Senate before 2.30 p.m., thereby securing Fraser's position.

The private drama came at Yarralumla that afternoon when Kerr faced a situation he had not anticipated. The House of Representatives had voted 'no confidence' in Fraser, the new prime minister, and had called upon the governor-general to commission Whitlam 'to form a government'. The issue for Kerr became: did he continue to exercise the reserve powers in the teeth of this demand or did he succumb to the House of Representatives resolution and reinstate Whitlam? The governor-general was determined to press ahead. But he was anxious to ensure the legal foundation for whatever he did – and herein lay the problem. The law officers began to query whether Kerr should revise his strategy. The political earth was briefly shaken by this new crisis.

Unlike Whitlam, Fraser returned immediately to Parliament House after leaving Yarralumla. On his return, Liberal Party federal director Tony Eggleton was already waiting in his office. He had received a phone call from Government House informing him Fraser was now prime minister. 'I was surprised but relieved,' Eggleton said. 'With the benefit of this momentous intelligence, I hurried down to the Parliament House kerbside to await Malcolm Fraser's return from Government House. As Malcolm stepped from his car, I shook his hand and simply said, "Welcome, Prime Minister." He smiled and asked me to summon the shadow cabinet.' The opposition, aware the dismissal could go wrong, now acted with speed.[1]

'Malcolm rang me,' Doug Anthony recalls. 'I was having a sandwich in my office . . . He said, "You're now deputy prime minister." And I said, "What?" He said, "I've just been made prime minister."'[2]

While at the Lodge, the Prime Minister's Department head John Menadue was phoned by Fraser's office chief, Dale Budd, and told the new prime minister wanted to see him 'urgently'. He left Whitlam and arrived at Fraser's office at 1.50 p.m. Menadue said: 'He [Fraser] informed me that he had been sworn as Prime Minister, and that he proposed to obtain passage of the appropriation bills through the Senate as quickly as possible, their presentation for Royal Assent in order that the parliament could be dissolved.' Fraser, unlike Whitlam, was focused on the supply bills in the Senate.[3]

The Senate had resumed at 2 p.m. in a state of confusion. The government leader, Ken Wriedt, was not told of the dismissal. The Senate president, Justin O'Byrne, was not informed. Nor did the manager of government business, Doug McClelland, know. The opposition senators, however, led by Reg Withers, did know. Withers had just come from a meeting with Fraser and senior Liberals. He knew his mission. Having blocked the bills for a month, Withers now had to pass supply as fast as possible for the Fraser government. 'How long will it take you to get supply?' Fraser asked. 'Just leave it to me, Malcolm,' Withers replied.[4]

There was a touch of bravado in this remark. But Labor's ineptitude saw Withers deliver his pledge with astonishing speed. The Labor senators were exceptionally unlucky. News of Whitlam's dismissal swept around King's Hall just a few minutes after they had walked into the Senate chamber. Veteran journalist Alan Reid, who had just heard of the dismissal, saw McClelland and called out to him, but McClelland got diverted. He missed the moment when Reid would have told him. There must have been other such stories.

Withers and Wriedt now faced each other, yet again, across the main bench. The irony, however, was supreme. This time they were both trying to secure supply but only Withers knew the government had changed hands. Withers told Wriedt the Coalition would pass the bills. Wriedt was astonished. He turned and spoke to his deputy, Don Willesee, and McClelland. 'There's something strange here,' he said. 'I can't understand why they've changed their minds.' Wriedt walked across to speak to John Button. 'There's a story going around that the government's been sacked,' Button told him. 'Don't be bloody ridiculous,' Wriedt said. 'Send someone out to check it.'[5]

Withers recalled the situation: 'I said to Wriedt, "Put the question, we'll vote for it this time." He looked stunned. Just couldn't believe it.'[6] McClelland had been handed a sheet of paper saying the government had been dismissed. He couldn't believe it. According to Reid's version, McClelland and Willesee asked Withers what had happened. He confirmed Whitlam was dismissed; they thought it was a joke.[7]

A note for file prepared by the Senate parliamentary liaison officer, MJ Hanson, dated 20 November 1975, described a pervading sense of 'confusion' in the Senate that afternoon.[8] At 2 p.m. he had been phoned by his counterpart in the House with the news of the dismissal. He told Wriedt's office. They were to seek clarification from the prime minister's office. Hanson said he went into the Senate chamber and told McClelland. But he could not confirm the news. At about 2.10 p.m., Hanson noted, clarification arrived from Whitlam's office that the government had been dismissed. This was conveyed to Wriedt and McClelland. Hanson said: 'At no stage had they received any communication from Mr Whitlam's office advising that Mr Fraser was now Prime Minister and that they were no longer Ministers.'

Withers asked Wriedt: 'Are you going to move these bills or will we?' Wriedt was in an impossible situation. Having had no contact with Whitlam or anybody from the lunchtime Lodge meeting, he was in ignorance of any agreed strategy and was still shaken by events. At 2.20 p.m., Wriedt reintroduced the supply bills. The president of the Senate put the motion. In just four minutes, at 2.24 p.m., the bills had passed with the support of both sides of the chamber, on the voices. Labor had voted for supply for Malcolm Fraser. The Senate was then suspended. Labor's only hope of thwarting Fraser had been extinguished.

If Wriedt had confirmation about the dismissal he would have asked the president, O'Byrne, to delay the vote. This would have given Labor time to consider an alternative strategy. But Wriedt doubted this would have made much difference.[9] Hanson, however, suggested in a later note, dated 24 November 1975, that all ALP senators knew Whitlam had been dismissed by 2.20 p.m.: 'Senator Wreidt went ahead with his motion without query from any Senator as to whether or not he should be moving such a motion on behalf of the new "government".'[10]

McClelland recalled these events in a previously unpublished interview with Troy Bramston. If he had known about the dismissal before the Senate resumed, there were options available to frustrate Kerr's actions. 'I think it is terribly sad that there was no discussions with any Senators that took place with Whitlam at the Lodge,' McClelland said. 'I have no doubt that whilst in the end we may have caved in, I have no doubt that for at least twenty-four hours we could have held up the Senate passing supply and put Kerr in an invidious position.'[11]

Ian Sinclair, who had been manager of opposition business in the House of Representatives, says he was 'absolutely alive' to the possibility the dismissal might unravel. 'I was very worried about it,' Sinclair said in an interview.[12] 'I was trying to make sure we got the House up at the end of the day for an election. If Gough had told his Senate leader, Ken Wriedt, about the dismissal, it could have been a difficult situation for us. It was Gough's great failure to advise his senators what had happened. If we didn't have supply, there was no government. If supply was not passed, then we had not fulfilled the essential remit from Kerr. The outcome on that day may well have been different.'

Hanson's contemporaneous note outlines how Kerr's dismissal action could have been thwarted in the Senate.[13] 'Had Senator Wriedt not proceeded with his motion and had the initiative for passing the bills been left to the Liberal–National Country Party Senators, then it may have been possible for the Labor senators to have delayed passage of the bills until the following day,' Hanson wrote. 'This is because the restoration of the bills would have been denied to the Liberal–National Country Party Senators as they would not have had an absolute majority in the Senate (assuming that Senators Steele Hall and [Cleaver] Bunton would have continued to vote with the Labor senators).' In this situation, surmised Hanson, 'The Speaker could then have informed the Governor-General not only of the want of confidence motion in the new prime minister but also the fact that supply had not been granted.'

This event highlights the prescience of advice from the Prime Minister's Department and the Attorney-General's Department before supply was blocked when they advised on a procedure requiring the supply bills to be resubmitted to the House of Representatives before becoming law. If that idea had been taken up, it is difficult to see how Fraser could have secured supply.

As head of the Prime Minister's Department, Menadue believed Kerr took a 'pretty big gamble' in assuming supply would be passed. In a note written soon after the dismissal, Menadue said: 'The Governor-General could not be certain that supply would be passed before a motion of no-confidence was adopted. He was taking a gamble that Mr Fraser could obtain supply through the Senate as quickly as possible, and that he could dissolve parliament before acute embarrassment occurred. As it happened, the Labor Senators were not prepared for this eventuality. If they had been, they could perhaps have delayed passage of the money bills for 24 hours. If this had happened the position could have become critical and perhaps even explosive.' Menadue argued that Kerr could not have 'turned back' from his commissioning of Fraser yet he could have been confronted with unpalatable options.[14]

The reality is that Kerr was dismissing Whitlam because he did not have supply. He could not, therefore, accept a Fraser government that did not have supply. The pivotal question on the afternoon of 11 November was supply. Fraser knew this. He needed to secure supply to advise Kerr to call a general election. And he did.

The trigger for the second crisis was the House 'no confidence' resolution in Fraser as prime minister. When the House resumed at 2 p.m. there was no mention of dismissal. Fraser did not inform the House that he had been commissioned as prime minister until 2.34 p.m., another astute move. By that time he had obtained supply in the Senate. The House was engulfed in shock and uproar. In a note for file dated 20 November the House parliamentary liaison officer, AE Dyster, said there was 'disbelief of all "government" members especially ministers' at the news of dismissal.[15]

Fraser moved that the House adjourn and saw his motion defeated sixty-four to fifty-five. The leader of the House, Fred Daly, then moved suspension of standing orders to allow Whitlam to move a motion. That was carried sixty-four to fifty-five. Whitlam then moved a motion of 'no confidence' in the prime minister and demanded the governor-general recommission him. That was carried sixty-four to fifty-five. The Speaker, Gordon Scholes, announced he would convey the message of the House to the governor-general as soon as possible. The House was suspended at 3.15 until 5.30.

Fraser had lost every division. These events demonstrated it was a gross violation of responsible government for a minority leader to be made prime minister on the condition that he obtain supply. Nor was it necessarily achievable. Kerr displayed contempt for the authority of the House of Representatives upon which majority democratic government in Australia depends. There was no justification for him to commission a minority leader without exhausting every other option.

During this period Scholes had contacted his private secretary, Mary Harris, and asked her to phone Government House to request a meeting with Kerr. With supply obtained the crisis was over and Labor now sought to have Whitlam recommissioned, given the House vote. Scholes returned to the Speaker's suite to find that no appointment had been made. David Smith had said the governor-general might be too busy to see Scholes. The Speaker asked Harris to tell Smith that if no appointment were secured, he would reconvene the House. An appointment was made for 4.45 p.m.

When Menadue returned to the Prime Minister's Department, he was told by officials it usually took several days to prepare bills for the governor-general's assent. But they did not have two days; they had two hours. Fraser was edgy, impatient and insistent. Soon after Menadue arrived back at his department, Fraser rang to inquire about 'process'. And he kept ringing. 'There were several urgent calls from Mr Fraser,' Menadue said. Fraser told Menadue it was 'essential' that all documents be with him by 3.40 p.m., in time to get them to Kerr for his signature at 4 p.m.

In Fraser's office, a bevy of officials from the prime minister's and attorney-general's departments were on hand to finalise the documentation before they went to Government House. Before they left,

Fraser, as caretaker prime minister, signed the letter to the governor-general recommending a double dissolution accompanying the proclamation.[16]

An anxious governor-general, watching events unfold from Yarralumla, said he now took an important call – from the deposed prime minister. Kerr documented the call in a note for his papers and in his memoirs. Supply had been passed and the House of Representatives had voted against Fraser.

Kerr said: 'He [Whitlam] said that as supply had been granted I should terminate the prime minister's commission and recommission him. He wanted to attend upon me to put this point of view.' According to Kerr, Whitlam said, 'You saw Fraser before, so I suppose you will see me.' Kerr told Whitlam that he would have to secure Fraser's approval for such a meeting. After all, Fraser was now the prime minister. The tables had turned: 'I said I would speak to him and let Mr Whitlam know the position.'[17] This was Kerr stalling Whitlam until the parliament was dissolved and it was too late to consider any alternate action. It was the method Kerr used with Scholes. A second meeting between Kerr and Whitlam on 11 November never took place. Whitlam never spoke to Kerr ever again.

Whitlam later denied making the call. Yet Kerr made a note including the details of the conversation. Whitlam's principal private secretary, John Mant, said it was entirely plausible that Whitlam rang. 'He could well have,' Mant said. 'It's a possibility, yes.'[18]

Any such call would have reinforced Kerr's anxiety about the legal foundation for his ongoing decisions. 'I wanted to have the benefit of legal advice,' he said about events from this stage of the afternoon. 'I knew what had happened that afternoon in Parliament. The consequences of my earlier decision and action could not be blocked nor could I be turned from my course by it.'[19] Kerr's course was set: he was not interested in seeing Scholes. His aim was to dissolve the parliament for the general election campaign.

The head of the Attorney-General's Department, a shocked and unhappy Clarrie Harders, arrived at Fraser's office at about 3.45 p.m. Fraser took Harders into an adjoining room and Harders made a note of their discussion: 'He [Fraser] said that it was possible that the Governor-General would wish to have advice regarding the resolution that had been adopted by the House of Representatives earlier in the afternoon expressing want of confidence in Mr Fraser.'[20]

In short, Kerr had to negotiate his way around the House resolution. He had not anticipated the 'no confidence' motion against Fraser. Fraser understood that Kerr needed to ensure a firm legal foundation for everything he was about to do. Fraser now said he wanted Harders to accompany him to Government House. Harders said that Solicitor-General Maurice Byers should come with them. But there wasn't sufficient time. Fraser could not wait. Harders went with him. They rushed across a crowded King's Hall and outside to a waiting car. 'The crowd was pressing around the car and the driver drove off immediately,' Harders recalled. The car left at 3.50 p.m.

In his note Harders recalled his discussion with Fraser en route: 'I spoke to the prime minister about the point he had raised with me. I said that it appeared that the Governor-General had acted on the basis that he had a reserve power, that the Governor-General had previously exercised a discretion that he regarded as residing in him and that the question whether he should change his decision in the light of the resolution adopted that afternoon by the House of Representatives was one for the Governor-General to consider, in the exercise of his discretion.'

In short, Harders was telling Fraser the transition of power was not yet a done deal. He was saying Kerr had to consider whether he 'should change his decision' given the 'no confidence' resolution in the House.[21] Kerr, of course, had not the slightest intention of changing his decision. But he had to be careful.

Arriving at Government House, Fraser went in to see Kerr alone while Harders made several calls, including to Byers. They discussed the impact of the House resolution and what Harders should advise

Fraser and Kerr. Harders then joined the governor-general and the prime minister.

Kerr's first task was to give royal assent to the supply bills. He then turned his attention to the dissolution of both houses. This action was based on the twenty-one bills – Whitlam's bills blocked by the Coalition opposition over the life of the parliament – that met the section fifty-seven criteria for a double-dissolution election. Fraser advised Kerr the bills satisfied the constitutional requirements for a double-dissolution election. In his note, however, Harders said he raised the consequences of the House of Representatives resolution.

'I stated the view that I had put to the Prime Minister during the journey to Government House,' Harders said. How hard did he press Kerr? In his note Harders did not provide any details of the words he actually used in cautioning the governor-general at such a momentous meeting. Harders said he and Byers had the same view. But Kerr's account is different and detailed.

Kerr said Harders advised 'that in law I could act under section 57 on this oral advice which I had been given by the Prime Minister and by him. I agreed with this. My Official Secretary was present during this conversation and he and I, as well as Mr Fraser, believed that Mr Harders had said that Mr Byers agreed with him not only about the validity of my continuing to carry out, under the reserve power, the "forced dissolution" procedure, but also as to the availability of the twenty-one bills to support a double dissolution.'[22]

The governor-general's account goes to the crux of the issue: 'Mr Harders said he had spoken to Mr Byers and both of them were of the view that, as I had exercised the reserve power in the morning, I could complete its exercise and could accept the advice of the Prime Minister in favour of a double dissolution. I was in effect being told that I did have a reserve power to exercise which would justify a dissolution.'

Harders and Byers believed the reserve powers existed but they had serious doubts about their use in this situation. In his memoirs Kerr said that if Harders and Byers believed he had no valid power to dismiss the Whitlam government they had an obligation to tell him then and there, say it was an invalid act and that it should be undone by recommissioning Whitlam. 'This they did not do,' Kerr said. This is pure sophistry: even if Harders and Byers had said this, Kerr would have proceeded anyway. His memoirs make plain he was not asking the law officers whether they agreed with his decisions – but merely for their views about the validity of the powers he was exercising.

Interviewed later Harders said: 'I didn't doubt that the Governor-General had such a discretion. The problem was the way it was done.'[23] But Kerr was not interested in any Harders view about the way it was done. He cared only for the legal advice on the powers.

The governor-general was anxious yet firm in his own mind. He said that having exercised the reserve power to dismiss Whitlam, he was entitled to continue to exercise the reserve power 'to sustain Mr Fraser in office and to get an election'. Kerr wrote: 'I had a Prime Minister who did not have the confidence of the House but who was prepared in accordance with convention to recommend an election. This was pursuant to his earlier undertaking and I was prepared to accept this advice.'[24]

At 4 p.m., Kerr signed the proclamation dissolving both houses of parliament on the basis of the twenty-one bills. There would be an election on 13 December. Harders journeyed back to Parliament House with Fraser.

Any idea that Kerr at that time would have recommissioned Whitlam was nonsense. Whitlam's argument to this effect is unconvincing. That would have constituted a betrayal of Fraser. Having commissioned Fraser as a caretaker prime minister subject to obtaining supply and advising an election, Kerr could not then turn around and dismiss Fraser after he had fulfilled the terms of his commission as set down by Kerr. The Senate had passed supply only because Fraser was prime minister. The House vote demonstrated what Kerr had known – that Whitlam had its confidence. Kerr knew he was commissioning Fraser as a minority prime minister to advise an election.

If Kerr had reversed his position, he would have had no option but to resign. No governor-general could betray two prime ministers on the one day and still survive.

The public servants were slow to grasp the dynamics of what had happened. This is no surprise since they had not planned for this contingency.

In the morning Kerr had sought tactical advice from Sir Garfield Barwick on how to handle Whitlam in his study when he terminated his commission. Now, in the afternoon, Kerr sought advice from Sir Anthony Mason about how to handle the Speaker. Scholes was carrying a no-confidence motion in Fraser that had been passed by the House. According to Mason, he told Kerr to hold his nerve. 'I said that the resolution was irrelevant as he had commissioned Mr Fraser to form a caretaker government for limited purposes to hold a general election,' Mason recalled.[25] Here was Kerr relying again for reassurance on that 'arch of advice' with Mason at its centre.

Scholes arrived at Government House at 4.25 p.m. and was kept waiting. When the Speaker was ushered in to meet with Kerr at 4.45 p.m., he was promptly told that the parliament had been dissolved.[26] Scholes recalled these events in an interview with Troy Bramston. 'I was at the gate of Government House with a letter that said the House of Representatives had expressed no-confidence in the new prime minister.'[27] Scholes was angry at being 'locked out' by Kerr. 'I told him that he had acted in bad faith,' Scholes recalled. 'I told him that he had acted improperly. I told him he should recommission Gough Whitlam as prime minister.' But Kerr told Scholes it was too late: 'It was done.' Scholes told Kerr he should have 'taken a different course of action'.

Kerr, however, remained anxious the entire afternoon. When Harders returned to his office at about 4.50 p.m., the phone rang. It was Kerr. He had rung through directly himself. He was replaying the events in his mind. 'He referred to the resolution that had been passed by the House of Representatives,' Harders wrote of the phone call.[28] 'The reason for the call was not clear to me. So far as I could sense, however, the call was made for the purpose of asking me to recapitulate the advice I had given to him earlier in the afternoon at Government House. I repeated what I had said.' Harders speculated that Kerr may have had 'some concern' that he 'should have seen' the Speaker before signing the proclamation. But the deed was now done.

As Smith was travelling to Parliament House to read the proclamation he passed the car taking the Speaker to his meeting with the governor-general.[29] At 4.45 p.m. Smith stood on the steps of Parliament House and read the proclamation dissolving both houses. The crowd was now loud and unruly as it swelled in size. Whitlam weaved through the crowd and stood behind Smith, his presence looming large.

'May God save the Queen,' said Smith, concluding his statement. The official secretary exited; Whitlam stepped forward. 'Ladies and gentlemen,' he said. 'Well may we say God save the Queen, because nothing will save the governor-general.' The crowd roared. Whitlam, though defeated, was unbowed. He gave a speech of defiance tinged with bitterness. It was his song of martyrdom. The curtain fell on a day of high drama.

Any hope Whitlam had entertained of being recommissioned lay in ruins. Once again, he had misjudged the power realities.

In truth, Whitlam could have seriously undermined Kerr's game plan after he was dismissed. He failed for three reasons. Whitlam was taken by surprise and did not think fast enough. He had no contingency plan available. And luck ran with Kerr and Fraser.

Whitlam's response to the dismissal was conventional yet ineffective: to move 'no confidence' in Fraser and then approach Kerr. He failed to grasp there had been a complete reversal. The best Whitlam tactic, therefore, was to deny supply to Fraser for as long as possible. There were several delaying options Whitlam could have deployed.[30] The House 'no confidence' resolution would only have traction when combined with Fraser's inability to get supply – and that option had been lost.

On 13 November, parts of the draft Byers legal opinion on the reserve powers were published after being leaked to the *Australian Financial Review*. The report was highly misleading and conveyed the impression Byers advised the powers did not exist. Kerr was immediately concerned. At his initiative the attorney-general in the caretaker government, Senator Ivor Greenwood, convened a meeting on Monday, 17 November at 2.30 p.m., six days after the dismissal. Held at Government House, it involved Kerr, Greenwood, Harders and Byers. The focus was the legal foundation for Kerr's action and, beyond that, his reputation and historical standing.[31]

That afternoon Harders told Kerr that his termination of Whitlam's government had not been justified. Accounts of this meeting illustrate it was highly charged.

Kerr's notes suggest his motive: he wanted to clarify that Harders and Byers accepted the legal basis for the dismissal, and to 'lock' them into his action, as far as possible. But with the deed a week old, Harders and Byers were firm: they accepted the legality but not the justification for the dismissal.

Concerned that his views had been distorted, Byers got Kerr's permission to have his opinion released in full. Kerr then raised with Harders an earlier discussion they had held about the reserve powers on 28 October at a reception for a Public Service Board course. During this discussion Harders had told Kerr he believed the reserve powers existed. 'That was my view and always has been my view,' Harders said later.[32]

Harders reminded Kerr, however, that at this reception the governor-general had said 'that there would surely be a reserve power if there were fighting in the streets'. Kerr quickly replied he meant that 'only as an illustration'. Yet Harders was not persuaded. His memory was Kerr had implied it was only in such extreme circumstances that the reserve powers would be used.

This exchange had had an impact on Harders at the time and he had told Menadue about it. Menadue had made a note of what Harders told him and raised it with Whitlam. Menadue wrote: 'The Governor-General apparently expressed the view that if there was fighting in the streets it might be necessary for him to intervene.' When told, Whitlam retorted: 'If the Governor-General thought that there would be fighting in the streets over the refusal of supply, which might force him to act, there would be even more fighting in the streets if he dismissed the prime minister.'[33]

According to Kerr's record of the 17 November meeting, Harders agreed 'the reserve power of the Crown existed' but he also 'thought a forced dissolution could only be precipitated in extreme circumstances'. Harders was blunt: 'He did not himself believe that the circumstances in which I had acted were serious enough.' The head of the Attorney-General's Department was telling Kerr to his face that his action was unjustified. The tension must have been palpable.

But Kerr would not wear it. He went on the offensive: 'I said to him [Harders], "I have never asked you for your opinion about the seriousness of the circumstances warranting a forced dissolution." ' Kerr continued: 'I said to him that I had to take the responsibility for exercising the discretion which only I possessed and the fact that there might be difference of opinion about circumstances in which it might be exercised was something about which I did not ask his advice or the advice of the law officers of the Crown.'

Much of the discussion then focused on the meeting at Government House during the afternoon of 11 November and the advice given that day by Harders and Byers. Kerr's understanding was that they had told him, having exercised the reserve powers, he could continue to exercise them and accept Fraser's advice to dissolve parliament for an election. According to Kerr's notes: 'Mr Harders then said he had not meant to be expressing approval of what I had done in the morning, as his own view was that things were not serious enough on 11 November for the exercise of the reserve power, but as I had done it I ought to go on to the end.'

Kerr and Greenwood then turned up the pressure on Harders and Byers. They asked them to justify their earlier advice on 11 November: 'Why, if they believed that the power to force a dissolution no longer existed, had they not said so on the afternoon of 11 November?' Harders, according to Kerr's note, said 'the power did exist' but again questioned 'the seriousness of the situation'. Byers said the reserve power existed but expressed doubt over its use regarding 'forced dissolutions'.

Closing the discussion, Kerr went to what he felt was his winning point: 'I said that I thought if either had been of the view that the power had been wrongly used in the morning because of its non-existence they should have said so in the afternoon but that on the contrary they had advised that having been exercised in the morning I need undo nothing but could proceed in logical continuity with what I had done in the morning.'

Kerr's lack of respect for Harders and Byers was obvious. Contempt may be a better word. He felt, having advised him on 11 November that he had the legal power, they were post-event becoming critics. Yet his sensitivity, a touch paranoid, was on display. The quest for justification would consume much of the rest of his life. Meanwhile the tension was now rife with the senior legal officers believing the governor-general had misused his powers.

Harders offered a tortuous explanation for his advice on the afternoon of 11 November saying it appeared to him and Byers that Kerr 'had asked for advice on the basis that he had a reserve power'. This is true. Harders, it seems, merely told Kerr the House resolution was 'an additional circumstance' to be taken into account by the governor-general in the exercise of his discretion.[34] Nowhere does Harders say or imply he told Kerr on 11 November the situation did not justify the use of the reserve powers in either the morning or afternoon.

Harders understood Kerr's motive for the 17 November meeting. 'Looking back,' Harders said. 'I sense here a desire on the part of the Governor-General to seek protection in the circumstances he had been faced with and to endeavour to enlist others in supporting the action he had taken.'[35] Kerr could count on the support of Fraser, Menzies, Barwick, Mason, Ellicott and the conservative establishment. But he would not be able to enlist Harders or Byers as his defenders.

In fact, Harders' view of the dismissal was damning. In a later oral history interview for the National Library, Harders said while he accepted the reserve power, 'I could not agree that the power should have been exercised in the circumstances existing on 11 November ... if my views had been sought I would have said so.'[36] Harders' views were not sought prior to dismissal. He also felt Kerr should not have acted without first warning Whitlam: 'I did not wish to be taken as agreeing that any reserve power should have been exercised in the way that it was exercised without first raising the Governor-General's concern directly with the Prime Minister.'[37]

The conventional public-service view was far distant from that of Kerr. Harders' department, for example, prepared a document on the governor-general's powers dated 10 October 1975, a week before supply was blocked. Marked in pen across the top is Harders' annotation that it is 'an important note'. In the event that supply was blocked, the Attorney-General's Department was 'reasonably clear' about Kerr's role: 'The governor-general would be entitled and indeed bound to act on advice from his ministers that all the possibilities of parliamentary government should be exhausted. Examination of the possibilities would certainly not appear to be any ground for dismissal'.[38]

The gulf between the Kerr and Harders–Byers positions was a chasm. The moral Kerr drew from these discussions with them was that seeking advice from Barwick had been prudent and essential.

Kerr then ensured that Harders' advice on 11 November prevailed in the official record. The day after the 17 November meeting, Kerr wrote to Fraser in response to the prime minister's letter on 12 November forwarding Byers' opinion in respect of the double dissolution. Keen to 'lock in' Harders, Kerr wrote: 'I note that this now confirms the advice given orally to us both by Mr Harders on his own behalf and on behalf of the Solicitor-General.'[39]

Attorney-General Greenwood moved to 'kill' any debate about the reserve powers spilling into the election arena. On 20 November he issued a statement.[40] 'The question whether the Governor-General had the power to act as he did in dismissing the Whitlam government has become a lawyers' question,' Greenwood said. 'There is no question that the reserve power of the Crown exists. It has been dramatically asserted and used. The attempt to build up some controversy about the Solicitor-General's opinion is nit-picking.' He made public the joint opinion dated 23 October written by Keith Aickin, Murray Gleeson and Pat Lane that upheld the notion of the reserve powers.

Greenwood engaged in some indulgence about the dismissal power. 'The people most surprised were some of the commentators and journalists in Canberra,' he said. 'They had deluded themselves that the Governor-General would not act. They were "snowed" by Mr Whitlam's office. There is no refuge in questioning the power of the Governor-General.' Greenwood said the issue of the reserve powers was 'unproductive as an election issue'. This was correct on all counts.

On 12 November 1975, the day after the dismissal, Speaker Scholes wrote to the Palace.[41] It was an understandable but extremely embarrassing letter. Scholes tried to draw the Queen into the crisis. 'I wrote to The Queen to tell her she should reconsider the action of the Governor-General,' Scholes recalled in 2015. 'We were trying very clearly to reverse the decision. We wanted her to act.' Scholes said there was a belief that the Queen could 'override' a governor-general.[42] This was soon proven to be nonsense.

In his letter, Scholes argued Kerr acted as her 'representative' and suggested she take responsibility for his actions. He accused Kerr of 'acts contrary to the proper exercise of the Royal prerogative' by sustaining Fraser in power despite the House voting no confidence in him. '[This] constitutes a danger to our parliamentary system and will damage the standing of your representative in Australia and even yourself,' he implored. 'I would ask that you act in order to restore Mr Whitlam to office as Prime Minister in accordance with the expressed resolution of the House of Representatives.'

The Palace was unmoved. On 17 November 1975, Scholes received a reply from Sir Martin Charteris that was copied to Kerr.[43] 'I am commanded by The Queen to acknowledge your letter of 12th November about the recent political events in Australia,' he wrote. 'As we understand the situation here, the Australian Constitution firmly places the prerogative powers of the Crown in the hands of the Governor-General as the representative of The Queen of Australia.' Only Kerr could commission and remove a prime minister. 'Her Majesty, as Queen of Australia, is watching events in Canberra with close interest and attention, but it would not be proper for her to intervene in person in matters which were so clearly placed within the jurisdiction of the Governor-General by the Constitution Act.' Labor's misjudged appeal to the Queen was a farcical end to its tragedy.

On 26 December 1975, Whitlam wrote to Charteris on leader of the opposition letterhead.[44] The letter was drafted by Graham Freudenberg.[45] 'In no way,' he argued, 'do the elections resolve the legal and constitutional questions raised by the conduct of the Crown's representative on and before 11 November. Nor could the election result of itself legitimise that conduct.' Whitlam's concern was 'the manner in which the Governor-General chose to invoke and exercise the reserve powers' which have 'put in jeopardy the future of the Crown in Australia'. He said confidence in the monarchy was undermined by 'any intervention, or appearance of intervention, on behalf of the contending political parties'. Whitlam detailed what he believed were Kerr's 'political decisions' to assist the Coalition parties. His accusation was that Kerr's actions 'have been such as to call into question on the part of many millions of Australians, particularly the younger majority, not merely the limits of the powers of the Crown, but its whole future role in Australia'.

On 12 January 1976, Whitlam received a reply from Charteris.[46] He said the Queen had read the letter, thanked him for it and 'taken note' of the views. 'I am sure you will neither wish nor expect me to enter into argument about the constitutional propriety of Sir John Kerr's actions,' Charteris wrote. 'I hope, however, you will allow me to make one comment on what you say. It is this. The constitutional role of the Governor-General and his reserve powers stem not from his position as The Queen's personal representative, to which he is appointed on the advice of the Prime Minister, but rather from what is written in the Constitution Act as applicable constitutionally. This point has, I think, particular relevance to the position of the Queen as Queen of Australia.' The Palace was washing its hands of the dismissal.

Whitlam's death as prime minister was confirmed during the afternoon of 11 November amid a series of dramas: allowing the Senate to pass supply, the House voting 'no confidence' in Fraser, a worried Kerr securing the legal advice he needed from law officers who later took a stand against him, the governor-general's rejection of the Speaker and, subsequently, the Queen's cool repudiation of the Speaker acting on Labor's behalf.

This long list of mini-crises testifies to the unsatisfactory nature of Kerr's solution. There is no doubt Kerr's strategy could have been delayed and disrupted with uncertain consequences. But Labor, under Whitlam, was not prepared for such a task or able to seize the opportunities when presented.

PART FIVE

The Aftermath

The British View

Nine days after the dismissal, the British high commissioner to Australia, Sir Morrice James, despatched a secret report to London. The message was clear: the British diplomats in Canberra did not endorse Sir John Kerr's decision to terminate the government. 'It seems open to question whether the situation on 11 November was so desperate, so extreme, that such a drastic exercise of the vice-regal reserve power was both justified and likely to be seen to be justified,' wrote James.[1]

In short, the British view from Canberra was that the political circumstances did not warrant dismissal. They could not imagine the Queen acting in this way. This was the message from the British High Commission to the United Kingdom government. The assessment came at the end of a long series of reports over previous weeks on Australia's constitutional crisis. The High Commission was concerned about the impact of Kerr's decision on the standing of the Crown in Australia, the role of the governor-general, the position of state governors and the future for Australia's political institutions. These records are held at the UK National Archives in Kew, outside of London, and were accessed for this book.

James also relayed to London a discussion with Kerr that took place just one week after Malcolm Fraser's crushing electoral victory on 13 December 1975.[2] Over tea at Government House, Kerr made an extraordinary comment to James. 'Sir J Kerr thought it no bad thing that the public in Australia (and perhaps also those in other monarchical Commonwealth countries, not excluding Britain) should have been reminded that the Crown possessed reserve powers,' James wrote. The use of such extraordinary powers, Kerr argued, was a good thing and should be seen throughout the Commonwealth as a sign of the Crown's authority.

Kerr was undeterred by the reaction to his exercise of the dismissal power as the Queen's representative. Indeed, he was recommending that voters need 'a reminder' that the powers exist and he suggested they be used perhaps 'every twenty-five or fifty years'. Invoking the royal prerogative would reinforce the point that 'the Crown's functions were not merely titular and/or ceremonial'. Kerr said Whitlam was wrong to assume the governor-general 'had no power to act save as the Prime Minister advised'. Here was Kerr, one month after the dismissal, arguing to British government representatives that each generation needed reminding about these unique powers. It seemed more than slightly mad.

This British surprise about the dismissal was echoed in Whitehall and Downing Street. Whitlam had met Prime Minister Harold Wilson in London several times, in government and opposition, and they got along reasonably well. Their last meeting in London had been in December 1974. There was shock inside Number 10 when they heard that Kerr had exercised the reserve powers to dismiss Whitlam. Wilson's press secretary, Joe Haines, referred in his memoir to Whitlam 'being dismissed from office by the unelected governor-general' and noted that he did so 'using powers that everyone thought had fallen into disuse'.[3]

Bernard Donoughue ran the policy unit at Number 10. He was part of the so-called kitchen cabinet with Haines and Marcia Williams, the prime minister's personal and political secretary. In an interview for this book, Donoughue remembered the reaction in Number 10. 'I recall the shock at his dismissal,' Donoughue told Troy Bramston.[4] 'Wilson was always very interested in Australia, he got on well with Whitlam and was a great Commonwealth man.' He agreed with Haines that the view in Number 10 was the reserve power to dismiss a prime minister had fallen into disuse and was redundant.

Wilson had responded to a question in House of Commons about the dismissal on 11 November 1975. Conservative Party politician Tim Renton asked Wilson, somewhat cryptically, when he next planned to visit Australia.[5] 'Would not such a visit provide the prime minister with a salutary lesson? Does not what is happening in Australia at the moment show the dangers of a federal or devolved form of government?'

Wilson brushed off any comparison with Whitlam. He did not condemn or endorse Kerr's actions. 'The Hon. Member is wrong, I think, to draw any conclusions for our own affairs from any problems which arise in Australia, for which there is no ministerial or parliamentary responsibility at Westminster,' Wilson said. He would not be publicly drawn on the crisis. 'It would be highly improper for any of us to enter into these very difficult problems – constitutional and others – which have arisen in Australia,' he said.

But the nine-page, 20 November 1975 report from James to the Secretary of State for Foreign and Commonwealth Affairs revealed a robust and discerning view of the dismissal. James identified the problem of timing as central to the governor-general's intervention:

> Had Sir John Kerr waited until essential government services had ground to a halt, until real hardship began to be felt, then there could have been little argument about the need for his intervention. Perhaps he acted in the belief that if he postponed his intervention fresh elections would have had to wait until the end of the Australian summer holiday period in February, leaving an unacceptably long delay before the people's decision could

resolve the deadlock. But by moving when he did, he laid himself open to the charge that he jumped the gun.

James wrote that Kerr 'acted with courage from the highest motives'. He did not doubt his 'legal skill' in doing so. But his assessment of Kerr's intervention is damning:

> The Senate had not yet actually rejected the Bills, only deferred action on them. The opinion polls were exerting growing pressure on Mr Fraser or the Liberal Senators to find a way of climbing down: perhaps in another few days they would have done so. Existing appropriations had not yet run out: Mr Whitlam still had two or three weeks in hand. His threats of impending economic and financial hardship as a result of the opposition's actions could have been regarded as bluff, designed to pile on the pressure for an opposition surrender, rather than as scientific predictions for an inescapable future. Even if the opposition had stood firm for another two weeks, perhaps Mr Whitlam would have adopted some other tactic – even agreeing to a dissolution of the House – rather than merely staying in office and finding debatable means of spending public money without parliamentary authority.

James also suggested that Kerr had alternatives to dismissal, including warning Whitlam, available to him:

> Perhaps a straightforward demand by the Governor-General that Mr Whitlam should take some more positive step, or else face dismissal, might have broken up the log jam. Certainly Sir John Kerr's action seems to have been based on a series of assumptions, any one of which might legitimately have been regarded as unwarranted.

From mid-October 1975, the Foreign and Commonwealth Office, through the British High Commission in Canberra, monitored developments closely. The British government's main concern was to ensure that neither the government nor the Queen was involved in the crisis. The Queen's private secretary, Sir Martin Charteris, asked to be informed of any potential situation where the Queen might be involved. The British were concerned about the possibility that state premiers might advise their governors not to issue writs for any half-senate election requested by Whitlam. NSW governor Sir Roden Cutler raised with the British the notion that Whitlam, in this situation, might advise the governor-general to ask the Queen to instruct state governors to issue the writs. Cutler told British diplomats that 'he would feel obliged to resign' if that happened while expressing confidence that the situation would not arise.[6]

On 17 December, James met with Whitlam in Canberra and passed on a sympathetic message from Wilson. Whitlam gave James his assessment of the legacy from the crisis. 'Speaking reflectively and with no particular heat,' James reported, 'he said that it had come as a great shock to the whole Labor movement to find that the Crown's reserve powers of (he had thought) long ago could be resuscitated at this late stage to the advantage of those forces here who were opposed to social progress.'

Whitlam said he did not believe the Queen would have acted as Kerr did. He warned that henceforth the monarchy was 'at risk' in Australia and republican sentiment would be energised. He said Kerr would be subject to hostile demonstrations. Whitlam said he believed Fraser had had prior warning of Kerr's intentions and speculated this had come from Sir Garfield Barwick to Bob Ellicott. In his report James dismissed these comments from Whitlam as 'a reflection of his own deep-seated disappointment and bitterness' rather than 'an objective forecast' of the future.

Whitlam also shared his views with Wilson. In a remarkable letter, written on 31 December 1975, Whitlam opened a window into his state of mind a fortnight after Labor's election defeat.[7] 'No one knows better than you the penalties paid by social democratic governments in times of economic difficulty,' Whitlam wrote. 'We take heart from the example you set between 1970 and 1974 in leading the Labor Party to a successful and, I believe, long-lasting restoration of its fortunes.'

On the dismissal – the real purpose of the letter – Whitlam was blunt: 'It is, in my view, quite simply intolerable that an elected government should have its term cut short at the behest of an unrepresentative upper house through the exercise of the reserve powers of the Crown.' He urged Wilson to 'look carefully at the dangerous implications' of what had happened in Australia on 11 November 1975. The truth, of course, is that the dismissal had no consequences for the monarchy in Britain.

In his 20 November report to London, James reflected on 'the lamentable dramas' that had gripped Australia in the weeks preceding the dismissal. James said 'the real villain' was the Australian Constitution, which sought to combine an upper house, the Senate, on the American model, with a lower house based on the Westminster model that determined the right to form a government. He said this contradiction, sooner or later, was likely to 'come unstuck'.

Referring to the principal protagonists, James said: 'Certainly the naked ambition for power of Mr Fraser, and the obduracy of Mr Whitlam, have contributed to the crisis, and it is impossible to dismiss completely the suspicion that Sir John Kerr's judgement has been open to question.' His harshest assessment fell on Kerr.

The British high commissioner said Kerr's dismissal 'took the entire nation by surprise'. Its timing and manner disturbed the representatives of Her Majesty's government in Canberra, more accustomed to the wisdom, caution and impartiality of the Queen. 'Not for many years can there have been so bold and controversial an exercise of the reserve powers of the Crown in a constitutional monarchy of the Westminster pattern,' James wrote. 'And not for many years to come will there be an end to the political and constitutional reverberations of Sir John Kerr's action.'

The CIA:
The Great Myth

In the years following the dismissal of the Whitlam government, a conspiracy industry emerged that tried to conflate a political crisis with a security crisis. It propagated the notion that Sir John Kerr acted on instructions from, or to satisfy, the US Central Intelligence Agency (CIA), the British security service (MI5) or its foreign section (MI6), or even Australia's own Australian Security Intelligence Organisation (ASIO). While devoid of evidence and fanciful, the notion of an intelligence or security conspiracy behind the dismissal has nevertheless permeated subsequent reporting and writing about these events.

As this book shows, the entire story of the dismissal and its motivations is explained by political and constitutional events tied to the personalities and characters of the main players: John Kerr, Gough Whitlam and Malcolm Fraser. This story is fantastic enough in terms of intrigue and deception. There is no need to create a conspiracy about intelligence and security events.

The dismissal, however, occurred at the same time as a crisis erupted in the Australian–US intelligence relationship. It sprang from concern in the United States that the Whitlam government would not renew the agreement covering the Pine Gap intelligence facility near Alice Springs. Kerr was sometimes assumed to have intelligence involvement because of his role during the war as deputy director of the Directorate of Research and Civil Affairs at Land Headquarters in Melbourne. And the CIA was known to have intervened in the domestic affairs of several countries in the 1970s, most notably Chile.

The attempt to join these elements into a theory to satisfy Kerr's dismissal of the government on 11 November 1975 has spawned a cottage industry sustained by a range of figures such as documentary filmmaker and UK-based Australian journalist John Pilger and legendary investigative journalist Brian Toohey, among others. This bizarre take on the dismissal has also been immortalised in fiction, most recently by Peter Carey in his novel *Amnesia*.

In his memoirs, Kerr repudiated one of the pivotal claims of the conspiracy theorists – that he had been associated with the intelligence community. He said of the World War Two organisation the Directorate that 'it never did intelligence work, nor did I'. Referring to the wider claims, Kerr said:

> An absurd story was put about that I became some kind of intelligence operative in the war years and maintained some intelligence affiliations thereafter. Alleged later connections with the CIA have been the subject of rumour and gossip. This is and always has been false in relation to the CIA and to all US and other intelligence activity. I have had no direct or indirect connections at any time, during or after the war, with any intelligence organisations including our own. Only the more gullible subscribers to the conspiracy theory of history could believe or want to believe such nonsense.[1]

The central problem with the conspiracy theory has been the absence of any link between the 1975 security/intelligence crisis and the 1975 political/constitutional crisis. They exist as parallel yet unrelated events. Whenever a story emerges about the security/intelligence crisis, the question is invariably posed: was it related to the dismissal? Yet there has never been any evidence produced that Kerr's motive in dismissing Whitlam was about security issues concerning the CIA or any other agency.

A bizarre meeting twenty months after the dismissal between opposition leader Gough Whitlam and the United States' deputy secretary of state for Asia and the South Pacific, Warren Christopher, has been cited by former Whitlam aide Richard Butler as evidence of a conspiracy of some kind. The meeting took place at the Qantas VIP room at Sydney Airport at 8 a.m. on 27 July 1977.[2]

Christopher, a high-ranking member of Jimmy Carter's administration, was on his way to New Zealand for ANZUS talks. Also present were Philip Alston, the United States' ambassador to Australia, who arranged the meeting, his aide, and Whitlam's aide, Butler. Whitlam recalled: 'He made it clear to us that he had made a special detour in his itinerary for the sole purpose of speaking to me.'

Christopher had a message for Whitlam from President Carter. The message, according to Whitlam, was that the president had asked Christopher to say:

1. That he understood the Democrats and the ALP were fraternal parties;
2. That he respected deeply the democratic rights of the allies of the US;
3. That the US Administration would never again interfere in the domestic political processes of Australia; and
4. That he would work with whatever government the people of Australia elected.[3]

In 2014, Butler told journalist and former Fairfax chief editorial executive Max Suich that Christopher's cryptic message was tantamount to an admission that the United States had been involved in

Whitlam's dismissal. 'It seemed obvious to me that the US had a role in the dismissal,' Butler said.[4] He was short on any substantiating detail.

In August 2015, Troy Bramston interviewed Carter. This interview is believed to be his only response to the question of alleged CIA involvement in Whitlam's dismissal and the Whitlam–Christopher meeting. Carter said he was not aware of any CIA involvement in Australia under the previous Republican administration of Richard Nixon and Gerald Ford, or their Democratic predecessors:

> **Bramston:** It is a curious meeting. Do you recall sending Mr Christopher to Australia to give this message to Gough Whitlam?
> **Carter:** In a hazy way. I had a very strong feeling of commitment to both Australia and to other countries like Canada, for instance, as they chose over a period of historic length to express more clearly their own independence rather than their dependence upon, or subservience in any way, to the British monarch. And so that was a basic commitment of mine . . .
> **Bramston:** Were you concerned at all that the CIA had been involved in Australian politics under the Nixon–Ford administration?
> **Carter:** I don't remember that concern.
> **Bramston:** Okay. Were you concerned at all that the CIA may have been involved in Gough Whitlam's dismissal?
> **Carter:** There was no doubt about the fact that the CIA had done some dastardly things before I was elected president. Those revelations occurred in the so-called Frank Church senatorial investigating committee when Gerald Ford was in office and earlier when Richard Nixon was in office. But even some other presidents had permitted or ordered the CIA to commit crimes of violence against political leaders with whom we had a difference. But that was obviously the things I had known about earlier. If you look at the record, I issued a directive when I became

president prohibiting any sort of improper or illegal activity by the
CIA or other American agencies overseas.

Bramston: I guess there might have been some concern in your
administration that these things had been going on in Australia
and other overseas countries previously?

Carter: Well, they had been. There's no doubt. I don't know about
Australia specifically. But I know in Chile, for instance, Iran and
Cuba, and so forth, there had been examples of improper actions
by the security forces of America, yes.[5]

This indicates that Carter – who campaigned for the presidency
in 1976 on a platform to restore integrity to the White House in the
aftermath of the Watergate scandal – was sending a message that CIA
interference in the politics of other countries would no longer be tolerated. There would be no more dirty tricks. Carter made no specific
reference to Australia. It is possible that Christopher was communi-
cating a blanket statement to Whitlam linked to Carter's presidential
directive.

In 2014, Bramston engaged a researcher to examine the Warren
Christopher Papers at the Hoover Institution Archives at Stanford
University in California. There is no record of the meeting with
Whitlam or any documentation that sheds light on it.

If anyone had cause to fan speculation about a CIA link to the dismissal it might be Whitlam. Yet he never thought the United States
intelligence agency had any involvement in his downfall. 'I have
always resisted the notion that the Central Intelligence Agency was
responsible for the dismissal,' he wrote. 'I take the view that all the
events of October and November 1975, including Kerr's conduct and
motives, are sufficiently explained by the internal record; there is no
need to introduce an external conspiracy.'[6]

This is a position founded in common sense and historical
evidence.

To examine how these claims of conspiracy got traction, it is useful to unpack the elements that gave rise to a crisis in Australian–US intelligence relations at the time of the dismissal. The context is important. There were fears inside the CIA about the future of the Pine Gap agreement governing the intelligence/defence installation near Alice Springs. This concern was heightened when Whitlam threatened to name CIA personnel who had operated in Australia.

In the months before the dismissal, Whitlam had become deeply disenchanted with Australia's security agencies. In October 1975, he removed the head of the Australian Secret Intelligence Service (ASIS), William T Robertson, the final trigger being ASIS activities in East Timor. Whitlam had also been angered to find that ASIS officers had worked with the CIA in undermining the left-wing Allende government in Chile. He had also removed the head of ASIO, Peter Barbour, partly as a result of damaging material discovered by Mr Justice Hope during his Royal Commission on Intelligence and Security.[7]

A flashpoint came when Labor staffers began to investigate the role of the CIA in Australia. This included staff from Whitlam's office. In particular, they received a tip that the American who had established the Pine Gap base, Richard Lee Stallings, had been employed by the CIA. An initial line of inquiry was the suspicion that Stallings may have handed over funds to political parties. Suspicions deepened when it was discovered that Stallings, at one point, had been renting the Canberra house of the leader of the National–Country Party, Doug Anthony.

Whitlam's office decided the only way its information about Stallings could be verified was by asking the bureaucracy for a list of CIA agents who had operated in Australia. Accordingly, Whitlam asked both the foreign affairs department and the defence department. Stallings' name was on the defence list but not the foreign affairs list. This was extremely sensitive information – while Pine Gap was publicly stated to be the responsibility of the US defence department, it was overseen by the CIA because of its vital intelligence functions.

Whitlam now went public in a calculated political strike. On 2

November 1975, he casually suggested at a Labor Party rally at Port Augusta that Anthony and the National–Country Party had received funds from the CIA and that Anthony had personal connections with the agency. It was followed by reports by Toohey in the *Australian Financial Review* on 3 and 4 November that named Stallings, outlined the connection with Anthony and tied Stallings to Pine Gap.

These stories and Whitlam's comments created a sensation in the US embassy, the intelligence community and the defence department. Revelations that Stallings had been employed by the CIA and not the US defence department left the implication that the CIA was running Pine Gap.[8]

The events sent alarm bells ringing at the CIA in Washington and with the head of Australia's defence department, the legendary Sir Arthur Tange. A guardian of the US defence and intelligence relationship with Australia, Tange realised the relationship was coming under threat. Deeply worried, Tange spoke with Defence Minister Bill Morrison, who then saw Anthony in an effort to defuse the public Whitlam–Anthony brawl that risked bringing more sensitive material into the public arena.

But the political genie was out of the bottle. Anxious to defend himself and clear his name, Anthony asked Whitlam in parliament to prove his house had been rented by a CIA official. Anthony, in fact, was an innocent party and did not realise that Stallings, whom he knew, had been CIA. On 5 and 6 November, Anthony pursued the matter in letters to, and articles in, newspapers rebutting the allegations made by Whitlam.

On 6 November, Anthony gave notice of a question in parliament to Whitlam that sought evidence Stallings was a CIA employee. This was prompted by a report in *The Australian* by John Raedler which quoted a state department official denying Stallings had worked for any US intelligence agencies. The issue came to a climax over the weekend of 8–9 November. A draft answer to Anthony's question, prepared by Whitlam's office, in effect confirmed that Stallings had been a CIA employee. When Whitlam read this proposed answer to Tange over the phone, Tange was horrified and was convinced it would inflame the Americans to the point of 'jeopardising the alliance'.[9]

Tange urged Whitlam to stick to the Pentagon's proposed statement that Stallings was employed by them and not by the CIA. He spent much time in phone contact with Whitlam's office chief, John Mant, seeking to persuade the prime minister to use a different form of words from those drafted. At one point on 10 November, Tange said to another staffer from Whitlam's office: 'This is the gravest risk to the nation's security there has ever been.' He issued another warning to his minister.[10] Whitlam was due to give his answer in the afternoon of 11 November; it was never delivered. Tange said later his efforts to warn of the dangers were 'treated with derision' by Labor staffers.[11]

At this point, one of the most dramatic cables in Australia's political history was sent from the ASIO liaison officer in Washington DC to the acting director-general at ASIO headquarters in Melbourne, marked 'top secret'. It was based on a briefing the head of the East Asia Division of the CIA, Ted Shackley, had given to the Washington DC ASIO officer. Two main themes run through the cable: that open discussion in Australian politics threatened to 'blow the lid off' US bases operating in Australia, particularly Pine Gap, and second, that the revelation about CIA employees would destroy the trust and cooperation between the two services.

The cable pointed out that many news agencies had made inquiries of the Pentagon about the Stallings allegations. It reported the CIA was deeply troubled and was wondering whether Whitlam's public statements signalled a change in Australia's attitude towards the bilateral security/intelligence relationship. The cable said: 'The CIA feels that . . . if this problem cannot be solved they do not see how our mutually beneficial relationships are going to continue . . . The CIA does not lightly adopt this attitude.' Shackley expressed 'grave concern' about the renewal of the Pine Gap agreement (Whitlam had already stated publicly that the agreement would be renewed). The CIA was alarmed about possible public disclosures about the operations at Pine Gap and the true nature of the US installations in Australia.

In those days there was no official disclosure of any of the functions at Pine Gap, a highly sophisticated facility tied into a series of secret US satellite programs involving intelligence gathering and early-warning arrangements. The cable suggested that the CIA felt diplomatic channels had failed to contain the issue and that it was now time to appeal to ASIO. This was intended as a 'service-to-service' message. But the acting head of ASIO, given the sensitivity, sent the cable to Whitlam's office.

Paul Kelly read the cable in early 1976 and included a chapter on the security crisis in his book that year on the Whitlam government and the dismissal. Kelly said the security crisis 'provided the necessary material for a pervasive conspiracy theory surrounding Whitlam's dismissal' but concluded there was 'no evidence' to sustain the theory. Kelly said the security crisis was never discussed at any of the meetings involving Kerr and Fraser or Kerr and Whitlam. He dismissed any suggestion that Tange had briefed Kerr on the intelligence issue.[12]

Mant said he was contacted several times in the lead-up to the dismissal by American 'spooks' concerned about the renewal of the Pine Gap agreement. In an interview for this book, Mant said, 'I don't believe' the 'conspiracy version' of the dismissal but it 'makes us all feel better'.[13] He recalled being given a 'private letter' by the Americans to give to Whitlam in Melbourne on 10 November that outlined their concerns. Mant recalled: 'Whitlam said: "I've never seen them like this, I've never seen it like this." He was sort of shocked, amazed and stunned. That was the general feeling . . . amongst the intelligence organisations, the sense of real panic.' This reveals Whitlam's naivety: he didn't grasp the alarm his public statements were generating in US intelligence circles.

The CIA was easily alarmed by developments in Australian politics. Nevertheless the recklessness of Whitlam's campaign was guaranteed to produce such alarm. The CIA was not alone. The Australian intelligence community and Tange, as the government's principal defence adviser, were panicked about the future of the alliance and the security surrounding Pine Gap. Beyond that, the CIA had paranoid fears that Jim Cairns, the left-wing ALP minister destroyed by the loans affair, might threaten Whitlam's hold on the prime ministership and imperil the ANZUS alliance.[14]

An article about the 10 November cable by Toohey in the *Australian Financial Review* in February 1976 prompted the preparation of a briefing note for Prime Minister Malcolm Fraser. 'As it stands, the article does not make any explicit connection between the Governor-General and the CIA, only raising questions about it,' the note summarised. 'It will feed conspiracy theories.'[15] The reality is that there is no evidence in Fraser's papers to lend any weight to the idea the cable was linked to the dismissal.

The conspiracy theory, however, was recycled on a regular basis over the next couple of decades. The focus now fell upon Tange and the suspicion that he had briefed Kerr in the days before the dismissal. The implication was that Tange or another defence official had supposedly communicated concerns about the security relationship to Kerr, acting as a conduit of the CIA and/or British intelligence. None of these accusations has ever been substantiated.

Writing in the *Australian Financial Review* in April 1977, Toohey claimed that a defence department official briefed Kerr on 8 November about concerns in the CIA. The official was Chief Defence Scientist Dr John Farrands, who spoke to Toohey over drinks one bright afternoon at a splendid parliamentary garden party in the Senate rose garden. This encounter became the subject of many reports for many years, with Toohey and Farrands disagreeing over what was said.[16]

However, the idea that Tange or Farrands had briefed Kerr about security issues, including possibly Pine Gap, just three days before the dismissal seemed too irresistible a notion to abandon. The broader context was that Whitlam was a threat to the alliance. The point sometimes made explicit, sometimes implied in journalistic reports, was that

Whitlam was sacked in the name of intelligence and security. But in most of his reports, Toohey included the critical qualification: the lack of hard evidence tying the security crisis to the dismissal. On the other hand, the gullible in the arts community swallowed the entire mythology.

Farrands denied he had briefed Kerr on 8 November. Yet the story would not die, fed by many ALP figures, still angry about the dismissal and ready to inflate the magnitude of the 'crime' against them. Writing in the *National Times* in March 1982, Toohey reheated his allegations and claimed that Farrands had briefed Kerr via phone on the weekend prior to the dismissal, 8–9 November, with Tange's but without Whitlam's knowledge.[17]

Farrands issued a comprehensive denial, in particular saying he had never discussed with Kerr any American activities in Australia. Farrands and Tange, both in retirement, launched legal action against Fairfax over the article. Both were insulted at what they believed was the implication: their disloyalty to the elected Australian government. For Tange, who had served both Labor and Coalition governments, this was an unforgivable slur. The newspaper backtracked in part on the allegations.[18] It published a denial from Farrands and later a letter from Tange, which read: 'I did not conceive in my own mind, much less take any action directed towards, any communication whatsoever with the Governor-General, then or at any other time on any matter canvassed in your article.'[19]

Tange's denial was as comprehensive as possible. In the end, Tange had his letter published and his costs paid. He decided not to pursue the issue further.

Writing in the *National Times* in November 1985, Toohey repeated the central allegation 'that Kerr was briefed on the CIA concern' but did not name Tange or Farrands, and noted Kerr's denial of any briefing.[20]

Tange's biographer, the historian Peter Edwards, had unfettered access to Tange's papers and concludes he is 'innocent' of any impropriety. 'It was utterly foreign to his character and his credo as a public

servant to be involved in a conspiracy against his elected government,'
Edwards writes. 'Moreover, he was never one to give uncritical alle-
giance to Washington or to any supposed secretive club of cold war
intelligence operatives.'[21]

The matter, however, was resurrected when, in 1988, Pilger claimed:
'British intelligence, which means both MI6 and MI5, played a significant part in the downfall of the Whitlam government. During 1974
and 1975 senior British intelligence officers were contacted by the CIA
through conduits and directly in London and Washington, and asked
to assist in bringing about Mr Whitlam's political demise.'[22]

Pilger's research assistant, William Pinwill, told Tange before the
documentary went to air that he had been named by a CIA official
as the link between the CIA and Kerr. But when it went to air, given
Tange's mention of previous legal action, he was not named. Indeed,
there was no documentary evidence or on-the-record interviews to
support this assertion. These claims were made in Pilger's documentary
The Last Dream and in his book *A Secret Country* the following year.[23]

Paul Kelly spoke to Tange at length at this time and subsequently
wrote in *The Australian* that Tange was the suspected figure in the
documentary named, according to Pilger, by a 'very senior source in
the CIA'. Tange vigorously denied the allegation. In January 1988,
Kelly wrote: 'Pilger's latest recycling of this conspiracy theory fails,
just as every previous attempt has failed, to establish any new conspiracy – to show that Sir John's dismissal notice had anything to do with
the CIA, intelligence links with the US or the Pine Gap base.'[24]

Political commentator Gerard Henderson put the Pilger allegations directly to Kerr in an interview for the *Weekend Australian* in
1988.[25] 'I did it myself in 1975,' Kerr said. 'I sacked Whitlam. Nobody
else did. Nobody else inspired me to do it, nobody else asked me to do
it.' Kerr disputed reports he was briefed by security officials on Pine
Gap or other intelligence installations by any Australian intelligence
agency in the weeks prior to the dismissal. 'I was getting ready to deal
with the biggest constitutional crisis Australia had ever faced,' Kerr

told Henderson. 'As far as I was concerned the joint facilities were of no relevance to this crisis.'

Following Whitlam's death in October 2014, Pilger returned to this theme in an article, predictably, for *The Guardian*.[26] Again, Pilger referred to his interview in the 1980s with a former CIA officer, Victor Marchetti, who was involved in the establishment of Pine Gap. 'This threat to close Pine Gap caused apoplexy in the White House . . . a kind of Chile [coup] was set in motion,' Marchetti told Pilger. A deputy director of the CIA – unnamed – told Pilger: 'Kerr did what he was told to do.'

Unfortunately for the mythologists, Kerr was agonisingly busy on the constitutional crisis. Once again, there was no smoking gun, no evidence to sustain a conspiracy theory.

Another element in the CIA conspiracy theory was provided by Christopher Boyce, who worked for the CIA-contracted aerospace firm TRW Incorporated, decoding and distributing messages from Pine Gap.[27] Boyce spent nearly twenty-five years in jail for selling CIA secrets to the Russians in the 1970s. In 1982, Boyce told journalist Ray Martin, then with *60 Minutes*, that the CIA was involved in the dismissal. He claimed that Kerr was a CIA 'flunkey' and known as 'our man Kerr' in the intelligence community. Mark Davis interviewed Boyce in 2014 for the SBS *Dateline* program. Boyce claimed the United States was concerned that Whitlam would withdraw from the Pine Gap agreement, threatening intelligence cooperation. Whitlam 'was viewed as a threat to the program', he said. There was 'jubilation' and 'relief' in the CIA when Whitlam was dismissed. However, Boyce acknowledged he could not 'prove' the CIA had any direct involvement in the dismissal.

A comprehensive account of the Australian–US security relationship is provided by Australian academic James Curran in his book *Unholy Fury: Whitlam and Nixon at War*.[28] Curran shows, from the documents, that Australia came close to losing the alliance due to a dramatic shift in foreign policy initiated in the early days of the

Whitlam government that upset the Nixon administration.[29] But Curran's examination of US government files, including declassified CIA documents, concludes there is no evidence to support claims of CIA involvement in Whitlam's dismissal.

Rumours of a foreign intelligence link to Whitlam's dismissal have not abated and probably never will. That testifies to the allure of the idea. Even Margaret Whitlam thought the CIA was involved in the dismissal. She told journalist Candace Sutton in April 1991: 'I do. He [Gough] doesn't. As an old thriller reader I'm prepared to believe it.'[30]

And that's the point: it is a tantalising idea that excites the imagination. It has the attraction of being a sinister explanation for events that otherwise testify to human frailties and ineptitude. The CIA conspiracy theory is emotionally convenient. It exempts us all as Australians from the mess of 1975 and means we can resort to the xenophobia of the 'foreign bogy' yet again as the driving force actually responsible for the dismissal. It has a deep psychological appeal that exploits the cultural cringe still beating in the heart of a nation that is close but has yet to attain full maturity.

In truth, the 1975 security crisis and constitutional crisis were parallel but unconnected events. The concerns about the Whitlam government in the intelligence community and the CIA were real and deep. If there was any connection between these crises, it would have emerged well and truly before now, given the obsession with this issue over the past forty years. The origin, course and resolution of the dismissal are explained, yet again, in this book within the operation of the political and constitutional system. If radicals are searching for something to fume about, there is no shortage of material in this narrative. It does not need embellishment from the CIA.

A mature nation should be able to see its history in an authentic and honest light rather than fabricate conspiracies to excuse its failures. In the absence of new and definitive evidence, the CIA explanation for the dismissal will remain exactly where it sits today: as nothing but a myth.

18

The Liberal
Judgement

The Liberal Party judgement on the events of 1975 is largely sympathetic to Sir John Kerr's predicament and solution, offers qualified support to Malcolm Fraser's decision to block supply to remove the Whitlam government and is mixed about the role of Sir Garfield Barwick. There is an undefined yet pervasive view that the 1975 crisis and dismissal was an inhibiting impact on Fraser and may have restrained him in office. There is agreement that because the crisis provoked such community divisions, the blocking of supply is most unlikely to be repeated. There is no appetite in the Liberal Party today for the multiple breaches of convention that 1975 involved.

The authors conducted new interviews for this book with every Liberal leader since Fraser – Andrew Peacock, John Howard, John Hewson, Alexander Downer, Brendan Nelson, Malcolm Turnbull and Tony Abbott. The book also includes interviews with former treasurer Peter Costello and a number of Fraser's close confidants.

The Liberal leader most critical about the events of 1975 is Turnbull – he offers a robust rejection of the roles of Kerr and Barwick. 'I was surprised and shocked that Kerr did it,' Turnbull said.[1] 'Kerr should have given Whitlam full notice of what he was proposing to do.' He recalled a post-1975 discussion with Kerr in London. Turnbull said: 'Kerr of course said to me, "If I had done that, Whitlam would have sacked me." I think that's a very poor excuse. You know, you have got to do your job . . . all of us should be fulfilling our duty and not having regard to self-interest like that.'

As a student and journalist, Turnbull was familiar with the reserve powers. He had interviewed former NSW premier Jack Lang, who was sacked by Governor Philip Game in 1932, and also William McKell, a former NSW premier and governor-general. Turnbull's view was formed early. He wrote a perceptive article for the paper *Nation Review*, published in mid-November 1975, saying Whitlam was now assured 'of the foremost place in the hagiography' of Labor and that Kerr's mistake was his failure to give Whitlam 'the choice' of going to the election as prime minister.

Turnbull said while Fraser's decision to block supply was constitutionally sound, the real test becomes a political judgement: 'The public were completely fed up with the Whitlam government. They wanted to be rid of it, as was evidenced in the election, even though my sense was that Kerr's sacking of Whitlam was very unpopular.'

With the benefit of hindsight, would he have adopted Fraser's strategy and blocked supply? 'My judgement would have been probably not,' Turnbull said. 'The Whitlam government was irretrievable. Fraser was clearly going to win an election. How soon it happened was whether it happened in '75 or '76. It couldn't have gone further than '77, of course . . . I think Fraser underestimated the level of division and bitterness.' Turnbull believed Fraser paid a price for pushing the political system to the brink. 'The prize was coming into his lap,' he said. 'With the benefit of hindsight, it would have been better not to push it that hard.'

But Turnbull also offered a defence of Fraser. 'You can't blame Fraser for what Kerr did,' he says. 'I mean, Fraser pushed the envelope. In some respects, Fraser wears some of the consequences of a misjudgement by Kerr.' He added: 'I think that the opprobrium that attached to him [Fraser] and blocking supply would have been much, much less if Kerr had not sacked Whitlam in the way that he did.'

Turnbull believed it was a mistake for Kerr to seek advice from Barwick, and for Barwick to provide it. 'I don't think he [Kerr] should have sought advice from the Chief Justice,' Turnbull said. 'I don't think the chief justice or a justice of the High Court should be giving advice to the governor-general . . . I am not saying it was illegal or unconstitutional . . . But, you know, Barwick of course [was] a highly political character [and] he would have been itching to get himself into the middle of this. I mean, if Kerr hadn't asked him for advice, Barwick would have sent it unsolicited, if necessary, in a plain envelope.' Turnbull does not believe Barwick's role damaged the standing of the High Court but says it was not his 'finest hour'.

In every respect Abbott, perhaps unsurprisingly, has the opposite view to Turnbull. It is an insight into their contrasting backgrounds that the two most prominent Liberals of the current age have such conflicting assessments of the 1975 crisis. Abbott finds no fault with Fraser, Kerr or Barwick.

'Whitlam was a great ex-prime minister,' Abbott said in the interview. 'But he was a terrible prime minister. The government was shambolic.'[2] Abbott saw the dismissal as a 'watershed' event for the 1970s political generation, an event that was 'polarising, opinion forming, even character changing'. He said that Fraser made the test for blocking supply 'extraordinary and reprehensible circumstances' and in the end that test was met.

'So did John Kerr do the right thing?' Abbott asked rhetorically. 'My judgement then was, "Yes, he did." Am I inclined to change that judgement today? No, I am not. It was right for Fraser to do what he did with supply. And given how Whitlam was reacting to it, I think the governor-general as umpire in these sorts of matters had to resolve the situation. I think he did the right thing.' Unlike Turnbull, Abbott wouldn't be 'critical' of Kerr and accepted Kerr's argument that he did not warn Whitlam because the governor-general believed he would be sacked. Asked about Barwick, Abbott said: 'Kerr was entitled to ask him and Barwick was entitled to accede to the request.'

Abbott was finishing his HSC at the time of the dismissal. 'It was certainly the highest of drama at the time,' he recalled. 'I was an eighteen-year-old schoolboy. I certainly got swept up in the whole thing.' He remembered Kerr presenting the prizes at the Saint Ignatius' Riverview speech day just a few weeks before the dismissal. 'We all saw Kerr as a Whitlam appointee who was basically going to find ways of allowing Whitlam . . . to stare down the Senate.' Abbott joked with his mates about what they would say to Kerr when they went to collect their prizes.

'I was the only one who [was] silly enough to say something to him,' he recalled. 'I said, "Sir John, I've got a fast car here and I am happy to drive you over to the Liberal Party rally in town later this afternoon."' The headmaster was displeased. Abbott later chatted to Kerr over afternoon tea and found the governor-general was 'very genial with me'. Within weeks Abbott was 'electioneering' against Labor in Queensland. 'I got completely swept up in the drama,' he said and recalled attending pro-Kerr demonstrations.

Abbott repudiated the view that the 1975 crisis ruptured Australian politics and society. 'The system coped,' he said. Fraser proceeded to govern for three terms and Labor 'for all its sound and fury did learn the lessons of Whitlam'. Abbott points out that the next Labor government, the Hawke–Keating era, became Labor's 'best government'. He is convinced the political system 'not only emerged unscathed but indeed has been strengthened'.

Peacock and Howard were members of the Liberal Party front bench in 1975, served in the Fraser cabinet and became Liberal Party leaders. Despite their rivalry for many years, their assessments of 1975 as younger colleagues in the Fraser era are remarkably similar. Their view, then and now, is that Fraser's strategy was justified.

'We believed in what we were doing,' Peacock said.[3] 'We didn't regard it as a crisis. We regarded it as something that had to be done . . . I recall well being strongly in support of what Malcolm was doing. And I read over the years about some people getting the wobbles. Well, some of them were.' Peacock said Fraser was 'committed to the strategy' and the party room gave him 'a lot of leeway' to pursue it. Peacock had no regrets about the strategy or the outcome. 'I haven't rethought my position,' he said. 'It would be difficult for people to comprehend the degree of alarm in the community. We took action that was tangible and all these years later I still believe it was correct. I am probably one of the few who still do.'

Howard had no doubt the strategy was justified. 'It was a very deliberate decision of the entire front bench,' Howard said.[4] 'I was very conscious that [blocking supply] was a big thing. Like a lot of the members [I was] nervous about what the impact would be on the body politic and the fabric of the system. I thought it was justified in the circumstances. I thought the context justified it. I was not gung-ho. I didn't think that we should be too triumphal about it. I thought some signs of celebration which emerged after Whitlam was dismissed were unwise.'

Howard, a thirty-six-year-old rising star at the time, thought the Whitlam government was 'very bad' and 'beset by division and scandal'. It is easy to forget today that it was 'an unprecedentedly disrupted period'.

But when news came through that Whitlam had been dismissed, Howard said he was 'flabbergasted'. He later saw Fraser in the lobbies, with Eggleton in tow, carrying a bible 'on which he had been sworn'. Howard offered a strong defence of Kerr. He believed Kerr had 'no alternative'. He said: 'I belong to the school that Kerr suffered unduly – that Kerr was the meat in the sandwich – it was left to him to break the deadlock. He was caught between two extremely egotistical men who wanted an irreconcilable outcome and neither of them was going to give an inch and it was left to him.'

Howard rejected speculation the opposition would have cracked. 'I find that hard to believe,' he says, 'If they were going to crack, they'd have cracked before.' He defended both Kerr's consultation with Barwick and Barwick's advice. 'I thought it was appropriate and I thought it was persuasive and I thought it was certainly very necessary,' he said.

Like Abbott, Howard believed the 1975 crisis did not 'fundamentally damage the social fabric'. He made the pivotal point – the 1975 and 1977 election results were emphatic. He provided a keen insight into the real legacy of the crisis. 'I think it had an impact on the elite political culture of the country,' Howard said of the crisis. 'It infected Labor people for years, this sense of being robbed . . . I don't believe their lingering resentment was justified. I think they have overdone it.' Howard said Hawke's 1983 victory 'assuaged' these sentiments and the way Hawke won was 'beneficial' to Labor. He remained convinced, however, that there was no 'permanent impact on the social contract in this country'.

Peacock and Howard agreed the dismissal had an influence on Fraser and on the character of his government. 'It had a particular impact on Malcolm,' recalled Peacock. 'On confrontations with the other side, he was more wary than he had been. I think it had a significant political cum personal impact on him much greater than people realise. I would not say it fazed him. I would not go that far. But I knew him pretty well.' Peacock, in short, thought the dismissal made Fraser cautious and wary.

'It is more of an intuitive thing,' Howard said, adding there is little evidence on the subject. 'But I had the impression that on some occasions [Fraser] held back from doing things he might otherwise have done, on the basis that he had stretched the fabric a lot in getting there . . . he was conscious that he had really pushed things to the limit and therefore it did have some impact on him. On occasions he would pull back from doing things even though he had control of the Senate until 1981.'

But Howard added an important caveat. Fraser, by nature, was not a free-market economic reformer and he tended to be cautious anyway. Howard injected a note of warning in assessing Fraser: it was difficult to discern how much came from the 1975 crisis and how much was in his nature as a reform-shy leader on the economy.

Hewson worked as an adviser on Howard's staff when he was treasurer and later succeeded Peacock as leader. At the time of the dismissal, he was travelling with the governor of the Reserve Bank, Sir Harold Knight, in the Middle East. They cancelled the trip and came straight home. Hewson said the Whitlam government was 'out of control' but he saw the blocking of supply as 'an extreme option' by Fraser. 'Ever since it's been off the agenda to deny a government its financial resources even if you totally disagreed with their policies,' he said.[5]

When Kerr died, in March 1991, Hewson was Liberal leader and spoke in the condolence motion in parliament after Hawke. He lavished Kerr with praise, describing him as 'a great Australian' who had become the 'focus of blame' for the crisis. Hewson's view has not changed. 'I think he [Kerr] obviously had his foibles – and some pretty telling performances at race meetings and so on – but I think he was a pretty effective governor-general in very difficult circumstances.' Hewson agreed with the Liberal orthodoxy: that Kerr made the right call. 'I don't think he had any choice,' Hewson said. Yet he did concede that 'a better way' may have been to call Fraser and Whitlam together and tell them his decision, rather than dismissal by ambush.

Hewson believed the dismissal did have a psychological impact on Fraser. 'The electorate backed them for what they [the Liberal Party] had done,' Hewson said. 'But Fraser said to me he never quite felt legitimate about 1975. So he went to an early election in 1977 to see if he could get a firm mandate. Yes, it [the dismissal] probably did make him cautious. He probably felt there had been enough disruption and he wanted a stable government . . . I think Malcolm was very cautious about reform.'

For the next generation of Liberal leaders, Downer and Costello, the 1975 crisis was a formative step in their political development and they took important lessons from it. They are more critical of Fraser than the Howard/Peacock generation.

Downer, who later worked in Fraser's prime ministerial office as a speechwriter, called the blocking of supply 'a ruthless and divisive thing to do'. He justified it 'because of the perception across the country of the complete incompetence and dysfunctionality of the Whitlam government'. Downer said the election result showed the nation wanted a new government: 'the public cast their verdict'.[6]

He believed Fraser was 'very shaken' by the divisions caused by the dismissal. He argued 'the way Malcolm Fraser came to power' had the effect of 'psychologically constraining' him in office. Downer was alert to the negative consequences of the dismissal. He saw the dismissal as a handbrake on reform, especially in the area of workplace relations because it meant challenging the labour movement. 'It made them more cautious and more timid,' Downer said of the Fraser government. 'They were less reformist than they might have otherwise been. And by being less reformist they came under a growing criticism from within the Liberal Party and particularly from the business community.'

Costello, a first-year undergraduate student at Monash University at the time of the dismissal, said he was 'shocked' by the news. He didn't support the Whitlam government. But he didn't support Fraser's strategy to block supply either. 'I just wasn't quite sure it was the right thing to do,' Costello said.[7] 'I voted for the Liberal Movement in the Senate, as a result of that.[8] I didn't have any doubt that it was legal, I just thought it was pretty hardball politics.' Costello said this view has only strengthened over time. Given his experience as treasurer, he believes a government is entitled to have the Senate pass its budget. He is uncomfortable with the Senate power to block supply. 'If the Senate had blocked my money bills [as treasurer], I would have gone off my tree,' he said. 'Completely off my tree.'

Downer and Costello, who formed a leadership ticket and successfully challenged Hewson in 1994, agreed the modern Liberal Party would not repeat Fraser's strategy of blocking supply. 'I don't think anyone would block supply again,' Downer said. 'I can't imagine a circumstance where they would block supply. I just can't. I suppose if a government became, just went off the reservation, just completely off the reservation, there might be some attempt to try and force an election and that might be one way of doing it. But I don't think people want to relive the acrimony of November 1975.'

Costello said: 'There has been no suggestion in my time in parliament of blocking supply or delaying supply or deferring supply . . . Now, you say to me, "should it never", well, maybe if there is some massive illegality. But if it is just, you know, as part of trying to force an election because a government is on the nose, I don't think that's right.' Costello's view is distant from Fraser's on this issue.

Who did Downer blame for the dismissal? 'If anybody is to be criticised for the dismissal, it should be Malcolm Fraser,' he said. 'If you're against the dismissal and you think the dismissal was a hugely bad thing to do, then criticise Fraser for it. The governor-general wasn't appointed to protect the Labor Party or for that matter the Liberal Party. The job of the governor-general was to try to resolve the situation as best as he possibly could.' On balance, Downer was more critical of Fraser than Kerr – the opposite of Turnbull's view.

Costello believed, like Downer, that Kerr was demonised for the dismissal. 'I actually feel a bit sorry for him,' Costello said of Kerr. 'Because I actually feel he did, given the circumstances, what was required . . . I think the Liberal Party found him quite expendable, actually. I think within the confines of the choices he had, he did the right thing and he was pilloried for the rest of his life as a consequence.'

But Costello was less forgiving about Barwick and Mason. 'I am a little troubled by that,' said the former barrister. 'I do think the High Court's got to be very careful. If a case is possibly going to come before it, they have to be very careful they haven't given what is called an advisory opinion. And it's possible some part of this could have come before the High Court. I think if I had been a High Court judge, I would have been very, very careful about that . . . I'm not sure the High Court's judges should have been giving the legal advice.'

For Brendan Nelson, who succeeded Howard as Liberal leader in 2007, the election victory on 13 December 1975 offered judgement on the dismissal. 'There was no doubt that the electorate was extremely concerned about the Whitlam government,' he said.[9] 'The election victory gave the Fraser government a mandate after the dismissal. The Whitlam government did many good things, particularly in social policy, that needed to be done. But in terms of economic management and governance, it was perhaps the worst government we had and the electorate made that judgement.'

Like Downer and Costello, he thought blocking supply was a tactic that would not recur. 'In life, as in politics, you can never say never,' Nelson said. 'But in my lifetime I don't think the Coalition, or the Labor Party, would ever block supply again. I just can't see that happening. The circumstances were unique in 1975 . . . It did cast a long shadow over Fraser as prime minister and his actions for the rest of his life.'

Howard and Peacock also shared this view. Asked if he could envisage the Senate's power being used again, Howard said: 'Hugely unlikely. But you can never rule it out. It still exists.' Peacock would not advocate any repeat but said: 'If the circumstances were the same, they [the Liberal Party] would have to consider it . . . It is a tough game, governing a country. It's not for wimps.'

Fraser's closest advisers rejected the orthodoxy that the dismissal unnerved him and generated excessive caution. Tony Eggleton, Liberal Party federal director through the Fraser years, said the dismissal did not 'overshadow' his prime ministership.[10] 'He had three terms as prime minister, which is not too bad. I don't think it poisoned his approach or thinking. I think he just got on with the job of being prime minister. The most interesting thing is that he and Gough became such good friends.'

David Kemp, a senior adviser to Fraser, believed the dismissal was part of a wider misinterpretation of Fraser as prime minister. Kemp, who saw Fraser at close quarters, disagreed the dismissal hung over Fraser like a cloud. 'Fraser was a man of action and this did not diminish after the dismissal,' he said.[11] 'The reforms and policies he took to the 1975 election, and his actions later, showed a man who was bold in action.' He offered the insight that the dismissal may have influenced Fraser's later behaviour in 'his reaching out to Whitlam'.

'Fraser was not cautious on reform,' Kemp said. 'It is simply that his reform record is judged by the ideas of a later time. Its content reflected his own thinking, not ideas that had yet to become widespread, such as deregulation of the industrial relations system, or floating the dollar.'

Fraser's private secretary, Dale Budd, reinforced the views of Kemp and Eggleton. Budd disagreed that Fraser was personally affected by the dismissal. 'Did I see the dismissal as influencing the way he operated? I don't think so. I never saw that.'[12] Budd offered another perspective: 'The main reaction after the election was: we've got this huge majority, we don't want to misuse it, we don't want to be heavy-handed, we're not going to trample over people just because we've got this huge majority. But I don't think that was a reaction to the dismissal. I think for many Liberal voters the dismissal was a statement of approval. It was an endorsement.'

Tony Staley, a Liberal minister after the dismissal and confidant of Fraser, argued, surely correctly, that Whitlam's post-dismissal reaction assisted Fraser. This is because the deposed prime minister focused much of his attack on Kerr, who was not contesting the election. 'In one sense there was remarkably little impact on Fraser because of Gough's concentration on Kerr,' Staley said.[13] 'The concentration on Kerr from Gough helped enormously. There were those who thought that we were somewhat illegitimate but I put them in the category of irritations rather than major problems.'

In his retirement Fraser bristled at suggestions the dismissal had weakened the character and performance of his government. Troy Bramston put this question to Fraser in a 2002 interview:

> **Bramston**: It is said that the dismissal – by John Howard and others – that the dismissal made you perhaps timid and maybe cautious in government.
> **Fraser**: I don't think so. If it had made me timid or cautious, I would not have led my own party in opposition to apartheid. Why would I bother? I would not have passed land rights legislation in 1976, which potentially was very unpopular with the National Party and some Liberals. No, I reject that.[14]

In the end, the extent to which the dismissal constrained Fraser in office is contested. The arguments for and against will never be resolved. The deeper point is that the events of 1975 were unique. The Liberal judgement that no subsequent leader is likely to block supply is because they cannot imagine another government as inept as the Whitlam government.

The further point, however, is that Fraser was not required to deny supply and force the crisis. His decision triggered a series of events that placed the constitutional, parliamentary and political system under enormous strain for partisan gain. For that reason also, the legacy of 1975 is that another denial of supply is unlikely to occur, though the power still exists.

19

The Labor
Judgement

The ultimate Labor judgement on the Whitlam government and dismissal, forty years after the event, is that Labor recognised the need to lift its game, leave behind the histrionics of Whitlam and govern in a different way. In the end, Labor saw the dismissal as an unforgivable action by a discredited governor-general yet inexorably linked to the excesses and brinkmanship that marked Whitlam's style. In a sign of maturity, the party condemned Kerr yet recognised it must reform itself.

The three Labor leaders after Whitlam, Bill Hayden, Bob Hawke and Paul Keating, drove this conception. This troika spanned the period from 1977 to 1996 – in effect, the entire post-Whitlam generation. While repudiating Kerr's actions, these leaders were dedicated to transforming the ethos, content and style of Labor as a party. They ensured Labor did not succumb to a self-defeating victim mentality, blaming everyone but itself for the flaws of the Whitlam era.

Labor became a more realistic, tougher and pragmatic party. Economic responsibility became the overarching imperative. The post-Whitlam generation, unlike Whitlam, saw Fraser as the real enemy. With Kerr's retirement they were no longer preoccupied with a departed governor-general whose historical record seemed discredited. They had no interest in reconciliation with Fraser. They knew that Fraser had triggered the crisis and their contempt for him deepened the longer he governed.

The post-Whitlam leaders, above all, had a profound conviction about Fraser: that he represented a conservative establishment that was far weaker than it seemed, that the 1975 crisis illustrated the overreach of the conservatives and that once in office Fraser had failed to effectively meet the challenges of the country. The Hawke ministry that came to office in 1983 was far superior to Whitlam's in grasping the power dynamics and policy needs of the nation.

In short, the origins of the Hawke–Keating era of government – the longest in Labor history – reside in Whitlam's failures and the humiliation of the dismissal. The post-Whitlam leaders drew three brutal lessons: that Labor was primarily responsible for its failures, that Fraser's ruthless outlook on politics had to be met by a similar Labor ruthlessness, and that Labor must win its political legitimacy by its actions rather than alarming voters with discredited policies.

Hayden, who was treasurer in 1975, was informed by his staff of the dismissal before 2 p.m., but didn't believe the news until it was confirmed when he sat next to Joe Berinson in the House of Representatives after lunch. Hayden felt Whitlam's speech on the Parliament House steps on the afternoon of 11 November was his 'most magnificent moment' but he knew that electoral annihilation beckoned.[1] Hayden believed Kerr should have resigned after the election 'for the sake of [the] reputation of the office he occupied and for the comity of the Australian community'.[2] In a decision that surprised many, Hayden became governor-general in 1989, an appointment that reaffirmed the practice of former politicians in the office. It gave him a unique perspective on Kerr: as a former dismissed Labor minister and as one of Kerr's successors.

The upshot was that Hayden formed a sympathetic but not

uncritical view of Kerr. He said Kerr 'acted within his authority' and he could not fault the decision to accept Fraser's advice about a double-dissolution election. But Hayden said Kerr was 'wrong' in two respects. First, it was a mistake to believe that if a prime minister 'cannot get supply he must resign or advise an election' and if that does not happen, then it is the governor-general's 'authority and duty' to terminate heir commission.[3] Second, Hayden said Kerr failed to manage his relationship with Whitlam. Kerr did not 'candidly discuss' the crisis with Whitlam and he dismissed the government 'without any warning at all'.[4]

Hayden said Kerr's role and the dismissal was discussed when he visited Buckingham Palace. He refused to reveal the detail of such discussions but said: 'I felt no reason to change my attitude on it based on everything that was said to me.'[5]

In retrospect, Hayden thought Kerr deserved to be 'looked upon in a kinder and less subjective light'. Hayden wrote: 'There may have been weaknesses in his character and defects in his judgement, which is to say he was human, but I have no evidence that his motives were sinister. I believe John Kerr was a good man who, at worst, erred on this occasion; it would be a mark of maturity if more of us would acknowledge that he was far from an evil man.' It is an assessment remarkable for its generosity.[6]

Hawke was in Melbourne, about to eat a T-bone steak for lunch, when he heard the news of Whitlam's dismissal from the restaurant owner and promptly flew to Canberra. But Hawke, as ACTU president and Labor's national president, brought an unusual view to the crisis – he believed it was a time for cool heads to prevail. The dismissal had no decisive impact on Hawke's political formation.[7]

'I was staggered, like most people were,' Hawke said. There was 'a great deal of pressure' from unions and Labor MPs for Hawke to call an immediate national strike. 'I was resolutely against that,' Hawke said. 'I argued that here you are complaining about proper processes not being followed in determining the course of constitutional events.

It didn't make sense in those circumstances to talk about national stoppages. I was able to persuade the ACTU this was the right course and Gough agreed with that.' Addressing the crowd outside Parliament House on 12 November, Hawke warned that 'hatred and violence is (not) going to be substituted for the processes of peaceful debate'.[8]

Hawke believed Kerr was a bad choice as governor-general. He had complained to Whitlam at the time: 'What are you doing appointing this bastard? He's just a DLP stooge. He'll just look after their interests all the time.' Whitlam asked him who he would appoint and Hawke nominated Richard Eggleston, then at the Melbourne Bar and a former ACTU advocate, as a desirable choice. 'He had a great traditional Labor background,' Hawke said. The Kerr appointment 'didn't make sense' to Hawke. He didn't trust Kerr.

Hawke's contempt for Kerr was undisguised. 'I just don't think he [Kerr] was objective in any way,' Hawke said. 'His interests were anti-Whitlam, anti-Labor, it's as simple as that.' Sometime after the dismissal, Whitlam said to Hawke: 'You were right, you bastard, weren't you?' The appointment of Hayden meant Yarralumla was in safe hands.

A year after the dismissal, Hawke gave a lecture at Monash University arguing that Labor needed to understand the conservative nature of the electorate and embrace 'gradualism' in implementing a reform agenda.[9] He foreshadowed his strategy for revival – Labor must address its past 'weakness in . . . economic strategy', improve relations with the bureaucracy, adopt more effective administrative techniques and be more persuasive in 'communication with the electorate'.

'I was terribly upset by the economic incompetence of the Whitlam government,' Hawke said. He warned Whitlam ahead of the 1972 election that his government would 'live or die' on its economic policies. 'It was just such a tragic waste of opportunity,' Hawke said. 'So while one had the great sense of frustration with the dismissal and the feeling that injustices had been done, it was all mixed up with the fact that you had this feeling of gross inadequacy in terms of economic reforms.'

Hawke saw the flaws beneath Fraser's victories in 1975 and 1977: that Fraser remained a symbol of division. Hawke believed the 'deep divisions' in the community over the dismissal were perpetuated by the confrontational approach of the Fraser government. The insight that drove Hawke's 1983 campaign was his pledge to bring the country together, with 'consensus' becoming the message of his leadership. There could not have been a greater contrast with the Whitlam–Fraser confrontational tactics in 1975.

In 1987, at the midpoint of the Hawke government, Keating as treasurer surveyed what Labor had learned from the dismissal: 'For my part, what gives the memory of 1975 relevance are the lessons for Labor as the party of government in the 1980s. As we rake through the embers of his period in office, we are reminded of Gough's success in refurbishing Labor and returning it to relevance; but we must also be struck by the vulnerability of any party which maintains a static political or economic posture in rapidly changing times. This, I believe, is one of the principal lessons of the period.'[10]

Keating was outraged by the dismissal. He was having lunch at the Lobby restaurant across from Parliament House when he was told by journalist Fred Brenchley that the government had been sacked. His instant reaction was that Whitlam had been 'shanghaied' by Kerr. For Keating, it was a 'premeditated and elaborate deception', an act of pure betrayal.[11] The story that Whitlam saw Keating soon after returning from Government House and told him 'you're sacked' before quickly walking off is 'a complete myth', he says. After Whitlam, Keating is far and away the Labor leader most affected by the dismissal. His anger is contained yet palpable four decades later.

That afternoon, at about 4 p.m., Keating walked into Fred Daly's office, where Frank Crean was also present, and said of Kerr: 'This guy's a pseudo crim and what you do with pseudo crims is you lock them up.' Asked in July 2015 if he would have put Kerr under house arrest at the time, Keating said: 'Look, I probably would have.'

He described the dismissal as a 'lynching'. It was 'a true breach of everything that was constitutionally proper', he said. In short, Keating believed Whitlam and the cabinet went too meekly to their deaths. They accepted 'too readily' Kerr's edict.

Although Hawke and Hayden went to Kerr's funeral in April 1991, Keating refused to go. 'I was the last minister in the cabinet, not the second or the third, I was the last,' Keating said of his appointment as minister on the eve of the 1975 crisis. 'I knew that Kerr brought down the guillotine on Whitlam.' He called Kerr 'a toady and a fool'. In retrospect, however, Keating saw Kerr as 'the great sufferer from the whole crisis' because his judgement about having an 'independent' role to play was so deeply flawed.

Keating was critical of Whitlam's approach. 'For a start I would have had a strategy,' Keating said. 'I don't say this with any measure of deprecation to Gough, but I would never have confronted a guy like Kerr without thinking of his options.' It is the obvious point that Whitlam ignored. Keating would have assessed Kerr's strategic choices alongside his personality. If confronted with dismissal, Keating would have challenged it. 'Gough was a classic player of the constitutional game,' Keating says. 'I would have used the power far more forcibly than Gough.' Keating said that Kerr was 'a rogue personality' and had to be dealt with accordingly.

Hawke and Keating are unforgiving of Fraser. Hawke accused Fraser of being 'very devious' and Keating said he engaged in 'crude political opportunism'. Hawke believed that Fraser was adversely affected by the dismissal and saw his reconciliation with Whitlam as evidence that 'he obviously had regrets'.

But Keating's critique of Fraser was more far-reaching. 'In the end it was a high misadventure for Fraser, and he never recovered from it,' Keating said. 'Fraser let the dog off the leash with the second chamber [the Senate]. I think the system has been internally corrupted and a party in the House of Representatives can only have faith in the longevity of its mandate if it remains popular.'

Keating also told the authors that Fraser's action had 'poisoned' the political system. Pushing the system to the brink 'destroyed the equanimity' in Australian politics and, Keating said, left 'a set of black clouds in the polity'. He branded Liberal Senate leader Reg Withers' strategy of blocking supply as reaching out for 'the naked flame'. Keating said the bitter 'enmities' between the political parties today are a 'consequence' of the dismissal. The 'brutality of the dismissal' ended any sense of goodwill, he said. 'The poison went into the bloodstream and it's never come out of it.' For Keating, the Senate remains permanently emboldened, with any attempt to circumscribe its power facing certain defeat.

Hayden, Hawke and Keating were critical of Sir Garfield Barwick and Sir Anthony Mason and the involvement of the High Court. Hayden said Barwick and Mason should not have advised Kerr. 'I think it was unwise in case it ended up before them on the court,' he said.[12] Hawke said Barwick acted 'deviously and improperly'. Keating said: 'I find against Barwick.' He said even though Barwick may have been convinced the matters would never come to the court, he advised Kerr knowing that he 'carried the weight of the office, which he really shouldn't have done'.

As a Labor historian, Graham Freudenberg said of the dismissal: 'What happened on 11 November was simply the crowning point of all that had gone before: the denial of legitimacy of a Labor Government . . . It remained a government under siege, under question, under doubt as to its legitimacy.'[13]

For those who lived through these events, this is a persuasive proposition. Yet a strange and magnificent political response followed. The Hayden–Hawke–Keating era, finally, put down the legitimacy bogy that had plagued Labor for so much of its existence. The upshot was apparent in the Rudd–Gillard era: they had no real interest in the dismissal and treated it as an irrelevance. The enduring legacy is now apparent: from the ashes of the Whitlam government and tumult of the dismissal, the building blocks of the next Labor government emerged.

Epilogue

IN THE SHADOW
OF THE DISMISSAL

On the morning after the dismissal, 12 November 1975, Gough Whitlam summoned members of Labor's campaign team and his personal advisers to the Lodge. They were to begin planning the campaign for the double-dissolution election on 13 December. Whitlam, however, did not emerge from his upstairs bedroom until long after everybody had arrived. Dressed in his pyjamas and dressing-gown, Whitlam muttered obscenities about Sir John Kerr as he paced around the room. The leader had been stripped of his power. He was in 'a state of shock', recalls Labor's pollster, ANOP's Rod Cameron:

> I remember Gough coming down the stairs. He was wearing a
> short dressing-gown. He looked at me but his eyes were focused
> somewhere else. He just paced around the room, muttering "the
> cunt", referring to John Kerr. He must have said it ten times. And
> then he left. We then began a fairly desultory planning session.
> The birth of the slogan came then: 'Shame, Fraser, Shame'. This
> was never going to win us an election. We were going to get

trounced. The idea was to keep the Labor sympathies up and the passions up. But there was nothing else to go on.[1]

There was a sense of hopeful delusion at the meeting – some people felt the dismissal might become an electoral asset. They decided on a campaign predicated on 'the survival of Australian democracy' as Whitlam insisted. It was doomed to fail, yet Labor, as a vanquished government, had nothing else as a campaign peg. Cameron, who had been Labor's pollster since 1972, believed that memories of the dismissal would quickly fade during a campaign despite the fact that voters did not approve the blocking of supply and many did not approve the dismissal. Labor's dilemma was highlighted in a memo Cameron had written for Whitlam back on 21 October, five days after supply was blocked:

> I believe there is some confusion in the minds of many Labor Party people that is operating to equate the new found apparent reaction against the Opposition's stance with an increase in the likely vote for Labor in an early election. The two are by no means any more than marginally related. I would suggest that voting for Labor is by no means the same thing as supporting an emotional bandwagon movement which is for the preservation of the democratic system as we know it . . . I would urge you strongly not to assume that such support automatically transfers to a vote for Labor in a 1975 election.[2]

Cameron argued that any election in 1975 would soon become about the respective merits of the two sides. He said:

> The major issue, as I have suggested previously, is competent government . . . Labor may hope to divert some attention away from competent government as an issue. It is unlikely, however, to be able to completely to defuse it. We cannot hope, no matter how

impressive the Prime Minister will be on the campaign trail, no
matter how skilful the ALP communications effort can be made,
to defuse in a short period a year's worth of constant, repetitious
reinforcement of the incompetent government theme. Other
things being equal, we have a show of doing it in six
months – not in six weeks.

This analysis of Labor's position was remarkably similar to that
made by the Liberal Party. Indeed, it was one reason Malcolm Fraser
had forced the election.

Yet, everywhere the dismissed prime minister went, in every
electorate and every city, he met huge and emotional crowds,
unprecedented in a Labor campaign. He was mobbed on stages and
platforms, people reached out to touch him, some crying, others
thrusting money into his hands. An estimated 30 000 people gathered
in Sydney's Domain at the start of the campaign, ahead of a thunderous 7500 packed into Melbourne's Festival Hall for the campaign
launch. Whitlam's policy speech was unique: no new promises, no
new spending. It was a polemic to stir the hearts and spirits of the
Australian people as the dismissed prime minister declared: 'Men and
women of Australia, the whole future of Australian democracy is in
your hands . . .' His staffers said the Festival Hall meeting was the
greatest political rally they had experienced.

The reality, beyond the Labor faithful, was different. Whitlam's dismissal was a major boost to the Coalition campaign. The dismissal was
seen as an adverse judgement on his government and on his prime ministership. Labor's position would have been significantly stronger had
Whitlam been campaigning as prime minister. But Fraser now held
that title, though he had to avoid any impression of prejudging the
vote. Kerr's refusal to give Whitlam a choice on 11 November was a tangible factor in the campaign. The governor-general's action generated
a sense of legitimacy around Fraser and illegitimacy around Whitlam.

On election day, Labor suffered a 6.5 per cent primary vote swing and lost thirty seats. It was left with just thirty-six seats in the 127-seat House of Representatives. Labor was not spared anywhere, with sizeable swings shown in every state. The Liberal and National Country Party coalition had a fifty-five-seat majority, the largest in Australian history. Fraser had won the most sweeping mandate in political history. Fraser had a senate majority of eight, thereby guaranteeing the Coalition full control of the Senate for two terms. The size of his House of Representatives majority pointed to the certainty of his re-election, though nobody anticipated a 1977 result that would essentially repeat the 1975 wipe-out.

The day after the election, Whitlam offered the leadership of the party to Bill Hayden, who was too shell-shocked to consider it. He was the only Queensland Labor MP to hold his seat. Whitlam then offered the leadership to Bob Hawke, who did not have a seat in parliament. Whitlam remained leader and led Labor to defeat, again, in December 1977.

The ALP recovery began when Hayden became leader in December 1977 and laid the foundations for a party looking to the future, not the past. Hayden's leadership was pivotal in restoring the Labor brand and the party's economic credentials after Whitlam. At the October 1980 election, Hayden put Fraser under serious pressure just five years after the dismissal. Labor won a two-party vote of 49.6 per cent and increased its seats from thirty-eight to fifty-one in the House of Representatives. It was an impressive comeback, though short of triumph. In February 1983, Hawke replaced Hayden as leader and defeated Fraser at the March 1983 election.

In the aftermath of the greatest political crisis in Australian history, the principals lived, to a greater or lesser extent, in its shadow. Former NSW premier Neville Wran, speaking at a conference on the twentieth anniversary of the dismissal said: 'I do not believe that the curtain will come down on this chapter of Australian history until all the actors in the drama which led to this unique and unprecedented event have left this earth to become members of a larger parliament, in a different firmament, in which our mortal clay is of little relevance.'[3]

Now all gone, Whitlam, Fraser, Kerr and Sir Garfield Barwick each defended their actions until the end of their lives. Sir Anthony Mason failed to reveal to the public his own participation until Kerr revealed his counsel during the crisis in his papers made public in 2012. The Queen, as to be expected, has kept a stoic silence about these events, although members of the royal household have spoken about their reactions.

Sir John Kerr

Kerr relocated to England in the years after the dismissal and remained there, effectively in exile, until the mid-1980s, when he returned to live in Sydney. As governor-general he had been trapped between staying to defend his actions and leaving so the nation could move forward. Anne Kerr called the situation they confronted after the 1975 crisis a 'new irrational scene swarming with instant enemies'. John Menadue, who still periodically visited Kerr, said: 'My impression of John Kerr afterwards was that he was a beaten man . . . There was a sense of physical fear, that people might jump the walls.' Menadue said Lady Kerr was a much-needed support.[4]

Kerr offered his resignation to Fraser on several occasions. Fraser, as prime minister, had given Kerr little personal support, later confessing that 'I probably should have tried to talk to him more about it'.[5] Kerr eventually resigned in 1977. Public outcry over Fraser's appointment of Kerr as ambassador to the United Nations Educational, Scientific and Cultural Organization (UNESCO) meant that he never assumed the diplomatic post.

His memoir, *Matters for Judgment*, was published in 1978, and a second manuscript, *The Triumph of the Constitution*, was written but never published. It sits among his papers in the National Archives of Australia, unreleased to the public. The foreword is written by Australian academic, educational leader and adviser to the Abbott government Don Markwell. It captures Kerr's view that history would be on his side:

'The serious debate on 1975 has shifted more and more in his [Sir John's] favour. I believe that any fair-minded person who reads a substantial part of the serious writing on 1975 will be struck by how strong the case for Sir John's action is.'[6]

After the dismissal, Kerr entertained the idea that he make a further statement to the nation. In his papers is a draft typescript of this statement which defends his actions and blames Whitlam and Fraser. In an annotation to the document, Kerr says the address 'was prepared about a week after 11/11/75' but was 'never used because an election campaign was in progress'. The draft suggests that Kerr wanted to justify his actions and secure public acceptance of them.

Kerr said the precedent established by the dismissal should be embraced, not spurned. 'I do not think we should shrink from the precedent just established simply because we may find it difficult to live with now, and even more inconvenient to live with in the future.' At the end of his proposed address, Kerr said: 'Let us resolve to go forward and look carefully at our constitution . . . If we find that it needs amendment, to have the courage as a nation to make those amendments so that never again will stubborn men be able to produce the divisive situation which we have experienced here.'

While not delivered, the statement reveals Kerr's anxiety for vindication and his desire that the Australian public hold the political leaders responsible. He said that in using the reserve powers he had 'come to our aid as a nation'.[7]

In the unpublished book, Kerr urged that his correspondence with Buckingham Palace be made public. He also proposed a number of constitutional reforms, including a maximum four-year term for the House of Representatives, the requirement that if supply is denied for thirty days there would automatically be an election for both houses of parliament and greater security of tenure for governors-general.

Markwell, who was based at Oxford University, befriended the

Kerrs and spent considerable time with them. He said they lived a life not of 'desolation in exile' but of 'richness'. Markwell said Kerr would have welcomed a 'reconciliation' with Whitlam, but didn't push for one.[8] Ken Gee, a friend of Kerr's over several decades, suggested a reconciliation meeting with Whitlam in the evening of their lives. Kerr was ambivalent. He agreed but asked: 'What is the point?' When Kerr's health deteriorated, Gee did not proceed.[9]

Until his death, in March 1991, Kerr looked for reassurance, just as he did during the 1975 crisis. The authors have had access to hundreds of pages of Kerr's documents, memos, diaries and handwritten notes available from the National Archives. They reveal a man forever obsessed about the dismissal and its justification. In 1980 in Britain he started a short-lived journal that described his social interactions, yet the underlying theme remained the dismissal and its consequences. Kerr maintained an extensive correspondence, often with the principal players from 1975. Some of the handwritten notes running to more than a dozen pages, presumably written late at night with increasingly illegible writing, evoke the spectre of a man unable to leave the issue alone. The legacy of the dismissal and the quest for vindication haunted Kerr for the rest of his life.

Following the 1983 television mini-series *The Dismissal*, Kerr wrote to his son, Philip, about his depiction: '[John] Meillon managed to portray me as a pretty weak sort of person, struggling to comprehend it all, worried about what was happening, anxious to do his best to play his role, but not having any real strength. It is hardly for me to say what sort of personality I have, but I have no doubt that the rather old, drab, worried person that Meillon made me out to be is very different from the sort of person I really am.'[10] Kerr was correct about the depiction. Yet it is a sad letter, a lament to his son over the way his personality had been misrepresented to the nation.

One of Kerr's correspondents in these years was Sir Robert Menzies, the principal founder of the Liberal Party, and strong supporter of Fraser as Liberal leader. Indeed, it was Fraser's leadership that had helped to reconcile Menzies to the Liberal Party after his disillusionment with John Gorton, Billy McMahon and Billy Snedden.[11] They corresponded at length about the dismissal. 'I want to tell you,' Menzies wrote to Kerr eight days after the dismissal, 'if I may do so without appearing to be impertinent, that your conduct in this matter has been, in my opinion, beyond reproach. You were right as a matter of constitutional law.' Menzies praised Kerr's 'remarkable moral courage in doing what I believe to have been your duty'. He offered 'my congratulations and my profound admiration'.

In January 1976, Menzies wrote an unpublished article and sent it to Kerr. He described Whitlam as 'a complete fool' with 'a rather superficial knowledge of the Constitution' who was now acting as 'a bad loser'. In words that would have buoyed Kerr, Menzies described Whitlam as 'a kind of Hitler' and branded his 1975 campaign launch speech to the faithful as 'like a Nuremberg Rally'. He said Goebbels would have been proud. In reply Kerr said: 'Your letter was a great comfort to me. I have, as you would realise, been through a very difficult period but I am in a state of reasonable calm, being convinced that I have done the only thing possible and also that what I have done is right.'

In retirement, Kerr was sustained by a group of academics, retired judges and friends. He corresponded and enjoyed visits with Barwick, Mason and Ellicott. He was supported by the academic John Paul, old friends such as Gee, new friends like Markwell and a range of Liberal politicians. Writing about 'the madness and shocking desire for revenge' among parts of the community, Kerr found another comfort. 'Christianity,' he wrote in his journal, 'has helped me, however, to resist my hatred of Mr Whitlam because of actions and statements of his.'

Barwick and Kerr became kindred spirits. Barwick, who died in July 1997, was proud of his advice as chief justice and believed he had put the steel into Kerr, an idea Kerr rejected. The more they were demonised, the more mutually supporting became their relations. Writing to Kerr in 1976, Barwick said: 'May I say to you, John, how much you are admired for your steadfastness at the present time. All may not realise, but I do, how difficult the situation is proving for you.'[12] In their letters they revisited the dismissal: the blocking of supply, the reserve powers, the role of the governor-general, the chief justice and the monarchy.

Whitlam was their permanent target. 'Whitlam has again attacked me publicly,' Barwick wrote to Kerr in 1979. 'He has, and has displayed, little or no political "nous". I am inclined to think the ordinary man has come to realise what a burden he has been.' In another letter, Barwick described Whitlam's 1979 book, *The Truth of the Matter*, as 'larded with falsehoods'. In 1980, Kerr wrote to Barwick, about the denigration each was suffering and the 'series of myths' that were being promulgated about their actions in 1975.

In a 1983 exchange of letters, Kerr and Barwick poured scorn on the idea that Whitlam should have been warned about dismissal. 'It was galling for me to have to put up with the ready assumption by academics, journalists and others that my caginess in dealing with Whitlam was due to a desire to hang on to my job and not to the need to avoid involving the Queen,' Kerr wrote. 'It was my duty therefore to do what I did and . . . not to run away from this by craven or reckless activity and, thus by staying, to avoid a puppet taking over.'[13]

For decades Mason failed to disclose publicly his own role and Kerr protected his friend. Bob Hawke and Paul Keating both told the authors that, had they known of Mason's role in advising Kerr, the cabinet would not have appointed him as chief justice. The conclusion from the comments of Hawke and Keating is that Mason's silence was integral to his elevation to the highest judicial office.

'As to what you say about Mason,' Kerr wrote to Barwick in 1982, 'I feel with you that "the younger man should not be involved". I have no desire to bring forward Mason's name, certainly not at this stage, though I feel that it may be desirable, before the history is finally written, for it to be known what he actually believed, but not until after our deaths.'[14]

Kerr's final defence became the 'scapegoat' plea – that Whitlam blamed Kerr because he could not blame an entire nation for rejecting him. 'Other people's sins were heaped upon my head,' Kerr said.[15] How, Kerr asked, could he be blamed when the Senate triggered the crisis and he had to deal with two headstrong leaders? He seemed not to grasp that a governor-general is supposed to have the wisdom to manage a parliamentary crisis. That is the job description.

Kerr enjoyed the prestige of being a retired governor-general, but the evolution of the office in Australia constituted a strong and unmistakable critique of Kerr's conduct. His two immediate successors, Sir Zelman Cowen and Sir Ninian Stephen, knew their task was to rehabilitate the office, a project conducted under the label of 'the healing process'. There was near universal recognition that the office of governor-general had been damaged by Kerr's extraordinary decisions and behaviour. Governors-general no longer talked about the reserve powers.

Kerr's great mistake was his misunderstanding of the reserve powers. They exist to be used only in the most exceptional circumstances as a last resort. Kerr abused this monarchical convention. He used the reserve powers not as a final solution but at his convenience, when his obligation was to obtain a political solution short of their application. He did not operate as an impartial governor-general representing the Queen but as a quasi-judge imposing an answer. For too long he pretended to be 'on side' with both leaders, a stance that encouraged their intransigence and drove him, finally, into a self-defeating constitutional ambush, an admission of his failure as governor-general.

Malcolm Fraser

Fraser, as prime minister and in retirement, hated talking about the dismissal and the 1975 crisis but never regretted any of his actions. He called the subject 'exhausted'. For Fraser, however, there is no escape from the historical judgement. He engaged in the serial smashing of conventions that had long underpinned stable government in Australia. He exploited the abuse of the Senate's casual vacancy procedure. He relied upon a tainted Senate. He broke convention by using the Senate's power to block the budget and force an election. And he resorted to a mixture of persuasion and intimidation in the quest to have Kerr dismiss Whitlam. It is no surprise Fraser preferred not to discuss the subject for the rest of his life.

The irony of Fraser's political life is that, having precipitated the crisis in a display of unparalleled political violence, he marched to the left in his retirement, became a fierce critic of the Howard government, resigned from the Liberal Party in 2009 and became a hero of sorts for the progressive side of politics. This revealed as much about the left as it did about Fraser.

The unexpected personal rapprochement between Fraser and Whitlam was a triumph of human reconciliation over political hostility. They agreed on many issues, from media reform to the republic. The reconciliation enhanced Fraser's image as a man of compassion – in contrast to the ruthlessness he displayed throughout the 1975 crisis. It also revealed a strange attitude from Whitlam. He blamed Kerr and Barwick for the dismissal but forgave Fraser, the initiating agent and the man he branded as 'Kerr's cur' on the Parliament House steps on the afternoon of 11 November. When Fraser presented his last book, *Dangerous Allies*, to Whitlam in 2014, he inscribed the inside page with the words: 'To Gough with affection and respect.'

It is significant, however, that the Fraser–Whitlam reconciliation came without Fraser making the slightest tangible concession about the events of 1975. He offered instead inconsistent and contradictory gestures. For example, in a 1987 oral history interview Fraser recorded with former Labor minister Clyde Cameron for the National Library of Australia – and made available to the authors – he said Kerr's actions had tarnished the office of governor-general. 'It's a fact of life that what John Kerr had done had resulted in damage to the office,' Fraser said.[16] He omitted to say his entire 1975 strategy was to persuade the governor-general to dismiss the prime minister.

Fraser knew he had pushed the political system to the brink, placing institutions under strain. But he always believed it was justified. 'I still feel that he [Kerr] had no option but to act in the way he did, and the person who really damaged the office was Gough Whitlam because Gough behaved in a way that no prime minister had ever . . . dreamed possible.'[17] Fraser revealed that if supply had not been passed, then he would not have returned his commission. 'I think it would have been a little difficult sacking a second Prime Minister and re-appointing the first one sacked,' Fraser said. 'I couldn't really see that happening.'[18] He would have recommended an election anyway.

His condemnation of the Whitlam government never died. That was essential for his 1975 self-justification. Beneath his subsequent friendship with Whitlam, Fraser's patronising contempt for Whitlam's darker side never disappeared. 'I'm not sure what mad things Gough Whitlam might have got up to,' Fraser told Cameron when justifying his effort to terminate the government.[19] Fraser even made the bizarre suggestion, since Whitlam had defied the Senate's bid to force an election, that he might not even have recommended an election at the end of the parliamentary term.[20]

Fraser enjoyed the story showing him outsmarting Menzies during the crisis. Menzies had told Fraser ten days before the dismissal: 'Malcolm, you're going to have to retreat. You're not going to get an election out of this man.' Fraser replied: 'Sir, I don't know how to retreat. We're right; and we're going to have to give him a lashing, and I believe we will.'[21]

The political skill and willpower Fraser displayed during the 1975 crisis was extraordinary. It remains one of the most astonishing acts of brinkmanship in our history, culminating in the December 1975 election victory. At every point Fraser prevailed. This was the 'great man' theory of history in action. But Fraser's performance as prime minister never matched the 'great man' expectations aroused by his coming to power.

Fraser, who died in March 2015, represented the last sighting of the 'born to rule' Liberal Party of another age. While he won three elections (two against a depleted Whitlam), Fraser was a stable but disappointing prime minister. He misread the 1980s winds of change and, in the end, lost to a far more astute leader, Bob Hawke, who prevailed on an agenda calling for national reconciliation and consensus.

Gough Whitlam

Gough Whitlam, who died in October 2014, never retreated from his view that the dismissal was 'a coup conceived in secret and executed by ambush'. Post-dismissal, Whitlam was unbowed. He believed history would affirm that he was wronged by Kerr, Barwick and Fraser.

His fire was focused on Kerr and, to a lesser extent, Barwick. In countless interviews, speeches and newspaper articles, Whitlam sought to destroy their reputations and repudiate their arguments. His attacks on Kerr were personal and always went to character. He accused Kerr of being a drunkard[22], who was obsessed with secrecy[23] and had blindsided him with deception. Whitlam did not blame Fraser for exploiting Kerr's weaknesses, but he did disapprove of him telling Kerr what his constitutional duty was. At the National Press Club in November 1995, Whitlam said he was not 'preoccupied with the dismissal'. Rather, his 'chief interest' in the events of 1975 was 'their relevance to the development of Australia as a republic'.[24] And, if anyone was inclined to 'maintain the rage', he said, it should be directed towards rage for 'parliamentary democracy'.

Whitlam wrote *The Truth of the Matter*, his account of the dismissal, published in 1979. Revised editions were published in 1983 and 2005. It was, in part, a response to Kerr's memoirs published in 1978. No book authored by a former prime minister has sold more copies – over 150 000. Whitlam never believed the dismissal was illegal but he did marshal the arguments to suggest it was improper and immoral.

He railed against Kerr's failure to advise, counsel or warn before dismissal; the veracity of Barwick's advice; its provision against his instructions; the replacement of Labor senators by non-Labor senators by the Queensland and NSW governments; his belief that the Senate was on the verge of cracking; that supply had not 'run out' when Kerr terminated his commission; and that he was not 'restored as Prime Minister' after supply was passed by the Senate and the House had declared 'no confidence' in Fraser. This, said Whitlam, was 'the ultimate constitutional outrage' perpetrated by Kerr on 11 November 1975.[25]

The dismissal converted Whitlam into a martyr. But it was not a title he embraced. 'I want to be remembered as an achiever, not as a martyr,' he often said.[26] The risk was that the dismissal, not his achievements in office, would define Whitlam's career. This fear was despatched with Whitlam's death when, over many days of assessments and tributes, it was his achievements in office, not his dismissal, that dominated.

The 1975 constitutional crisis revealed, on the grandest stage, the glory and blunder in Whitlam's character. He waged an electric and inspiring campaign on behalf of responsible government and the rights of the House of Representatives, the People's House, against the Senate. Yet Whitlam's ineptitude in his conduct of the crisis is almost beyond belief. He bears a serious share of responsibility for the dismissal.

Like other protagonists, Whitlam was unable to accept criticism of his actions. He could never admit, in intellectual or emotional terms, that he contributed to the unsatisfactory outcome on 11 November that damaged him so much. It is not just that he failed to manage Kerr effectively or assess him psychologically. Whitlam's tactics with Kerr were based upon a refusal to engage in private and a compulsion towards intimidation in public. Whitlam drove Kerr's distrust of the prime minister, convinced Kerr his position was at risk and, instead of reassuring the governor-general, frightened and alienated him.

Whitlam refused to realise the real issue was about the reserve powers, declined to provide Kerr with formal advice, engaged in deluded strategies about the half-senate election and the alternative financial arrangements and was blind to the signs pointing to Kerr's intervention. He undertook no contingency planning. Whitlam believed Kerr should have been 'open, frank and honourable' with him. Yet he was not open, frank and honourable with Kerr. The moral, as ever, is that Whitlam was his government's greatest strength and its greatest weakness.

The dismissal is inexorably linked to Whitlam's political and personal character. It is a reminder that this contest was not just about parliamentary and constitutional powers and conventions. It was a contest shaped and defined by the three extraordinary personalities at its heart, Whitlam, Fraser and Kerr. Its course and outcome can be grasped only by the personality and human factor.

Contrary to many dire predictions, the political, parliamentary and constitutional system recovered and proved its resilience. None of the major powers exercised has been cancelled. The Senate can still block or reject supply bills. The governor-general can still dismiss a prime minister. A High Court chief justice can still furnish the governor-general with an advisory opinion.

The deeper lesson, however, has been absorbed by the political and legal culture – institutions and powers must not be pushed to breaking point. Democracy relies upon a degree of restraint in the pursuit of partisan interest, and that restraint was lost in 1975. Changing norms mean the Senate is unlikely to block supply in future, the dismissal power in these circumstances will not be exercised by the governor-general again and a chief justice is unlikely to advise the governor-general again on the reserve powers.

While Labor did 'maintain its rage', it avoided any descent into myopic radicalism about the system. The Hawke government displayed a maturity in dealing with the institutions, and the Keating

government chose to pursue the republic as its governance priority. Labor has shifted its long-run reform focus from the Senate and
reserve powers to the transition from constitutional monarchy to
republic. That will be a distant journey.

In the long interim, the system that generated the 1975 crisis
remains intact – yet that event is altogether too fantastic to become
anything but a monumental reminder of how not to run a country.

Appendix A

AUTHORS' NOTE ON SIR JOHN KERR'S CORRESPONDENCE WITH BUCKINGHAM PALACE

During 1975, Sir John Kerr had an extensive correspondence with Buckingham Palace, writing letters that he believed would be fundamental to understanding the political and constitutional crisis, and also serve as an important record for Australian history. While Kerr revealed in his papers that he wanted this correspondence to be made available to the public at a later date, these letters remain secret and their release, in effect, is hostage to the attitudes of Buckingham Palace in London and Government House in Canberra. They remain sealed and are unlikely to, at this stage, be publicly released. This seems to be an insult to Australian independence and our historical memory.

Kerr referred to this correspondence in his autobiography, *Matters for Judgment* (1978), and in a second, unpublished book, *The Triumph of the Constitution*. A near-final draft manuscript of this subsequent book, written in 1987–90, has been given to the authors by Don Markwell, who befriended Kerr while studying at Oxford University in the 1980s. It sits in Kerr's papers at the National Archives of Australia and will not be released in full until at least 2025. In this unpublished book, Kerr discussed the letters at great length.

In Chapter Twenty of *Matters for Judgment*, Kerr wrote: 'The Governor-General reports regularly to the Queen. There are no rules about how often or in what detail reports are to be made: the duty is simply to send dispatches which keep Her Majesty informed. The supply crisis of 1975 was a crucial event in Australia and as it unfolded the Queen had been receiving full reports on what was happening.'

Further, Kerr writes there were 'two risks' he had to guard against in his relationship with the Palace: 'On the one hand, the Queen could become involved in our crisis if she were asked to recall me when I was in the process of dismissing Mr Whitlam or threatening to do so. Equally, she could become involved if she had advance knowledge of my intention to exercise the reserve power.'

In Chapter Eleven of *The Triumph of the Constitution*, Kerr reveals new details about his correspondence with the Palace:

> There has been some real interest in what is in the Palace correspondence between myself and the Queen covering my governor-generalship. That correspondence consists of letters and enclosures from me addressed to the Queen's Private Secretary [Sir Martin Charteris] and intended for her eyes and the replies from the Palace written on her behalf by him. The Palace archives contain one set of the correspondence and the Australian National Archives has and will have the other. Each set has been embargoed from inspection for long periods of time. Indeed I have been told that it is within the discretion of the monarch of the time whether and when the contents of the correspondence in the Palace archives such as this, or parts of it, will be allowed to be published or used for research.

Kerr writes that his correspondence consists of 'three large, thick, foolscap volumes'covering his term as governor-general. He gives an insight into the correspondence:

I proceeded in writing my 1978 book on the basis that history would ultimately be able to test what I said in my book and other publications against my detailed reports to the Queen which will become available in time to come. I decided quite early in my period of office that I would cover happenings, relevant public statements and statements in the press, not, certainly, on a daily or even weekly basis, but factually and thoroughly. I sent a reasonably comprehensive collection of relevant press cuttings and copies of selected editorials, feature articles and magazine articles, and included accounts of and comments on the passing parade of happenings in Parliament and the Courts. Important of course were my reports of conversations with the Prime Minister and less frequently other ministers.

I was sensitive about going into great detail but the growing crisis, certainly from December 1974 onwards, made it necessary. I thought to do this to an extent reasonable in the circumstances.

My main need was to give a reasonably full account such as would provide a story of the arguments and the passionate controversy, in a deepening constitutional crisis – the biggest ever, so it was said, in Australian history.

Kerr describes the style of writing that aided him as much as, he hoped, the Palace:

The resulting correspondence, from my end, took on a character, dictated by events, which was characterised largely by the technique of diary or journal writing. This technique grew naturally by design, in a conscious not a completely fortuitous, accidental way. So much so that I deliberately used the correspondence as a diary with my copies able to be used by me and others from which I could when necessary refresh my memory.

Kerr makes it clear that, for the sake of history, his correspondence should be available to public scrutiny:

> I would myself be entirely willing to see my Palace
> correspondence, or my copies of it which will be in the
> Australian National Archives – or at least my contribution to the
> correspondence – available now to historians, constitutionalists,
> lawyers and political theorists. If this were to happen I would not
> expect to be hailed as a great literary and political letter-writer and
> showered with praise on that score, but as a participant in a great
> constitutional controversy I would have to be judged in a real
> sense partly on the basis of a real record.

Finally, Kerr asks who has jurisdiction over the correspondence and in what interest they serve:

> Since the dissolution of the British Empire and the independence
> of its once imperial parts, since the modern development of the
> Monarchy in the Commonwealth of Nations in which the Queen
> plays such an important role . . . who is to decide what is to be
> done about such material as my Palace correspondence? Should
> a policy be devised as to such archives in the separate countries?
> Are the archives in the Australian National Archives, to the extent
> that they relate to the relations of the Queen of Australia and her
> Australian governor-general, to be opened up solely at her personal
> discretion, or the discretion of the future monarchs?

The correspondence is not only extensive; it also offers insights into Kerr's public duties. Moreover, he believed this correspondence should be made available so Australians could form their own opinions of how he carried out those duties. And Kerr asks whether his correspondence concerning the affairs of an independent nation should be determined for public access by a foreign monarch at their sole discretion.

In Kerr's handwritten journal written in England in 1980 – accessible to the public as part of his papers in the National Archives – he noted that he had made it clear to the Palace that his correspondence 'should for history's sake be available' to future generations.

Despite his firm views, Buckingham Palace and Government House have refused to make Kerr's correspondence available to the public.

The authors have obtained the two instruments of deposit governing Kerr's papers. In August 1978, the official secretary to the governor-general, Sir David Smith, deposited into the National Archives of Australia a package of Kerr's 'personal and confidential correspondence' with the Queen. In part, it reads: 'In accordance with The Queen's wishes and Sir John Kerr's instructions, these papers are to remain closed until 60 years after the end of his appointment as Governor-General, i.e. until after 8 December 2037.'

There is an additional stipulation: 'Thereafter the documents are subject to a further caveat that their release after 60 years should be only after consultation with the Sovereign's Private Secretary of the day and with the Governor-General's Official Secretary of the day.'

In 1991, Douglas Sturkey, the official secretary to the governor-general, noted: 'The Queen has now reduced this period to 50 years, subject to the approval in each case of the Sovereign's Private Secretary and the Official Secretary to the Governor-General.'

Kerr's correspondence will be available for an assessment for public release after 8 December 2027. This means that even the youngest voters in 1975 will be seventy years old when these documents are released, while most Australians who lived through the crisis will be long gone.

In May 2015, the authors met with the director-general of the National Archives, David Fricker, and requested access to the correspondence. Mr Fricker said under the *Archives Act 1983*, Commonwealth records comprise records of the 'official establishment of the Governor-General'. These are, it was explained, the documents produced in the performance of duties by the governor-general as the representative of the monarch in Australia. However, the Archives classify Kerr's correspondence to the Palace as 'personal records' rather than Commonwealth records.

Therefore, the correspondence is not subject to the normal access requirements. Kerr's other personal papers, many of which are quoted in this book, are subject to a thirty-year rule. Yet it seems nonsense to classify documents as private records that were sent by the governor-general to the Palace in the discharge of his responsibility during the nation's most serious political and constitutional crisis. The Archives have also denied access, or full access, to several of Kerr's notes and correspondence that make even the slightest mention of the Palace or the Queen, even though they were written on Government House letterhead.

Access decisions, however, have not been consistent. The Archives have provided public access to 'extracts' from six of Kerr's letters to the Palace, including one written on 11 November 1975. Kerr had cut out paragraphs from copies of the original letters and pasted them onto blank sheets of paper. These extracts are quoted in this book, but their full context is not known as the entire letters have not been released.

Anne Twomey, Professor of Law at Sydney University, addressed this issue of the Palace correspondence in an article for the *Spectator Australia* magazine on 4 April 2015:

> The letters are held by a Commonwealth Government body,
> having been written by a Commonwealth officer in his capacity
> as Governor-General concerning the exercise of his powers as an
> officer of the Commonwealth. They do not amount to personal
> correspondence about his garden, his family or the Queen's corgis.
> They are about a critical event in Australia's history. They could
> not possibly be regarded as "personal correspondence" under
> any stretch of the imagination, let alone any legal definition.
> Yet Ministers refuse to release them.

There has been a flawed categorisation of Kerr's letters to the Palace as personal records. Other correspondence between governors-general, the monarch and members of the royal household is available for public access. Moreover, there is undue discretion afforded to Government House and the Palace to determine access to the correspondence. There is, however, no appeal process and this unorthodox arrangement is in defiance of Australian practices concerning the release of official documents.

In July, we raised this matter formally with the then prime minister, Tony Abbott, and the attorney-general, George Brandis. We made it clear these policies, in our view, are not consistent with Australia's independence.

We now have a situation where public access to Kerr's correspondence with the Palace, as part of his official duties during the 1975 political and constitutional crisis, is being kept secret under an agreement by Buckingham Palace and Government House. This issue now has the potential to become a matter of serious embarrassment for Australia. Forty years after the dismissal, it is time this correspondence was released.

Appendix B

FORTY YEARS
OF DISMISSAL MYTHS

This essay was first published in
The Weekend Australian *on 26 December 2015.*

Gough Whitlam's dismissal by Sir John Kerr in November 1975 was the single most dramatic event in our political history.

Contrary to many predictions at the time, Australia's parliamentary and constitutional system recovered from the 1975 crisis and proved its resilience. The lesson was absorbed: namely, that institutions and constitutional powers must not be pushed towards breaking point.

Our democracy was tested in 1975 in a brinkmanship involving Whitlam, Malcolm Fraser and Governor-General Kerr in a contest startling in its lust for power that exposed the elemental impulses in human nature.

Forty years later, however, it is tempting to ask whether the current lethargy and entrenched deadlock in our politics is actually a deeper and more systemic problem than the 1975 eruption, an event that is unlikely to recur.

The present political malaise is more insidious. Indeed, many people insist there is no problem, while the political system for much of a decade has failed to deliver the public policy outcomes essential for Australia's progress.

As an event the dismissal exists to be reinterpreted by each generation and this phenomenon has been on display again.

The fortieth anniversary occasioned the publication of our book, *The Dismissal: In the Queen's Name*, based on about forty new interviews and one thousand pages of new historical documents. Our book and the reaction to it testifies to a range of old and new mythologies about the crisis.

There are three that are conspicuous: that the dismissal was really a conspiracy driven from the US by the CIA; that the Queen and Buckingham Palace were 'in the know' and Kerr's co-agents in the dismissal; and that Whitlam was actually going to prevail on 11 November and had his triumph stolen from him by Kerr. It is past time, in this fortieth anniversary year, to engage with these mythologies.

Each of these ideas is astonishing and, on the available evidence, completely false. But such ideas reveal much about this event. To an extent, it transcends history and rational analysis. Whitlam's dismissal has become part of our culture and that culture loves nothing more than conspiracy. The paranoid strand in our political culture may be isolated but it runs deep. The 1975 crisis, a fantastic event in its own right, becomes the cradle for another bunch of improbable fantasies.

During the many public meetings we experienced in the marketing campaign for our book there was always one certainty: the inevitable question about the CIA. It seems too spectacular a story to throw away. We quote Margaret Whitlam in a 1991 interview saying she thought the CIA was involved. 'Gough doesn't,' she said. But as a reader of thrillers she was 'prepared to believe it'. And that's the point. It is an idea that excites the imagination.

There was a documented crisis in security intelligence relations between Australia and the US in November 1975 but there is no credible evidence from a reliable source that the intelligence crisis precipitated the dismissal.

Whitlam denied the CIA theory; Kerr repudiated it. The authors, in reading hundreds of pages of Kerr's intimate revelations after 1975, have found nothing on the CIA. The notion that the governor-general was so corrupt that he would secretly sack Whitlam at the behest of the CIA is the ultimate proof of a debased political system – and this is the motive that inspires the mythology.

There are many criticisms that can be levelled against Kerr but selling out his country at the behest of a foreign power is not among them. However, don't expect the myth to die.

A potentially more powerful myth has gained currency this year courtesy of historian Jenny Hocking, Whitlam's biographer and author of a slim book published this year, *The Dismissal Dossier* (MUP). Hocking has propagated the view that the Queen not only had prior warning of Kerr's dismissal but also supported his vice-regal intervention.

Once again, this is an astonishing claim made on the thinnest evidence. It is tenuous and fleeting. It is disputed by other records and interviews. In recent weeks Hocking has amplified her view that the Queen knew of and supported the dismissal.

This contradicts the accounts of Kerr and Palace officials. Whitlam never claimed the Queen was a party to Kerr's intervention.

In *Gough Whitlam: His Time* (MUP), Hocking writes that before supply was blocked in October 1975, 'the governor-general had already conferred with the Palace on the possibility of the future dismissal of the prime minister, securing in advance the response of the Palace to it'.

Hocking argues there were 'several critical conversations and understandings reached' between the Palace and Kerr concerning Whitlam's dismissal. In *The Dismissal Dossier* she claims the Palace had 'advance knowledge' that Kerr planned to dismiss Whitlam. She says there was a 'secret arrangement' between Kerr and the Palace about 'a well-advanced plan'.

Hocking says Palace officials gave what could only be called 'an unqualified green light to Kerr's dismissal of Whitlam'. Hocking says the Queen herself was 'aware' that Kerr was considering dismissal and did not dissuade him from doing so.

These are explosive claims. If true, they transform our understanding of the dismissal. Whitlam always argued the Queen would never have done what the governor-general did. Any notion that the Queen was party to the dismissal and through this awareness endorsed Whitlam's dismissal could only prejudice the position of the monarchy in this country.

The main evidence for this claim is a few paragraphs Kerr wrote by hand in a short-lived 1980 journal. The authors have read and evaluated this account.

In this journal Kerr ruminated at length on the prospect in 1975 that Whitlam might have recalled him as governor-general. He wrote that in September 1975 he had a conversation with a young Prince Charles in Papua New Guinea. Kerr, apparently, told Charles he may have to exercise the reserve powers of dismissal and conveyed his fear of being recalled by the Queen on Whitlam's advice. According to Kerr, Charles said: 'But surely, Sir John, the Queen would not have to accept advice that you should be recalled at the very time should this happen when you were considering having to dismiss the government.'

Kerr's journal says Charles reported this discussion to the Queen's private secretary, Martin Charteris. The following month, Charteris wrote to Kerr. According to Kerr the 'advice' from the Palace was 'that if the kind of contingency in mind were to develop, although the Queen would try to delay things in the end she would have to take the Prime Minister's advice'. Kerr made the point he already knew this – if Whitlam wanted him removed then the Palace would act on such advice.

The suggestion by Kerr five years later in a journal that he told Charles before supply was blocked that he might have to dismiss Whitlam is astonishing. Its credibility must be doubted. This full account is not mentioned in Kerr's two volumes of memoirs, one published and one unpublished, or in any of his other contemporary papers and files.

Even assuming, however, that it happened, this cannot constitute what Hocking claims.

The budget had not been blocked at this stage. There was no certainty of a crisis. The sequence of future events was not known. Kerr is not informing Charles or the Palace of any intention to dismiss Whitlam. It is preposterous to draw this conclusion. What comes through is Kerr's well-known obsession that Whitlam might try to remove him as governor-general.

The advice Charteris conveys by letter – if such a letter exists it has not been located – is merely that Whitlam would be able to remove Kerr. This does not amount to a prior agreement by the Palace on Kerr's dismissal of Whitlam. Nor is there any documentary evidence to this effect.

Hocking's view is not verified by any other document in Kerr's many thousands of pages of files at the National Archives or any interview with a participant in these events. If it had been Kerr's intention to secure the prior agreement of the Palace, why would he not reveal this?

The answer, of course, is that this was not Kerr's intention, as he explains at length. His golden rule in the crisis was to cultivate the Palace, keep the Palace informed by letter of the progress of the 1975 events, outline his thinking and possible options, but not tell the Queen of his intent or the timing of any dismissal.

Indeed, as a proud man Kerr wanted to ensure the dismissal was his responsibility. He also wanted to protect the Palace from being implicated in the dismissal. Fearing that Whitlam would try to remove him, Kerr sacked Whitlam in an ambush.

Interviewed by the authors, the Queen's assistant private secretary, William Heseltine, said his reaction was 'stunned surprise' when rung in the middle of the night and informed about Whitlam's dismissal. This was also the reaction of Charteris as private secretary.

Asked about the Queen's reaction, Heseltine said: 'I think she was indeed surprised, as surprised as we had been. She certainly gave no indication to me that there had been any thought that something like this would happen.

'I would hesitate to say that she was shocked. It would be true to say that none of us at the time thought that this was an ideal solution to the crisis.'

Every principal involved in the dismissal has rejected the notion that the Palace was a party to it. Not only was the Palace taken by surprise but there was a distinct sense of disquiet about Kerr's action. This did not fit the Buckingham Palace culture of no surprises and no partisanship.

The effort, 40 years later, to construct a narrative about the Queen's involvement in the dismissal, with the Palace giving the 'green light' to Kerr, is not sustained by the evidence. If true, it would be extremely damaging to both the office of governor-general and the position of the Queen of Australia. The cause of the republic does not need or justify such a misleading historical account.

The third great mythology about the dismissal, again promoted by Hocking, is that Whitlam on 11 November was about to resolve the crisis in a glorious victory with his proposal for a half-Senate election. This is but the latest version of misplaced Whitlam idolisation unjustified by the facts.

As is well known, when Whitlam went to Yarralumla at lunchtime on 11 November he carried a recommendation for the governor-general for a half-Senate election. Hocking says once this became known 'the opposition senators would have passed the budget'. She claims there is 'no doubt' the Senate election 'would (have been) both a resolution of the crisis and a successful outcome for Whitlam'.

These are ludicrous claims. They misunderstand the fundamentals of the 1975 crisis.

Whitlam spent a month after the blocking of supply in mid-October trying to pressure Fraser and the Senate to crack and pass his budget. He was unsuccessful. It was only after this lack of success that Whitlam resorted to the half-Senate election option, given such an election was due before July 1976. This was a sign of Whitlam's weakness. And Kerr understood.

When Kerr spoke to Whitlam by phone on the morning of 11 November, the prime minister indicated his intention to recommend the Senate poll. They discussed what time Whitlam would arrive at Government House. Kerr asked Whitlam whether supply would be available for the campaign period and Whitlam confirmed that it would not.

For Kerr, this was a crucial point. Whitlam, in effect, was advising a half-Senate election knowing the government would run out of funds during the campaign. Kerr later wrote that his acceptance of this advice would have led to 'financial chaos'. Whitlam was telling Kerr he planned to govern through a Senate campaign after supply was exhausted. No responsible governor-general would accept this advice. Certainly, Kerr had no intention of accepting it.

By 11 November the half-Senate election was a dead-duck option. Far from being the resolution to the crisis and a Whitlam victory, it offered nothing to advance a solution. That Whitlam was promoting this option on 11 November reveals his defective tactics, his misunderstanding of the crisis and his misreading of Kerr. Hocking cannot grasp the obvious – that Whitlam's only window of opportunity for a half-Senate election was earlier in mid-October, when supply would have been available for the campaign.

Kerr would have granted a request for a Senate election at that early stage. But he could not have honoured the obligations of his office and granted Whitlam a Senate poll on 11 November, an elementary point in vice-regal thinking about elections.

The final bizarre claim about Whitlam as the deserved 11 November victor is Hocking's argument that Kerr should have recommissioned Whitlam as prime minister in the afternoon after the House of Representatives had voted 'no confidence' in Fraser as caretaker prime minister.

Whitlam has long advanced this argument to justify his failed tactics after the dismissal. It is unconvincing and untenable.

The truth is that Whitlam had no contingency plan in case Kerr dismissed him. A prudent prime minister would have devised plans to respond to various scenarios, including the worst-case scenario of dismissal. Whitlam didn't. The upshot is that Whitlam was completely outfoxed on the afternoon of 11 November.

He failed to grasp that the key to thwarting Kerr lay in the Senate – in denying supply to Fraser's caretaker government. Whitlam's tragedy is that Labor senators voted supply to the Fraser government by 2.24 p.m. That action meant Fraser could meet the terms of his commission and now recommend a double-dissolution election, ensuring that Kerr's plan was carried to success.

Whitlam's tactic, on the other hand, was to pass a no-confidence motion in Fraser in the House of Representatives and, with supply now granted, ask the governor-general to recommission him.

According to Hocking, passage of the no-confidence motion meant 'Kerr's action in dismissing Whitlam had completely derailed'.

Hocking says Kerr's refusal to act on the no-confidence motion was tantamount to a 'second dismissal' of Whitlam.

She claims there was 'no barrier' to Whitlam re-forming government and there should have been 'no quandary' for the governor-general against the recommissioning of Whitlam as PM.

It is utter nonsense. Kerr sacked Whitlam in order to get a new prime minister who would advise an election. He knew Fraser lacked the confidence of the House of Representatives. Having commissioned Fraser on the basis that he would obtain supply and advise an election, Kerr could not turn around to dismiss Fraser after he had fulfilled the terms of his commission.

The Senate passed supply because Fraser was PM. The house vote demonstrated what Kerr knew. Kerr was wrong to dismiss Whitlam in an ambush without warning. Having done that, he could not betray Fraser and sack a second prime minister on the same day for doing what he asked.

The dismissal sees historical reality and myth in a complex interaction. After 40 years, however, the evidence remains clear: the CIA wasn't responsible, the Palace didn't know and Whitlam was not the thwarted victor on 11 November 1975.

Appendix C

CONSPIRACIES — KERR'S SECRET MEMOIR

In his second unpublished book, *The Triumph of the Constitution*, Sir John Kerr covered a range of historical issues dealing with the 1975 crisis, the Palace, the politics of constitutional change and included two chapters (12 and 13) on Conspiracies Galore. The authors have a near final draft of this manuscript written over 1987–90.

In these chapters Kerr deals at length with the elaborate conspiracy theories that surrounded the dismissal and that, in some ways, only grew over time. He writes that he included these two chapters 'somewhat reluctantly' since they concerned 'myth making' about 1975 and his 'basic desire' was to avoid spreading false stories. In the end, though, he said: 'I believe that we owe it to Australia and to Australians to repudiate the exercise in disinformation.'

'I feel the need to have my denials clearly on the record,' Sir John wrote. This was because 'a vocal minority' was disposed to accept such myths. He was particularly aware of the ability of the Labor Party to allege 'conspiratorial doings' among its class enemies or in the 'Establishment'. Indeed, he spent several pages recalling the conspiracy theories advanced by former ALP leader Dr HV Evatt during the 1950s concerning the Petrov affair.

Proceeding to the events of 1975, Kerr wrote:

> The pattern, so far as I understand it, consisted of at least four
> separate vaguely alleged political 'conspiracies', namely:
>
> 1. That I as governor-general conspired with the leaders of the
>   armed forces with the intention, as the commander-in-chief of
>   those forces, 'to bring out the troops' to support my decision of
>   11 November 1975 or in any event had formed a 'conspiratorial'
>   intent to do so if I judged it to be necessary;
> 2. That I had as governor-general conspired in vaguely expressed
>   ways with the leader of the Opposition, [Malcolm] Fraser;
>   [Bob] Ellicott, former solicitor-general and in 1975 a shadow
>   minister in Fraser's shadow cabinet; and with the chief justice
>   of Australia, Sir Garfield Barwick to dismiss the Whitlam
>   Government; or one or more of them;
> 3. That I had as governor-general conspired with Sir Arthur Tange,
>   the secretary of the defence department, and Dr JL Farrands, the
>   scientific head of the defence department, to accept a briefing
>   from Farrands a few days before 11 November 1975 on the CIA's
>   alleged view that Whitlam was a security risk, all of this being
>   without the knowledge of the prime minister; and
> 4. That I had conspired with the CIA and the United Kingdom
>   security services to destabilise and destroy the Whitlam
>   Government and had dismissed it, pursuant to that conspiracy,
>   at the behest of the CIA and British security.
>
> I entirely repudiate all of this nonsense and have so far generally
> managed substantially to ignore it. These 'conspiracy theories' are
> fantastic, absurd and incredible. They have been put forward with
> varying degrees of vagueness and have been repeated or referred
> to over and over again by the media, often simply by using the
> formula, after referring to me in one way or another, that 'he is

the man widely believed in the Labor Party (or in Australia) to have dismissed the Whitlam Government at the behest of the CIA' or 'the UK security forces' or words to that effect. The 'conspiracies' were whispered from mouth to mouth, repeated over and over again, and with participants who differed in various allegations. They were recycled with growing or dying vigour according to circumstances and supported by the argument 'where there is smoke there is fire'. How gullible do the proponents of such nonsense believe the people to be? How insulting it all is to Australia and its people.

Kerr dealt, in turn, with each claim. In relation to the first claim he referred to a press conference held by Gough Whitlam in London on 11 June 1977 when the former prime minister said that Kerr 'would have called out the Army if the Labor Government had not taken its dismissal quietly'. Sir John pointed out that there had been no fighting in the streets, civil commotion or industrial trouble. He said the only act that might have inspired violence on 11 November was Whitlam's own 'maintain your rage' speech on the stairs of Parliament House.

Kerr wrote:

> My mind did not turn, even for a passing moment, to the prospect of real street fighting. In my talks with Fraser on 11 and 12 November the subject was never mentioned by either of us; nor was it mentioned to me by any of the new caretaker ministers.
>
> Mr Whitlam as quoted above takes credit for the fact that the Labor Government had 'taken its dismissal quietly on November 11, 1975'. What alternative did it have except insurrectionary action, violence and civil commotion and street fighting tending possibly to civil war – to revolutionary conduct? There never was any risk of this.
>
> What Whitlam was really saying in London at the book

launching was that if violence in the streets had broken out so as to require military action the Governor-General individually and on his own sole authority would have brought out the troops and been able to do so. Not so. What would have happened during or after the election in such a situation would have been that the existing prime minister and government, whether caretaker or not, would have doubtless advised the governor-general what they proposed to do.

Any action which followed involving the troops would have taken place on the responsibility of the prime minister and his government.

When he made his 'maintain your rage' speech, Whitlam was living in a dream world, and when he made his above-quoted speech in London 18 months later he was living out a fantasy.

In relation to the second alleged conspiracy, Kerr repudiated any notion that he had conspired with other figures. He said that at no time during the crisis did he talk to his friend, the senior Liberal, Robert Ellicott. He said he had no discussion with Chief Justice, Sir Garfield Barwick, from the time of their 20 September talk at the Union Club dinner to their contact on 9 November at which point Kerr had made up his mind.

Reviewing his dealings with Fraser, Kerr said:

He was quite unlike Whitlam who had also gambled everything on the outcome. I saw both of them on 6 November. Fraser was worried. Whitlam was not. Fraser is said now to have, because of the 'conspiracy', known what was going to happen from the beginning, but he never acted in his talks with me like a man who believed he had the whole thing sewn up, and of course he did not. He did not act as a man talking to a fellow conspirator and talking as one 'in the know' and 'in a conspiracy'. The reality was quite different.

The second alleged conspiracy did not exist. There was no conspiracy, no agreement, between Fraser, Ellicott, Barwick and myself or any of us about what was going to happen. We each did what we did – acting on our separate views at the relevant time of what had to be done.

In relation to the third and fourth conspiracy theories Kerr said he would deal with them as one. He branded the idea that he had received a secret briefing about the CIA's alarm before 11 November 'a wicked falsehood'. Kerr asked: 'Who invented it? Who knows? It is a typical piece of disinformation maliciously conjured up by someone and equally maliciously circulated and re-circulated.'

In his unpublished book Kerr quoted at length from two letters, the first written by former chief defence scientist, Dr John Farrands, to *The National Times* of 4–10 April 1982 and the second by the former head of the defence department, Sir Arthur Tangle, to the same newspaper of 16–22 May.

Farrands referred to claims that he briefed Kerr on Tange's instructions on 8 November 1975 and that Farrands and Tange kept this material from the Whitlam Government. Farrands said he met Kerr on 28 October as part of the 'common custom' of senior official seeing the governor-general. He said there was no discussion about US installations in Australia. 'There was no reference made to Pine Gap, Nurrungar, the CIA or any other matters of a security nature,' Farrands wrote.

At the conclusion of his letter Farrands said:

Let me set the matter straight by unequivocally stating that:
1. At no time on or before November 11, 1975, did I discuss with Sir John Kerr any American activities in Australia;
2. I have never had any communication with any Governor-General relating to the security standing of any prime minister or any other minister; and

3. I did not communicate in any way with Sir John Kerr on the
   weekend of November 8–9, 1975.'

In the Tange letter, Sir Arthur stated:

I did not conceive in my own mind, much less take any action
directed towards, any communication whatsoever with the
Governor-General, then or at any other time on any matter
canvassed in your article. To suggest it to someone who has served
successful [sic] Labor and Coalition governments since the 1940s,
and who has occupied the Secretaryship of both the Departments
of External Affairs and Defence, attacks and slurs my integrity as a
loyal servant of elected government.

Kerr said that despite 'the splather of nonsense' circulated about
the CIA intervention as a factor in the dismissal the story was 'false'.
He invoked Whitlam who also denied the CIA conspiracy theory. Kerr
wrote that the 'killing final comment' came from Whitlam's interview
with journalist Peter Hastings, published in *The Sydney Morning
Herald* of 24 March 1984. Did Whitlam think the CIA had got to the
governor-general? Whitlam replied: 'No, I don't. I never have.'
Kerr wrote:

It is very understandable that Whitlam is not prepared to endorse
the notion that the CIA had 'got to me' because this would involve
his acceptance of the theory that he, 'The Great Leader' as Hastings
calls him ironically in his interview, had been finally sacked and
defeated as a result of CIA efforts.

It would be unbearably humiliating for him to do so and, of
course, he is right to repudiate it.

Kerr set out to demolish the conspiracy theories that had enveloped
the story of the dismissal because they diminished his role in it. Kerr

was a vain and proud man. In this unpublished memoir, he described the dismissal as 'a great personal as well as political and constitutional drama' and cast himself as the principal actor. 'I was neither weak nor conspiratorial,' Kerr wrote.

Appendix D

THE DISMISSAL DOCUMENTS

Confidential

👑

GOVERNMENT HOUSE
CANBERRA

for P. M

Hon Frank Crean
Hon K. E. Beazley
David Derham
John Kerr
Sir Kenneth Wheare
Sir Vincent Fairfax
mr — Kenneth Myer
H. J. Souter .

Sir Paul Hasluck's confidential list of possible governors-general to Gough Whitlam
(June 1973).
Source: The Whitlam Institute

THE GOVERNOR-GENERAL'S POWERS

In a statement issued in Canberra today Opposition Front-Bencher,
Mr R. J. Ellicott, Q.C., said:

"The Governor-General's basic role is the execution and
maintenance of the Constitution and of the laws of the
Commonwealth.   He performs this role with the advice of
Ministers whom he chooses and who hold office during his
pleasure.

The Prime Minister is treating the Governor-General as a
mere automaton with no public will of his own, sitting at
Yarralumla waiting to do his bidding.

Nothing could be further from the truth.   It is contrary
to principle, precedent and common sense.   The Governor-
General has at least two clear constitutional prerogatives
which he can exercise - the right to dismiss his Ministers
and appoint others, and the right to refuse a dissolution
of the Parliament or of either House.

These prerogatives, of their very nature, will only be
exercised on the rarest occasions.   They have been exercised
in the past and the proper working of the Constitution
demands that they continue.   One only has to think of
extreme cases to realise the sense behind them, e.g.
the case of an obviously corrupt Government.

The maintenance of the Constitution and of the laws of the
Commonwealth require that the Government have authority
from Parliament to spend money in order to perform those
functions.   A Government without supply cannot govern.

..2

Bob Ellicott's legal opinion on the constitutional crisis (16 October 1975).
Source: The Whitlam Institute (Graham Freudenberg Papers)

The refusal by Parliament of supply, whether through the
House or the Senate, is a clear signal to the Governor-
General that his chosen Ministers may not be able to
carry on.   In the proper performance of his role, he
would inevitably want to have from the Prime Minister
an explanation of how he proposed to overcome the situation.
If the Prime Minister proposed and insisted on means which
were unlawful or which did not solve the problems of the
disagreement between the Houses and left the Government
without funds to carry on, it would be within the Governor-
General's power and his duty to dismiss his Ministers
and appoint others.

In the current situation now facing us, the Governor-
General, in the performance of his role, would need to
know immediately what steps the Government proposes to
take in order to avert the problem of it being without
supply in the near future, so endangering the maintenance
of the Constitution and of the laws of the Commonwealth.
He is not powerless and the proper exercise of his
powers demands that he be informed immediately on this
matter.   The Prime Minister should inform him on his
own initiative.   If he does not, the Governor-General
would be justified in sending for him and seeking the
information.

..3

The Governor-General is entitled to know:

(1) when it is that the Government will or is likely
    to run out of funds under the current Supply Acts;
    and

(2) how the Government proposes to carry on after those
    funds run out; and

(3) how the Government proposes that the disagreement
    between the two Houses should be resolved.

These questions cannot properly be left to be considered
at a later date because of the consequences which lack
of authorised appropriations will have on the Government's
capacity to govern, the public service of the Commonwealth
and public order.

If he is informed by the Prime Minister that the Government
proposes that a half Senate election be held and that by
this means (as a result of the election of Territory
Senators) the Government hopes to have a majority in the
Senate the Governor-General will need to be satisfied:-

(i) that having regard to the proposed date of the election,
    the Government will have sufficient supply to carry
    on until the result of that election has been ascertained.

(ii) that the election is likely to resolve the difference
    between the two Houses by giving the Government a
    majority in the Senate.

In being satisfied of the first matter a number of factors
would be relevant and he would be entitled to be informed
about them e.g.

(i)   The date when the Government would or would be likely
       to run out of supply.   Because of the seriousness
       of the Government not having supply the Governor-General

should not be expected to rely nor should he rely
on mere estimates. He is entitled to and should be
satisfied what supply the Government still has
and when it will in the ordinary course run out.

(ii) the date when the result of the poll is likely to
be known having regard to possible events such as
a large number of candidates or postal voting.
Because of the seriousness of the Government being
without supply before that date the assessment
should err on the conservative side.

In being satisfied of the second (the likelihood of the
Government obtaining a majority in the Senate as a result
of the election) he will need to have information which
justifies that conclusion.   He would also be entitled
                                        immediately
to consider, how those who will be in the Senate/after
the election are likely to vote if the Appropriation Bills
were re-submitted.   If it was thought that some of the
States were not prepared to hold the elections he would
be entitled to consider, for instance, the likely votes
of those casual Senators who would remain, e.g. Senator
Field.   The fact that Senator Field's seat is under
challenge would only add uncertainty as to whether the
Government can hope to get a majority as his replacement
would be a matter for the Queensland Government.

In view of the Government's complaint that the Senate
has consistently blocked its legislation the Governor-
General would be entitled to consider whether the
dispute would really be solved by a half term election or
whether the only practicable course was for the Government
to seek a double dissolution so that the matter could be

resolved by the people.

If the Governor General was not satisfied that the Government would have supply until the election result in the Territories was known he would only have one option open to him in the interests of good government. He is entitled to and should ask the Prime Minister if the government is prepared to advise him to dissolve the House of Representatives and the Senate or the House of Representatives alone as a means of ensuring that the disagreement between the two Houses is resolved.

If the Prime Minister refuses to do either it is then open to the Governor General to dismiss his present Ministers and seek others who are prepared to give him the only proper advice open. This he should proceed to do. The proper advice in the circumstances is to dissolve both Houses of the Parliament or the House of Representatives alone with or without a half Senate election."

$\mathscr{D}r\!=\!\!\mathscr{ft}$ OPINION (3)

Mr R.J. Ellicott, Q.C., M.P. at the Attorney-General's request made available to him a copy of a press statement relating to the Governor-General's powers. We have been asked by the Prime Minister to provide an opinion upon the legal propositions which that statement contains or assumes. The statement expresses Mr Ellicott's view that His Excellency is legally obliged to take certain steps because of, and as a result of, the current dispute between the House and the Senate. A short recapitulation of that dispute is necessary so that our view of what the situation is which confronts His Excellency may be understood.

2.   We set out hereunder a statement in chronological order of the formal steps taken in relation to the introduction and disposition of the Bills by the Representatives and the Senate including the relevant resolutions passed by each of the Houses.

1975

19 August   Appropriation Bill (No. 1) 1975-76 and Appropriation Bill (No. 2) 1975-76 were introduced into the House of Representatives, accompanied in each case by a message from the Governor-General, in accordance with the requirements of section 56 of the Constitution, recommending an appropriation of the Consolidated Revenue Fund for the services set forth in the Bills.

'Draft' joint opinion by Maurice Byers and Kep Enderby on the constitutional crisis, presented to Sir John Kerr on 6 November 1975, with the governor-general's annotations (4 November 1975).
Source: National Archives of Australia (Kerr Papers)

8 October	The House of Representatives passed Appropriation Bills (No.1) and (No.2) 1975-76.
16 October	The Senate, after reading Appropriation Bill (No.1) a first time, amended a motion by the Leader of the Government in the Senate "that the Bill be now read a second time" by leaving out all words after "that" and inserting:

"this Bill be not further proceeded with until the Government agrees to submit itself to the judgment of the people, the Senate being of the opinion that the Prime Minister and his Government no longer have the trust and confidence of the Australian people because of -

(a) the continuing incompetence, evasion, deceit and duplicity of the Prime Minister and his Ministers as exemplified in the overseas loan scandal which was an attempt by the Government to subvert the Constitution, to by-pass Parliament and to evade its responsibilities to the States and the Loan Council;

(b) the Prime Minister's failure to maintain proper control over the activities of his Ministers and Government to the detriment of the Australian nation and people; and

(c) the continuing mismanagement of the Australian economy by the Prime Minister and this Government with policies which have caused a lack of confidence in this nation's potential and created inflation and unemployment not experienced for 40 years".

Appropriation Bill (No.2) was similarly dealt with.

On 16 October the House of Representatives adopted a resolution in the following terms:

"Considering that this House is the House of the Australian Parliament from which the Government of Australia is chosen;

Considering moreover that on 2 December 1972 the Australian Labor Party was elected by judgment of the

people to be the Government of Australia; that on
18 May 1974 the Australian Labor Party was re-elected
by judgment of the people to be the Government of
Australia; and that the Australian Labor Party continues
to have a governing majority in this House;

Recognising that the Constitution and the
conventions of the Constitution vest in this House the
control of the supply of money to the elected
Governments;

Noting that this House on 27 August 1975 passed
the Loan Bill 1975 and on 8 October 1975 passed the
Appropriation Bill (No.1) 1975-76 and the Appropriation
Bill (No.2) 1975-76 which, amongst other things,
appropriate moneys for the ordinary annual services of
the Government;

Noting also that on 15 October 1975, in total
disregard of the practices and conventions observed in
the Australian Parliament since Federation, the Leader
of the Opposition announced the intention of the
Opposition to delay those Bills, with the object of
forcing an election of this House: that on 15 October
1975 the Leader of the Opposition in the Senate announced
that the Opposition parties in the Senate would delay the
Bills; and that on 15 October 1975 the Senate, against
the wishes of the Government, decided not to proceed
further with consideration of the Loan Bill 1975;

Considering that the actions of the Senate and of
the Leader of the Opposition will, if pursued, have the
most serious consequences for Parliamentary democracy in
Australia, will seriously damage the Government's efforts
to counter the effect of world-wide inflation and
unemployment, and will thereby cause great hardship for
the Australian people:

1.   This House declares that it has full confidence
     in the Australian Labor Party Government.

2.   This House affirms that the Constitution and
     the conventions of the Constitution vest in this
     House the control of the supply of money to the elected
     Government and that the threatened action of the
     Senate constitutes a gross violation of the roles
     of the respective Houses of the Parliament in
     relation to the appropriation of moneys.

3.   This House <u>asserts</u> the basic principle that
a Government that continues to have a
majority in the House of Representatives has
a right to expect that it will be able to
govern.

4.   This House <u>condemns</u> the threatened action of
the Leader of the Opposition and of the non-
government parties in the Senate as being
reprehensible and as constituting a grave
threat to the principles of responsible
government and of Parliamentary democracy in
Australia.

5.   This House <u>calls upon</u> the Senate to pass
without delay the Loan Bill 1975, the Appropriation
Bill (No.1) 1975-76 and the Appropriation Bill
(No.2) 1975-76.

<u>21 October</u>   The House of Representatives resolved as follows:

(1) That the House of Representatives having
considered Message No.276 of the Senate asserts that the
action of the Senate in delaying the passage of the
Appropriation Bill (No.1) 1975-76 and the Appropriation
Bill (No.2) 1975-76 for the reasons given in the Senate
resolution is not contemplated within the terms of the
Constitution and is contrary to established constitutional
convention, and therefore requests the Senate to re-consider
and pass the Bills without delay.

(2) That a message be sent to the Senate acquainting
it of this resolution.

<u>22 October</u>   The Senate, having received by message the

resolution adopted by the House of Representatives

on 21 October, resolved as follows:

"Leave out all words after 'That', insert - 'the
Senate having considered Message No.380 of the House of
Representatives asserts

(a) That the action of the Senate in delaying the
passage of the Appropriation Bill (No.1) 1975-76
and the Appropriation Bill (No.2) 1975-76 for
the reasons given in the Senate Resolution as
communicated to the House of Representatives in
Message No.276 is a lawful and proper exercise
within the terms of the Constitution of the
powers of the Senate.

(b) That the powers of the Senate were expressly conferred on the Senate as part of the Federal Compact which created the Commonwealth of Australia.

(c) That the legislative power of the Commonwealth is vested in the Parliament of the Commonwealth which consists of the Queen, the Senate and House of Representatives.

(d) That the Senate has the right and duty to exercise its legislative power and to concur or not concur, as the Senate sees fit, bearing in mind the seriousness and responsibility of its actions, in all proposed laws passed by the House of Representatives.

(e) That there is no convention and never has been any convention that the Senate shall not exercise its constitutional powers.

(f) That the Senate affirms that it has the constitutional right to act as it did and now that there is a disagreement between the Houses of Parliament and a position may arise where the normal operation of Government cannot continue, a remedy is presently available to the Government under section 57 of the Constitution to resolve the deadlock.

(2) That the Senate reaffirms to the House of Representatives its resolution set out in Senate Message No.276 in respect of each of the two Appropriation Bills, namely - 'this Bill be not further proceeded with until the Government agrees to submit itself to the judgment of the people, the Senate being of the opinion that the Prime Minister and his Government no longer have the trust and confidence of the Australian people because of -

(a) the continuing incompetence, evasion, deceit and duplicity of the Prime Minister and his Ministers as exemplified in the overseas loan scandal which was an attempt by the Government to subvert the Constitution, to by-pass Parliament and to evade its responsibilities to the States and the Loan Council;

(b) the Prime Minister's failure to maintain proper control over the activities of his Ministers and Government to the detriment of the Australian nation and people; and

(c) the continuing mismanagement of the Australian economy by the Prime Minister and this Government with policies which have caused a lack of confidence in this nation's potential and created inflation and unemployment not experienced for 40 years.'

(3) That the foregoing Resolutions be transmitted
to the House of Representatives by message."

> Bills identical with the original Appropriation
> Bills and entitled Appropriation Bill (No.1)
> 1975-76 /No.2/ and Appropriation Bill (No.2)
> 1975-76 /No.2/ were introduced in and passed
> by the House of Representatives and forwarded to
> the Senate. These Bills were accompanied by
> messages from the Governor-General recommending
> the appropriation of the Consolidated Revenue
> Fund accordingly as required by section 56 of
> the Constitution.
>
> The Senate read the /No.2/ Bills for the first
> time.

23 October
> The motion of the Leader of the Government in
> the Senate that the /No.2/ Bills be now read a
> second time was amended to the effect that the
> Bills were not to be further proceeded with
> until the Government agreed to submit itself
> to the judgment of the people. The motion as
> amended and passed then went on to refer to the
> same matters as were contained in the Senate's
> motion of 16 October.

28 October
The House of Representatives resolved as follows:

"(1) That the House of Representatives, having considered
Message No.279 of the Senate -

    (a) again asserts that the action of the Senate in
delaying the passage of the two Appropriation
Bills is contrary to established constitutional
convention;

(b) denounces the blatant attempt by the Senate to violate section 28 of the Constitution for political purposes by itself endeavouring to force an early election for the House of Representatives;

(c) resolves that it will uphold the established right of the Government with a majority in the House of Representatives to be the Government of the nation; and

(d) again calls on the Senate to re-consider and pass the Bills without further delay in order to avoid the possibility of widespread distress occurring within the Australian community.

(2) That a message be sent to the Senate acquainting it of this Resolution."

3.   We conclude this recital with the list of Appropriation

and Supply Bills which had been passed by the Senate where the

Government of the day did not have a Senate majority.

Appropriation and Supply Bills

1913 -
```
Appropriation 1913-14
Appropriation (Works and Buildings) 1913-14
Supplementary Appropriation 1911-12
Supplementary Appropriation (Works and Buildings) 1911-12
Supplementary Appropriation 1912-13
Supplementary Appropriation (Works and Buildings) 1912-13
Supply (No.1) 1913-14
Supply (No.2) 1913-14
Supply (No.3) 1913-14
Supply (No.4) 1913-14
Supply (No.5) 1913-14
```

1930 -
```
Appropriation 1930-31
Appropriation (Works and Buildings) 1930-31
Supply (No.1) 1930-31
```

1931 -
```
Appropriation 1931-32
Appropriation (Unemployment Relief Works)
Appropriation (Works and Buildings) 1931-32
Supplementary Appropriation 1927-30
Supplementary Appropriation (Works and Buildings) 1927-30
Supply (No.1) 1931-32
```

1956 -
     Appropriation (No.2) 1955-56
     Appropriation 1956-57
     Appropriation (Works and Services) (No.2) 1955-56
     Appropriation (Works and Services) 1955-57
     Supplementary Appropriation 1954-55
     Supplementary Appropriation 1955-56
     Supplementary Appropriation (Works and Services) 1954-55
     Supplementary Appropriation (Works and Services) 1955-56
     Supply (No.1) 1956-57
     Supply (Works and Services) (No.1) 1956-57

1957 -
     Appropriation (No.2) 1956-57
     Appropriation 1957-58
     Appropriation (Works and Services) (No.2) 1956-57
     Appropriation (Works and Services) 1957-58
     Supply 1957-58
     Supply (No.2) 1957-58
     Supply (Works and Services) 1957-58
     Supply (Works and Services) (No.2) 1957-58

1958 -
     Appropriation (No.2) 1957-58
     Appropriation 1958-59
     Appropriation (Works and Services) (No.2) 1957-58
     Appropriation (Works and Services) 1958-59
     Supply 1958-59
     Supply (Works and Services) 1958-59

1962 -
     Appropriation (No.2) 1961-62
     Appropriation 1962-63
     Appropriation (Works and Services) (No.2) 1961-62
     Appropriation (Works and Services) 1962-63
     Supply 1962-63
     Supply (Works and Services) 1962-63

1963 -
     Appropriation (No.2) 1962-63
     Appropriation 1963-64
     Appropriation (Works and Services) (No.2) 1962-63
     Appropriation (Works and Services) 1963-64
     Supply 1963-64
     Supply (Works and Services) 1963-64

1964 -
     Appropriation (No.2) 1963-64
     Appropriation 1964-65
     Appropriation (No.2) 1964-65
     Appropriation (Special Expenditure) 1964-65
     Appropriation (Works and Services) (No.2) 1963-64
     Supply 1964-65
     Supply (Special Expenditure) 1964-65

1965 -

Appropriation (No.3) 1964-65
Appropriation (no.1) 1965-66
Appropriation (No.2) 1965-66
Appropriation (Special Expenditure) (No.2) 1964-65
Supply (No.1) 1965-66
Supply (No.2) 1965-66

1966 -

Appropriation (No.3) 1965-66
Appropriation (No.4) 1965-66
Appropriation (No.1) 1966-67
Appropriation (No.2) 1966-67
Supply (No.1) 1966-67
Supply (No.2) 1966-67

1967 -

Appropriation (No.3) 1966-67
Appropriation (No.4) 1966-67
Appropriation (No.1) 1967-68
Appropriation (No.2) 1967-68
Supply (No.1) 1967-68
Supply (No.2) 1967-68

1968 -

Appropriation (No.3) 1967-68
Appropriation (No.4) 1967-68
Appropriation (No.1) 1968-69
Appropriation (No.2) 1968-69
Supply (No.1) 1968-69
Supply (No.2) 1968-69

1969 -

Appropriation (No.3) 1968-69
Appropriation (No.4) 1968-69
Appropriation (No.1) 1969-70
Appropriation (No.2) 1969-70
Supply (No.1) 1969-70
Supply (No.2) 1969-70

1970 -

Appropriation (No.3) 1969-70
Appropriation (No.4) 1969-70
Appropriation (No.1) 1970-71
Appropriation (No.2) 1970-71
Supply (No.1) 1970-71
Supply (No.2) 1970-71

1971 -

Appropriation (No.3) 1970-71
Appropriation (No.4) 1970-71
Appropriation (No.1) 1971-72
Appropriation (No.2) 1971-72
Appropriation (No.3) 1971-72
Supply (No.1) 1971-72
Supply (No.2) 1971-72
Supply (No.3) 1971-72

1972 -
      Appropriation (No.4) 1971-72
      Appropriation (No.5) 1971-72
      Appropriation (No.1) 1972-73
      Appropriation (No.2) 1972-73
      Supply (No.1) 1972-73
      Supply (No.2) 1972-72

1973 -
      Appropriation (No.3) 1972-73
      Appropriation (No.4) 1972-73
      Appropriation (No.5) 1972-73
      Appropriation (No.6) 1972-73
      Appropriation (No.1) 1973-74
      Appropriation (No.2) 1973-74
      Supply (No.1) 1973-74
      Supply (No.2) 1973-74
      Supply (No.3) 1973-74

1974 -
      Appropriation (No.3) 1973-74
      Appropriation (No.4) 1973-74
      Appropriation (No.5) 1973-74
      Appropriation (No.1) 1974-75
      Appropriation (No.2) 1974-75
      Appropriation (Urban Public Transport) 1974
      Supply (No.1) 1974-75
      Supply (No.2) 1974-75

1975 -
      Appropriation (No.3) 1974-75
      Appropriation (No.4) 1974-75
      Appropriation (No.5) 1974-75
      Appropriation (No.6) 1974-75
      Appropriation (No.1) 1975-76
      Appropriation (No.2) 1975-76
      Appropriation (Development Bank) 1975
      Supply (No.1) 1975-76
      Supply (No.2) 1975-76

4.   The resolutions we have set out define the conflict

between the Houses. The Senate asserts that it may consistently

with the Constitution and the practices or conventions governing

the relations between the Houses defer Supply to compel an

election of the Representatives. This the Representatives deny.

That House says the Senate's action violates its position relative

to the Senate under the Constitution and the practices and

conventions necessary for its working. The reasons referred
to in the Senate's resolution are themselves matters of
political dispute as to the truth of which opinion is divided.
There has been no authoritative determination upon any one of
them. Indeed there cannot be, for they are stated not as
matters of law upon which a Court could pass but as matters
only determinable politically. To accept one or more of them
as established is therefore to enter the area of political
dispute.

5.   The question thus is whether the deferring of Supply
by the Senate solely to procure the resignation or, failing
that, the dismissal of the Ministry as a step in a forced
dissolution of the Representatives compels His Excellency to
dissolve that House. The existence, nature or extent of the
Governor-General's reserve powers of dismissal or dissolution
in other circumstances does not arise. On those questions we
express no opinion. By forced dissolution we mean one
occurring "when the Crown insists on dissolution and, if
necessary, dismisses Ministers in order to procure others who
will tender the desired advice".: Forsey: The Royal Power
of Dissolution of Parliament in the British Commonwealth,
1943, page 71.

6.   We have set out in paragraph 4 what may be regarded
as the essence of the dispute between the Houses. But a closer
analysis of the opposing contentions is called for. It will be
remembered the Representatives first resolution of 21 October
says "that the action of the Senate in delaying the passage of
Appropriation Bill (No.1) 1975-76 and Appropriation Bill (No.2)

12.

1975-76 for the reasons given in the Senate resolution is
not contemplated within the terms of the Constitution and is
contrary to established constitutional convention". The Senate's
reply of 22 October denies this and in doing so refers in
paragraph (c) to the undoubted fact that the legislative power
of the Commonwealth is vested in the Queen, the Senate and the
House of Representatives. That, of course, is the language of
section 1 of the Constitution and reference to it but emphasises
the validity of the Representatives' complaint set out at the
beginning of this paragraph. For the Senate's resolutions of
16 and 22 October made clear its refusal to participate with
the Representatives in relation both to these Bills and their
successors in the exercise of legislative power with which the
Constitution entrusts both Houses except upon satisfaction of a
condition which it has no express constitutional authority to
impose. Nor is there any implied authority. What justification
under the Constitution would there be for the Representatives
to refuse to perform its part in law-making unless the Senate
agreed to a periodical election of half its members?

7.   This is not to say that the Senate's actions are in
any way invalid or inoperative. It is but an assertion of the
view that the Constitution envisages the Houses of Parliament
as engaged in legislative action alone, and that save perhaps
to the extent that a refusal to embark upon consideration of the
measure may amount to a failure to pass it for the purposes of
section 57, does not contemplate either House as refusing to
undertake that task whether conditionally or unconditionally.
But when one says that a refusal to entertain consideration
of a measure may amount to a failure to pass it for the
purposes of section 57, the necessary consequence follows, we

think, that that dispute between the Houses has a
constitutional solution which envisages the interposition of a
period of three months between the first and second failures
to pass the measure. To this we later return.

8.   It clearly cannot be said that the Representatives
in asserting the existence of the convention are acting
unreasonably or without the most solid foundation. This
particular power of the Senate has never before been exercised -
a fact suggesting the convention exists. There is no doubt
that the principles of responsible government permeate
the Constitution: Amalgamated Society of Engineers v. Adelaide
Steamship Co. Ltd. (1920) 28 C.L.R. 129 at 146-147. Indeed a
number of the principles of responsible government, for
example that Supply is voted only on message from the Crown,
and that appropriation and taxation laws may only originate in
the popular House, are expressly provided for by the Constitution.
Neither the existence of the Prime Minister nor the necessity
for his membership of the Representatives is the subject of
express provision, but that such requirements exist and have
been observed for the same period as has the disputed convention
or practice is incontrovertible.

9.   The Senate's resolution indicates an intention to
defer passage of the Appropriation Bills until either the
Ministry resigns or the Governor-General acting against its
advice dismisses it and, upon advice of Ministers in a minority
in the Representatives, dissolves it. The Ministry has not
resigned (and will not do so.) That leaves only a forced
dissolution. Dr Jennings (Cabinet Government, 3rd ed. 1969)

observes (at page 403) that "No Government has been dismissed
by the Sovereign since 1783", and points out that there was no
dismissal in 1834 of Lord Melbourne's Government (pages 403-405).
Dr Forsey (The Royal Power of Dissolution of Parliament, 1943)
says that "In the overseas Empire there appears to have been
only one instance of this: New Brunswick in 1853" (page 71).
The passage continues -

> "The dissolutions in Newfoundland in 1861, New
> Brunswick in 1866, Quebec in 1878 and 1891, British
> Columbia in 1900, Queensland in 1907 and New South
> Wales in 1932, like the British dissolution of 1807,
> were not true forced dissolutions. Ministers were
> not dismissed because they refused to advise
> dissolution; they were dismissed for quite other
> reasons, and dissolutions granted to their successors
> because they could not hope to carry on government
> with the existing Lower House."

10.   We have referred to forced dissolutions only to
indicate that their very rarity and the long years since their
exercise cast the gravest doubt upon the present existence of
that prerogative.

11.   But we would emphasise that we understand the question
for His Excellency to be not which of the disputants is correct
in its views, but rather that the two Houses are in real dispute
about momentous matters. For it can hardly be doubted that the
Crown will not as a general rule take sides in such disputes
for "while it should be the governor's earnest desire to
contribute, as far as he can properly contribute, to the removal
of existing differences between the two Houses, it is clearly
undesirable that he should intervene in such a manner as would
withdraw these differences from their proper sphere, and so
give to them a character which does not naturally belong to them,
of a conflict between the majority of one or another of the two

Houses, and the representative of the Crown:" Todd: Parliamentary Government in the British Colonies 2nd ed. 1893 page 722. To this we later return.

12.   Before turning to a consideration of Mr Ellicott's press statement, we think it relevant to observe that by section 28 of the Constitution every House of Representatives shall continue for three years from the first meeting of the House and no longer but may be sooner dissolved by the Governor-General. Whether the power of dissolution referred to in section 28 is independent of that conferred by section 5 is not, we think, material to resolve. What is significant is that, while the power to refuse a dissolution is one "for which the representative of the Crown is alone responsible, although it is sometimes stated that the incoming Ministry assumes the responsibility of the refusal by undertaking to carry on the Queen's Government for the time being", it is equally clear that "A grant of a dissolution is an executive act, to which the Crown assents, and for which the Ministry tendering the advice and doing the act are responsible to Parliament and the country" Quick and Garran, section 118, page 464. A passage to the same effect appears in section 63 of the Annotated Constitution of the Australian Commonwealth by the same authors at page 407. The point of this, of course, is that the Crown in dissolving the House of Representatives acts upon ministerial advice - that is to say, upon the advice of Ministers chosen from the political party with the majority in the Representatives. The only exception presently material is the doubtful case of the forced dissolution. In such cases the Crown in dissolving has acted upon advice of a minority Ministry.

13.   The central point taken by Mr Ellicott is that a
Government without Supply cannot govern, for the maintenance of
the Constitution and of the laws of the Commonwealth require
that the Government have authority from Parliament to spend
money to perform those functions. The Governor-General is
sought to be immediately engaged upon a refusal of Supply by the
assertion that His Excellency's basic role is the execution
and maintenance of the Constitution and Commonwealth laws, one
which he exercises upon the advice of a Ministry chosen from
the majority party in the Representatives, but holding office
during His Excellency's pleasure.

14.   Before proceeding further some comments should be
made. Section 61 of the Constitution enacts that -

> "61. The executive power of the Commonwealth is
> vested in the Queen and is exerciseable by the Governor-
> General as the Queen's representative, and extends to
> the execution and maintenance of this Constitution, and
> of the laws of the Commonwealth."

Section 62 provides for a Federal Executive Council to advise
the Governor-General "in the government of the Commonwealth"
who shall hold office during his pleasure and section 64 for
the appointment of officers to administer such departments of
State as the Governor-General in Council may establish. These
officers must be members of the Federal Executive Council and
hold office during the Governor-General's pleasure. They are
the Queen's Ministers of State for the Commonwealth and must
sit in the Parliament. In this way the Cabinet system was
incorporated into the Constitution. What these sections make
clear is that the Executive power of the Commonwealth

exerciseable by the Governor-General may only be so exercised on advice of a Ministry which, because responsible government permeates the Constitution, will be drawn from the majority party in the Representatives.

15. The point of this is that section 61 affords no ground for the conclusion that upon the Senate deferring or rejecting Supply solely to procure the resignation or dismissal of the Ministry possessing a majority in the Representatives, His Excellency is constitutionally obliged immediately to seek an explanation of the Prime Minister of how he proposes to overcome that situation.

16. Nor do we agree with the suggestion that were the Prime Minister unable to suggest means which would solve the disagreement between the Houses and left the Government without funds to carry on, it would be His Excellency's duty to dismiss his Ministers.

17. We do not suggest that, should a case exist for his intervention, His Excellency in considering the course he will take must disregard the fact that the Senate's deferring or refusal of Supply will impede the business of government. We do suggest that His Excellency is not confined to a consideration of that fact. He may consider others. After all the constitutional provisions but recognise that the Ministry holds office during His Excellency's pleasure (section 64) and that he may dissolve the Representatives before the expiry of its term (sections 28 and 5); they do not, considered alone, afford any guide as to the circumstances when the extreme and abnormal reserve powers of dismissal of a Ministry and consequent

dissolution of the Representatives should or may be exercised or even that they still exist. This is the field of convention and discretion.

18.   But it is, we think, not correct to treat the exercise of those powers as demanded when refusal of Supply is threatened or when it occurs. To do so is to deny, for example, a Vice-regal authority to offer suggestions where the circumstances have reached a stage sufficiently grave to warrant His Excellency's adoption of that course, bearing in mind that the cardinal rule is that the Crown should not "withdraw these differences from their proper sphere": Todd, supra.

19.   We have quoted in paragraph 11 above the view expressed by Governor Bowen in relation to his duty where a conflict between the two Houses arose in the State of Victoria in 1877. We shall later refer to Mr Asquith's memorandum to His Majesty the King containing more recent and more forceful observations to like effect. Dr Jennings remarked of this memorandum (Cabinet Government 3rd ed. 1969) that it "so far as it goes, is incontrovertible" (page 409).

20.   It is perhaps relevant to bear in mind that the Legislative Council in that dispute, possessing an express constitutional power to reject financial measures, in fact rejected the Appropriation Bill and that the response of the Government of Victoria was the dismissal of civil servants, an act in which the Governor acquiesced. The important consideration for present purposes is that the Governor was

advised by/the Colonial Secretary, Sir Michael Hicks Beach, that
he must follow his Ministers' advice though in case of
necessity he should take legal opinion: Jennings: Cabinet
Government 3rd ed. 1969 p.407. This, of course, supports the
view we have expressed that the mere threat of or indeed the
actual rejection of Supply neither calls for the Ministry to
resign nor compels the Crown's representative thereupon to
intervene.

21.   It is, we think obvious enough that since the
Imperial Conference of 1926 the Governor-General is the
representative of the Crown and holds in all essential respects
the same position in relation to the administration of public
affairs in the Dominion as is held by His Majesty the King in
Great Britain, and that he is not the representative or agent
of His Majesty's Government in Great Britain or of any
Department of that Government. Thus, as Sir Kenneth Bailey
suggested in his introduction to the first edition of Dr Evatt's
work The King and His Dominion Governors, it is necessary in the
Dominions now to discover the principles which have underlain
the action of the King himself in recent constitutional crises
and that the most important sections of Dr Evatt's book are
those which analyse the action of the Crown in Great Britain
during the critical years 1909-14: Evatt: The King and His
Dominion Governors, 2nd ed. 1967 pages xxxvi-xxxvii. We would
not suggest, of course, that the constitutional authority of the
House of Lords is as great as that of the Senate for, amongst
other factors, the power to reject money measures has been

removed. But when that power still existed and was exercised the constitutional crisis thus caused continued for a number of years. It could hardly be disputed that a factor of the first importance is the relationship between the Governor-General and the two Houses and that that relationship is the stronger when a judicious abstention from intervention is exercised, as the present crisis perhaps indicates.

22.   It is with such considerations in mind that Mr Asquith, in his memorandum on the King's position in relation to the Home Rule Bill, wrote:

> "Nothing can be more important, in the best interests of the Crown and of the country, than that a practice, so long established and so well justified by experience, should remain unimpaired. It frees the occupant of the Throne from all personal responsibility for the acts of the Executive and the legislature. It gives force and meaning to the old maxim that 'the King can do no wrong'. So long as it prevails, however objectionable particular Acts may be to a large section of his subjects, they cannot hold him in any way accountable. If, on the other hand, the King were to intervene on one side, or in one case - which he could only do by dismissing ministers in de facto possession of a Parliamentary majority - he would be expected to do the same on another occasion, and perhaps for the other side. Every Act of Parliament of the first order of importance, and only passed after acute controversy, would be regarded as bearing the personal imprimatur of the Sovereign. He would, whether he wished it or not, be dragged into the arena of party politics; and at a dissolution following such a dismissal of ministers as had been referred to, it is no exaggeration to say that the Crown would become the football of contending factions.
>
> This is a constitutional catastrophe which it is the duty of every wise statesman to do the utmost in his power to avert."
> Jennings: Cabinet Government 3rd ed. 1969 page 408.

23.   To the above positive considerations, in themselves
perhaps compelling enough, another remains to be added, one
valid whether or not our analysis of the nature of the dispute
be right or not. There is or is threatening a legislative
deadlock. Section 57 of the Constitution enshrines the
constitutional solution "of the spectre of legislative deadlock"
which possession by the Senate of the power to reject
legislation including money bills necessarily gave rise to.
The language we use has been borrowed from the judgment of the
Honourable Mr Justice Stephen delivered in the case of The
State of Victoria and Her Majesty's Attorney-General for the
State of Victoria v. The Commonwealth and another (not yet
reported). As His Honour said in Cormack v. Cope: (A passage
quoted with approval by the Honourable Mr Justice Mason in his
judgment in the first mentioned case)

> "It (section 57) serves an obviously
> useful purpose: avoidance of deadlock is what
> the section is concerned with and the interval
> of three months, in providing a time for attempted
> reconciliation of differences must begin after the
> deadlock occurs."

24.   That the section applies to money bills is obvious
not only from its language ("any proposed law") and the
opinion of the most persuasive writers upon the Constitution
("It covers every proposed law which may have been passed by
the National Chamber": Quick and Garran page 685) but also,
explicitly (the Honourable Mr Justice Gibbs and the Honourable
Mr Justice Stephen and, perhaps, the Honourable Mr Justice
Mason) and implicitly in the judgments of the other Justices who
considered that case first referred to.

25.   It seems likely that the refusal of the Senate
to entertain consideration of the Appropriation Bills may
have amounted to a failure to pass them within the meaning
of the section. But, if that is or may be so, the full
operation of the section requires that a period of three
months elapse between that failure to pass by the Senate
before the first limb of the section has fully operated.
The section "relies, after the first occurrence of deadlock,
upon providing opportunity for second, and perhaps wiser,
thoughts and for negotiation and compromise between the
chambers", to use again the language of the Honourable Mr
Justice Stephen in the case first cited.

26.   If such be the section's purpose and intended
operation, how is it possible consistently with the
Constitution that a reserve power of uncertain existence
and unknowable constituents must be exercised in a way
necessarily denying effect to the one constitutional
provision expressly directed to the solution of deadlock
between the Houses? We do not find it possible ourselves
to accept that view and to the extent that Mr Ellicott does
so he is, we think clearly wrong.

27.   That neither or either House intends to compromise
is not to the point, should it be the fact. The section exists
to permit that opportunity and to allow a joint sitting to be
held whose decision finally resolves the difference.

28.   We have, so far, confined our remarks to what the
press release expressly says. We turn now to consider what
it assumes. Those assumptions include at least the following:

(1) that the Senate's legal power to reject
Supply may in point of law be exercised
whenever and for whatever reason commends
itself to the Senate and whatever the consequences;

(2) the express provisions of the Constitution,
construed taking into account the principle
of responsible government which pervades
it (to use the language of the High Court
in the Engineers' Case (1920) 28 C.L.R. 129
at pages 146-147) contain nothing which implies
any restraint upon the untrammelled use of the
Senate's legal power to reject Supply for any
reason; and lastly

(3) that no practice or convention relating to
the exercise of that power solely to determine
the life of the Representatives exists, or,
if existing, is relevant for Vice-regal
consideration.

29.   We have referred to an untrammelled use of the
power to reject Supply. By that expression we mean one legally
and in point of constitutional practice of the nature we have
described in (1) above and naturally intend to include an
exercise solely to determine the Representatives' term. Such
is the present exercise, as the Senate's resolution makes clear.
It is not, we think, unfair or inaccurate on our part to suggest
that the press statement demands the making of such an
assumption amongst others. For if the Senate's power to reject

is subject to any restraint, that restraint is not in words
imposed upon the power which section 53 contains and thus
must be found in a practice or convention which would then
become a factor offsetting the weight that would otherwise
attach to a denial of funds and the hardships necessarily
thereby involved without a forced dissolution. None such is
suggested. The power which Mr Ellicott assumes in the Senate
must, therefore, be one legally and conventionally untrammelled.

30.   How does this assumption accord with other provisions
of the Constitution? We have already mentioned section 57 and
do not here repeat what we have said of it. We would wish
again to refer to sections 5 and 28. The relevant part of
section 5 is in the following terms:

> "5.   The Governor-General may appoint such times
> for holding the sessions of the Parliament as he thinks
> fit, and may also from time to time, by Proclamation or
> otherwise, prorogue the Parliament, and may in like
> manner dissolve the House of Representatives."

Section 28 provides as follows:

> "28.   Every House of Representatives shall continue
> for three years from the first meeting of the House, and
> no longer, but may be sooner dissolved by the Governor-
> General."

31.   We have also referred to the voting of Supply only
on a message from the Crown and to the Representatives'
exclusive authority to initiate laws imposing taxation and
appropriating revenue or moneys. This last is the subject of
express Constitutional provision for section 53 provides
(and we quote the relevant parts):

"53. Proposed laws appropriating revenue
or moneys, or imposing taxation, shall not
originate in the Senate. But a proposed law
shall not be taken to appropriate revenue or
moneys, or to impose taxation, by reason only
of its containing provisions for the imposition
or appropriation of fines or other pecuniary
penalties, or for the demand or payment or
appropriation of fees for licences, or fees for
services under the proposed law."

32.   The second paragraph denies to the Senate power
to amend proposed laws imposing taxation or proposed laws
appropriating revenue or money for the ordinary annual
services of the Government. The Senate's power to reject
appropriation (which for the purpose of this Opinion we
assume to exist) arises from that part of section 53 enacting
that except as the section provides the Senate shall have
equal power with the Representatives in respect of all
proposed laws.

33.   The object of section 56 of the Constitution
(providing that proposed laws appropriating revenue or
moneys may not be passed unless the purpose of the
appropriation has been recommended by message of the
Governor-General to the House in which the proposal originated)
is to retain to the Ministry drawn from the party with a
majority in the Representatives (and therefore advising the
Governor-General in the exercise of the Executive power which
section 61 of the Constitution confers) control over the means
to give effect to the maintenance of the Constitution and the
execution of the laws of the Commonwealth.

34.   What emerges from the provisions? In our opinion
it is clear enough that the financial provisions (sections
53 and 56) both in terms and in their implications commit
to those advising the Governor-General as the Queen's
representative and exercising the Executive power of the

Commonwealth, authority to decide the amounts necessary for the
ordinary annual services and to obtain from the Representatives
(for they are envisaged by the Constitution as there
possessing a majority) legislation for those amounts. The
Senate is denied authority to amend any proposed law giving
effect to that decision. It is denied also the authority
to make that decision itself. It may ask the Representatives
to consider its suggestions as to the omission or amendment
of any items (section 53, third paragraph). Again, those
advisers alone by virtue of their majority in the
Representatives may initiate laws imposing the taxation
necessary to obtain those amounts. Further, the Constitution
envisages in section 28 that the Representatives will normally
enjoy a term of three years. Any decision for a shorter term
will be taken by the Governor-General on the advice of those
from the Representatives' majority.

35.   To treat the Senate's power to reject Supply as
untrammelled by convention or practice means that sections
28 and 53 are deprived of their intended harmonious co-operation
and that continuity in the exercise of the Executive power is
disrupted and thus the power itself is weakened.

36.   It is germane to recall that several Australian
federalists of eminence considered that the Cabinet system
of Executive Government which the Constitution enshrines was
incompatible with a true Federation. Their contentions are
thus described by Quick and Garran at page 706 of their work
on the Constitution:

"In support of this contention it is argued
that, in a Federation, it is a fundamental rule
that no new law shall be passed and no old law
shall be altered without the consent of (1) a
majority of the people speaking by their representatives
in one House, and (2) a majority of the States speaking
by their representatives in the other House; that the
same principle of the State approval as well as popular
approval should apply to Executive action, as well as to
legislative action; that the State should not be forced
to support Executive policy and Executive acts merely
because ministers enjoyed the confidence of the popular
Chamber; that the State House would be justified in
withdrawing its support from a ministry of whose policy
and executive acts it disapproved; that the State House
could, as effectively as the primary Chamber, enforce
its want of confidence by refusing to provide the
neeessary supplies. The Senate of the French Republic,
it is pointed out, has established a precedent showing
how an Upper House can enforce its opinions and cause a
change of ministry. On these grounds it is contended
that the introduction of the Cabinet system of
Responsible Government into a Federation, in which the
relations of two branches of the legislature, having
equal and co-ordinate authority, are quite different
from those existing in a single autonomous State, is
repugnant to the spirit and intention of a scheme of
Federal Government. In the end it is predicted that
either Responsible Government will kill the Federation
and change it into a unified State, or the Federation
will kill Responsible Government and substitute a new
form of Executive more compatible with the Federal
theory. In particular, strong objection is taken to
the insertion in the Constitution of a cast-iron
condition that Federal Ministers must be members of
Parliament. Membership of Parliament, it is argued,
is not of the essence of Responsible Government, but
only an incident or an accidental feature, which has
been introduced by modern practice and by statutory
innovation."

The underlining is ours. But as those learned authors said:

"Their views have not been accepted, and for
better or worse, the system of Responsible Government
as known to the British Constitution has been practically
embedded in the Federal Constitution in such a manner
that it cannot be disturbed without an amendment of the
instrument."
Quick and Garran pages 706-707.

In the first passage which we have quoted "the State House"

is,.of course, the Senate.

37.   The point of quoting the first passage is that
those eminent Federalists included Sir Samuel Griffith and
Mr Justice Inglis Clark and that the defeat of their
objections involved in the minds of those responsible for
the Constitution rejection of the notion that the Senate
would "enforce its want of confidence by refusing to provide
the necessary supplies".

38.   It seems to us, if we may respectfully say so, that
assumptions underlie Mr Ellicott's press statement which
present dangers to the orderly working of Government. Those
dangers are significant ones. That the possibility of their
existence is a disquieting one cannot, we venture to think,
be seriously doubted. For they may be indefinitely repeated
and may involve deleterious consequences to the working of
the constitutional provisions. That that working requires
restraint on the part of both Houses is hardly open to doubt.
A view which looking only to the existence of the legal power
disregards or ignores constitutional practices hitherto
apparently governing the exercise of those powers, requires,
we venture to think, the gravest consideration before its
adoption could even be contemplated.

39.   We have found ourselves for the reasons we have
stated firmly of opinion that Mr Ellicott's expressed views are
wrong.

Kep. Enderby
Attorney-General of Australi

M.H. Byers
Solicitor-General of Australi

4 November, 1975

CHAMBERS OF THE CHIEF JUSTICE
TAYLOR SQUARE
DARLINGHURST, N.S.W. 2010

10th November, 1975.

Dear Sir John

In response to Your Excellency's invitation I attended this day at Admiralty House. In our conversations I indicated that I considered myself, as Chief Justice of Australia, free, on Your Excellency's request, to offer you legal advice as to Your Excellency's constitutional rights and duties in relation to an existing situation which, of its nature, was unlikely to come before the Court. We both clearly understood that I was not in any way concerned with matters of a purely political kind, or with any political consequences of the advice I might give.

In response to Your Excellency's request for my legal advice as to whether a course on which you had determined was consistent with your constitutional authority and duty, I respectfully offer the following.

The Constitution of Australia is a federal Constitution which embodies the principle of Ministerial responsibility. The Parliament consists of two houses, the House of Representatives and the Senate, each popularly elected, and each with the same legislative power, with the one exception that the Senate may not originate nor amend a money bill.

Two relevant constitutional consequences flow from this structure of the Parliament. First, the Senate has constitutional power to refuse to pass a money bill; it has power to refuse supply to the Government of the day. Secondly, a Prime Minister who cannot ensure supply to the Crown, including funds for carrying on the ordinary services of Government, must either advise a general election (of a kind which the constitutional situation may then allow) or resign. If, being unable to secure supply, he refuses to take either course, Your Excellency has constitutional authority to withdraw his Commission as Prime Minister.

Sir Garfield Barwick's formal advice to Sir John Kerr (10 November 1975).
Source: National Archives of Australia (Kerr Papers)

There is no analogy in respect of a Prime Minister's duty between the situation of the Parliament under the federal Constitution of Australia and the relationship between the House of Commons, a popularly elected body, and the House of Lords, a non-elected body, in the unitary form of Government functioning in the United Kingdom. Under that system, a Government having the confidence of the House of Commons can secure supply, despite a recalcitrant House of Lords. But it is otherwise under our federal Constitution. A Government having the confidence of the House of Representatives but not that of the Senate, both elected Houses, cannot secure supply to the Crown.

But there is an analogy between the situation of a Prime Minister who has lost the confidence of the House of Commons and a Prime Minister who does not have the confidence of the Parliament, i.e. of the House of Representatives and of the Senate. The duty and responsibility of the Prime Minister to the Crown in each case is the same: if unable to secure supply to the Crown, to resign or to advise an election.

In the event that, conformably to this advice, the Prime Minister ceases to retain his Commission, Your Excellency's constitutional authority and duty would be to invite the Leader of the Opposition, if he can undertake to secure supply, to form a caretaker government (i.e. one which makes no appointments or initiates any policies) pending a general election, whether of the House of Representatives, or of both Houses of the Parliament, as that Government may advise.

Accordingly, my opinion is that, if Your Excellency is satisfied in the current situation that the present Government is unable to secure supply, the course upon which Your Excellency has determined is consistent with your constitutional authority and duty.

Yours respectfully,

(GARFIELD BARWICK)

His Excellency The Honourable Sir John Kerr, K.C.M.G.,
Governor-General of Australia,
Admiralty House,
SYDNEY.

1) Double Dissol All?
2) Canberra
3) No police charges
4) No Royal Comm
5) + Supply.
5) Dissolution Today.

9.55 11 Nov
1975

Malcolm Fraser's handwritten note after a telephone call with Sir John Kerr
(9.55 a.m., 11 November 1975).
Source: The Malcolm Fraser Collection, University of Melbourne

PARLIAMENT OF AUSTRALIA

HOUSE OF REPRESENTATIVES

OPPOSITION WHIP
PARLIAMENT HOUSE
CANBERRA, A.C.T. 2600
TEL. 72 1211

JOINT PARTY MEETING

10.00 A.M. TUESDAY, 11 NOVEMBER 1975

A G E N D A

1.   TACTICS

2.   LEGISLATION

3.   MEMBERS LEAVING THE HOUSE DURING
     QUESTION TIME   (Bourchier)

Reverse side of Malcolm Fraser's handwritten note after a telephone call with Sir John Kerr
(9.55 a.m., 11 November 1975).
Source: The Malcolm Fraser Collection, University of Melbourne

Government House,
Canberra.   2600.

11 November 1975

Dear Mr Whitlam,

      In accordance with section 64 of the
Constitution I hereby determine your appointment
as my Chief Adviser and Head of the Government.
It follows that I also hereby determine the
appointments of all of the Ministers in your
Government.

      You have previously told me that you
would never resign or advise an election of the
House of Representatives or a double dissolution
and that the only way in which such an election
could be obtained would be by my dismissal of you
and your ministerial colleagues. As it appeared
likely that you would today persist in this
attitude I decided that, if you did, I would
determine your commission and state my reasons for
doing so. You have persisted in your attitude and
I have accordingly acted as indicated. I attach a
statement of my reasons which I intend to publish
immediately.

      It is with a great deal of regret that I
have taken this step both in respect of yourself
and your colleagues.

      I propose to send for the Leader of the
Opposition and to commission him to form a new
caretaker Government until an election can be held.

Yours sincerely,

The Honourable E.G. Whitlam, Q.C., M.P.

Sir John Kerr's letter to Gough Whitlam terminating his commission as prime minister
(11 November 1975).
Source: The Whitlam Institute

Statement by the Governor-General

I have given careful consideration to the constitutional crisis and have made some decisions which I wish to explain.

Summary

It has been necessary for me to find a democratic and constitutional solution to the current crisis which will permit the people of Australia to decide as soon as possible what should be the outcome of the deadlock which developed over supply between the two Houses of Parliament and between the Government and the Opposition parties. The only solution consistent with the Constitution and with my oath of office and my responsibilities, authority and duty as Governor-General is to terminate the commission as Prime Minister of Mr Whitlam and to arrange for a caretaker government able to secure supply and willing to let the issue go to the people.

I shall summarise the elements of the problem and the reasons for my decision which places the matter before the people of Australia for prompt determination.

Because of the federal nature of our Constitution and because of its provisions the Senate undoubtedly has constitutional power to refuse or defer supply to the Government. Because of the principles of responsible government a Prime Minister who cannot obtain supply, including money for carrying on the ordinary services of government, must either advise a general election or resign. If he refuses to do this I have the authority and indeed the duty under the Constitution to withdraw his Commission as Prime Minister. The position in Australia is quite different from the position in the United Kingdom. Here the confidence of both Houses on supply is necessary to ensure its provision. In the United Kingdom the confidence of the House of Commons alone is necessary. But both here and in the United Kingdom the duty of the Prime Minister is the same in a most important respect – if he cannot get supply he must resign or advise an election.

If a Prime Minister refuses to resign or to advise an election, and this is the case with Mr Whitlam, my constitutional authority and duty require me to do what I have now done – to withdraw his commission – and to invite the Leader of the Opposition to form a caretaker

.../2

Sir John Kerr's statement of reasons for the dismissal (11 November 1975).
Source: The Whitlam Institute

government - that is one that makes no appointments or dismissals and initiates no policies, until a general election is held. It is most desirable that he should guarantee supply. Mr Fraser will be asked to give the necessary undertakings and advise whether he is prepared to recommend a double dissolution. He will also be asked to guarantee supply.

The decisions I have made were made after I was satisfied that Mr Whitlam could not obtain supply. No other decision open to me would enable the Australian people to decide for themselves what should be done.

Once I had made up my mind, for my own part, what I must do if Mr Whitlam persisted in his stated intentions I consulted the Chief Justice of Australia, Sir Garfield Barwick. I have his permission to say that I consulted him in this way.

The result is that there will be an early general election for both Houses and the people can do what, in a democracy such as ours, is their responsibility and duty and theirs alone. It is for the people now to decide the issue which the two leaders have failed to settle.

Detailed Statement of Decisions

On 16 October the Senate deferred consideration of Appropriation Bills (Nos. 1 & 2) 1975-1976. In the time which elapsed since then events made it clear that the Senate was determined to refuse to grant supply to the Government. In that time the Senate on no less than two occasions resolved to proceed no further with fresh Appropriation Bills, in identical terms, which had been passed by the House of Representatives. The determination of the Senate to maintain its refusal to grant supply was confirmed by the public statements made by the Leader of the Opposition, the Opposition having control of the Senate.

By virtue of what has in fact happened there therefore came into existence a deadlock between the House of Representatives and the Senate on the central issue of supply without which all the ordinary services of the government cannot be maintained. I had the benefit of discussions with the Prime Minister and, with his approval, with the Leader of the Opposition and with the Treasurer and the Attorney-General. As a result of those discussions and having regard to the public statements of the Prime Minister and the Leader of the Opposition I have come regretfully to the conclusion that there is no likelihood of a compromise between the House of Representatives and the Senate nor for that matter between the Government and the Opposition.

.../3

The deadlock which arose was one which, in the interests of the nation, had to be resolved as promptly as possible and by means which are appropriate in our democratic system. In all the circumstances which have occurred the appropriate means is a dissolution of the Parliament and an election for both Houses. No other course offers a sufficient assurance of resolving the deadlock and resolving it promptly.

Parliamentary control of appropriation and accordingly of expenditure is a fundamental feature of our system of responsible government. In consequence it has been generally accepted that a government which has been denied supply by the Parliament cannot govern. So much at least is clear in cases where a ministry is refused supply by a popularly elected Lower House. In other systems where an Upper House is denied the right to reject a money bill denial of supply can occur only at the instance of the Lower House. When, however, an Upper House possesses the power to reject a money bill including an appropriation bill, and exercises the power by denying supply, the principle that a government which has been denied supply by the Parliament should resign or go to an election must still apply - it is a necessary consequence of Parliamentary control of appropriation and expenditure and of the expectation that the ordinary and necessary services of government will continue to be provided.

The Constitution combines the two elements of responsible government and federalism. The Senate is, like the House, a popularly elected chamber. It was designed to provide representation by States, not by electorates, and was given by Sec. 53, equal powers with the House with respect to proposed laws, except in the respects mentioned in the section. It was denied power to originate or amend appropriation bills but was left with power to reject them or defer consideration of them. The Senate accordingly has the power and has exercised the power to refuse to grant supply to the Government. The Government stands in the position that it has been denied supply by the Parliament with all the consequences which flow from that fact.

There have been public discussions about whether there is a convention deriving from the principles of responsible government that the Senate must never under any circumstances exercise the power to reject an appropriation bill. The Constitution must prevail over any convention because, in determining the question how far the conventions of responsible government have been grafted on to the federal compact, the Constitution itself must in the end control the situation.

Sec. 57 of the Constitution provides a means, perhaps the usual means, of resolving a disagreement between the Houses with respect to a proposed law. But the machinery which it provides necessarily entails a considerable time lag which is quite inappropriate to a speedy resolution of the fundamental problems posed by the refusal of supply. Its presence in the Constitution does not cut down the reserve powers of the Governor-General.

I should be surprised if the Law Officers expressed the view that there is no reserve power in the Governor-General to dismiss a Ministry which has been refused supply by the Parliament and to commission a Ministry, as a caretaker ministry which will secure supply and recommend a dissolution, including where appropriate a double dissolution. This is a matter on which my own mind is quite clear and I am acting in accordance with my own clear view of the principles laid down by the Constitution and of the nature, powers and responsibility of my office.

There is one other point. There has been discussion of the possibility that a half-Senate election might be held under circumstances in which the Government has not obtained supply. If such advice were given to me I should feel constrained to reject it because a half-Senate election held whilst supply continues to be denied does not guarantee a prompt or sufficiently clear prospect of the deadlock being resolved in accordance with proper principles. When I refer to rejection of such advice I mean that, as I would find it necessary in the circumstances I have envisaged to determine Mr Whitlam's commission and, as things have turned out have done so, he would not be Prime Minister and not able to give or persist with such advice.

The announced proposals about financing public servants, suppliers, contractors and others do not amount to a satisfactory alternative to supply.

Government House,
Canberra.   2600.

11 November 1975

11 November 1975

Your Excellency,

You have intimated to me that it is your Excellency's pleasure that I should act as your Chief Adviser and Head of the Government.

In accepting your commission I confirm that I have given you an assurance that I shall immediately seek to secure the passage of the Appropriation Bills which are at present before the Senate, thus ensuring Supply for the carrying on of the Public Service in all its branches. I further confirm that, upon the granting of Supply, I shall immediately recommend to Your Excellency the dissolution of both Houses of the Parliament.

My Government will act as a caretaker Government and will make no appointments or dismissals or initiate new policies before a general election is held.

Yours sincerely,
(J. M. Fraser)

His Excellency the Honourable Sir John Kerr,
A.C., K.C.M.G., K.St.J, Q.C.,
Governor-General of Australia,
Government House,
CANBERRA A.C.T. 2600

Malcolm Fraser's letter accepting his commission as prime minister (11 November 1975).
Source: National Archives of Australia (Kerr Papers)

PRIME MINISTER

CANBERRA

that this House declares
that it has confidence
in the Whitlam govt
and that this House
informs HM the Queen
that, if ~~the~~ HE the G·G
proposts to commission
the hon member for Wannon
as PM, the House does
not have confidence in him.
or in any govt he forms.

Gough Whitlam's handwritten motion of no-confidence in Malcolm Fraser
(1.50 p.m., 11 November 1975).
Source: The Whitlam Institute

written at the
Lodge   —   1.50 p.m.
                          11 November 1975

                          Present:
                             E. G. W.
                             Frank Crean
                             Fred Daly
                             Kep Enderby
                             -
                             John Menadue
                             -
                             John Mant
                             G. Freudenberg
                             -
                             David Coombe

Reverse side of Gough Whitlam's handwritten motion of no-confidence in Malcolm Fraser
(1.50 p.m., 11 November 1975).
Source: The Whitlam Institute

11 November, 1975

Your Excellency,

I write further to our discussions and to my letter to you of today in which I confirmed to you in accepting your commission that I had given you an assurance that I would immediately seek to secure the passage of the Appropriation Bills before the Senate. I confirmed also that upon the granting of Supply I would immediately recommend to Your Excellency the dissolution of both Houses of the Parliament.

I can now inform Your Excellency that the Senate has passed *Appropriation Bill (No. 1) 1975/76* and *Appropriation Bill (No. 2) 1975/76*. These Bills are being presented to you for assent.

In the light of my earlier undertaking I now recommend to Your Excellency that you exercise the power of the Governor-General under section 57 of the Constitution and dissolve simultaneously the Senate and the House of Representatives.

A proclamation for that purpose is attached which specifies the 21 Bills that have satisfied the requirements of section 57 of the Constitution.

Yours sincerely,
(J. M. Fraser)

His Excellency the Honourable Sir John Kerr,
A.C., K.C.M.G., K.St.J, Q.C.,
Governor-General of Australia,
Government House,
CANBERRA A.C.T. 2600,

Malcolm Fraser's letter proposing dissolution of both houses of parliament (11 November 1975).
Source: National Archives of Australia (Fraser Papers)

P R O C L A M A T I O N

Australia

Governor-General.

By His Excellency the

Governor-General of

Australia

WHEREAS by section 57 of the Constitution it is provided
that if the House of Representatives passes any proposed
law, and the Senate rejects or fails to pass it, or passes
it with amendments to which the House of Representatives
will not agree, and if after an interval of three months
the House of Representatives, in the same or the next session,
again passes the proposed law with or without any amendments
which have been made, suggested, or agreed to by the Senate
and the Senate rejects or fails to pass it, or passes it
with amendments to which the House of Representatives will
not agree, the Governor-General may dissolve the Senate and
the House of Representatives simultaneously:

AND WHEREAS the conditions upon which the Governor-General
is empowered by that section of the Constitution to dissolve
the Senate and the House of Representatives simultaneously
have been fulfilled in respect of the several proposed laws
intituled -

Health Insurance Levy Act   1974
Health Insurance Levy Assessment Act   1974
Income Tax (International Agreements) Act   1974
Minerals (Submerged Lands) Act   1974
Minerals (Submerged Lands) (Royalty) Act   1974
National Health Act   1974
Conciliation and Arbitration Act   1974
Conciliation and Arbitration Act (No.2) 1974
National Investment Fund Act 1974
Electoral Laws Amendment Act 1974
Electoral Act 1975
Privy Council Appeals Abolition Act 1975
Superior Court of Australia Act 1974
Electoral Re-distribution (New South Wales) Act 1975
Electoral Re-distribution (Queensland) Act 1975
Electoral Re-distribution (South Australia) Act 1975
Electoral Re-distribution (Tasmania) Act 1975
Electoral Re-distribution (Victoria) Act 1975
Broadcasting and Television Act (No.2) 1974
Television Stations Licence Fees Act 1974
Broadcasting Stations Licence Fees Act 1974

Sir John Kerr's proclamation dissolving parliament, countersigned by Malcolm Fraser
(11 November 1975).
Source: The Whitlam Institute

NOW THEREFORE, I Sir John Robert Kerr, the Governor-General of Australia, do by this my Proclamation dissolve the Senate and the House of Representatives.

Given under my Hand and the

Great Seal of Australia on

11 November 1975.

By His Excellency's Command,

Malcolm Fraser

Prime Minister

GOD SAVE THE QUEEN!

SPEAKER'S OFFICE
HOUSE OF REPRESENTATIVES
CANBERRA

12 November 1975

Your Majesty,

  I am compelled by events involving yourself through your representative in Australia, His Excellency the Honourable Sir John Kerr, A.C., K.C.M.G., K.St.J., Q.C., to communicate my concern at the maintenance in the office of the Prime Minister of the Hon. Malcolm Fraser, M.P. despite his lack of majority support in the House of Representatives.

  Immediately following the announcement of the dismissal of the former Prime Minister, Mr. Whitlam, and Mr. Fraser's appointment, the House of Representatives carried a resolution expressing want of confidence in the Governor-General's nominee and requesting the re-instatement of the former Prime Minister in whom the House expressed confidence.

  I am seriously concerned that the failure of the Governor-General to withdraw Mr. Fraser's commission and his decision to delay seeing me as Speaker of the House of Representatives until after the dissolution of the Parliament had been proclaimed were acts contrary to the proper exercise of the Royal prerogative and constituted an act of contempt for the House of Representatives. It is improper that your representative should continue to impose a Prime Minister on Australia in whom the House of Representatives has expressed its lack of confidence and who has not on any substantial resolution been able to command a majority of votes on the floor of the House of Representatives.

  It is my belief that to maintain in office a Prime Minister imposed on the nation by Royal prerogative rather than through parliamentary endorsement constitutes a danger to our parliamentary system and will damage the standing

Speaker Gordon Scholes' letter to the Queen (12 November 1975).
Source: The Whitlam Institute

of your representative in Australia and even
yourself.

I would ask that you act in order to
restore Mr Whitlam to office as Prime Minister
in accordance with the expressed resolution of
the House of Representatives.

For Your Majesty's information I would
point out that Supply was approved by the Senate
prior to 2.25 p.m. Mr Fraser announced that
he had been commissioned as Prime Minister in the
House of Representatives at 2.35 p.m. The House
expressed its view at 3.15 p.m. by 64 votes to 54.
I sought an audience with the Governor-General
immediately following the passage of that
resolution. An appointment was made for me to
wait on the Governor-General at 4.45 p.m. The
Governor-General prorogued the Parliament at
4.30 p.m.

The House expressed its view after the
passage of the Supply Bills and was and is entitled
to have that view considered.

Yours sincerely,

(G.G.D. SCHOLES)
Speaker

Her Majesty Queen Elizabeth the Second

BUCKINGHAM PALACE

17th November, 1975.

Dear Mr Scholes

        I am commanded by The Queen to acknowledge your letter of 12th November about the recent political events in Australia. You ask that The Queen should act to restore Mr. Whitlam to office as Prime Minister.

        As we understand the situation here, the Australian Constitution firmly places the prerogative powers of the Crown in the hands of the Governor-General as the representative of The Queen of Australia. The only person competent to commission an Australian Prime Minister is the Governor-General, and The Queen has no part in the decisions which the Governor-General must take in accordance with the Constitution. Her Majesty, as Queen of Australia, is watching events in Canberra with close interest and attention, but it would not be proper for her to intervene in person in matters which are so clearly placed within the jurisdiction of the Governor-General by the Constitution Act.

        I understand that you have been good enough to send a copy of your letter to the Governor-General so I am writing to His Excellency to say that the text of your letter has been received here in London and has been laid before The Queen.

        I am sending a copy of this letter to the Governor-General.

Yours sincerely

Martin Charteris

The Honourable G.G.D. Scholes.

Sir Martin Charteris' reply to Speaker Gordon Scholes (17 November 1975).
Source: The Whitlam Institute

Leader of the Opposition

<u>COPY ONLY</u>

26 December 1975

Dear Sir Martin (sgd)

Since Her Majesty the Queen will soon be receiving His Excellency the Governor-General, I feel it is my duty to request you to place before Her Majesty certain matters relating to the recent constitutional crisis which in my opinion have serious implications for the future of the Crown in Australia.

The very clear result of the elections convincingly settles Australia's immediate political future. In no way, however, do the elections resolve the legal and constitutional questions raised by the conduct of the Crown's representative on and before 11 November. Nor could the election result of itself legitimise that conduct.

It is not my present purpose to canvass the legality, or even the propriety, of the Governor-General's actions. These are and will certainly continue to be the subject of great juridical and academic argument. My immediate concern and contention is that the manner in which the Governor-General chose to invoke and exercise the reserve powers of the Crown has put in jeopardy the future of the Crown in Australia and has already gravely undermined the respect and regard attaching to the office of the representative of the Crown and therefore to the Crown itself.

I assert that the Crown can have no enduring future in Australia except by the continuing consensus and assured assent of the overwhelming majority of the people. I further assert that that majority must transcend traditional political allegiances and temporary political attitudes. I finally assert that these conditions can apply only if the Crown continues to avoid any intervention, or appearance of intervention, on behalf of any of the contending political parties. I fear that these conditions no longer apply in Australia.

.../2

Parliament House, Canberra, ACT 2600

Gough Whitlam's letter to Sir Martin Charteris (26 December 1975).
Source: The Whitlam Institute

The Governor-General used the reserve powers of the Crown to make at least five political decisions. All these decisions favoured one political combination against the other, which happened to be the party with an assured majority in the Lower House. At no time did he inform me as Prime Minister of the resolution he had formed to dismiss my government. He refused not merely to accept but even receive my advice recommending steps to bring about an election for half the Australian Senate. He rejected the opinion of the Crown Law officers and accepted the contrary opinion of a private member of Parliament, albeit a former Solicitor-General. Against my express advice, and contrary to all proper practice, he consulted the Chief Justice on a matter that could well have become a matter for judgement by the full High Court itself. He refused to receive the Speaker of the House of Representatives, acting on the express instructions of the House, until Parliament had been dissolved.

The events leading up to 11 November were essentially a political crisis, a political deadlock between the two Houses which was capable of political solution. The Governor-General chose to make a political judgement to the effect that his constitutional advisers had exhausted all political means to solve this political crisis by procedures legally and constitutionally open to them. He refused to receive the advice which would have shown that such a conclusion was unwarranted.

My concern at the damage done to the future standing of the Crown is in no way lessened by any argument that the Governor-General's action may have been within the letter of the Constitution. It is a very clear case of a power being tolerated only on condition that it is not exercised. For I believe it would be thoroughly unacceptable to a majority of the Australian people if in fact the reserve powers of the Crown were so potent that the representative of the Crown could legally intervene so decisively against any duly elected government retaining its majority in the House of Representatives.

Far from resolving the constitutional issues, the
recent political crisis in Australia has only obscured
them. They must await future clarification. I regret
to say, but am in duty bound to say, that the actions
of Sir John Kerr, as representative of the Crown in
Australia, have been such as to call into question on
the part of many millions of Australians, particularly
the younger majority, not merely the limits of the powers
of the Crown, but its whole future role in Australia.

With best wishes,

Yours sincerely,

E. G. Whitlam (sgd)

Lt. Col. the Rt. Hon. Sir Martin Charteris, K.C.B.,
        K.C.V.O., O.B.E.,
Private Secretary to H.M. the Queen,
Buckingham Palace, S.W.1,
LONDON, ENGLAND

OFFICE OF THE

Leader of the Opposition

19th Floor,
Westfield Towers,
100 William Street,
SYDNEY, N.S.W.

31 December 1975.

The Right Hon. Harold Wilson, C.H., M.P.,
Prime Minister of the United Kingdom,
House of Commons,
LONDON, U.K.

Dear Harold,

Thank you very much for the kind message you conveyed to me through your High Commissioner in Canberra. It was good to hear from you. I am reminded that just over a year ago I was with you in London. Our election in Australia was held on the anniversary of the day I departed for Britain.

No one knows better than you the penalties paid by social democratic governments in times of economic difficulty. No one understands better the problems we have faced in Australia. We take heart from the example you set between 1970 and 1974 in leading the Labor Party to a successful and, I believe, long-lasting restoration of its fortunes.

You will understand if I betray some natural feeling – though not, I hope, any bitterness – at the outcome of the election, but more especially at the events that brought it about. They could never have happened in Britain, and as I said more than once, "the Queen would never have done it" – a feeling I know you will share. It is, in my view, quite simply intolerable that an elected government should have its term cut short at the behest of an unrepresentative Upper House through the exercise of the reserve powers of the Crown. I should hope that other parliamentary democracies, particularly those of the Commonwealth, will look carefully at the dangerous implications of what happened in this country on 11 November.

I made a fundamental mistake in recommending to the Queen that she appoint a judge as her viceroy. In Australia judges suffer the corruption of knowing that on the High Court they can with impunity make propositions and dispositions of a political nature. The Governor-General was persuaded that he could do the same. He deceived me – realising, I'm sure, that I would have been in touch with the Queen if my suspicions had been aroused. Moreover, I believe he connived with the Chief Justice and indirectly with the Leader of the Opposition and the Establishment. If the Crown in Australia has reserve powers such as the Governor-General used, no elected government, particularly a reforming government, can be safe under it. The upshot is that republicanism has received a very significant boost in Australia.

Gough Whitlam's letter to Harold Wilson (31 December 1975).
Source: The National Archives, United Kingdom

I do want to stress one further point: despite our heavy loss of seats, due largely to the peculiarities of our complicated electoral system, the Labor Party's share of the vote in the recent election held up remarkably well. Our basic percentage of 43 per cent was in fact higher than that polled by the Liberal Party. We have a very strong basis for future recovery.

Thank you for your message and for the warm welcome you have always given me in London. I take satisfaction from everything the Labor Government was able to achieve in the past three years. The British Labor Party was always an example to us; you at least will be able to judge the rather silly accusations that Australia was turning away from Britain or growing hostile to our British traditions. We did strive for a more independent foreign policy, but our admiration for the best things in Britain never faltered. In many ways we have faced the same problems as all other western countries; I can only wish that our democratic institutions were as strongly equipped to deal with them.

My fraternal thoughts and good wishes remain with you in the many challenging and difficult tasks that lie before you.

Yours ever,

Gough.

E. G. WHITLAM

BUCKINGHAM PALACE

12th January, 1976

Dear Mr Whitlam

Thank you for your letter of 26th December which did not reach me until 8th January.

Any one who has served The Queen as her Prime Minister has, I have no doubt, a perfect right to make his views known to her on any subject, and certainly on one which he holds to be of national importance. I have of course therefore, as you requested, placed your letter before Her Majesty.

The Queen, who knows your letter was written out of concern at any damage which you consider may have been done to the future standing of the Crown in Australia, has told me to thank you for having written. She has taken note of your views.

I am sure you will neither wish nor expect me to enter into argument about the constitutional propriety of Sir John Kerr's actions. I hope, however, you will allow me to make one comment on what you say.

It is this. The constitutional role of the Governor-General and his reserve powers stem not from his position as The Queen's personal representative, to which he is appointed on the advice of the Prime Minister,

Sir Martin Charteris' reply to Gough Whitlam (12 January 1976).
Source: The Whitlam Institute

but rather from what is written in the Constitution Act as applicable constitutionally. This point has, I think, particular relevance to the position of The Queen as Queen of Australia.

Before ending this letter I should like to say how much I have appreciated your kindness and consideration to me personally whilst you have been Prime Minister of Australia.

Yours very sincerely

Martin Charteris

The Hon. Gough Whitlam, Q.C., M.P.

CONVERSATIONS WITH SIR JOHN KERR RELATING TO HIS TERMINATION OF THE COMMISSION OF THE PRIME MINISTER (THE HON E G WHITLAM AC QC) ON 11 NOVEMBER 1975

Introduction

1.   This statement records my recollection of my conversations with Sir John leading up to the termination of the Prime Minister's commission on 11 November 1975 and conversations thereafter relating to that event. I make the statement in response to documents placed by Sir John Kerr in National Archives which were recently released and have been discussed by Professor Hocking in vol.2 of her biography of Mr Whitlam. The documents relate to conversations with me in October – November 1975 preceding the dismissal of the Whitlam government. They incorporate a shorter version prepared on 21 October 1975. The documents are neither a complete nor an accurate record of our conversations, particularly of our conversations on 9 November.

2.   Sir John prepared the documents in 1981 for future publication without showing them to me or checking their accuracy with me. Nor did I become aware of their contents until after they were released by National Archives. In responding to them some thirty or so years later I note that other documents lodged by Sir John are still to be released.

3.   I was, as Sir John says, a close friend, as was my wife. He had discussed with me whether he should accept appointment as Governor-General. So I was willing to talk to him about the issues that were to confront him in October-November 1975 and to give him my views on the exercise of the Governor-General's reserve powers to dismiss a Prime Minister.

4.   In our conversation relating to the offer of appointment as Governor-General, he told me that he was discussing the matter with me at the request of his first wife. He wanted to accept the appointment because he thought it would be interesting and he had achieved as much as he could in the Supreme Court of New South Wales by introducing important administrative reforms in the short time he had been Chief Justice. In response to my view that appointment as Governor-General would not present a challenge and that he would find himself formally rubber-stamping decisions made by others, he did not agree. He thought that there would be opportunities to contribute to policy issues and he

Sir Anthony Mason's statement on his conversations with Sir John Kerr relating to the dismissal (23 August 2012).
Source: National Library of Australia

referred to the reserve powers and the possibility that an occasion could arise for their exercise. I did not understand this to be a prediction but rather an argument that I was underestimating the importance of the office of Governor-General. Our discussion ended with my saying that I could not advise what he should do and that he would have to make up his own mind whether or not to accept the appointment.

5.   After his appointment as Governor-General, I saw Sir John from time to time at Admiralty House and Yarralumla, some times elsewhere, at official functions and once at least at our home in Mosman and our place in the Blue Mountains. Our conversations relating to, and preceding, the events of 11 November 1975 took place at Yarralumla, Admiralty House, what I understood to be Lady Kerr's house at North Sydney and by telephone.

6.   In his autobiography "Matters for Judgment", Sir John said in 1978 of our conversations leading up to his termination of Mr Whitlam's commission as Prime Minister

> "The conversation(s) did not include advice as to what I should do but sustained me in my own thinking as to the imperatives within which I had to act, and in my conclusions, already reached as to what I could and should do."

That statement was an accurate description of the substance of our conversations on 9 November and on other occasions, except in so far as I informed Sir John that he should warn the Prime Minister that, if he did not agree to hold a general election, his commission would be terminated.

The conversations

7.   There are a number of inconsistencies between Sir John's version of our relevant conversations and my recollection of them. The major points of disagreement are:

- The relevant conversations began before 12 October 1975.
- I said to Sir John that he should warn the Prime Minister that he would terminate his commission if he did not agree to hold a general election. The warning was not heeded.
- I did not encourage Sir John to dismiss Mr Whitlam.
- I did not volunteer or agree to give a written opinion on Mr R J Ellicott QC's press statement or document of 16 October 1975 and the draft Law Officers' opinion and allow my opinion to be made public.

- I played no part at all in the preparation of Sir John's statement of decision, nor was I asked to do so, though I prepared, at his request, a draft letter terminating Mr Whitlam's commission (which Sir John did not adopt).

8.   My first conversation in 1975 with Sir John with reference to the reserve powers was at Yarralumla in August, not 12 October, as Sir John says. In that conversation he mentioned that an occasion might arise for him to exercise the reserve powers, dismiss Mr Whitlam and commission Mr Fraser to form a caretaker government for the purpose of securing supply and holding an election. He referred to Dr Evatt's monograph "The King and his Dominion Governors" relating to the reserve powers which, as "Matters for Judgment" records, he re-read before accepting his appointment as Governor-General.

9.   I said that, in my view, the incumbent Prime Minister should, as a matter of fairness, first be offered the option of holding a general election to resolve any dispute over supply between the two Houses and informed that if he did not agree to do so his commission would be withdrawn. I pointed out that it would be to the advantage of the Prime Minister to hold such an election as the serving Prime Minister rather than contest it as a Prime Minister who had been dismissed by the Governor-General. Sir John did not question my view then or at any time in his discussions with me.

10.   Shortly thereafter, Sir John told me that he had been informed confidentially by Mr (later Sir) Geoffrey Yeend, then a senior officer and later Secretary of the Department of Prime Minister and Cabinet, that the Government was planning to seek the termination by the Queen of his appointment as Governor-General if he indicated that he intended or was minded to terminate the Prime Minister's commission. I don't remember whether Sir John said that Mr Yeend conveyed this information directly or in coded words. Sir John did not inform me of his response to Mr Yeend.

11.   In his archival note of the conversation with Mr Yeend, Sir John attributes to Mr Yeend the inquiry

> "What would happen if you were to consider taking action yourself? Your own position could be in doubt. There could be a race to the Palace".

Sir John's reply as noted was

> "There would be no race to the Palace Geoff. I do not have to go
> to the Palace".

In the note Sir John records that he "regretted what he said in reply" to
Mr Yeend because it was not clear whether Mr Yeend was speaking in a
personal capacity. Sir John records that what Mr Yeend said "hit me
hard" and "shattered" me.

12.   In a subsequent conversation on or before 12 October Sir John
informed me that he had it in mind to consult the Chief Justice in the
event that it became necessary to resolve a crisis over supply, though he
had some concern over possible perceptions arising from the Chief
Justice's former association with the Liberal Party. He believed that the
Chief Justice would be willing to advise him. Sir John also said that, if
the Senate were to defer or fail to grant supply, it would be necessary to
allow some time to pass in order to test the Senate's resolve.

13.   Coming now to the October conversations and our discussion of
Mr Ellicott's view, as related to me by Sir John, that the Governor-
General should take immediate action to resolve the crisis, I said to Sir
John that, if he considered it legitimate or necessary to consult the Chief
Justice, it would be unwise to do so at that time as the Chief Justice might
agree with Mr Ellicott's view that immediate action be taken. But I did
not describe or regard that view as "radical". Nor did I describe the
consequences as "catastrophic" or "disastrous".

14.   I certainly did not agree to give a written opinion on the Law
Officers' advice or on the Ellicott document (which I had not seen), as Sir
John claims, though I had suggested that he should ask the Prime
Minister to obtain the Law Officers' opinion on the Governor-General's
power to terminate the commission of the Prime Minister. Sir John said
he would do that. I did not receive a copy of the Ellicott document,
despite Sir John's claim to the contrary.

15.   At about this time Sir John informed me that the Prime Minister
had agreed, at Sir John's request, to him seeing the Leader of the
Opposition (Mr Fraser). Sir John did not discuss with me how this came
about. Nor did he ever communicate to me his conversations with Mr
Fraser, except to say later that the Senate remained firm in its resolve in
not granting supply, a statement which I assumed was based on
information provided by Mr Fraser. Nor did Sir John ever discuss with

me his conversations with Mr Hayden about the Government's financial
position.

16.   Sir John was very much aware of the possibility that the Prime
Minister might seek to have him removed from office. Apart from his
account to me of his conversation with Mr Yeend, he told me of the
Prime Minister's remark before the State banquet in honour of the Prime
Minister of Malaysia, "It could be a question of whether I get to the
Queen first for your recall or you get in first with my dismissal".

17.   About a week before Sunday 9 November 1975, I had a
conversation with Sir John at Admiralty House. In this conversation he
said that he had not received the Law Officers' opinion and did not know
the reason for the delay. Sir John asked me whether, in the event that the
issue of the dismissal of the Prime Minister were to go to the High Court,
the Chief Justice would sit if he had given a written opinion on the
matter. I replied that I did not know the answer to that question. Sir John
did not ask me whether, in the event that the matter went to the High
Court, I would sit on the case. Nor did he ask me for my view on the
likelihood of the matter going to the High Court. There was no
discussion of either of these questions. Whatever may be thought now, at
the time I was of the view that the matter was unlikely to come before the
High Court.

18.   Towards the end of our conversation Sir John said that he would
resolve the crisis one way or the other without asking for a written
opinion from the Chief Justice or "another member of the High Court". I
think that it was in the course of that conversation and not later that Sir
John said that the Prime Minister had told him that he (Sir John) was not
to consult the Chief Justice but he did not disclose when and in what
circumstances the Prime Minister had made that statement.

19.   Our next conversation, the first conversation on 9 November, took
place at what I understood to be Lady Kerr's house in North Sydney,
where Sir John asked me to meet him. On my arrival, Sir John said that
we were meeting at the house because the Prime Minister was at Kirribilli
House (adjacent to Admiralty House) and he (Sir John) did not want the
Prime Minister to know of our meeting. That first conversation was in
the late morning or early in the afternoon but I am confident that it was
not in the late afternoon, as Sir John states. The second conversation,
which was fairly brief, took place at Admiralty House before and at the
end of dinner with Sir John and Lady Kerr that evening. My wife and I
were the only guests.

20.   The substance of the first conversation began with a statement by Sir John in which he said that, after careful consideration of all that happened he had decided that he had no alternative but to dismiss Mr Whitlam and to commission Mr Fraser to form a caretaker government. He said he had information from the Electoral Commission that if an election was to be conducted and completed before the Christmas vacation, it had to be held on 13 December. To enable such an election to take place instructions for it must be given no later than the next Wednesday. Sir John then handed me two opinions. The first was the "Draft" Opinion by the Law Officers; the second was the Solicitor-General's Opinion on alternative financing. Neither opinion was sent to me in advance, as the archival documents state.

21.   I then read the "Draft" Opinion and simply said "I don't agree with it". Sir John said "Will you give a written opinion to that effect that I can rely on?" I replied "I could not do that without consulting Barwick". I also said that it would not be appropriate for me rather than the Chief Justice to give such a written opinion. Sir John then said "Well, I will ask Barwick".

22.   After I read the Opinion on alternative financing, I said that I was not prepared to express a view as to its legal efficacy, but went on to say that I thought that the private banks would be unlikely to act on it. Sir John then left the room and telephoned the Chief Justice and was told that he was not in but would be available later in the day. I had no discussion with Sir John then or later about what he would or would not say to the Chief Justice.

23.   At the end of our first conversation I expressed my relief that Sir John had made a final decision to resolve the crisis by dismissing the Prime Minister because I thought that the crisis should be resolved by a general election to be held before the summer vacation and any further delay could lead to instability. I do not think that I expressed to Sir John the reason for my relief. I assumed that this reason lay behind Sir John's announced decision to terminate the Prime Minister's commission because that decision would facilitate the holding of a general election before the vacation. My comment was not, and should not have been understood as, encouragement to dismiss the Prime Minister as Sir John had already announced his decision to take that step.

24.   As I was about to leave I said to Sir John that unfortunately it was unfolding like a Greek tragedy whereupon he called out to Lady Kerr who was upstairs and asked her to join us. He explained to her what he had decided to do. When I said that the decision was bound to be controversial and attract strong criticism, he said "Tony, you don't know these people. I do. It will be much worse than you think". It was then that he invited my wife and me to dinner that evening.

25.   On our arrival at Admiralty House in the evening, in response to my inquiry, Sir John told me that the Prime Minister had left Kirribilli House earlier in the day. Sir John also said that he had spoken to the Chief Justice and would be seeing him the next morning. Later, at the end of dinner, Sir John told me that he would see Mr Whitlam and simply hand him a letter of dismissal. I then said that before doing so he should say that he had no alternative but to dismiss the Prime Minister unless he was willing to hold a general election.

26.   Sir John replied "I know that". I told him that, if he did not warn the Prime Minister, he would run the risk that people would accuse him of being deceptive. I also said that he would need to consider the possibility that the Prime Minister might ask for time to consider his position and, if so, what response should be made.

27.   Sir John made no comment but immediately asked me if I would draft a letter terminating the Prime Minister's commission which I agreed to do. The draft was delivered early the next morning at Admiralty House. The draft was short, consisting of about three sentences, identifying the failure to obtain supply as the critical event. The actual letter of dismissal was in very different terms. Sir John did not ask me to draft paragraphs for inclusion in his statement of decision. I played no part at all in its preparation. Nor was it ever shown to me or its contents discussed with me. Some time later Sir John returned the draft to me.

28.   In the course of the conversation which took place after dinner on 9 November, I said to Sir John that he would be criticised for not telling the Prime Minister that he (Sir John) was disregarding his instruction not to consult the Chief Justice. Sir John said that Barwick's attendance at Admiralty House the next day would appear in the Vice-Regal notes and that would constitute sufficient notice to the Prime Minister.

29.   Late on Monday 10 November 1975 Sir John telephoned me to ask whether the Chief Justice had discussed with me the advice he (Sir John) had received from the Chief Justice. I said that the Chief Justice had

shown me the letter and I had replied "It's OK". I also said to Sir John Kerr that I would have expressed the advice in slightly different terms but that was not a matter of importance. Sir John said that he had asked the Chief Justice to speak to me because he (Sir John) felt embarrassed that he had first discussed the question with me and he wanted the Chief Justice to know what my view was.

Later conversations

30.   On 11 November 1975 Sir John telephoned me to say that the Speaker and others wished to see him to present a resolution of the House of Representatives expressing no confidence in the Fraser government. I said that the resolution was irrelevant as he had commissioned Mr Fraser to form a caretaker government for limited purposes to hold a general election.

31.   On 19 November or thereabouts I had dinner at Yarralumla with Sir John and Lady Kerr – I may have stayed there overnight. After dinner Sir John said to me that our discussions should be made public for the sake of history and he reminded me that (in our first conversation on 9 November) I had expressed my relief that he had decided to dismiss Mr Whitlam. I replied by saying that if he were to publish our discussions he would need to record that I had said that he should warn the Prime Minister and give him the option of calling a general election. Sir John made no reply and the conversation turned to other matters. On that occasion Sir John spoke of leaving a letter with his executors giving them instructions as to publication.

32.   Some years later at a function at "The Quarterdeck", Sir John and Lady Kerr's apartment in Kirribilli, I had another conversation with Sir John about publication of our discussions, a conversation initiated by Sir John. It was in terms virtually identical with the discussion in the preceding paragraph, except that there was no reference to instructions to his executors. The conversation terminated after my reference to the need to record my remarks about warning the Prime Minister.

Concluding comments

33.   In his writings since 9 November 1975, Sir John has strongly defended his decision not to warn Mr Whitlam. Although he did not discuss his reasons for that decision with me before or after the dismissal, my impression is that Sir John thought that warning the Prime Minister

might lead to Her Majesty becoming embroiled in the Australian constitutional controversy and that he wanted to avoid such an outcome.

34.   Despite my disagreement with Sir John's account of events and his decision not to warn the Prime Minister, I consider that Sir John was subjected to unjustified vilification for making the decision which he made. I consider and have always considered that Sir John acted consistently with his duty except in so far as he had a duty to warn the Prime Minister of his intended action and he did not do so.

A. F. Mason

A. F. Mason
Dated: 23 August 2012

Acknowledgements

This book benefited by being able to draw upon nearly forty new interviews with many key players in the events of October-November 1975 from many vantage points. Some interviews conducted several years ago are used here for the first time. Other interviews by the authors are being republished and are included in the endnotes.

For agreeing to new interviews, the authors would like to thank: Tony Abbott, Doug Anthony, Sir Gerard Brennan, Dale Budd, Rod Cameron, Jimmy Carter, Peter Costello, Bernard Donoughue, Alexander Downer, Tony Eggleton, Bob Ellicott, Robert French, Graham Freudenberg, Vic Garland, Murray Gleeson, Bob Hawke, Bill Hayden, Sir William Heseltine, John Hewson, John Howard, the late Sir Kenneth Jacobs, Paul Keating, David Kemp, Tom Lewis, Geoffrey Lindell, John Mant, Don Markwell, Doug McClelland, Brendan Nelson, Andrew Peacock, Dennis Pearce, Gordon Scholes, Michael Sexton, Ian Sinclair, Sir David Smith, Tony Staley, Sir Laurence Street and Malcolm Turnbull.

In researching and writing this book, we drew on many new archival documents, including some held in private collections. Several documents are published in these pages for the first time. We wish to especially thank Dale Budd, Tony Eggleton, Nicholas Hasluck and Don Markwell for providing us with access to their personal papers.

Andrew Cairns at the National Archives of Australia was always prompt in responding to our very many queries and helpful in getting new material, particularly from Sir John Kerr's papers, cleared for access. Elizabeth Masters' assistance in sourcing photos from the National Archives collection was invaluable. We also made use of personal and official papers held in the National Archives of Sir Garfield Barwick, Malcolm Fraser, Gough Whitlam, Sir Clarence Harders, John Menadue, Sir Geoffrey Yeend and the staff of the departments of Prime Minister and Cabinet and Attorney-General's.

We appreciated the assistance provided by the staff of the National Library when accessing the personal papers of John Menadue, Sir Anthony Mason, Sir William Heseltine and Geoffrey Sawer. Marian Hanly and Duncan Felton at the National Library were helpful in facilitating our access to oral history interviews with Sir John Kerr, Malcolm Fraser, Sir Clarence Harders, Reg Withers and Sir Billy Snedden, among others. We also looked through the papers of Sir Roden Cutler at the State Records Authority of NSW, at Kingswood.

The personal archives of Gough Whitlam and Malcolm Fraser were invaluable for this book. We owe a special debt of gratitude to Katie Wood for helping us to navigate the Malcolm Fraser Collection at University of Melbourne; Lorraine West at The Whitlam Institute located at Western Sydney University; and Pixie Stardust for providing documents from the Bob Hawke Collection at the University of South Australia.

At The National Archives of the United Kingdom, we were able to access several documents from the Prime Ministerial Office files of Harold Wilson and also the Foreign and Commonwealth Office files, including material from the United Kingdom High Commission in Canberra.

We benefited from the valuable assistance, editorial advice and suggestions of many people, including: Hollie Adams, Michele Bramston, James Curran, Elena Douglas, Philippa Ellis, Malcolm Farnsworth, Josh Frydenberg, Margaret Kelly, Michael Kirby, Greg McIntosh, John Menadue, Chris Merritt, Linda Scott, Brett Odgers, Nicky Seaby, George Williams and George Wright.

We appreciated the support and encouragement provided by our colleagues at *The Australian*, including Chris Mitchell, Clive Mathieson, Michelle Gunn and Milan Scepanovic.

Penguin Random House was immediately enthusiastic when we began discussions about this book in detail earlier this year. Our many thanks goes to Ben Ball and his team, especially Arwen Summers, Rebecca Bauert, Heidi McCourt and Alysha Farry.

Notes

CHAPTER ONE

1   This is a reference to Anne Robson as Lady Kerr.
2   Memorandum by Paul Hasluck, 10 August 1977, Hasluck Collection, Perth.
3   David Kemp, interview with Troy Bramston, June 2015.
4   David Smith, interview with Paul Kelly and Troy Bramston, July 2015.
5   Dale Budd, interview with Paul Kelly and Troy Bramston, July 2015.
6   Tony Staley, interview with Troy Bramston, July 2015.
7   Hasluck Memorandum.
8   Ibid.
9   John Kerr, *Matters for Judgment*, Macmillan, South Melbourne, 1978, pp. 395–99.
10   John Kerr Papers, 'Menzies Correspondence', M4524, 1 Part 4, 19 November 1975–14 July 1977, National Archives of Australia.
11   Bill Hayden, *Hayden: An Autobiography*, Angus & Robertson, Sydney, 1996, p. 294.
12   John Kerr Papers, 'The Queen's visit and the position of the Governor-General', M4524, 28 March 1977, National Archives of Australia.
13   John Kerr Papers, 'Assessment of position up to the Queen's visit and relevant conversations', 20 April 1975, M4524, 34, National Archives of Australia.
14   Kerr Papers, 'The Queen's visit and the position of the Governor-General'.
15   Malcolm Fraser and Margaret Simons, *Malcolm Fraser: The Political Memoirs*, Miegunyah Press, Carlton, 2010, pp. 335–36.
16   Kerr Papers, 'The Queen's visit and the position of the Governor-General'.
17   David Smith, interview with Paul Kelly and Troy Bramston, July 2015.
18   John Kerr Papers, 'Correspondence between The Prime Minister and The Governor-General on the Governor-General's Resignation', M4524, 31, National Archives of Australia.
19   William Heseltine, interview with Paul Kelly, May 2015.
20   William Heseltine, interview with Paul Kelly, quoted in *100 Years: The Australian Story*, Allen & Unwin, Sydney, 2001, p. 26.
21   Martin Charteris, interview with Paul Kelly, July 1995.
22   Paul Kelly, *November 1975: The Inside Story of Australia's Greatest Political Crisis*, Allen & Unwin, Sydney, 1995, p. 314
23   William Heseltine, interview with Paul Kelly, May 2015.
24   Ibid.
25   Martin Charteris, interview with Paul Kelly, 13 July 1995; William Heseltine, interview with Paul Kelly, May 2015.
26   William Heseltine, interview with Paul Kelly, May 2015.

27   Ibid.
28   William Heseltine, interview with Troy Bramston, September 2015.
29   William Heseltine, interview with Troy Bramston, October 2014.
30   William Heseltine, interview with Paul Kelly, quoted in *100 Years: The Australian Story*, Allen & Unwin, Sydney, 2001, p. 26.
31   John Menadue Papers, 'Fax from Tim McDonald to John Menadue, 6 June 1997', Box 3, 'Dismissal, Fraser Government', MS Acc 11.054, National Library of Australia.
32   Ibid.
33   Hasluck memorandum.
34   Ibid.
35   William Heseltine, interview with Paul Kelly, May 2015.
36   Kerr Papers, 'The Queen's visit and the position of the Governor-General'.
37   John Kerr Papers, 'Menzies Correspondence'.
38   John Kerr Papers, 'Journal for 1980', M4523, 1 Part 17, National Archives of Australia.
39   William Heseltine, interview with Troy Bramston, September 2015.

CHAPTER TWO

1   Fraser and Simons, *Malcolm Fraser: The Political Memoirs*, p. 304.
2   Ibid.
3   Ibid., p. 305.
4   John Kerr, *Matters for Judgment: An Autobiography*, p. 355.
5   Fraser and Simons, *Malcolm Fraser: The Political Memoirs*, p. 305.
6   Reg Withers, Oral History Interview, 1997, ORAL TRC 3616, National Library of Australia, p. 389.
7   Vic Garland, interview with Paul Kelly, July 2015.
8   Dale Budd, 'D-Day', in Sybil Nolan (ed.), *The Dismissal: Where were you on November 11, 1975?*, Melbourne University Press, Carlton, 2005, p. 48.
9   Dale Budd, interview with Paul Kelly and Troy Bramston, July 2015.
10   Malcolm Fraser, Statutory Declaration, 2 June 2006, The Malcolm Fraser Collection, University of Melbourne.
11   It is the authors' view that Fraser has misread this part of his contemporaneous note. It is not 'police charges' but 'policy changes'.
12   Philip Ayres, *Malcolm Fraser: A Biography*, William Heinemann, Richmond, 1987, pp. 292–93.
13   Malcolm Fraser, Oral History Interview, 1987, ORAL TRC 2162, National Library of Australia, pp. 381–82. In 1992, Fraser attached a letter to this interview stating that it 'will give an inaccurate view' of events as Cameron 'seemed to be using me as a sounding board for his views . . . that were detrimental to Mr Whitlam.' Fraser gave Troy Bramston permission to access the interview in 2013.
14   David Kemp, 'Red Felt Pen on Green Paper', in Nolan (ed.), *The Dismissal: Where were you on November 11, 1975?*, p. 42.
15   David Kemp, interview with Troy Bramston, June 2015.
16   Gerard Henderson, 'Sir John Kerr: The Dismissal – What I told Malcolm Fraser', the *Weekend Australian*, 14–15 November 1987. See also Gerard Henderson, *Menzies' Child: The Liberal Party of Australia: 1944–1994*, Allen & Unwin, St Leonards, 1994, p. 239.
17   John Kerr Papers, 'Notes by Sir John Kerr on discussions with Gough Whitlam and Malcolm Fraser', 16 November 1975, M4523, 1 PART 3, National Archives of Australia.
18   Henderson, *Menzies' Child: The Liberal Party of Australia: 1944–1994*, p. 240.
19   David Smith, 'Malcolm Fraser recalls what wasn't said', *The Australian*, 15 March 2010.
20   David Smith, the *Sydney Institute Quarterly*, Issue 27, Volume 9, Number 4, January 2006.

21 Alan Reid was standing in King's Hall when Malcolm Fraser passed by and said he was on his way to see Kerr. 'What's he want to see you about?' Reid asked. 'I don't know. I wasn't told. I suppose it's to get my version of this morning's discussions [with Whitlam, Crean and Daly]', Fraser reportedly said. See Alan Reid, *The Whitlam Venture*, Hill of Content, Melbourne, 1976, pp. 410–11.
22 Paul Kelly, *November 1975*, p. 251.
23 Henderson, *Menzies' Child: The Liberal Party of Australia: 1944–1994*, p. 241.

CHAPTER THREE

1 Kerr, *Matters for Judgment*, pp. 309–10.
2 Anthony Mason, 'Conversation with Sir John Kerr relating to his Termination of the Commission of the Prime Minister (The Hon. EG Whitlam AC QC) on 11 November 1975', MS Acc 12.118, National Library of Australia.
3 John Kerr Papers, 'Extracts from Letters dated 20 September 1975, 17 October 1975, 20 October 1975, 6 November 1975, 11 November 1975 and 20 November 1975', M4523, 1 PART 7, National Archives of Australia.
4 John Menadue Papers, 'The Governor-General and the Dismissal of the Labor Government', 11 December 1975, Box 3, 'Dismissal, Fraser Government', MS Acc 11.054, National Library of Australia.
5 John Menadue, interview with Paul Kelly, April 1995.
6 John Wheeldon, interview with Paul Kelly, July 1995.
7 Jim McClelland, interview with Paul Kelly, August 1995.
8 Graham Freudenberg, interview with Troy Bramston, July 2015.
9 Paul Keating, interview with Paul Kelly and Troy Bramston, July 2013.
10 Gough Whitlam, *The Truth of the Matter*, Penguin, Ringwood, Victoria, 1979, p. 89.
11 Jim McClelland, interview with Paul Kelly, February 1976; Gough Whitlam, interview with Paul Kelly, February 1976; Kelly, *November 1975*, p. 180.
12 Senate, *Hansard*, 18 February 1976, p. 56.
13 Whitlam, *The Truth of the Matter*, p. 91.
14 Kelly, *November 1975*, p. 147.
15 Kerr, *Matters for Judgment*, p. 311.
16 Bill Hayden, interview with Paul Kelly, June 1995.
17 Hasluck Memorandum.
18 John Kerr Papers, 'Kerr, Elizabeth and Philip', M4526, 24, National Archives of Australia.

CHAPTER FOUR

1 Garfield Barwick, interview with Paul Kelly, June 1995; see Henderson, *Menzies' Child*, p. 244.
2 Gerard Brennan, written interview with Paul Kelly and Troy Bramston, May 2015.
3 Robert French, written interview with Paul Kelly, May 2015.
4 Quoted in Robert French, 'Chief Justice and the Governor-General', speech, 29 October 2009, published in *Melbourne University Law Review*, p. 647.
5 Ibid.
6 Murray Gleeson, interview with Paul Kelly and Troy Bramston, April 2015.
7 Ibid.
8 Garfield Barwick, *Sir John Did His Duty*, Serendip Publications, Wahroonga, 1983, p. 77.
9 See Chapter Thirteen, 'Manipulating a Willing Chief Justice'.
10 Anthony Mason, 'Conversations with Sir John Kerr relating to his Termination of the Commission of the Prime Minister (The Hon E G Whitlam AC QC) on 11 November 1975'.

11 John Kerr Papers, 'Conversation with Sir Anthony Mason during October–November 1975', M4523, 1 PART 14, National Archives of Australia.

12 Bob Hawke, interview with Troy Bramston, August 2015.

13 Paul Keating, interview with Paul Kelly and Troy Bramston, July 2015.

14 For interviews with Duffy, Evans and Willis see Troy Bramston, 'Role with Kerr would have barred Mason as top judge', *The Australian*, September 1–2, 2012.

15 Bill Hayden, interview with Troy Bramston, October 2014.

16 Barwick, *Sir John Did His Duty*, pp. 76–80.

17 See Harry Gibbs, 'The dismissal and the constitution', in Michael Coper and George Williams (eds.), *Power, Parliament and the People*, The Federation Press, Sydney, 1997, pp. 146–54.

18 Ibid., p. 146.

19 Garfield Barwick, *A Radical Tory*, The Federation Press, Sydney, 1995, pp. 232–33.

20 Garfield Barwick Papers, 'Dismissal of the Labour [sic] Government, 1975–79', M3942/18, National Archives of Australia.

21 Ibid.

22 Michael Kirby to Troy Bramston, emails, 1 May 2015 and 2 July 2015.

23 Kerr Papers, 'Conversation with Sir Anthony Mason during October–November 1975'.

24 Paul Kelly, *November 1975*, p. 227.

25 'Sir Anthony was wrong to advise Barwick', *The Australian*, 5 January 1994.

26 Michael Sexton, interview with Troy Bramston, August 2015.

27 Barwick, *Sir John Did His Duty*, p. 78.

28 Murray Gleeson, interview with Paul Kelly and Troy Bramston, April 2015.

29 Robert French, written interview with Paul Kelly, May 2015.

30 Gerard Brennan, written interview with Paul Kelly and Troy Bramston, May 2015.

31 Ibid.

32 Ibid.

33 French, 'Chief Justice and the Governor-General'.

34 Paul Hasluck, *The Office of Governor-General*, Melbourne University Press, Carlton, Victoria, 1979.

35 Anne Twomey, 'List of occasions upon which judges have advised vice-regal officers in Australia', document provided to Paul Kelly.

36 Ibid.; interview between Richard Carleton and Sir Murray Tyrrell, 'State of the Nation', 30 October 1975.

37 French, 'Chief Justice and the Governor-General'.

38 Paul Kildea and George Williams, 'The Mason court', in Rosalind Dixon and George Williams (eds.), *The High Court, the Constitution and Australian Politics*, Cambridge University Press, Melbourne, 2015, p. 245.

39 Kerr, *Matters for Judgment*, p. 340.

40 Ibid., p. 339.

CHAPTER FIVE

1 John Kerr, Oral History Interview, 1974–76, ORAL TRC 440, National Library of Australia, p. 163. The authors obtained access to this interview in 2013. It is not available for public access until 2041 without written permission from Kerr's executor.

2 Ibid.

3 Ibid., pp. 157–58; Jim McClelland has a different version of this story. See Jim McClelland, *Stirring the Possum*, Penguin, Ringwood, Victoria, 1989, p. 135.

4 Kerr, Oral History, pp. 165–66.

5 McClelland, *Stirring the Possum*, p. 108.

6   Kerr, Oral History, p. 166.

7   Laurence Street, interview with Paul Kelly and Troy Bramston, April 2015.

8   Anne Kerr, interview with Paul Kelly, June 1995.

9   Letter from Patti Warn to Gough Whitlam, 11 December 1978. In the authors' possession.

10   Kerr, Oral History, pp. 26–29; Kerr, *Matters for Judgment*, p. 43.

11   Kerr, Oral History, pp. 22–24; Kerr, *Matters for Judgment*, p. 45.

12   Kerr, Oral History, p. 35.

13   Ibid., pp. 37–41.

14   Ibid., p. 29.

15   Ibid., p. 366.

16   Kerr, *Matters for Judgment*, p. 141.

17   Ibid., pp. 146–48.

18   Kerr, Oral History, pp. 126–27; Kerr, *Matters for Judgment*, p. 148.

19   Kerr, Oral History, pp. 126–27.

20   McClelland, *Stirring the Possum*, p. 109.

21   Kerr, Oral History, p. 128.

22   James McAuley writing in *Quadrant*, January 1976. See Kerr, *Matters for Judgment*, p. 149.

23   Kerr, Oral History, p. 125.

24   Ibid., p. 128.

25   Ibid., p. 116.

26   Kerr, *Matters for Judgment*, p. 157.

27   Elizabeth Reid, interview with Paul Kelly, August 1995.

28   Kerr, Oral History, pp. 156–61.

29   Ibid., p. 145.

30   Ibid., pp. 164–65.

31   Ibid., p. 194.

32   Ibid., pp. 150–51.

33   Roden Cutler, interview with Paul Kelly, August 1995.

34   Kerr, Oral History, p. 167.

35   Gough Whitlam, *The Truth of the Matter*, Melbourne University Publishing, Carlton, Third Edition, 2005, p. xvii.

36   *The Bulletin*, 24 September 1985.

37   Kerr, Oral History, pp. 175–76.

38   Whitlam, *The Truth of the Matter*, p. 22.

39   Mason, 'Conversation with Sir John Kerr relating to his Termination of the Commission of the Prime Minister (The Hon. EG Whitlam AC QC) on 11 November 1975'.

40   Kerr, *Matters for Judgment*, p. 16.

41   Ken Gee, interview with Paul Kelly, June 1995.

42   Whitlam, *The Truth of the Matter*, pp. 25–26.

43   Ken Gee, interview with Paul Kelly, June 1995.

44   Kerr, Oral History, pp. 175–76.

45   Menadue Papers, 'The Governor-General and the Dismissal of the Labor Government'.

CHAPTER SIX

1   Murray Gleeson, interview with Paul Kelly and Troy Bramston, April 2015.

2   Kerr, *Matters for Judgment*, pp. 39–41

3   Kerr, Oral History, pp. 35–37.

4   Kerr, *Matters for Judgment*, pp. 52–53.

5   Gough Whitlam, interview with Paul Kelly, June 1995.

6   Whitlam, *The Truth of the Matter*, Third Edition, p.259.

7   HV Evatt, *The King and His Dominion Governors*, Oxford University Press, London, 1936.
8   Kerr, *Matters for Judgment*, chapters 4 and 5.
9   Mason, 'Conversation with Sir John Kerr relating to his Termination of the Commission of the Prime Minister (The Hon. EG Whitlam AC QC) on 11 November 1975'.
10   Kerr, Oral History, pp. 123–25 and p. 368.
11   David Marr, *Barwick*, George Allen & Unwin, Sydney, 1980, pp. 75–76.
12   Barwick, *Sir John Did His Duty*, p. 77.
13   Kerr, Oral History, p. 377.
14   Jim McClelland, interview with Paul Kelly, February 1976.
15   Kerr, Oral History, pp. 378–79.
16   Barwick, *Sir John Did His Duty*, pp. 68–69.
17   John Howard, *The Menzies Era*, HarperCollins, Sydney, 2014, pp. 273–74.
18   Barwick, *A Radical Tory*, pp. 208–09.
19   Kerr, Oral History, pp. 379–81.
20   Kerr, Oral History, p. 169.
21   Barwick, *Sir John Did His Duty*, p. 85.
22   John Kerr Papers, Anthony Mason to John Kerr, 10 April 1976, 'Mason, The Honourable Mr Justice', M4541/27, National Archives of Australia.
23   Geoffrey Sawer Papers, 'Office of the Governor-General, 1975–1991', MS2688, Series 12, Folder 1, Box 7, National Library of Australia.
24   Geoffrey Lindell, interview with Troy Bramston, August 2015.
25   David Smith attended the sessions with Kerr and said in an email to Troy Bramston in August 2015: 'The meetings were organised to help Sir John get some scholarly advice on the Governor-General's role and powers, and he found them most helpful.'
26   Dennis Pearce, interview with Troy Bramston, August 2015.
27   Sawer Papers, 'Office of the Governor-General, 1975–1991'.
28   Barwick, *A Radical Tory*, pp. 289–90.
29   Maurice Byers, interview with Paul Kelly, June 1995.
30   Joe Riordan, interview with Paul Kelly, June 1995.

CHAPTER SEVEN

1   This chapter and a number of quotes draw upon Kelly, *November 1975*.
2   David Kemp, interview with Troy Bramston, June 2015.
3   Malcolm Fraser, 'Towards 2000: Challenge to Australia', The Fifth Alfred Deakin Lecture, 20 July 1971.
4   Malcolm Fraser, interview with Troy Bramston, April 2013.
5   The loans affair is discussed in detail in Chapter Eight.
6   *The Advertiser*, 11 April 1974.
7   Reg Withers, interview with Paul Kelly, June 1995.
8   Senate, *Hansard*, 10 April 1974, p. 902.
9   Tom Lewis, interview with Troy Bramston, March 2011.
10   Doug Anthony, email to Troy Bramston, September 2015.
11   Shadow Ministry Minutes, 15 October 1975, Malcolm Fraser Collection, University of Melbourne.
12   John Howard, interview with Paul Kelly, June 2015.
13   Kelly, *November 1975*, pp. 104–05.
14   John Quick and Robert Garran, *The Annotated Constitution of the Australian Commonwealth*, Angus & Robertson, Sydney, 1901, p. 706.

CHAPTER EIGHT

1   Kerr, *Matters for Judgment*, p. 254.
2   See John Kerr Papers, 'Notes on the Joint Sitting of Parliament and the Loan Crisis', M4524, 25, National Archives of Australia.
3   This chapter and a number of quotes draw upon Kelly, *November 1975*.
4   Clarrie Harders, Oral History Interview, 1996–97, ORAL TRC 3537, National Library of Australia, p. 35; and Clarrie Harders, interview with Paul Kelly, June 1995.
5   Kerr Papers, 'Notes on the Joint Sitting of Parliament and the Loan Crisis'.
6   Ibid.
7   *Kerr, Matters for Judgment*, p. 225.
8   Ibid., pp. 226–27.
9   Harders, Oral History, pp. 40–41.
10 Menadue Papers, 'The Governor-General and the Dismissal of the Labor Government'.
11 House of Representatives, *Hansard*, 9 July 1975, pp. 3644–5.
12 Whitlam, *The Truth of the Matter*, p. 49.
13 Kerr Papers, 'Notes on the Joint Sitting of Parliament and the Loan Crisis'.
14 Kerr, *Matters for Judgment*, pp. 239–40.
15 Whitlam, *The Truth of the Matter*, pp. 46–58.
16 Ibid., p. 59.
17 Harders, interview with Paul Kelly, June 1995.
18 Hasluck Memorandum.
19 Kerr, *Matters for Judgment*, pp. 238–40.
20 Ibid., p. 240.
21 Ibid., p. 254.
22 Ibid.
23 Walter Bagehot, *The English Constitution*, 1867, reprinted by Fontana, London, 1993, p. 113.
24 Kerr Papers, 'Notes by Sir John Kerr on discussions with Gough Whitlam and Malcolm Fraser'.
25 Whitlam, *The Truth of the Matter*, p. 95.

CHAPTER NINE

1   Gough Whitlam to Harold Wilson, 31 December 1975, Records of the Prime Minister's Office, PREM 16/1509, The National Archives, Kew.
2   Whitlam, *The Truth of the Matter*, p. 111.
3   Menadue Papers, 'The Governor-General and the Dismissal of the Labor Government'.
4   Michael Sexton, interview with Troy Bramston, August 2015.
5   John Mant, interview with Troy Bramston, August 2015.
6   Kerr Papers, 'Notes by Sir John Kerr on discussions with Gough Whitlam and Malcolm Fraser'.
7   Kerr, *Matters for Judgment*, p. 258.
8   *The Bulletin*, 10 and 17 September 1985; Anne Kerr, interview with Paul Kelly, June 1995; David Smith, interview with Paul Kelly, April 1995.
9   John Kerr Papers, 'Notes on a conversation with Malcolm Fraser on the occasion of a dinner for the Prime Minister of Malaysia', M4523, 1 PART 2, National Archives of Australia.
10 Malcolm Fraser, interview with Troy Bramston, April 2013.
11 Kerr Papers, 'Journal for 1980'.
12 Jenny Hocking, *Gough Whitlam: His Time*, The Miegunyah Press, Carlton, 2012, pp. 312, 319, 354 and 362.

13   Kelly, *November 1975*, p. 134.
14   Roden Cutler, interview with Paul Kelly, August 1995.
15   Martin Charteris, interview with Paul Kelly, June 1995.
16   David Smith, interview with Paul Kelly and Troy Bramston, July 2015.
17   Kerr, *Matters for Judgment*, pp. 263–64; Whitlam, *The Truth of the Matter*, p. 90.
18   Private discussions between Malcolm Fraser and Paul Kelly in October–November 1975.
19   Dale Budd, interview with Paul Kelly and Troy Bramston, July 2015.
20   David Kemp, interview with Troy Bramston, June 2015.
21   Laurence Street, interview with Paul Kelly and Troy Bramston, April 2015.
22   Kerr Papers, 'Notes on a conversation with Malcolm Fraser on the occasion of a dinner for
      the Prime Minister of Malaysia'.
23   Shadow Cabinet Minutes, 21 October 1975, Malcolm Fraser Collection, University
      of Melbourne.
24   Kerr, *Matters for Judgment*, pp. 267–68.
25   Dale Budd, interview with Paul Kelly and Troy Bramston, July 2015.
26   John Menadue, interview with Paul Kelly, August 1995.
27   Menadue Papers, 'The Governor-General and the Dismissal of the Labor Government.'
28   Ibid.
29   John Menadue, interview with Paul Kelly, April 1995.
30   Kelly, *November 1975*, p. 166.
31   Fraser and Simons, *Malcolm Fraser: The Political Memoirs*, pp. 297–98.
32   Philip Ayres, *Malcolm Fraser: A Biography*, p. 283.
33   David Kemp, interview with Troy Bramston, June 2015.
34   John Howard, interview with Paul Kelly, July 2015.
35   Dale Budd, interview with Paul Kelly and Troy Bramston, July 2015.
36   Fraser and Simons, *Malcolm Fraser: The Political Memoirs*, p. 294.
37   These interviews are drawn from Kelly, *November 1975*, pp. 219–22.
38   Graham Freudenberg, interview with Troy Bramston, October 2012.
39   Hayden, *Hayden: An Autobiography*, p. 294.
40   Kelly, *November 1975*, p. 136.
41   William Heseltine, interview with Paul Kelly, May 2015.
42   Kelly, *November 1975*, p. 217.
43   William Heseltine, interview with Troy Bramston, October 2014.
44   Hasluck Memorandum.

CHAPTER TEN

1   Menadue Papers, 'The Governor-General and the Dismissal of the Labor Government'.
2   John Mant, interview with Troy Bramston, August 2015.
3   Maurice Byers, interview with Paul Kelly, June 1995.
4   John Menadue, interview with Paul Kelly, April 1995.
5   Harders, Oral History, p. 71.
6   Ibid., p. 73.
7   John Mant, interview with Paul Kelly, May 1995.
8   Harders, Oral History, pp. 71–74.
9   Maurice Byers, interview with Paul Kelly, June 1995.
10   Harders, Oral History, pp. 71–73.
11   Anne Kerr, interview with Paul Kelly, June 1995.
12   Menadue Papers, 'The Governor-General and the Dismissal of the Labor Government'.
13   Michael Sexton, interview with Troy Bramston, August 2015.
14   Menadue Papers, 'The Governor-General and the Dismissal of the Labor Government'.

15 Harders, Oral History, p. 67.

16 Menadue Papers, 'The Governor-General and the Dismissal of the Labor Government'.

17 Ibid.; Harders, Oral History, p. 66–67.

18 John Menadue, interview with Paul Kelly, April 1995.

19 Menadue Papers, 'The Governor-General and the Dismissal of the Labor Government'.

20 Geoff Yeend Papers, 'Possible rejection of Appropriation Bills by the Senate – papers – 1975', M4810, 53, National Archives of Australia; 'The Dismissal – Governor-General – draft letter from the Prime Minister regarding blocking of Supply', M4081, National Archives of Australia.

21 During the crisis the prime minister used these words in private conversation with Paul Kelly.

22 Maurice Byers, interview with Paul Kelly, June 1995.

23 Bob Ellicott, interview with Troy Bramston, October 2014; email from David Smith to Troy Bramston, November 2014.

24 See John Kerr Papers, 'The Ellicott Memorandum – or Press Statement', 21 October 1975, M4525, 1 PART 12, National Archives of Australia and Kerr Papers, 'Conversation with Sir Anthony Mason during October–November'.

25 Bob Ellicott, interview with Troy Bramston, October 2014.

26 Kerr Papers, 'Conversation with Sir Anthony Mason during October–November 1975.'

27 McClelland, *Stirring the Possum*, p. 170.

28 Maurice Byers, interview with Paul Kelly, June 1995.

29 Graham Freudenberg, *A Certain Grandeur: Gough Whitlam in Politics*, Macmillan, Melbourne, 1977, p. 377.

30 Graham Freudenberg, interview with Troy Bramston, May 2014.

31 Michael Sexton, interview with Troy Bramston, August 2015.

32 Kerr, *Matters for Judgment*, p. 271.

33 Kerr Papers, 'Conversation with Sir Anthony Mason during October–November 1975'.

34 Kerr, *Matters for Judgment*, p. 272.

35 Harders, Oral History, p. 73.

36 Ibid., p. 72; Menadue Papers, 'The Governor-General and the Dismissal of the Labor Government'.

37 Clarrie Harders Papers, 'The Dismissal – Advice – Recommendation that the Prime Minister tender formal advice to the Governor-General', M4081, National Archives of Australia.

38 Kerr, *Matters for Judgment*, p. 302–03.

39 Ibid., p. 303.

40 Kep Enderby, interview with Paul Kelly, August 1995.

41 Michael Sexton, interview with Troy Bramston, August 2015.

42 Harders, Oral History, pp. 71–73.

43 Enderby, interview with Paul Kelly, August 1995.

CHAPTER ELEVEN

1 Kerr, *Matters for Judgment*, p. 341.

2 Here we draw on, inter alia, Kristen Walker, 'Mason, Anthony Frank', in Tony Blackshield, Michael Coper and George Williams (eds.), *The Oxford Companion to the High Court of Australia*, Oxford University Press, South Melbourne, 2001, pp. 459–61.

3 Kerr Papers, 'Conversation with Sir Anthony Mason during October–November 1975'. This note incorporates a previous note written by Kerr about his relationship with Mason. See Kerr Papers, 'The Ellicott Memorandum – or Press Statement'. In this chapter, Kerr's quotes about Mason come from these documents unless otherwise identified.

4   Mason, 'Conversations with Sir John Kerr relating to his Termination of the Commission of the Prime Minister (The Hon EG Whitlam AC QC) on 11 November 1975'. In this chapter Mason's quotes come from this document unless otherwise identified.

5   ABC TV, *Sir Garfield Barwick: A Life*, 5 January 1994.

6   Gerard Henderson, 'Kerr's matter of judgment', the *Sydney Morning Herald*, 8 January 1994. See also Henderson, *Menzies' Child*, pp. 242–43.

7   Hocking, *Gough Whitlam: His Time*.

8   Anthony Mason to Paul Kelly, letter, 25 May 2015.

9   'Vice-Regal', *The Age*, 13 November 1975, p. 26.

10   Kerr, Oral History, p. 147.

11   John Kerr Papers, 'The Honourable Sir Anthony, KBE, QC', 25 October 1978, M4526, National Archives of Australia.

12   Gough Whitlam, 'Truth, like the mede, immutable', the *Sydney Morning Herald*, 15 January 1994.

13   Cameron Stewart, 'Mason unblemished: Whitlam', *The Australian*, 5 January 1994, p. 1.

14   Whitlam, 'Truth, like the mede, immutable'.

15   Graham Freudenberg, interview with Troy Bramston, July 2015.

16   Michael Sexton, *On the Edges of History*, Connor Court, 2015, p. 128.

17   Michael Sexton, interview with Troy Bramston, August 2015.

18   Don Woolford, 'Dismissal dismissed at Sir John's memorial service', the *Canberra Times*, 7 April 1991, p. 1.

19   Commonwealth of Australia, *Service of Thanksgiving for the life of The Right Honourable Sir John Robert Kerr AK, GCMG, GCVO, QC*, The Parish Church of St James, King Street Sydney, 6 April 1991, The Whitlam Institute.

20   Anthony Mason, 'Eulogy delivered at the memorial service for the Right Hon Sir John Kerr AK, GCMG, GCVO', *Australian Bar Review*, Vol. 8, 1991, pp. 93–96.

CHAPTER TWELVE

1   Kerr Papers, 'Notes by Sir John Kerr on discussions with Gough Whitlam and Malcolm Fraser'.

2   Kerr Papers, 'Extracts from Letters dated 20 September 1975, 17 October 1975, 20 October 1975, 6 November 1975, 11 November 1975 and 20 November 1975'.

3   Paul Keating, interview with Paul Kelly and Troy Bramston, July 2015.

4   Tony Eggleton, interview with Paul Kelly and Troy Bramston, July 2015.

5   Ayres, *Malcolm Fraser*, p. 278.

6   Tony Eggleton, 'Record of Shadow Cabinet No. 27, 21 October 1975', Malcolm Fraser Collection, University of Melbourne.

7   Tony Eggleton, interview with Paul Kelly and Troy Bramston, July 2015.

8   Paul Kelly, *The Unmaking of Gough*, Allen & Unwin, Sydney, Revised Edition, 1994, p. 340.

9   House of Representatives, *Hansard*, 16 October 1975, p. 2206.

10   House of Representatives, *Hansard*, 21 October 1975, p. 2305.

11   Kerr Papers, 'Extracts from Letters dated 20 September 1975, 17 October 1975, 20 October 1975, 6 November 1975, 11 November 1975 and 20 November 1975'.

12   John Mant, interview with Troy Bramston, August 2015.

13   John Kerr Papers, 'Notes on talks with the Prime Minister, Gough Whitlam, the Treasurer, Bill Hayden and Malcolm Fraser', M4523, 1 PART 5, National Archives of Australia.

14   Kerr Papers, 'Notes by Sir John Kerr on discussions with Gough Whitlam and Malcolm Fraser'.

15   *The Australian*, 1 November 1975.

16   Malcolm Fraser, interview with Paul Kelly, May 1995.

17   Hayden, *Hayden: An Autobiography*, p. 270.
18   Bill Hayden, interview with Paul Kelly, June 1995.
19   Ken Wriedt, interview with Paul Kelly, July 1995.
20   Joe Riordan, interview with Paul Kelly, June 1995.
21   Michael Sexton, interview with Troy Bramston, August 2015.
22   Geoffrey Sawer, *Federation Under Strain*, Melbourne University Press, Melbourne, 1977, p. 216.
23   Kerr, *Matters for Judgment*, p. 289.
24   Kerr Papers, 'Extracts from Letters dated 20 September 1975, 17 October 1975, 20 October 1975, 6 November 1975, 11 November 1975 and 20 November 1975'.
25   Reg Withers, interview with Paul Kelly, June 1995.
26   Kerr, *Matters for Judgment*, p. 291.
27   Ayres, *Malcolm Fraser*, p. 288.
28   Kerr, *Matters for Judgment*, p. 292.
29   Kelly, *November 1975*, p. 191.
30   Kerr Papers, 'Extracts from Letters dated 20 September 1975, 17 October 1975, 20 October 1975, 6 November 1975, 11 November 1975 and 20 November 1975'.
31   Kerr Papers, 'Notes by Sir John Kerr on discussions with Gough Whitlam and Malcolm Fraser'; Kerr, *Matters for Judgment*, p. 310.
32   Kelly, *November 1975*, p. 186.
33   Roden Cutler, interview with Paul Kelly, August 1995.
34   Kelly, *November 1975*, p. 199.
35   Kerr, *Matters for Judgment*, p. 297.
36   David Kemp, interview with Troy Bramston, June 2015.
37   Malcolm Fraser, interview with Paul Kelly, May 1995.
38   Kerr, *Matters for Judgment*, p. 297.
39   Tony Staley, interview with Troy Bramston, July 2015.
40   Malcolm Fraser, interview with Paul Kelly, May 1995
41   Tony Staley, interview with Troy Bramston, July 2015.
42   Ibid.
43   Kerr, *Matters for Judgment*, p. 297.
44   Hayden, *Hayden: An Autobiography*, p. 277.
45   Bill Hayden, interview with Paul Kelly, June 1995.
46   Ibid.
47   Kerr, *Matters for Judgment*, p. 335.
48   John Kerr, Statement by the Governor-General, 11 November 1975, Government House.
49   Kerr, *Matters for Judgment*, p. 335.
50   Ibid., p. 333.

CHAPTER THIRTEEN

1   Kerr Papers, 'Conversation with Sir Anthony Mason during October–November 1975'.
2   Garfield Barwick, *Sir John Did His Duty*, p. 77.
3   Kerr Papers, 'Conversation with Sir Anthony Mason during October–November 1975'.
4   Mason, 'Conversations with Sir John Kerr relating to his Termination of the Commission of the Prime Minister (The Hon EG Whitlam AC QC) on 11 November 1975'. In this chapter Mason's quotes come from this document unless otherwise identified.
5   Kerr Papers, 'Conversation with Sir Anthony Mason during October–November 1975'.
6   Mason, 'Conversations with Sir John Kerr relating to his Termination of the Commission of the Prime Minister (The Hon EG Whitlam AC QC) on 11 November 1975'.
7   Kerr, *Matters for Judgment*, p. 341.

8   Barwick, *A Radical Tory*, p. 214.
9   Ibid., p. 290.
10   Ibid., p. 297.
11   Barwick Papers, 'Dismissal of the Labour [sic] Government, 1975–1979'.
12   Barwick, *A Radical Tory*, p. 291.
13   Barwick, *Sir John Did His Duty*, pp. 79–80.
14   Barwick Papers, 'Dismissal of the Labour [sic] Government, 1975–1979'.
15   Malcolm Fraser, interview with Troy Bramston, April 2013. See also Troy Bramston, 'Kerr not a strong man', *The Australian*, 19 April 2013.
16   Garfield Barwick, interview with Paul Kelly, June 1995.
17   Barwick, *A Radical Tory*, p. 298.
18   Kelly, *November 1975*, p. 227.
19   Whitlam, 'Truth, like the mede, immutable'; Whitlam, *The Truth of the Matter*, p. 126.
20   Kerr, *Matters for Judgment*, p. 339.
21   Murray Gleeson, interview with Paul Kelly and Troy Bramston, April 2015.
22   Malcolm Fraser, interview with Troy Bramston, April 2013.
23   Kerr Papers, 'Conversation with Sir Anthony Mason during October–November 1975'.
24   Barwick Papers, 'Dismissal of the Labour [sic] Government, 1975–1979'.
25   In his memoirs, Barwick writes that Kerr phoned him 'late in the afternoon of November 10' to ask if [Kerr] could disclose the advice (see *Sir John Did His Duty*, p. 87). Yet Barwick's contemporary note suggested this conversation in fact occurred on the morning of November 11.
26   Murray Gleeson, interview with Paul Kelly and Troy Bramston, April 2015.
27   Kerr, *Matters for Judgment*, p. 347.
28   Barwick, *Sir John Did His Duty*, p. 94.
29   Bob Ellicott, interview with Paul Kelly, June 1995.
30   Kerr, *Matters for Judgment*, p. 348.
31   John Kerr Papers, 'Barwick, the Right Honourable Sir Garfield', M4526, 4 PART 1, National Archives of Australia.

CHAPTER FOURTEEN

1   Kerr, *Matters for Judgment*, pp. 357–58.
2   Tony Eggleton, interview with Paul Kelly and Troy Bramston, July 2015.
3   Dale Budd, interview with Paul Kelly and Troy Bramston, July 2015.
4   Tony Staley, interview with Troy Bramston, July 2015.
5   Harders, Oral History, pp. 74–75.
6   Malcolm Fraser, interview with Troy Bramston, September 2002.
7   Fraser and Simons, *Malcolm Fraser: The Political Memoirs*, p. 304.
8   Kelly, *November 1975*, p. 246.
9   Ibid.
10   Doug Anthony, interview with Troy Bramston, July 2015.
11   Fred Daly, *From Curtin to Hawke*, Sun Books, South Melbourne, 1984, p. 230.
12   Ibid.
13   Andrew Peacock, interview with Troy Bramston, June 2015.
14   John Mant, interview with Troy Bramston, August 2015.
15   Brian Buckley, *Lynched: The Life of Sir Phillip Lynch*, Salzburg Publishing, Toorak, 1991, pp. 85–88.
16   John Menadue, 'Note for File: The Dismissal of Mr Whitlam, and appointment of Mr Fraser, as Prime Minister', in Department of Prime Minister and Cabinet, 'Double dissolution of Parliament – 11 November 1975', A1209, 1975/2448, National Archives of Australia.

17 Whitlam, *The Truth of the Matter*, p. 150.
18 Kelly, *November 1975*, p. 246–47.
19 Menadue, 'Note for File: The Dismissal of Mr Whitlam, and appointment of Mr Fraser, as Prime Minister'.
20 Anne Kerr, *Lanterns over Pinchgut: A Book of Memoirs*, Macmillan, South Melbourne, 1988, p. 284.
21 Kerr, *Matters for Judgment*, p. 355.
22 David Smith, *Head of State: The Governor-General, The Monarchy, The Republic and The Dismissal*, Macleay Press, Sydney, 2005, pp. 271–72.
23 Kerr, *Lanterns over Pinchgut*, p. 283.
24 Kerr, *Matters for Judgment*, p. 346.
25 Kerr, *Lanterns over Pinchgut*, p. 283.
26 Anne Kerr, interview with Paul Kelly, June 1995.
27 Kerr, *Matters for Judgment*, p. 349.
28 Barwick Papers, 'Dismissal of the Labour [sic] Government, 1975–1979'.
29 Tony Eggleton, Joint Party Meeting – Brief for Mr Fraser, 11 November 1975, Malcolm Fraser Collection, University of Melbourne.
30 Minutes of Joint Party Meeting, 11 November 1975, Malcolm Fraser Collection, University of Melbourne. See also Kelly, *November 1975*, p. 252.
31 Kep Enderby, interview with Troy Bramston, May 2014.
32 Mike Steketee, 'Driver dismisses Fraser conspiracy', *The Australian*, 31 October 2005, p. 1.
33 Whitlam, *The Truth of the Matter*, p. 153.
34 There are various eye-witness accounts of these events on 11 November 1975, but they often differ on precise timing. We draw on both Whitlam's and Kerr's accounts here in their respective memoirs.
35 David Smith, interview with Paul Kelly and Troy Bramston, July 2015.
36 Ibid.
37 Kerr, *Matters for Judgment*, pp. 358–59.
38 Whitlam, *The Truth of the Matter*, p. 157.
39 Kerr, *Matters for Judgment*, p. 358.
40 See Kelly, *November 1975*, pp. 258–59.
41 Kerr, *Matters for Judgment*, p. 364.
42 See Troy Bramston, 'John Kerr's wordplay masked his reasons behind Gough Whitlam's dismissal', *The Australian*, 22 November 2013, p. 2.
43 Kerr, *Matters for Judgment*, p. 365.
44 Budd, 'D-Day', p. 48.
45 'He was not the sort of bloke who was going to talk to you anyway,' Harry Rundle, Fraser's driver, recalled in 2005. See note 32 above.
46 Menadue and Yeend were the senior departmental officials. Dale Budd, interview with Paul Kelly and Troy Bramston, July 2015.
47 Susan Mitchell, *Margaret and Gough*, Hachette, Sydney, 2004, p. 234.
48 Whitlam, *The Truth of the Matter*, Third Edition, p. 158.
49 Daly, *From Curtin to Kerr*, p. 231.
50 John Mant, interview with Troy Bramston, August 2015.
51 Whitlam, *The Truth of the Matter*, p. 158.
52 David Smith, interview with Paul Kelly and Troy Bramston, July 2015.

CHAPTER FIFTEEN

1 Tony Eggleton, interview with Troy Bramston, May 2014.
2 Doug Anthony, interview with Troy Bramston, November 2014.
3 Menadue Papers, 'The Governor-General and the Dismissal of the Labor Government'.

4   Kelly, *November 1975*, p. 267.
5   Ken Wriedt, interview with Paul Kelly, July 1995.
6   Reg Withers, interview with Paul Kelly, July 1995.
7   Reid, *The Whitlam Venture*, pp. 416–17.
8   MJ Hanson, 'Note for File: Events in the Senate on 11 November 1975', in Department of Prime Minister and Cabinet, 'Double dissolution of Parliament – 11 November 1975', A1209, 1975/2448, National Archives of Australia.
9   See Michael Roe, 'Wreidt, Kenneth Shaw', *The Biographical Dictionary of the Australian Senate*, vol. 3, 1962–83, UNSW Press, Sydney, 2010, pp. 167–73.
10 Hanson, 'Note for File: Events in the Senate on 11 November 1975'.
11 Doug McClelland, interview with Troy Bramston, December 2012.
12 Ian Sinclair, interview with Troy Bramston, June 2015.
13 Hanson, 'Note for File: Events in the Senate on 11 November 1975'.
14 Menadue Papers, 'The Governor-General and the Dismissal of the Labor Government'.
15 AE Dyster, 'Double Dissolution – Events of 11 November 1975', in Department of Prime Minister and Cabinet, 'Double Dissolution of Parliament – 11 November 1975', A1209, 1975/2448, National Archives of Australia.
16 ID Emerton, 'Note for File: Double Dissolution – 11.11.75', in Department of Prime Minister and Cabinet, 'Double dissolution of Parliament – 11 November 1975', A1209, 1975/2448, National Archives of Australia.
17 John Kerr Papers, 'Notes on conversation between the Governor-General, Malcolm Fraser and Clarence Harders', M4523, 1 PART 8, National Archives of Australia.
18 John Mant, interview with Troy Bramston, August 2015.
19 Kerr, *Matters for Judgment*, p. 369.
20 Clarrie Harders Papers, 'Confidential: Constitutional Crisis – 1975' in 'The Dismissal – Governor-General – Discussions with Secretary of Attorney-General's Department', M4081, 2/17, National Archives of Australia.
21 Troy Bramston asked Malcolm Fraser about this conversation in an interview in Melbourne in April 2013. Fraser said he had no recollection of this conversation with Harders. Yet, Harders wrote a contemporary note about it. Other contemporary notes referred to here also identify Harders as travelling with Fraser to and from Government House in the afternoon.
22 Kerr, *Matters for Judgment*, p. 370.
23 Clarrie Harders, interview with Paul Kelly, June 1995.
24 John Kerr Papers, 'Notes on conversation between the Governor-General, Malcolm Fraser and Clarence Harders'.
25 Mason, 'Conversations with Sir John Kerr relating to his Termination of the Commission of the Prime Minister (The Hon EG Whitlam AC QC) on 11 November 1975'.
26 Scholes prepared a note for the 'parliamentary archives' that Whitlam refers to. See Whitlam, *The Truth of the Matter*, pp. 161–64. The authors have not been able to find this note.
27 Gordon Scholes, interview with Troy Bramston, June 2015.
28 Harders Papers, 'Confidential: Constitutional Crisis – 1975'.
29 Smith, *Head of State*, p. 255.
30 See Kelly, *November 1975*, pp. 276–79.
31 John Kerr Papers, 'Notes relevant to legal opinions and advice available to Governor-General in connection with the constitutional crisis', M4524, 8, National Archives of Australia.
32 Harders, Oral History, p. 83.
33 Menadue Papers, 'The Governor-General and the Dismissal of the Labor Government'.
34 Harders, Oral History, p. 84.
35 Ibid.

36 Ibid., p. 83.
37 Ibid., pp. 85–86.
38 Clarrie Harders Papers, 'The Dismissal – Governor-General – Position where the Senate rejects supply', M4081, 2/16, National Archives of Australia.
39 John Kerr to Malcolm Fraser, letter, 18 November 1975. See Clarence Harders Papers, 'The Dismissal – Double Dissolution – Tabling of documents', M4081, 2/11 PART 1, National Archives of Australia.
40 Ivor Greenwood, Statement by the Commonwealth Attorney-General, 20 November 1975. See Malcolm Fraser Papers, 'Dissolution', M1268, 80, National Archives of Australia.
41 See Troy Bramston (ed.), *The Whitlam Legacy*, The Federation Press, Sydney, 2013, pp. 431–33.
42 Gordon Scholes, interview with Troy Bramston, June 2015.
43 Bramston, *The Whitlam Legacy*, p. 434.
44 Ibid., pp. 435–37.
45 Graham Freudenberg, 'Draft of the Letter to the Secretary to HRH Queen Elizabeth II regarding the Dismissal dated 26 December 1975', Item 8128, The Whitlam Institute.
46 Bramston (ed.), *The Whitlam Legacy*, pp. 438–39.

CHAPTER SIXTEEN

1 Morrice James, 'The Australian Constitutional Crisis, 1975', 20 November 1975, Diplomatic Report No. 373/75, Foreign and Commonwealth Office, FCO 24/2051-2052, The National Archives, Kew.
2 Morrice James, 'Footnotes to the Constitutional Crisis', 20 December 1975, Foreign and Commonwealth Office, The National Archives, Kew.
3 Joe Haines, *The Politics of Power*, Jonathan Cape, London, 1977, p. 92.
4 Bernard Donoughue, interview with Troy Bramston, August 2015.
5 House of Commons Debates, 11 November 1975, Vol. 899, c1136.
6 Morrice James, 'The Australian Constitutional Deadlock: Possible Involvement of HMG', 20 October 1975, Foreign and Commonwealth Office, FCO 24/2079, The National Archives, Kew.
7 Whitlam to Wilson, 31 December 1975.

CHAPTER SEVENTEEN

1 Kerr, *Matters for Judgment*, pp. 99–100.
2 Gough Whitlam, *The Whitlam Government: 1972–1975*, Viking, Ringwood, Victoria, 1985, pp. 52–53. See also Gough Whitlam, *Abiding Interests*, University of Queensland Press, St Lucia, Queensland, 1997, pp. 49–50.
3 Ibid.
4 Max Suich, 'Sacking doubts re-emerge', the *Australian Financial Review*, 31 October 2014, Review, pp. 1, 6–7.
5 Jimmy Carter, interview with Troy Bramston, August 2015.
6 Whitlam, *Abiding Interests*, p. 49.
7 Kelly, *The Unmaking of Gough*, Revised Edition, Chapter Four.
8 Here we draw on Peter Edwards, *Arthur Tange: The Last of the Mandarins*, Allen & Unwin, Crows Nest, 2006, pp. 271–85.
9 Kelly, *The Unmaking of Gough*; and Edwards, *Arthur Tange*, p. 275.
10 Kelly, *The Unmaking of Gough*.
11 Edwards, *Arthur Tange*, p. 275.
12 Kelly, *The Unmaking of Gough*, p. 46.

13   John Mant, interview with Troy Bramston, August 2015.
14   See Troy Bramston, 'US feared Whitlam's "extreme left" allies', *The Australian*, 7 November 2014, pp. 1–2.
15   Malcolm Fraser Papers, 'CIA', 20 February 1976 – 24 May 1977, M1277/36, National Archives of Australia.
16   Brian Toohey, 'Pine Gap mystery deepens', the *Australian Financial Review*, 28 April 1977, p. 1.
17   Brian Toohey and Dale Van Atta, 'New Light on CIA Role in 1975', the *National Times*, 21–27 March 1982, p. 12.
18   In these paragraphs, we draw on Peter Edwards, 'No connection between the dismissal and Pine Gap', *The Australian*, 9 November 2005.
19   Edwards, *Arthur Tange*, p. 280.
20   Brian Toohey, 'The CIA feels grave concern…', the *National Times*, 8–14 November 1985, pp. 23–25.
21   Edwards, *Arthur Tange*, pp. 289–90.
22   John Pilger, 'Pilger: Why Whitlam was sacked', the *Weekend Australian*, 30–31 January 1988, p. 19.
23   John Pilger, *A Secret Country*, Jonathan Cape, London, 1989.
24   Paul Kelly, 'Tange denies briefing Kerr on CIA worries', *The Australian*, 29 January 1988, pp. 1–2.
25   Gerard Henderson, 'The Kerr testimony', the *Weekend Australian*, 30–31 January 1988, p. 17.
26   John Pilger, 'The British–American coup that ended Australian independence', *The Guardian*, 23 October 2014.
27   See Troy Bramston, 'Boyce still believes CIA dismissed Whitlam,' *The Australian*, 18 February 2014, p. 2.
28   James Curran, *Unholy Fury: Whitlam and Nixon at War*, Melbourne University Press, Melbourne, 2015.
29   See also Troy Bramston, 'US pact teetered over Nixon's contempt for Whitlam', *The Australian*, 1 May 2015, p. 2; and Troy Bramston, 'CIA didn't get Gough but Nixon mulled espionage', the *Weekend Australian*, 2–3 May 2015, p. 10.
30   Candace Sutton, 'Margaret Whitlam: CIA was involved!' the *Sun-Herald*, 28 April 1991, p. 27.

CHAPTER EIGHTEEN

1   Malcolm Turnbull, interview with Paul Kelly, July 2015.
2   Tony Abbott, interview with Paul Kelly, July 2015.
3   Andrew Peacock, interview with Troy Bramston, June 2015.
4   John Howard, interview with Paul Kelly, June 2015.
5   John Hewson, interview with Troy Bramston, July 2015.
6   Alexander Downer, interview with Troy Bramston, June 2015.
7   Peter Costello, interview with Troy Bramston, July 2015.
8   The Liberal Movement, as Costello described, was a breakaway group that opposed the blocking of supply but still directed preferences to the Liberal Party.
9   Brendan Nelson, interview with Troy Bramston, June 2015.
10   Tony Eggleton, interview with Paul Kelly and Troy Bramston, July 2015.
11   David Kemp, interview with Troy Bramston, June 2015.
12   Dale Budd, interview with Paul Kelly and Troy Bramston, July 2015.
13   Tony Staley, interview with Troy Bramston, July 2015.
14   Malcolm Fraser, interview with Troy Bramston, September 2002.

CHAPTER NINETEEN

1   Hayden, *Hayden: An Autobiography*, pp. 278–79.

2   Ibid., p. 294.

3   Ibid., p. 289.

4   Ibid., pp. 289, 292.

5   Bill Hayden, interview with Troy Bramston, October 2014.

6   Hayden, *Hayden: An Autobiography*, p. 295.

7   Bob Hawke, interview with Troy Bramston, August 2015. Other Hawke quotes, unless identified, are from this interview.

8   Bob Hawke, speech at rally outside Parliament House, 12 November 1975.

9   See Troy Bramston, 'The Hawke Leadership Model', in Susan Ryan and Troy Bramston (eds.), *The Hawke Government: A Critical Retrospective*, Pluto Press, Melbourne, 2003, p. 60.

10 Paul Keating, '1975, Lessons for Labor in the 1980s', in Gary Jungwirth (ed.), *Snapshots of Hope: The Making of Modern Labor*, Pluto Press, Annandale, 1988, pp. 43–54.

11 Paul Keating, interview with Paul Kelly and Troy Bramston, July 2015. Other Keating quotes, unless identified, are from this interview.

12 Bill Hayden, interview with Troy Bramston, October 2014.

13 Freudenberg, *A Certain Grandeur*, pp. 402–03.

EPILOGUE

1   Rod Cameron, interview with Troy Bramston, August 2015. See also Kelly, *The Unmaking of Gough*, pp. 366–67.

2   David Combe, 'Report by Mr David Combe, National Secretary of the Australian Labor Party, on the 1975 Double Dissolution Election', Bob Hawke Collection, University of South Australia.

3   Neville Wran, Speech at the Australian National University, 9 November 1995.

4   Kelly, *November 1975*, p. 283.

5   Malcolm Fraser, interview with Paul Kelly, May 1995.

6   Provided by Don Markwell to the authors.

7   John Kerr Papers, 'Draft typescript of notes with annotations relating to a possible statement to the nation by the Governor-General', M4524/2, National Archives of Australia.

8   Don Markwell, interview with Troy Bramston, August 2015.

9   Kelly, *November 1975*, p. 316.

10 Kerr Papers, 'Kerr, Elizabeth and Philip'.

11 Heather Henderson, interview with Troy Bramston, September 2014. See Troy Bramston, 'The Mighty Robert Menzies: Prime Minister, statesman, my father . . .', the *Weekend Australian*, 27–28 September 2014, p. 20.

12 John Kerr Papers, 'Barwick, the Right Honourable Sir Garfield Part 1', M4526, 4 Part 1, National Archives of Australia.

13 Ibid.

14 Ibid.

15 Kelly, *November 1975*, p. 285.

16 Fraser, Oral History, p. 197.

17 Ibid.

18 Ibid., p. 379.

19 Ibid., p. 388.

20 Ibid., p. 389.

21   Ibid., p. 384.
22   Tony Stephens, 'Kerr was dried out twice: Whitlam', *The Age*, 1 November 2002.
23   Gough Whitlam, 'Soundproofing episode shows how secrecy was essential', the *Sydney Morning Herald*, 15 January 1994.
24   Gough Whitlam, speech to the National Press Club, 8 November 1995.
25   Whitlam, 'Truth, like the mede, immutable'.
26   Gough Whitlam, conversation with Troy Bramston, November 2013.

Index